GLOBAL MATRIX

Nationalism, Globalism and State-Terrorism

Tom Nairn and Paul James

Pluto Press

LONDON · ANN ARBOR, MI

First published 2005 by
Pluto Press 345 Archway Road, London N6 5AA
and 839 Greene Street, Ann Arbor, MI 48106

www.plutobooks.com

British Library Cataloguing in Publication Data
A catalogue record for this book is available from the British Library

ISBN 0 7453 2291 3 hardback
ISBN 0 7453 2290 5 paperback

Library of Congress Cataloging in Publication Data applied for

10   9   8   7   6   5   4   3   2   1

Designed and produced for Pluto Press by
Chase Publishing Services, Fortescue, Sidmouth, EX10 9QG, England
Typeset from disk by Stanford DTP Services, Northampton, England
Printed and bound in Canada by Transcontinental Printing

Contents

To Alan Roberts

Preface: In Search of a Name

Paul James and Tom Nairn

Globalization is the latest moment of high modernity, but one way to approach this moment is via classically early-modern satire. Our Introduction to this volume attempts this in a moment via Goya's evocation of 'El Coloso', the weird Giant that appeared to loom over the Iberian landscape after Napoleon's invasion, and the outbreak of 'total war' (see cover of paperback edition). And long before that, Jonathan Swift's tales of 'Gulliver in Laputa' conjured up a world where the leaders are philosopher-rationalists. They are so taken by the speculation on things other than the human that they need *flappers* – in contemporary terms, human-relations consultants – to keep them in touch with the world around them. Redolent of the world of Blair's reliance on spin-doctors and Bush's love of autocues, the *flappers* run around with bladders tied to the end of a stick, touching their masters' mouths and ears to arouse their senses when it is time to talk and time to listen. These Laputian technocrats live with their monarch on a floating island above the king's dominions:

> If any Town should engage in Rebellion or Mutiny, fall into violent Factions, or refuse to pay the usual Tribute; the King hath two Methods of reducing them to Obedience. The first and the mildest Course is by keeping the Island hovering over such a Town, and the Lands about it; whereby he can deprive of the Benefit of the Sun and the Rain, and consequently afflict the Inhabitants with Dearth and Diseases. And if the Crime deserve it, they are at the same time pelted from above with great Stones, against which they no Defence, but by creeping into Cellars and Caves, while the Roofs of their Houses are beaten to Pieces. But if they still continue obstinate, or offer to raise Insurrections; he proceeds to the last Remedy, by letting the Island drop directly on their Heads.[1]

This is an enticing metaphor for contemporary economic globalization, and the War on Terror. It is as if Swift was writing allegorically about the floating parliament of Bush, Blair, Howard and Sharon. The trouble is that some readers might take it all too literally. Despite some of its more reductive critics and advocates, globalization is not reducible to economic and military hegemony – the Coalition of the Willing and the International Monetary Fund notwithstanding. As Jonathan Swift carefully wrote into his satire, letting the Island drop directly onto its enemies is fraught with the danger that the Island itself could crack up. The people know how far to take their resistance. And when the king 'is highest provoked, and most determined to press a City to Rubbish, [he] orders the Island to descend with great Gentleness, out of a Pretence of Tenderness to his People, but indeed for fear of breaking the Adamantine Bottom'.[2] Both the conspiracy critics and the proponents of invasions in Afghanistan and Iraq seem to have forgotten how complex international politics is.

In the end, in naming this book we went for a more elusive concept, one that has re-entered the lexicon through a popular cultural film – *The Matrix*. 'No-one can conceive it … No-one can be told what it is … It has to be seen … to be understood. This is the kind of future that you don't dream about.'[3] The blurb resonates with the confusions of explanation that abound in relation to globalization. However, rather than treating globalism and nationalism as part of an elaborate simulacra, in using the term 'matrix' we want to carry forward the concept's fuller meaning. In its most general sense a matrix is a setting in which something takes form, has its origin or is enclosed. In obstetrics 'matrix' refers to the body of the womb. By contrast, in mathematics it refers to a regularized array of abstract elements. And in engineering – a personal favourite given the current expressions of globalism – it refers to a bed of perforated metal placed beneath an object in a machine press against which the stamping press operates. The concept of a matrix thus carries in its multiple meanings the contradictory intersection of embodied and abstracted social relations, contingent events and systematic processes that the book takes as its field of discussion.

It is a concept that even in its trivialization gives insight into the nature of globalization. In Malaysia during Merdeka month, the month celebrating postcolonial nationalism, the Japanese Hyundai Corporation – advertising itself as the official partner of the World Cup in Germany – launches the Pinifarina as the 'Matrix', a car designed to be a 'lifestyle partner'.[4] A car as a *lifestyle partner* in an Islamic capitalist and self-consciously nationalist country! Where is this matrix heading? In the United States a second advertisement appears – this time for the Toyota Corporation. A car again called the 'Matrix' is featured. Featuring an ideology that, as we will describe, is closely associated with contemporary globalization: 'Matrix … was sent to here to set you free … The freedom to leave it all behind. The freedom to bring it all with.'[5] While the focus in this book is on international politics and culture we are interested in both the hard and the soft side of globalization, both 'the sell' and the structures of feeling and practice, and globalization as freedom is one of the dominant ideologies of our time.

Between the two of us we have accumulated many debts of gratitude to many people over many years: Shahram Akbarzedeh, Ben Anderson, Perry Anderson, Ien Ang, Sigrid Baringhorst, Anthony Barnett, Jerry Bentley,

Andy Butfoy, Joe Camilleri, Peter Christoff, Allen Chun, Joan Cocks, Bill Cope, Kate Cregan, Phillip Darby, Robyn Eckersley, Jonathan Friedman, Bernard Giesen, Gerry Gill, David Goldsworthy, James Goodman, John Hutchinson, Micheline Ishay, Damian Kingsbury, Tim Luke, David Lyon, David McCrone, Walter Mignolio, Ashis Nandy, Monika Naslund, Brendan O'Leary, Andrew Phillips, Chris Reus-Smit, Alan Roberts, Gyorgy Scrinis, Geoff Sharp, Jukka Siikala, Manfred Steger, Alison Tate, Stephanie Trigg and Ben Wellings.

Earlier versions of the chapters were tried out in a number of journals and at recent conference presentations in Australia, Greece, Scotland, Ireland, Taiwan and the United States. We have to thank the editors of *Arena Journal*, *New Left Review*, *Open Democracy*, *Communal/Plural*, *London Review of Books* and *National Identities* for publishing earlier versions of some of the chapters or sections within. Special thanks goes to the Arena publications group – Alison Caddick, Simon Cooper, John Hinkson, Guy Rundle, Matthew Ryan, Chris Scanlon and Geoff Sharp – not only for giving early life to some of our ideas in print, but for also for providing an intellectual milieu in Melbourne for debate and critique.

The foundational setting for our writing is the Globalism Institute at RMIT in Melbourne where we both work. How many other universities in the world would let such a motley gaggle of people gather together with the brief to be critical, engaged and disruptive of easy mainstream assumptions? The Institute's 'Manifesto' reads:

> At a time of acute sensitivity to questions of social dislocation, economic inequity and political upheaval, the Globalism Institute is committed to rethinking the relationship between the global and the local. The Institute's primary intellectual task is to understand the processes of change *and* continuity in order to think through cultural-political questions about sustainable living in a globalising world. In particular, it is concerned to facilitate and enhance activities of cultural dialogue across the continuing and positive boundaries of cultural diversity in the world today. This entails responding to key political issues of the new century across all levels of community and polity: from the remaking of institutions of global governance and global civil society through to the reconstitution of the nation-state and the reformations of local regions and communities. It entails working across the lines of critical theory, applied research and political debate. We begin with the place in which we live and seek to draw lines of co-operation and reciprocal connection with others – locally, regionally, nationally and internationally.

Working along these lines we have been well supported with generous grants from both RMIT and the Australian Research Council. We'd like to thank our wonderful colleagues in the Globalism Institute – Kate Cregan, Damian Grenfell, Douglas McQueen-Thomson, Martin Mulligan, Yaso Nadarajah,

Peter Phipps, Leanne Reinke, Chris Scanlon and Chris Ziguras – as well as those who have strongly supported the Institute: Mary Kalantzis, Peter Kell, Michael Singh, Neil Furlong and others. Hariz Halilovich, a colleague of the Institute, must be thanked for completing the index. This book is part of a much larger project on 'The Sources of Insecurity' that is being developed in conjunction with these scholars and others such as Jonathan Friedman, Walter Mignolo and Ashis Nandy.

We also thank family and friends for grounding our lives, almost out of the reach of Laputa – Stephanie and Joel Trigg, Millicent Petrie; also Robyn Eckersley, Peter Christoff, Alan Roberts and others. However, it is to Alan that we must specially dedicate this book. As we wander between our interconnected backyards discussing the meaning of the matrix, it is he who has repeatedly brought us back to earth with coffee and conversation, and assorted tales about this world and its ever-weirder alternatives – including grapevines, dogs, cats, z-net listings, *Arena* articles, films, eucalyptus trees and interminably protracted building extensions.

1
Introduction:
Mapping Nationalism and Globalism

Tom Nairn and Paul James

Most commentators, scholars and journalists suggest that the dominance of one age (or epoch, or time, or whatever) ended in the 15 years between the dismantling of the Berlin Wall and the present. There are already so many expressions of this that even to list them would be hard; but to help locate the ideas in the present volume, some examples may be useful. Historian John Lukacs' *The End of an Age* argues that a 500-year 'modern' period is ending, after being originally voiced by the 'confused excrescences' of postmodernism, and will be replaced by what some readers must have found even more confusing: an odd mixture of theoretical physics and rekindled Christianity.[1] William H. McNeill and his son J.R. McNeill have followed with a general reinterpretation of history founded upon 'the notion of the centrality of webs of interaction in human history'. Their title *The Human Web* voices this contemporary insight, deriving of course from the impact of the communications revolution, the internet and a world in which 'peasant patterns of life and labor are in full retreat'.[2] They perceive us as being on 'the crest of a global breaking wave' that will either make or demolish the human species. The McNeills replace Lukacs' preoccupation with physics by an analogous focus upon biology and the biosphere, as if post-1989 globalization may be responding to the pressures of a deeper 'symbiosis'. The third, still more recent, reinterpretation of the historical process is that of anthropologist Emmanuel Todd: his *Après l'Empire* is a fiery polemic, founded on a primarily anthropological retrospect.[3] Todd denounces US leadership since 2001 as a futile, self-destructive attempt to recover the lost hegemony of pre-1989 – to arrest the reality of globalization in its tracks, and avoid its spreading into the wider delta of an uncontrollable, multipolar diversity where no single state or culture can hope to be in command. Here, physics and biology give way to a speculative anthropology, grounded on Todd's previous demographic studies. The most important was *La Diversité du Monde: Structures Familiales et Modernité*, an argument that humankind's socio-cultural variation is determined by an inherited diversity of familial types and (hence) of intimate relationships and emotive dispositions. These may be 'memes' rather than genes, but the point is that such diversity is of

1

the human-social essence, not just a series of contingent accidents. The implication is then that the truly 'global' must be the affirmation of such diversity, not its 'overcoming' or suppression.

The studies gathered together in the present volume have a different emphasis again, perhaps closer to Todd than to Lukacs or the McNeills, but also unconvinced by the anthropological determinism of his underlying philosophy. It is true that the dominance of one 'matrix' of development is receding, and that the events of 2001 to 2004 have dealt it a shattering blow. It also seems apparent that another matrix is in formation, overlaying older developments in contradictory ways – the first comprehensive 'global' matrix, as our title suggests. However, our own emphasis is upon a cultural-political theme, which at the same time embraces a variety of other factors – ecological, anthropological, and the condition of being human – and seeks to link them together. This is an 'ecumenical' approach: in other words, closer to the overview given by Manfred Steger in his *Globalism: The New Market Ideology*, and sharing his insistence there is nothing inevitable or 'irreversible' about market ascendancy and deregulation.[4] This counter-view is forced upon us, rather than being just a bland choice. We have also been influenced by cautious distrust of all the single-issue or portmanteau explanations that have crowded the shop-front of theory since the 1990s. There undoubtedly is an emergent global matrix; but it calls for detective work and some house-to-house enquiries, rather than (as British tabloids love to say) a 'swoop' upon the presumed guilty party. A case has to be patiently built up, beyond premature rushes to judgement.

One feature of this deeper alteration in course is – and ought to be – a profound and long-running reaction against those shadows from which the globe began to free itself, when the Cold War at last ended. Masterful yet phoney monotheism dominated that shadow-world. We faced a supposed choice between command-economy socialism and liberal-capitalism. The choice of worlds had narrowed down, from the competitive spectrum of former would-be empires to a basic 'either–or'. Only two of Goya's 'Giants' were left, as it were, capable of devouring (and indeed destroying) everything and everyone else.[5] These Giants, it went without saying, were capable of *explaining* everything, in one or other omnivorous, all-encompassing fashion. The '-isms' of such a world were apologies for claimed omnipotence: fantasies extolling a brute authority which (fortunately) no actual modern empire has ever had.

Now, even that claim has foundered: this is part of what globalization is about. However, ideological authoritarianism did not vanish in 1989–90, alongside the ex-Communist imperium. The inherited memes of gigantism persist, and indeed still demand that humankind acknowledge the dominance of the one '-ism' that remains – as if, deprived of Colossi, the species might indeed turn into the scared, fleeing rabble in Goya's picture. In fact (as

Todd shows), this is a Giant with no clothes, dependent upon a mixture of craven self-subjection by inherited satrapies, grossly exaggerated military threats, and an almost equally exaggerated economic credo – the secular religion of neo-liberalism. The truth, or rather our political hope, is that 'globalization' must lead *in the overall direction* of a Giant-less world. It will not lead (naturally) to a globe without large states or nations, or without uneven economic development, or social conflicts, but at least it presumes one where it becomes increasingly difficult to naturalize such inequities and sustain the constant deferral of legal/ideal senses of recognition and human status. Though foreshadowed in the formal structure of the United Nations organization, whose General Assembly ranks Andorra alongside China, this equality stood little real chance in a world of Giant contests. But in a post-Giant world, ought there not to be some possibility of reality growth?

We have assumed that clearing the way towards such a big shift calls for clearing the way for a different theoretical approach. *Global Matrix* doesn't offer still another key to the universe. Our assumption is that while 'keys' are not helpful, new lines of understanding are crucial, and can only be composed collectively over a period to come, by those who will be 'natives' of the globalized world – those who have been born into it and will take its deeper undertow and instincts for granted, as the present authors are unable to. We have been formed by the world of nationalism, and our way of contesting that age was (primarily) via theorizing about these older structures. Of course, such theorizing bears its marks of origin: in this case, the distant edge-lands of Scotland and Australia. Critics will not be slow to point these out, usually ignoring (or simply not perceiving) their own marks of descent as they do so. However, we can take some comfort here from what is actually a minor formative principle of globalism: in human discourse (unlike that of the Gods) the stigmata of contingent origin are universal, and, at a certain level, ineffaceable. Every theorist bears an axe to grind – social theory would not be any use if this were not so.

Two and a half centuries ago, David Hume made the same point in a book that fell stillborn from the press: 'We speak not strictly and philosophically when we talk of the combat of passion and of reason. Reason is, and ought only to be the slave of the passions, and can never pretend to any other office than to serve and obey them.'[6] As he goes on to explain, 'passions' are original existence, the drivers of society's discourse and of the reason this requires. One crucial task for the latter is the recognition and delineation of its own limits. Rational*ism* is a systematic evasion of this – the promotion of reason into a religion, or substitute religion, a secular magic capable of making humanity's crooked timbers all straight, preferably by this time next week. Globalization, by contrast, should encourage greater diffidence and uncertainty. This is why *Global Matrix* is also a founding member of the 'crooked timbers' club. Giants are not admitted, naturally; all '-isms' must be consigned to the cloakroom upon entry; and the only members' oath commits them to an anti-crusade against 'fundamentalist' delusions – religious and secular alike.

THE '-ISM' OF NATIONS

The lineages of nationalism and globalism are messy and cross-cutting. National*ism* begins in the take-off period of modern imperial globalization with its proponents and critics alike looking forward to a new cosmopolitan and humanized world. 'Its course will be marked with material as well as moral ruin, in order that a new invention may prevail over the works of God and the interests of mankind', snarled the good traditionalist Lord Acton in 1862 in his essay 'On Nationality'.[7] However, contrary to a later received idea, the celebrated essay was not a denunciation of 'nationalism'. The term does not appear there. What Acton attacked was 'the nationality principle' and 'the theory of nationality'.

The '-ism' arrived only later, after the War of Secession in America, and the Franco-Prussian War in Europe. Once this Pandora's Box was opened, however, its contents proved to be all-conquering. By the end of the nineteenth century, the world was ready for it. All tongues adapted the concept from the original French, and it imbued the air we still breathe today. Like the concepts of 'ethnicity' and 'globalization' a century later, it not only caught on in the words we speak, but was also part of a swift transformation of the way that people think and feel. That transformation involved nothing less than a covenant with the grand narratives and practices of modernity. It was never totalizing, yet by the middle of the twentieth century no one was really outside it, and, despite decades of scholarly attention, even today nobody comfortably understands it.

Just as the power of nationalism remains something of a mystery, a new phenomenon is moving in to change the rules – globalism.[8] From a term that almost nobody used until the 1980s, everybody has now discovered globalization. As we discuss in the first section of the book, across the turn of the twenty-first century, globalization is treated mythically as the latest thing, the all-encompassing process that itself explains all that happens on this planet. Overstatement remains a condition of our time. Alternatively, moving from the ridiculous to the sublimely stupid, some of its ideologues have just begun proclaiming its 'true meaning' as the natural condition of the planet, pushing globalization back to the beginning of time and naturalizing as if it has always been with us. Alan Shipman, the author of *The Globalization Myth*, begins his defence of globalization thus: 'Life on planet earth was global from the outset, as one fragile lonely planet huddled for comfort against cold and empty space.' The parochializing move to set up local boundaries 'came later', says our neo-liberal author in his

Tower of Babel story – 'after manners started to fragment over space, and memories over time. Many efforts have since been made to turn back the dispersing tide and restore our cross-border connections', he says in right-wing cosmopolitan fashion.[9]

Like many other neo-liberal tracts *The Globalization Myth* treats the role of the nation-state either as part of the problem as it slides back to a parochializing past, or as part of the solution in which nations, like backward children, are called upon to work extra hard to transcend their own history, notably in the realm of the market. By contrast, this book treats nationalism and globalism much more ambiguously and ambivalently. As social phenomena, globalism and nationalism, at least in their modern expressions, are bound up with each other. As Steger points out in *Globalism*, our era of globalization has resemblances to the period from 1870 through to the First World War, though as yet (fortunately) without a prevailing philosophical narrative like Social Darwinism. New narratives remain to be thought out, in terms of a new dialectic of discontinuity and continuity. In their ethical implications both nationalism and globalism are Janus-faced. Whether they are good or bad, we argue, can only be understood in terms of how they come to be practised in the emergent conditions.

NATIONALISM IN GLOBAL CONTEXT

One layer of the reality is that nation-states and classical modern globalization grew up together across the course of the eighteenth century and into the nineteenth century – the latter was known as 'imperialism' and became the glorious mission of the former. It was the White Man's Burden. The formation of political entities called 'nation-states' was framed by the globalizing industrial and commercial revolutions. There were of course nations before the affirmation of capitalism, but few were self-conscious or self-guided collectivities like those gathered into the modern nation-states of the late nineteenth century. The older terrestrial landscape was characterized by tribalism and clanship, despotic and multicultural empires, missionary faiths and trading city-states. When Isaac Newton formulated the law of gravity, much of the globe was still occupied by hunter-gatherers. Yet in an astonishingly short time, this elaborate magma was overlaid by today's World Cup contest, consumer capitalism and Bill Gates, a globe of relatively uniform and comparable states, all claiming to be mystically extended families equipped with the same rights and sovereignty. *Overlaid*, we say, because as one undercurrent of the book maintains, the world is layered in complexity. It is not the one-dimensional liberal-democratic market (albeit one beset by a network of terrorist recalcitrants hiding under every bed) as George Bush, Tony Blair and Francis Fukuyama would have us believe.

Marx's 'sorcerer' of capitalist modernity was partly responsible for the new dominant layer – in particular the unleashed market forces of the nineteenth century, at once hymned and condemned in the *Communist Manifesto*. In their wake came a vast tidal wave of destruction, combined with societal reordering. The globe warped into wildly uneven development, where survival and identity had to be fought for, economically, and very often militarily as well. The political recasting, now institutionalized as the nation-state, was a necessary part of this. Modernist theorists of nationalism have established that this was not an accident, or the work of loose-cannon intellectuals, or a resurgence of prehistoric unreason. 'Made by Capitalism' is on its label, as much as on those of the Invisible Hand, Enron, dot.com lunacy or the British monarchy. Eric Hobsbawm, Benedict Anderson and the other modernist theorizers who followed Gellner's lead in his 1964 'Nationalism' essay, have been able to deconstruct thoroughly the mechanisms that created the world of nations.[10]

They rescued us from Lord Acton. However, the escape from fogeydom could not help posing another and much profounder question. For much of the globe, 'modernization' has been an accelerated bum's rush from totem pole to George W. Bush. It can be seen *how* this happened. We have a far more partial understanding of *why* it happened. But this is the question that has grown more important, as the age of 'nation-ism' gives way to something else. The globe is walking backwards into 'globalism': what on earth have we walked through up to this point, especially from 1870 to 1989? Such formative epochs don't just lapse. They are 'contributing' to (that is, partly forming) the initial phase of globalization, in ways we don't understand (because nationalism remained partly mysterious).

The socially driven inevitability and omnipresence of modern nationalism has been established; but not its deeper sources in the nature of human community – that is, in those long-accumulated cultures which were hurled into the maelstrom from the eighteenth century onwards. Mythologies of 'blood' descent and solidarity were stories, but not stories about nothing. They continue to entrance in the age of the information revolution and the human genome. It is now known that genetic constitution had astonishingly little to do with ethnic or national identity. But of course this simply amplifies the problem. It means that socio-cultural differentiation must possess its own social logic, a cultural compulsion so great that the sorcerer's latest conjuring trick – 'globalization' – appears to be awarding it a new lease of life.

As we write, identity politics is back on the international stage, if it ever went away. Suicide-bombers are making their way both into Iraq and Israel, the Israeli army is poised for further atrocities in the West Bank or Gaza; Pakistan and India are mobilizing over the broken nation of Kashmir in what may become the world's first nuclear war; North Korea is attempting to join the club of war-machines with nuclear capability; China is rejoining the world economy on a tide of rejuvenated chauvinism; and the British Prime Minister has become a latter-day Lord Acton, ceaselessly air-freighting the spent fuel-rods of UK wisdom from one 'trouble spot' to the next.

As Perry Anderson commented a decade ago, in *A Zone of Engagement*, Gellner and the modernizers tell us everything we need to know about nationalism, except what we need to know about nationalism: 'The overpowering dimension of collective *meaning* that modern nationalism has always involved: that is, not its functionality for industry, but its fulfillment of identity.'[11] Anthony Smith's distinction has always lain in recognizing the same thing. From his *Ethnic Origins of Nations* in 1986 down to his latest intervention, *Nationalism: Theory, Ideology, History*, he has weighed in on the side of meaning and origination as keys to the apparent chaos of the present.[12] This has been overlooked by the various schools of shamanism who believed in the primacy of economics, whether of the Left or Right, either that of free trade marketry, or of state control of production and commerce. Both these Colossi of Predetermination perceived the history that *mattered* as starting in the eighteenth century or (stretching things a bit) the setting up of the Westphalian state-system in the previous century. Previous history was therefore but raw material, the world before the Flood. Romantic nationalists may have imagined 'nations' back there, awaiting the sorcerer's transforming touch, but this was retrospective delusion. Everything that counts comes from the economic flood itself, though (admittedly) it often presents itself in obscure cultural disguise. But then, what is to be expected from Kant's 'crooked timber' of the pre-Enlightened?

At this point it may be relevant to say more about the present writers' respective places in these battlelines. Formerly a left half-back (reserves) with Team Modern's one-world economania, Tom Nairn switched sides in the 1990s and tentatively join the neo-primordialists, at least for the after-match discussions. His former stance is correctly described in Anthony Smith's *Nationalism: Theory, Ideology, History* (2001) but was abandoned some years ago. Paul James was born too late to be a modernist, and born too early to join the ranks of the postmodernists. His approach is informed by an antipodean theory associated with the journal *Arena* that has been playing in the Third Division for many years. In the meantime, one side-effect of marketolatry's dismal hegemony has been to suck much of both modernization and postmodern theory down with it, into the lower depths of political turpitude and journalistic scumbaggery. Every postmodern fairground hustler is now bursting to tell you that nationalism was 'invented', and that the 'nation-state' is hopelessly out of date. We have both been arguing against these contentions, albeit in our different ways.

Though not yet a butterfly, counter-theory is wriggling out from the cocoon of hard-line 'modernization', without necessarily coming under the spell of the bright lights of postmodernism. Today it more clearly can be seen how that cocoon was also a straitjacket. The opposition squad to Gellner's modernism consisted of theorists who found it impossible to credit the 'industrialism-plus' yarn, or to accept that the pre-1688 world was essentially a half-asleep 'ethnic patchwork' awaiting the steam engine and modern artillery.

In *Imagined Communities*, Benedict Anderson underlined the enduring significance of a revolution long preceding industrialism: the advent and effects of the written word, which could only be made flesh through nations. Despite this rewriting there is still a tendency, following a long tradition from Hans Kohn onwards, to treat the analytic distinction between 'territorial nations' and 'ethnic nations' as the basis of two distinct modern templates for the nation. It leads to a tortured narrative about the historical sequence of nation formation. In this story, first came the 'territorial nations' in the West. For some unspecified time, territoriality formed the only concept of the nation. Then, those European states found that it only worked if they also developed a shared culture of myths and symbols. Alongside this development but more gradually there emerged ethnic nations on the basis of pre-existing ethnic ties: Germany, which was also a bit territorial; and Eastern Europe and the Middle East, more prominently ethnic. Later, when the political elites of Asia and Africa decided to create nations they first tried the Western model, but then they were compelled by the logic of the situation to form their own myths of nationhood.

NATIONALISM AND GLOBALISM IN HISTORICAL CONTEXT

Who were these first 'territorial nations' that could take their ethnic elements for granted? Firstly, it should be said that they were territorial *states*, not territorial *nations*. Secondly, these states could not take ethnicity for granted before the nineteenth century, because ethnicity as distinct from blood ties (genealogy) was not for anyone at that time an active category of self-identification. The 'ethnic revival' and the positive use of the concept of 'ethnicity' occurred in these states *as* they became nation-states. If we take one of the oft-used examples, the French, we find an amalgam of cultures and regions brought together across the nineteenth century. It was evidenced in such apparently banal processes as military conscription (beginning in the late eighteenth century), railways (from the 1850s), compulsory and secular education (from the early 1880s) and the generalization of print distribution and radio broadcast from the end of the nineteenth century. However, even despite the self-conscious territorial organization of the nation-state it was not until the beginning of the twentieth century that this could be taken for granted.

Even then we can list the continuing ethnic-territorial cultures that could have become nation-states:

1. the Burgundians in eastern France, a people of Scandinavian origin whose language had died out since their incorporation in the French state at the end of the fifteenth century, but who have carried forth a regional identity to the present day;
2. the Basques from the southwest border of France and Spain who have asserted for themselves the national legitimacy of a government of Euzkadi;
3. the Bretons, from the northwest peninsula of France, who revived the Breton language at the end of the nineteenth century as a response to Francification, not the other way round;
4. the Provençals, who still use the language of Occitan or *langue d'oc*, though as a private rather than public language, and sustain a sense of culture difference through folk revivals and tourism;
5. the Corsicans, who from the late 1960s have sponsored strong movements for regional autonomy or semi-autonomy;
6. the Catalans, from the southeast border of France and Spain (including Andorra), who still feel a strong cultural, though not political, nationalism drawing upon the distinct and old language of Catalan.

This tendency to treat patchwork Western territorial states such as France as if they were already territorial nations is related to a tendency to treat the features of being a nation as intrinsically Western. This is simply a category mistake. There is nothing about the notions of 'territoriality' or 'political culture' or 'legal codes', for example, that makes them 'Western'.[13] Certainly the dominant Western mode of organization involves a certain form of abstract territoriality and sovereignty over the landscape: however, the absolutist states (or what some writers too easily call 'the nations') of England and France did this by virtue of their transition to modern forms of juridical framing – not by virtue of being 'Western'. We only have to compare these to the approaches to territory and culture in the 'Eastern' state of Japan to see how shaky the categories become. Japan, like China, had long been a territorial state with established legal codes and conceptions of sovereignty.[14] The Tokugawa modernizing revolution of the late nineteenth century was certainly influenced in part by Western-educated intellectuals, but it also restored the traditional emperor as the essence of the national polity, or *kokutai*. This carries through our theme of the uneven intersection of formations of traditionalism and modernism.

When some writers argue that the earliest cases of territorial nations were in the West, England, France, Spain, the Netherlands, and later Russia, there is a further question of analytical anachronism here that needs to be addressed. Though these polities were certainly long-run territorial entities that later became nations, it does not make them continuous nations, or at least it does not make them nations back then. It should, however, be said that there *were* 'nations' prior to the nineteenth century, but they were not nation-states, and they were not 'territorial nations' as such. As a short-hand response to the existence of nations prior to the nation-state, the different 'stages' in the history of nations, nationalism and nation-states can be set out as a series of moments (alongside processes of globalization).

The concept of *natio* comes to us from Latin, but it meant something completely different from the modern sense of the word, 'nation': firstly, in archaic definitions the concept of *natio* was used as coextensive with 'tribe' (or what has been referred to as *ethnie*); secondly, it referred to *traditional* communities of strangers who found common purpose with each other under conditions of being lifted out of their locales into new settings of face-to-face *interaction*. This occurred in places such as mediaeval monasteries, universities and military barracks. The only commonality in this second case with the *modern nation* is that these communities – groups that we can call 'traditional nations', assuming all the unusual ontological weight that the adjective 'traditional' has to carry in this context – were abstracted communities forced to examine basic issues of embodiment, temporality and spatiality. They were communities of common fate but they were not territorial nations. Traditional globalization developed alongside this naming of 'national' difference carried by the old empires and sodalities, but it too was unrecognizable in modern terms.

From the sixteenth century in England, and to a lesser extent in other places such as the Netherlands, the concept of the 'nation' went through a period of politicization. However, it was associated with the genealogically connected aristocratic ruling classes or the emergent groupings of *men* of learning, the new intellectually trained of a country or region. Despite the language of 'nation'-ness, the predominant political structure remained from the top firmly that of a *traditional* kingdom or empire; or from the bottom, of village or parish. The unwashed masses did not care to be part of any putative nation, nor were they invited to be so. In this third manifestation of traditional communities of common fate, *traditional nations* were only territorial to extent that they were sometimes coextensive with kingdoms, sometimes counties, and sometimes language regions. This is the period of the expansion of Europe and the beginnings of modern imperialism (globalization).

From the late eighteenth century we started to get intellectual and political creeds about 'nationalism' and 'cosmopolitanism' as European philosophers, theologians and poets 'discovered' the concepts. However, as we have been implicitly arguing, it took a long time for those terms to enter the languages of the world. Moreover, naming a thing does mean that the thing is invented by the places that first name it. Nevertheless, this period marked the rise of *modern* 'nationality theory' as a self-conscious European philosophy.

The late eighteenth to mid nineteenth centuries saw the emergence of explicitly national movements in the Americas, Europe and parts of Asia. These movements rose *before* most of the old absolutist states, kingdoms and empires began to see themselves as territorial nations.[15] This simple fact is an important challenge to the idea of pre-nineteenth-century, pre-nationalist territorial nation-states. Across the nineteenth century, public spheres developed that broadened beyond the court or town square. This occurred in association with ideologies of public sovereignty, democracy and national citizenship, and was an important ideological backdrop to the still emerging nation-state system. They depended upon a changing mode of communication that drew a reading public into political consequence.

It was not until the late nineteenth century that the uneasy conjunction of national citizenry and abstract state really became established forming in some cases what can be now called the classical *modern* nation-states. It is important to remember that the old empires carried through into the next century as viable polities. And this was the period that has also been called the take-off stage of modern globalization. In other words, what was previously nationality or national-interest ideology acquired the harder cutting edge of national*ism* only under the aegis of great-nation advance and consolidation. Such an advance was also 'imperialism' or (as was often said at the time) the 'New Imperialism', the *modern* kind as distinct from the fuddy-duddy *anciens régimes* in Austria-Hungary, Tsarist Russia, India or China.

But of course, modernization then became mandatory. Both the fuddy-duddies and the smaller fry without hope of imperial outreach had to pretend they were 'nations', no longer in a simple popular-cultural or linguistic sense, but in the 'serious' mode of the successfully modern. They had to be (or to claim) 'viability', economic capacity and self-defensive capacity: *effective* 'sovereignty', as the big-leaguers never tired (and indeed, still rarely tire) of saying, particularly when 'threatened'. But in big-league terms, Sovereignty (the capital letter counts) is always under threat, potentially if not actually, and nationhood is less a 'daily plebiscite' than a daily rallying call to arms, 'mobilization' of the spirit if not of young uniformed bodies. This is of course the weird universe of 'Realism' in International Relations, and the source of its obsessions about Security (also best when capital-upgraded).

Such weirdness is that of Goya's devouring Giants, mentioned earlier. Sovereign Security is possible only among Giants, preferably Super-Giants or 'Powers' (or in more recent terminology, 'Hyper-Powers'). The 'short twentieth century' featured the world wars of these increasingly barbaric entities, invariably carried out in the name of universal this-and-that, and entirely legitimate by the rules of the prevalent '-isms', including nationalism. The liberation movements of *modern* tribalism and neo-traditionalism had to be nationalist too, in order to get anywhere. These were of course seen as relatively small, disruptive, noisy and deplorable; that is, until success was extracted. Whereupon the noisy ones oft became parts of the general chorus (or competing choirs) of civilization, under one or other of the Great Conductors. During this period many new nation-states emerged in the Third World, but also formed in Europe, including Yugoslavia, and its subsequent breakaways. The dominant trend in United Nations' membership is of course towards larger numbers of ever-smaller national states, minnows inherently incapable of 'classical' nationalism and its accompanying prescriptions.[16]

The late twentieth century and early twenty-first century saw the rise of a new subjectivity of nationalism – postmodern nationalism – where the emphasis moved to an aesthetic of choice. While there may still be no postmodern nations as such, during this period, particularly in the West, postmodern subjectivities of noticeably greater intensity have come to overlay the continuing modern foundations of the contemporary nation. Neo-liberal preaching saw only the lowering of borders, and nation-states losing former powers and status – this was another way of affirming the all-importance of economics, and its supposed human by-product, 'economic man' and 'woman'. It did not occur to the zealots that this might also be a formula for producing both elite and mass resentments, and a rising determination to make better (more aggressive) use of non-economic powers, as well as of whatever budgetary and financial influence remained.

In other words, the spreading general constraints of a global economy have not dissipated but magnified the importance of the non-economic. It has magnified 'identity politics', in the deepest sense meaning the delineation of traits (including borders) and a human thirst for significant contribution, 'fate', or acknowledgement by some transcendent Giant in the sky. 'Fundamentalism' is thus not an accident. Nor is it essentially a religious impulse, though it is hardly surprising that theocratic revivalism has made the most of it. Our joint concern for the dimension of culture and politics reflects this phenomenon: it is forced upon serious enquiry, not a matter of aesthetic or supposedly postmodern predilection.

While this book concentrates on the last two 'episodes' of nation-building and global formation mentioned above – postwar modernization and the overlay of processes of postmodernization – such a long-run episodic account provides crucial contextualization to our understanding of the present. Not surprisingly, social anthropologists have played a leading part in this rethinking. From Fredrick Barth and Jack Goody through to Hugh Brody and Chris Knight, parts of the larger story have emerged – that it is the social relations of cross-history that accounts for so much of the modern episode itself. In this wider narrative, culture, language, feeling and religion are as important as economics. Capitalism's Enlightenment was one key phase of this, now giving way to a weird spectrum of by-products, provisionally labelled 'globalization'. The 'X-factor' in this is nationalism, previously reckoned to be a leftover from the end of history.[17]

BEING NATIONAL, BECOMING GLOBAL

The same argument suggests strongly how extraordinarily unlikely it is that nationalism will evaporate from the 'One Market Under God' world. The blinkers of modernizing theory implied that uneven development – the supposed lever of nationalist impatience and mobilization – belonged exclusively to the novel circumstances of machine production, economic measurement and militarism. Hence it would diminish as these conditions 'worked themselves out' into some more equitable distribution of resources and lifestyles. By contrast, the longer-term perspective perceives uneven fate as endemic: it must have been rooted in the way that the species colonized the globe, and not merely in the way some parts of it sought to colonize others between 1650 and 1950. This entails what we might call a 'levels' argument,[18] one that takes seriously both the contemporary expressions of geo-political power as the outcome of very particular contemporary structures of practice, and the longer-run ontologies of meaning and practice that lie beneath the swirl of the dominant representations of the matrix. Like the 'sacred', boundaries and differentiation are embedded in the longest *durée* of human society rather than in the 'superstructures' of a single phase. 'Belonging' and the kaleidoscopes of human identification are only 'imagined' in the deeper sense of having to be imagined – eyes, not spectacles adjustable at will. Of course individuals may switch or choose among identities, but they are never at liberty to have no identity at all (save by a fall into the non-human, or into madness).

One analogy with this is Noam Chomsky's theory of language. Humans are by nature beasts of communication; they communicate over a fantastic range of wavelengths, in mutually incomprehensible patterns, but are also defined by the need for and capacity to be on one *given* wavelength ('deep grammar'). The particularity of tongues is itself a universal. So is the resultant nexus between community and identity. This means that we both eschew the post-structuralist sense that it is all surface. Here, for a moment, however, the two present authors part company, with Nairn calling this nexus 'nationality' and James calling it 'social identity'. In the latter's approach 'nationality' is treated as a distinct form of social identity being relevant to three dominant ontological formations: the traditional, modern and postmodern. Nevertheless, what we are both clear on is that the earlier version of the primordialist turn against modernization theory (including some of Anthony Smith's work) made the mistake of arguing that particular 'ethnicities' (or potential nations) had to be in place for each modern-period nation or state to arise. This view colluded with that of romantic nationalists, who naturally sustained their politics by contending that there must always have been Serbs, Inuits, Teutons or Welshmen – in waiting, as it were, but unfairly cheated of the opportunity to be themselves.

So much nonsense inhered in this view that it served mainly to fortify modernism. Sardonic tongues like those of Hobsbawm and Gellner were unlikely to miss such a target. However, it is now clearer that the proximate target was mistaken, but not the direction of aim. What was 'waiting' was not a range of pre-packaged nation-states but the accumulated and common power of human society to assert itself in political shape. National*ism* was global from the start. This is why it took over the world cranium from the 1870s, not before. Using the Chomskyan model again, it was from the eighteenth century onward waiting to 'speak': but the discourse that the sorcerer had made possible was, in the first instance, utterable solely out of the content of its traditional foundations. Here the distinction between form and content is crucial. The nineteenth century was the 'Babel' of future-time, ready to be transformed as the monolithic hold of past empires and faiths were themselves modernized. We are still far from guessing the whole story here, but we feel that elucidation is helped along by ranging across changing modes of formation from traditionalism to modernism (and more recently postmodernism), and by tracking the changing modes of practice from communication to production.

'What earlier century had even a presentiment that such productive forces slumbered in the lap of social labour?' mused Marx in 1848: 'All that is solid melts into air, all that is holy is profaned, and man is at last compelled to face with sober senses, his real conditions of life, and his relations with his kind.' Like most of modernism's progeny, Marx was over-impressed by economics, and by future-fantasies tinged with the apocalyptic. 'Sober senses' was always uncomfortably reminiscent of *Homo economicus.* In truth, the solid did not melt into air, nor was the holy profaned. Both were overlaid, but to an increasing extent then reconstituted themselves in terms of modernity, as expressions of identity politics. What Marx's radical, modernizing, progressive tunnel vision obscured was something vital – much the same thing as Perry Anderson discerned over a century later. Nationalism (and for that matter, globalism) was two-faced from the outset, and one of its demeanours was deeply conservative. It was 'conservative' in both senses of the word – with 'conservationist' being in some ways a more accurate take on what was meant.

All preceding history had been marked by a ragged, unceasing and uneven mutation of populations, bundling good and bad together in an itinerant's backpack. Peoples, countries, and cultures were characterized not by stable 'immemoriality', but by mutability and creative change on the one side, and on the other by forced migration, subjection or slavery, assimilation, and what today we charge as 'genocide'. The many-coloured coat was constantly being re-patched; and most of its parts never stayed around long enough to become part of the taken-for-granted fabric. Nationalism, by contrast, became like the weaving machine of history, bestowing *for the first time* at least a chance of permanence. This was historical permanence for peoples, that is, rather than just for the ruling crusts of fogeys, hustlers, ennobled *banditi* and Word-of-God men.

Nationalism and globalism were not 'made' by the industrial revolution in itself – rather they consolidated themselves through the way that humanity used industrial-commercial-technological-scientific development, for ends rooted in its changing but deeply embedded social nature. This is why Babel has not collapsed, and why – as Anthony Smith contends – it is inconceivable it will do so merely because of the internet, or because large numbers speak pidgin American, watch *ER* on television or devour Big Macs. More probably, its time is yet to come. Hysterical prophecies of plastic globalization tend to locate us near the end of history, or even 'post' everything. By contrast, what we are attempting to do in this book is to situate the contemporary period in the middle of the rapids of history, and to suggest that the sorcerer has nothing like concluded his business.

In presenting this argument, the book is divided into four parts. Part I begins with the question of globalization, because it has become the most generalizing framework of our time. Here we argue that globalization has to be understood in its full ambiguity, historical reach and social depth. The only significant divergence in our approaches is over how we are to understand the role of the United States of America in the current rapids. Is it part of the process of extending globalization, or is it being left behind? Here Nairn's 'Global Trajectories: America and the Unchosen' can be read against James' later chapter, 'Meta-War and the Insecurity of the United States'. Part II is conducted as a debate over the politics of nationalism, concentrating in particular on the question of civic nationalism. It asks 'Does a deeply democratized civic nationalism provide an adequate model for an alternative politics?' Here Nairn argues for a revised civic nationalism, while James is not so sanguine.

Part III discusses a series of case studies, Britain, Scotland, Australia, Canada and Central Asia, each time attempting to work through the patterns of continuity and change. And finally, Part IV takes up the question of globalization again in the context of the 'War on Terror'. Here we track the various crucibles of state terror from a mass meeting in the Hofbräuhaus – a city-centre beer cellar where Hitler first gained his political voice – to the hometown America where George W. Bush delivered his January 2003 State of the Union address. There is no suggestion here that these politicians have much explicitly in common politically or ethically. Nevertheless, their international interventions are not comfortably and completely distinct either. For all their profound differences, the outcomes of their effects upon the world come together as we map the dark and dangerous side of undemocratic states which have globalizing pretensions, whether they are bent on world domination or on proclaiming 'perpetual peace'. Goya's Giant may be on his knees, but is not yet reconciled to his final fall. The picture showed him squaring up like a blind boxer, to unseen challengers, a Terrorism still to come, somewhere outside the visible frame.

Global Matrix is part of what Manfred Steger calls 'the reformist project' to revise the neo-liberal scenario of early globalization, and to engender 'an ethical vision for a global society'. New meanings are needed to formulate such a vision, and give it institutional voice – that is, new constitutions for democracy, which in turn demand altered identities (including national identities) to make them live. Humanity can't jump out of its old, accumulated skin overnight. Not by armed 'shock and awe' tactics, certainly; but neither by committee decisions, religious pontification, or a recycled rhetoric of internationalism. Few would contest the Dalai Lama's urging of 'a sense of universal responsibility' upon twenty-first-century youth; but the *universal* is no longer a prerogative of faith (including his own), it depends upon particular transformations on earth (including Tibet's independence), and the formation of a global climate unintimidated by the legacy of Giantism.

Part I

Rethinking Globalism and Globalization

2
Global Enchantment:
A Matrix of Ideologies

Paul James

Contemporary globalization is remarkable creature. She is an agile, blousy Hollywood-style genie that rarely lives up to her promises yet all too often slips relatively unscathed between the legs of her fiercest critics.[1] Globalization evades critique through many manoeuvres, but I want to concentrate on just two key ways in which the critics themselves inadvertently contribute to capitalist globalization becoming seen either as inevitable or as a (contested) cultural commonsense. Firstly, to the extent that globalization is treated as a process of spatial extension only pertaining to the last two or three decades, we tend to overlook the long-term development of practices and ideas that underpin its contemporary power. Secondly, to the extent that globalism is reduced to an ideology of capitalist economic expansion, we tend to miss out on the way in which it is now carried by a matrix of ideological assumptions across the whole range of contemporary modes of practice from globalizing capitalism to disembodying techno-science.[2] A number of scholars such John Tomlinson, Arjun Appadurai, Manfred Steger, Roland Robertson and James Mittelman have recognized the broader dynamics of globalization, but when it comes to discussing globalism as an ideology-subjectivity most commentators critically focus on deconstructing ideologies that directly defend the globalizing market. Both of these critical moves contribute to reducing globalism to one of its expressions – neo-liberal globalism. To be sure, neo-liberalism is one of the dominant philosophies of our time. However, part of the power of neo-liberalism is, strangely, that it is at one level so contested. Its glaring prominence blinds us to the breadth and depth of a matrix of associated ideologies that are left relatively uninterrogated. In the process, some of the assumptions associated with globalism-in-general slip away unnoticed.

The usual approach is to concentrate on ideologies of progress and economic development, of instrumental management and economic rationalism, but this misses out on lots of others. Take for example the following ideologies. They are ideologies that are usually uncontested or taken for granted. They are sensibilities that affect different people in uneven ways, but they nevertheless constantly impinge upon the various life-worlds of modernized, globalized souls:

1. *interconnectivity*, the cultural imperative to be always available in a loop of potential communicative connection, preferably electronic. This message is being 'benignly' and constantly reinforced by the globalizing mobile-phone market.[3] We feel it in our bodies to the extent that most of us are uncomfortable with its opposite – unchosen isolation. Even when we are in the face-to-face presence of others, we feel the need 'to know', to be in mediated connection with what is happening in the world;

2. *mobility*, the imperative to develop a capacity to move across borders. Here the unease comes from an aversion to being relegated to a projected mire of parochialism. It is easy to see how these ideologies of mobility and interconnectivity intersect with globalism. Electronic interconnectivity, both as practice and idea, helps to sustain our sense of viable open mobility largely free of the attendant perceived risks of dealing with strangers face-to-face. As the world globalizes it simultaneously becomes full of strangers and full of people with whom communication is possible. This further relates to an ideology of security;

3. *security*, the imperative to manage one's place in the mobile risk society. This includes an imperative to manage rogue elements or processes that assail that sense of relative comfort. It is indicative that while opposition to the war on Iraq intensified, it would take a brave person in the West to say that Osama bin Laden is philosophically onto something of value. The definition of him as a rogue element, whether evil or merely criminal, has been almost totalizing;

4. *justice* and *democracy*, the imperative to couch any claims to action in the world in terms of human rights discourse. For example, the importance of deposing the Taliban was in part legitimized by the Bush administration in terms of Taliban oppression of Afghani women. In the aftermath of the war in Afghanistan the continuing oppression of women, documented by such groups as Human Rights Watch, is either glossed over or passed into irrelevancy by assertions of the importance of 'doing something in the first place'. In other words, we are drawn into the importance of a doctrine of war-making now known in the international relations literature as 'humanitarian intervention' in the name of freedom;

5. *freedom*, *autonomy* and *transcendence*, the imperative to overcome limits and oppressions. Does anything more need to be said to explain this set of assumptions?

Who in our modern/postmodern world but a few recalcitrants or neo-traditionalists would argue that any one of these imperatives could be intrinsically bad?[4] This, I argue, is precisely their power as ideologies. At one level, these ideologies are connected as cross-cutting and often contradictory precepts, shovelled up into a grab-bag of clichés that can be delivered out of context, out of contestation. At a deeper level, they form the cultural ground upon which we walk. While the many critics of corporate globalization have been addressing the problems of globalism as they directly confront us, neo-liberal and neo-conservative commentators, such as Francis Fukuyama, have, with minimal scrutiny, been quietly redefining the ground beneath.[5] This chapter addresses these tendencies by broadening out the concept of globalism. It does so across three related sections. Firstly, it broadens the definitions of globalization and globalism; secondly, it sets out a series of methodological arguments about how we might better understand them; and thirdly, it examines one intersection of ideological presuppositions around the concepts of freedom–autonomy–security as it relates to a contemporary example of globalization – the 'War on Terror'.

DEFINING GLOBALISM

The terms associated with 'globalism' appear to be the easiest set of concepts in the world to define. In one way, globalization is simply the spatial extension of social relations across the globe. It is literally evoked in the picture that we have become accustomed to seeing in satellite photographs. However, that definition leaves us concentrating on the last few decades. A working definition of the cluster of terms around 'globalism' begins by relating the various intersecting modes of practice, including the modes of communication, production and exchange, to their extension across world-space. Across human history, as those practices have at one level become more materially abstract, they have maintained or increased their intensity while becoming more extensive and generalized.

Globalization is thus most simply the name given to the matrix of those practices as they extend across world-space. Exemplary contemporary systems of materially powerful but disembodied extension include the stamping presses of finance capital, electronic warfare or electronic broadcast culture. There are, however, earlier or more concrete forms of globalization that need to be incorporated into any definition. There are lines of global connection carried by agents of the early expansionist imperial states, by traders on the silk routes, and by crusading war-makers going off to 'smash the infidels' simply because they were there, living in the same world.[6] These lines of connection were conducted through a quite different matrix of assumptions than those that sit behind contemporary globalization. The crusaders did not draw on ideologies of ideologies of justice or freedom to defend these activities, whereas, by a remarkable reversal of sentiments, George W. Bush began the 'War on Terror' by first calling it a crusade. Thus globalization can be defined as the unevenly structured manifold of social relations, materially enacted through one or more of the various dominant modes of practice – exchange, production, communication, organization and enquiry – and extended across *world-space*, where the notion of 'world-space' is itself defined in the historically variable terms in which it has been practised and understood phenomenally through changing *world-time*. It is thus a process, a matrix of ongoing material practices enacted in the name of historically changing sets of ideological clothing.

The associated concept of 'globalism' is defined as the dominant matrix of ideologies and subjectivities associated with different historical formations of global extension. The definition thus implies that there were premodern or traditional forms of globalism and globalization long before the driving force of capitalism sought to colonize every corner of the globe; for example, going back to the Roman Empire in the second century CE, and perhaps to the Greeks of the fifth century BCE.[7] As the Roman Empire drew lines of practical connection across vast expanses of the known world, Claudius Ptolemaeus (c.90–c.150 CE) revived the Hellenic belief in the Pythagorean theory of a spherical globe. He wrote systematically about a world-space stretching from Caledonia and Anglia to what became known as Java Minor. Alongside the secular empire, the Roman Catholic Church, as its name suggests – *katholikos*, 'universal'; *kata*, 'in respect of'; *holos*, 'the whole' – had globalizing pretensions.

This does not mean that globalism was the dominant or even a generalized understanding of the world. Sacred universalism is not necessarily the same as globalism. By contrast to the European clerics of globalization, the Chinese form of universalism was inwardly turned. For example, although the Celestial Kingdom had produced printed atlases that date long before the European Ortelius' supposedly first historical atlas, early maps of China show the world as fading off beyond the 'natural extent' of territory.[8] While evidence suggests that the Chinese may have travelled the world, this does not mean that they acted through a subjectivity of globalism. In other words, the Chinese centred their empire, whereas the Romans globally extended theirs. If the Roman Peutinger Table is any indication, the Roman world-view was globalizing to the extent that it travelled in geometric lines that stretched as far as the travelling eyes of the agents of empire could see.[9] In the current context, it does not matter whether or not the United States has the same territorial ambitions as the Romans. Globalizing imperialism, as I will argue in the final section, can in different historical contexts take the territorialized form of extending embodied or institutional power or, in the present period, the territorializing form of making the world safe for globalizing democracy.

THEORIZING GLOBALISM

Before moving on to the example of freedom as a totalizing yet contradictory ideology of globalization, I want to make five brief methodological points that carry forward the definitional discussion and help to generalize some starting points for an alternative theory of globalization.

1. Globalization involves extensions of social relations across world-space, defining that world-space in terms of the historically variable ways in which it has been practised and socially understood through changing world-time. In other words, long before that stunning satellite photograph of the globe hit us in the face with the obviousness of planet earth, there were different practices and conceptions of world-space. We may not have previously come close to the current condition of self-conscious globality – an unprecedented development in human history – but processes of globalization and the subjectivities of globalism were occurring, both intended and unintended, to the extent that social relations and subjectivities (together with their ecological consequences) were being given global reach. For example, *subjective* projections of the globe (globalism) emerged with the incipient development of a technical-analytical mode of enquiry by the ancient Greek philosophers. An understanding of the inhabited world-space (the *oecumene*) began to be debated during the sixth and fifth centuries BCE, combining information both from phenomenal experience such as oral testimony and from abstract principles such as geometry.[10] Lines of *objective* global spatial extension (globalization) developed in the traditional empires; arguably, for example, with the Roman Empire as it sought to control the known world.

   Here I am sensitive to the critical excursions of Justin Rosenberg in his raunchy polemic, *The Follies of Globalisation Theory*.[11] As he argues, some writers have elevated changes in the nature of time and space into a grand architecture of explanation that tends to dehistoricize the processes of global extension. Notwithstanding Rosenberg's telling methodological injunction that if globalization involves spatial extension it cannot be explained by invoking the claim that world-space is now global – the explanation and the thing-being-explained, he rightly says, are thus reduced into a self-confirming circle – it is still, I suggest, legitimate to treat globalization is a *descriptive* category referring to a process of extension across a historically constituted world-space. An explanation as to why the dominant modes of practice contribute to the genie of globalization is not contained inside the definition, even if a method for beginning such an enquiry is inferred. With a few refinements that is all that I am doing here.

2. The form of globalization has been, and continues to be, historically changing. This can be analytically understood in terms of globalization taking fundamentally different forms across world history, or even within one historical moment. In any particular period, globalization ranges from embodied extensions of the social, such as through the movements of peoples, to the disembodied extensions, such as through communications on the wings of textual or digital encoding. In terms of the present argument, across human history, the dominant forms of globalization range from the *traditional* (primary carried by the embodied movement of peoples and the projections of traditional intellectuals) to the *modern* and *postmodern* (primarily carried by disembodied practices of abstracted extension and the projections of a emergent cosmopolitan class of the intellectually trained).[12] The definition thus is also sensitive to Roland Robertson's argument that globalism is a deep historical and variable process. However, by including the Roman Empire as having both globalizing sensibilities and practices, it extends Robertson's chronicle of the 'germinal stage' back long before the beginning of *modern* forms of globalism in the fifteenth century with the *revival* of a spherical view of the world.[13] The earlier form of globalism is what might be called 'traditional globalism' – with all the attendant issues of social form that the concept of 'traditionalism' entails.

This means that the present approach fundamentally questions modernists like Anthony Giddens who suggest that globalism is a consequence of modernity, and utterly rejects theorists such as Martin Albrow who, in a fit of theoretical exuberance, claims that globality is now replacing modernity.[14] Giddens, in this view, does not have more than a single-layered sense of history, and Albrow makes a stunning category mistake. Albrow overlooks the issue that 'modernism' and 'globalism' come to us from two categorically different levels of analysis: 'globalization' is a descriptive term, an empirical generalization made about various processes of spatial extension, whereas 'modernism' is a categorical term that can only be understood in terms of positing either a kind of subjectivity/aesthetic or a general ontological formation. Processes of globalization developed long before modernity (understood provisionally in epoch terms only as a dominant, not totalizing formation), and they will probably continue long after its heyday. However, this does not mean that globality is replacing modernity. It means that the dominant form of globalization and globalism is changing, as is the once-assumed dominance of modernism. Even as modern forms of globalism and imperialism continue, they are overlaid with postmodern forms: from the globalization of capital as it commodifies future-time through speculative hedging, to the globalization of cinematic culture with its postmodern sensibility signalled, for example, in the title of a new magazine of Hollywood gloss – *Empire*.[15] Abstracted from history, the title carries no more than the most obvious superficial irony.

3. The driving structural determinants of *contemporary* globalization are capitalism (based on an accelerating electronic mode of production and an expanding mode of commodity and financial exchange), mediatism (the systemic interconnectivity of a mass-mediated world, based on a mode of electronically networked communication), and techno-scientism (based on a new intersection between the mode of production and the mode of enquiry). Contemporary globalization has reached its present stage of relative globality under conditions of the intersection of each of these modes of practice. For example, satellite transmission, cable networking and the internet were all developed techno-scientifically as means of communication within state-supported capitalist markets that rapidly carried globalization to a new dominant level of technological mediation.[16]

4. One of the driving ideological determinants of contemporary globalization is the contested philosophy of neo-liberalism. However, the ideological-subjective grounding of globalization also goes much deeper and wider than ideologies of the economic. Globalization is carried forward through the relatively uncontested territory of the taken-for-granted assumptions of our time. Ideologies of economic globalism, from notions of market freedom to the joy of a 'borderless world', have naturalized the techniques and technologies of global extension as the inevitable outcomes of material progress. However, more than that, globalism partakes of the excitement that surrounds generalized notions of autonomy, mediation and interconnectivity.

5. Globalization does not inevitably sweep all aside before it. All that is solid does not melt into air. For example, processes of globalization may eventually undermine the sovereignty of the nation-state, but there is no inevitability about such an outcome, in neither logic nor reality. It is salutary to remember that the institutions and structures of modern globalization and the modern nation-state were born during the same period; they were formed through the concurrent processes, with the tension between these two phenomena being over boundary formation and sovereignty rather than in general. This argument goes directly against those who would treat nation formation and global formation as the antithetical outcomes of respectively a 'first and second modernity', or those who would narrowly define globalization as that which undermines the nation-state.[17] In the context of contemporary globalization we have seen both nationalist revivals and reassertions of tribalism. In the present climate, nationalism is one of those too-easily-dismissed ideologies, one that keeps returning from the dead despite the confidence of the obituary writers.

F IS FOR FREEDOM, G IS FOR GLOBALISM AND P IS FOR PATRIOTISM

Continuing the theme of the relationship between globalism and nationalism, it is important to recognize how certain kinds of postnationalism or civic nationalism are comfortably presented as compatible with the globalization of the market. While critics of corporate globalization rightly point to the contradiction between the homeland emphasis on national integrity and the neo-liberal emphasis on 'no borders' versions of the capitalist market, such critique has little effect on the proponents of this dual projection. The dominant neo-liberal definition of the market as the open flow of commodities, commercial culture and capital across the world is treated, within this new dominant commonsense, as just the extension of the national interest outwards.

For an ideologue such as Lynne Cheney, overt nationalism is a bad thing, but patriotic support of America as the nation that exemplifies the virtue of global freedom, including freedom of the market, cannot be anything but a good thing. In her recent children's book, *America: A Patriotic Primer*,[18] the market – neoliberal or otherwise – does not get a mention. We travel from 'A is for America, the land that we love', to 'Z is for the end of the alphabet, but not of America's story. Strong and free we will continue to be an inspiration to the world', without any defence of capitalist globalization. Nevertheless, during that journey the abiding presumption is of *the* globalizing nation reaching out and carrying the possibilities of freedom to others. In this last section of the present chapter, discussing the ideology of freedom as one of the ideologies of globalism is thus intended as a way of showing the breadth of the ideologies that underpin globalization. It is also intended to carry one of the central themes of the present book, one that both Tom Nairn and I both consistently argue – namely, that *modern* globalism and *modern* nationalism are bound up with each other. Globalization does not necessarily mean the end of nationalism is nigh.

The notion of freedom includes a bevy of associated words that flock together, words such as 'autonomy', 'liberty', 'independence', 'emancipation', 'choice' and 'openness'. While the meaning of 'freedom to choose' has been rewritten by the marketeers with cars named 'Freedom' and 'Freelander', and with Ford's advertising in 2003 running under the slogan 'no boundaries' the subjectivity of freedom transcends Left and Right debates. Even neo-liberal notions of freedom are much broader than usually portrayed and related to such ideologies as 'making the world free for democracy'. Ronald Reagan expressed it beautifully as a divine assignment to spread the 'sacred fire of human liberty'. The only way potentially to enhance our sense of security and democracy is firstly to totalize the freedom of 'us', 'the good guys' (I cannot think of a better name for 'us') and secondly to objectify the others as abstract strangers and a potential threat. It is an apparent paradox because this particular concept of 'freedom' entails developing the infrastructure to defend the free movement and operation of some, and to strictly curtail the freedom of others. Examples abound. The Patriot Act of 2001 is a massive document extending powers that were already more than adequate for the purpose. Since September 11, 2001, secret hearings and detentions have been held for 1,200 persons in the United States, mostly Muslim persons arrested on immigration charges under the Act. Others have been detained in a military prison in a US-controlled section of Cuba without recourse to legal representation. And on 5 June 2002, we first heard the announcement of an intention to revive the long-dormant powers of the 1952 immigration law with tens of thousands of visitors from Islamic countries to be fingerprinted, potentially increasing to 5 million persons per year by 2005.

The failure of 'totalizing control' ever to attain static ascendancy gives us a way of explaining why the culture war over the concept of 'freedom' is so important (see also Chapter 15). Whether we are talking about the 'freedom/ fear' and 'freedom/terror' contrasts, or the 'global free trade/national closure' polarity, the concept of 'freedom' has become paramount. In the USA as the *home* of the *free*, all of those terms have become linked as coextensive. Totalizing security projections have been projected inward as 'homeland security'. This has involved organizational co-ordination and breathless announcements (6 June 2002) of a new single permanent department to secure the American homeland. The Secretary of Homeland Security is to be in cabinet, and to co-ordinate the FBI and CIA with an upgrading the status of the homeland security office currently headed by Tom Ridge. Careful language-use has permeated even the titles of bits of legislation: the title of the 'USA Patriot Act' acts as a form of cultural closure on the possibility that the intended changes can be criticized as curtailing freedoms. More than that, the title of the Act, an acronym for Uniting and Strengthening America by Providing Appropriate Tools Required to Intercept and Obstruct Terrorism (USA PATRIOT), ties the act of being American and the necessity of the War to Defend Freedom together. Speeches for home consumption continually posit a fight between willed freedom and weak fear with the repetitive use of phrases such as 'weapons of mass destruction' (WMD) 'rogue states' and the 'need for pre-emptive strikes', with pre-emptive intervention supposedly combating rogue states in order to make the world safe from WMD. George W. Bush's State of the Union address of 30 January 2003 is a case in point:

Our war against terror is a contest of will in which perseverance is power. In the ruins of two towers, at the western wall of the Pentagon, on a field in Pennsylvania, this nation made a pledge, and we renew that pledge tonight. Whatever the duration of this struggle and whatever the difficulties, we will not permit the triumph of violence in the affairs of men. Free people will set the course of history ... Now, in this century, the ideology of power and domination has appeared again and seeks to gain the ultimate weapons of terror. Once again, this nation and all our friends are all that stand between a world at peace and a world of chaos and constant alarm. Once again we are called to defend the safety of our people, and the hopes of all mankind ... We exercise power without conquest, and we sacrifice for the liberty of strangers. Americans are free people, who know that freedom is the right of every person and the future of every nation. The liberty we prize is not America's gift to the world, it is God's gift to humanity.

Even when projected externally and globally, much of the rhetoric is for domestic consumption in the West. The 'Axis of Evil' notion deliberately echoes Reagan's 'Evil Empire', and both have their origins in the Second World War period. Similarly, the concept of global action in the name of humanity has a history going back to the middle of the twentieth century: for example, the use of images of globalism has long been part of national US institutions of war-making or space exploration. The official badged icons for the US Department of Defense, the Navy SEALS and the Joint Special Operations Command, the Strategic Computing Program and the Defense Advanced Research Projects Agency (DARPA) as a whole, take the globe as their symbol of territorial reach. The war on terrorism is predicated on a rhetoric legitimizing attacking the source of evil in distant locations. In George Bush's terms, 'We must be ready to strike at a moment's notice in any dark corner of the world' (West Point speech, 1 June 2002). Overlaying that older rhetoric is a newer claim about the legitimacy of pre-emptive strikes to protect our way of life against totalizing evil. Donald Rumsfeld, speaking at the NATO headquarters in Brussels (6 June 2002), opened up this new convergence of the notions of 'freedom to act' and 'totalizing control'. 'Absolute proof cannot be a precondition for action', he said. He was supported by the British Defence Secretary talking about the possibility of using nuclear weapons against the threat of chemical and biological attack. This is part of a postmodern redefinition of the conventions of international law. Under the conventions of modern international law, *pre-emption* and *retaliation* become illegal as rationales for action. It became illegitimate to strike first just in case something might happen, or to respond to a single act of aggression by retaliating in kind to send a message. What we are seeing now is the neo-liberal rewriters of international relations attempting to recuperate traditional notions of 'an eye for an eye', notions that provided the map for earlier tracks of globalization, such as the religious crusades.

However, in these contradictory times retaliation has made a comeback in a reconstituted and more abstract form – this time as a pastiche of floating and *ad hoc* rationalizations. Retaliation is never explicitly enunciated as the motivational basis of action, much less revenge. Now, 'pre-emption' before the putative 'event', and 'humanitarian intervention' after the putative 'event', are used as a dynamic duo of legitimizing abstract signifiers. In the aftermath of September 11, it was claimed that the attack was so massive that in effect it could be taken as a declaration of continuous war, thus warranting continuous defence.[19] This was despite the fact that no one declared such war, no one even took responsibility for the act of terror, and only circumstantial evidence was available to decide upon whom the retaliation should be effected. Within no time the terrorists had a generic name – *terrorism*. They were all Islamic, and they were found in every primeval corner of the globe. The stakes are high, and the battlefield is global.

All of this makes seemingly academic tasks, such as adequately defining globalization and being clear about what it is, extremely important. Defining globalization as the uneven but structured manifold of connections across world-space, taking that space in the historically variable terms in which it has been *socially understood* through changing world-time, arguably helps us to recognize both its objective and subjective character. Furthermore, by broadening out the terms of analysis it is suggested that we are less likely to come to the conclusion that our globalization is good and theirs is bad. Globalization is always ethically ambiguous. Like all social practices, globalization is always structured as relations of power, and these relations of power – both structural and ideological – need to be analysed in the broadest possible way.

3
Global Trajectories: America and the Unchosen[1]

Tom Nairn

Why this sudden bewilderment, this confusion?
(How serious people's faces have become)
Why are the streets and squares emptying so rapidly,
Everyone going home lost in thought?
Because night has fallen and the barbarians haven't come.
And some of our men just in from the border say
There are no barbarians any longer.
Now what's going to happen us without barbarians?
Those people were a kind of solution.

C.P. Cavafy, 'Waiting for the Barbarians' (1898), in *Collected Poems* (1998)

Often the attack on Iraq is presented as a straightforward prosecution both of US neo-imperial foreign policy and of globalization. It may be the former, but is not automatically the latter. The two things are no longer the same. In fact, this war may represent the most serious blow *against* globalization, as that process has emerged and begun to define itself since the end of the Cold War. What the assault aimed to do was drag the process backwards, under 'Western' (but really American) leadership. Its aim was to force an awakened American nationalism into a more decidedly imperial mould – which can only be done by 'old-fashioned' techniques. Barbarians must be reinvented and patriots be turned into Homelanders in order to prop up a half-elected President, and to realign restive or dissident satrapies. With all its shortcomings and contradictions, globalization had been showing signs of escaping from US neo-liberal hegemony over the past few years. Tragically, it is believed in some places that a 'good war' will help to rein in such trends, by establishing a new kind of empire-boundary – the apocalyptic, and by definition, unceasing fight against terrorism. Paul James gets at this in his concept of the 'meta-war' (Chapter 17), and Gore Vidal has phrased it very well: 'perpetual war for perpetual peace'.[2] Like them, I want to argue that this effort stands no chance of long-term success – a fact unlikely to influence the policy makers in Bush's Washington.

In the context of recent incursions many writers have made convincing cases that US policy makers were motivated by a long-term strategic need, which they perceive as requiring control of Iraq's oil reserves. However, the very long-term nature of this interest means that it can't explain America's decision to move immediately to ensure its regional supremacy *now*. Why the implacable urgency, the sense of life or death, and the grotesque inflation of 'Terrorism' into an apocalyptic menace? It does feel like Cavafy's poem: barbarians are required to justify civilization in its chosen course. It may incline one to think that other factors must be in operation. Is it not America's role in the world, some important part of its inherited national identity, that since September 11, 2001, has been felt to be at stake?

Globalization is bigger than America. A ragged and confused divorce was well under way well before September 11. Since 1989, the underlying globalization process had begun to emancipate itself from a US hegemony that stemmed from the nature of the Cold War, and the way it ended. The 1990s may have initiated globalization, but they were also marked by something very anachronistic – the unusual, overwhelming domination of a single country. The latter drove forward the information stage of globalization (which I will define more precisely later). But the underlying drive of globalization was to decentre and share this out. It may be true that it could not have arisen without US dominance and hegemony. However, this in itself will not prevent the same nemesis as has affected all imperiums of the past. Beneficiaries are ungrateful by definition. They always think they will benefit most by ceasing to depend, and becoming equals. Now globalism will simply have to emancipate itself from its initial, but also primitive, American definition. The process was brusquely accelerated, or shocked onwards by the events of September 11 – above all, in consciousness. But an unavoidable part of this greater awareness is a determination to restore the disturbed equilibrium in the interests of those guiding it – the 'national interest' already indicated, the Cold War bequest underwritten (supposedly) by the post-1989 triumph of One Market Under God.[3]

Let me attempt to sketch how this may have been working out. Those who died on September 11 were 'ordinary people', identified with as such by (we must assume) a majority of the world's population. One common reaction was to feel it was 'like being in a disaster movie' made over into the real thing. However, what this film also reflected was 'real' in a sense that no epic adventure had ever been: individuals 'just like us' were indeed being put through it, and not in their or our dreams. Viewers entered hell by direct empathy, not via Harrison Ford. However, ordinary mixed-up people dwell by definition in an ordinary society – in this case a society, it turned out, visibly unprotected by either the CIA or Divine Providence. They do not dwell in the City on a Hill, beacon to and leader of all mankind, home of the free and the Cato Institute, but in, well ... just another country. A big country, of course, with an awful lot of resources and most of the world's military hardware – and with a dominant culture still beset by elite notions of centrality and chosen-ness. Such a nation – or, more to the point, such a *state* – presents big problems for everybody else. But these are problems of a recognizable, historically ordinary, kind.

In other words, the global meaning of the accident was contagiously greater than America itself. The very thing so many commentators and anchor persons so volubly expressed – 'a universal tragedy' touching everyone – meant that it would never be completely recuperable or possessed by the United States. The mental explosion had already encompassed the globe. Hence the problem for both Oval Office statehood and the neo-liberal clerics was more like shrinkage: how to cut it back to manageable size, thereby restoring their own definitional role. Heroism became one focus for the expression of their anxious efforts to appropriate and 'nationalize' the September 11 events. It in no way reflects upon the courage shown by so many, to consider whether among the normal individuals of diverse faith and hue who perished that day – the janitors, cleaners, secretaries, sandwich-makers, young executives and firemen – some may have been planning an early exit to the beach, or hoping that the boss had suffered a heart attack overnight. Were *none* of those managers putting in their daily call to Arthur Andersen Inc., or thinking of selling their shares in Enron? The point is not to impugn memories, but simply to point out that, even if solemnly expunged from iconic versions of the day, such humdrum thoughts must have figured in the shared worldwide reaction from the outset. Ordinary folk (of whom we are all specimens) know what we ordinary folk are like – and the poignancy of September 11 remains inseparable from this. What struck people to the heart was a shared, universal loss and fortitude, as well as the specific heroism 'of New Yorkers'.

What follows, by an instinct no less immediate than the amorphous shift behind it, is that an 'ordinary country', however large, may have all sorts of strengths and weaknesses. It is, however, by moral definition *without entitlement to being judge and gendarme of the international order*. In fact, no country or state can be entitled in that way. During the long preceding clash of quasi-religious ideologies, from the 1930s up to the 1980s, this was by no means so evident. Up to the 1990s, plausible if specious alibis still abounded – intact zealotries of race, blood, class or spirit, whose innate tendency was fallacious universalism. But now all these are sunk for good. As I have argued before, a 'really existing' internationality has come into existence, bearing warts, contradictions and all else human. The atrocious slaughter of September 11 was also the moment of their stage farewell. In the plainer arena a mounting preference for international regulation and action on international affairs is the sole possibility. This may have all sorts of shortcomings; indeed it may be more shortcomings than achievements.

But it is no longer just weakness or absence of moral fibre, as has been so consistently suggested by President Bush's accomplices. Thus the rest of the world is increasingly taking the opposite reaction to that of official America and its media. As the US proclaims a perpetual War on Terror starting with the Axis of Evil, Schroeder, Lula and Roe are elected in Germany, Brazil and South Korea on the strength of popular opposition to Bush's influence – a combination unimaginable during the Cold War. The President still has his dogs, naturally, reared in one or another 'special relationship' – Blair in London, Howard in Canberra, Berlusconi in Rome – but before long, I suspect that even they will be trailing back to their kennels.

On September 11 an identifiable order perished before the eyes of the rest of the world. This was a unique epiphany that engendered 'a loss for words'. However, meanings already in the air at once rushed into this void. The resultant tidal commotion of American nationalism only confirmed them. This was the reaction of a nation justifiably brought to passionate and civic life. But in the gaze of everywhere else, that is also *all* that it was: a nation, not humanity's beacon rekindled, or resumption of the State Department's divine right to reconfigure the rest of the world. The great nation itself was moved to action, pursued the forces that had assaulted it into Afghanistan, and toppled the regime supporting them. But Washington was unsatisfied. Now guided by a redemption-minded heartland, it represents the older, chosen nation – an elect and destiny-bearing contingent, intended by some higher authority to mark out Heaven's acre. This transcendent meaning of America, discussed by Paul James in Chapter 15, carries its own fundamentalism, and now called for far wider regime changes, and a worldwide mission – that is, an impossible war against Terrorism as such, with the subtext of imposition of one conception upon the globe. A national *redressement* passed straight into an outward-directed crusade.

Is it a crusade 'for democracy'? One acute commentary on this feature of post-2001 has been given by Anatol Lieven, who writes:

> When it comes to democracy, the American establishment's conscience flickers on and off like a strobe light in a seedy disco. The rest of the world can see this ... [but a] naïve belief in the universal, immediate applicability of US-style democracy, and America's right and duty to promote this, is an article of national ideological faith in the US. It easily shades over into a messianism which is, in itself, nationalist and imperialist.[4]

Nationalism is the most potent of social forces, and for that very reason the most in need of systemic *and contemporary* democratic rigidity. Otherwise (notoriously) a combination of external threat and autocracy causes it to default into populism, and in the American and British cases this has now come about. Their anachronistic, and indeed failing, representational systems are trying to compensate for blatant deficits by a combination of tabloid antics and external heroics.

The American administration calls this 'leadership'. The rest of the world begs to differ. In the 1990s the world witnessed a precipitous decline in the moral authority of the United States under Clinton. Then his replacement culminated in the non-election of a successor. In an astounding yet defining moment, a whole year before 9/11, the globalization process suddenly found itself captained by and dependent upon defective voting machines, gerrymandering and chicanery in the state of Florida. Worse was instantly to follow – a US Supreme Court that would stop at nothing to salvage this hopelessly outdated constitution from self-destruction. At which point, far from globalism being led by America towards democracy, it became hostage to a blatant democratic deficit – a partly familial *coup d'état* that was to put George W. Bush in charge of most of the globe's military power. To sum up so far: even without the seismic shift of 9/11 and after, no acceptable world order could conceivably have been led from this vantage point. Globalization had emerged as an approximately common *economic* terrain after 1989, and – as Anthony Giddens argues in his *Runaway World*[5] – started to develop a life-momentum of its own. No one now believes this will be halted, let alone reversed. Leadership of the process is a *political* question, however, and one about which, it should now be clear, will never merely emerge from the *Homo economicus* of neo-liberal superstition. Instead, it is being hijacked by a Texas Ranger and his hounds. All this involves more than economics and short-range political tactics. It raises deeper issues of *meaning*, and calls for a much broader perspective – a view of human and societal nature in fact, seeking to look beyond this disaster zone and explore the new common ground.

GLOBALIZATION TODAY

I argued earlier that America has now become the enemy of globalization. Of course 'America' here refers primarily and unfairly to the administration of George W. Bush. Many Americans have a more benign view of the rest of the world and a more cautious awareness of the limits of American wealth and power – suffering from a lack of the latter, as most of them do. The continuing Middle Eastern expeditionary force is an attempt to keep globalizing forces in safe hands. But the 'hands' are those of the state, and also of the now vast and influential neo-liberal clerisy of journalists, academics and corporate leaders who have so recklessly thrown in their lot with George W. Bush's foreign policy. These must not be confused with the hands, or the will, of the American people. In December 2001, the British journalist and writer Bonnie Greer made a moving and informative BBC2 documentary about the reaction to the September 11 events of the 'ordinary Americans' she had known, principally from the black community in Chicago. Even then, the result was strikingly at odds from what has become the standard patriotic litany: sceptical, and searching for better justifications than those handed out by the media. The American Left may have been temporarily overwhelmed by the orchestrated reaction of post-September 11, but no one should assume this will endure.

In their widely read debate on the Open Democracy website, two of the world's leading scholars of globalization, David Held and Paul Hirst, have surveyed its nature, their different interpretations and how they see the future.[6] Hirst argues that the concept is misconceived. He opposes the neo-liberal view that a global economic process is sweeping national politics into impotence; he insists that measured by the degree of trade and other economic indicators, the world has merely managed to recover the degree of internationalization it achieved in 1914, before the outbreak of the First World War; and he scorns the idea that global rules and institutions can replace the traditional power of great states. Held agrees with Hirst that the 'hyper-globalizers' are wrong to foresee the inevitable success of neo-liberalism and economic forces free from other motivations. But he places greater emphasis on the originality and extent of globalization today, and sees both the necessity and the possibility of creating a cosmopolitan response to it at the global level.

Few who have read the exchange are likely to be any longer either 'for' or 'against' globalization as such. While the two contenders thrash out the historic canvass and the international reach of the forces at work, it is clear to both that if the nature and meaning of globalization remains disputed, its existence has become rooted and irreversible. Around the same time as this debate was published, the World Social Forum prepared for its conference at Porto Alegre by calling for global justice. The Forum gathered together the 'anti-globalizers'. While their image as opponents of globalization has become an essential icon for media coverage, the press and television especially in the Anglo-Saxon countries actually failed to cover much of what it was about. The fact is that it was one step in globalization itself, a pioneering global movement with, as Chomsky put it, some claim to represent the truth of the process, as distinct from the giddy abstractions of neo-liberal apostles and their 'No Alternative' political drones.

Critics have also complained the Forum was like an interminable series of seminars. The judgement was accurate, but the censure was revealingly mistaken. The world desperately needs debate about the new turning, and the slow formulation of alternative stories and projected meanings is crucial. Open Democracy's Held–Hirst polemic and the present book are only more contributions to this ongoing 'seminar'. The aim of the seminar has perhaps been best put by Roberto Unger and Dani Rodrik in their admirable website at www.sopde.org (the Seminar on Progressive Democratic Economies).

What is needed is not desperate recuperation of has-been state socialism or garbled papier mâché concoctions like the 'Third Way'. As Unger says, the question boils down to formulation of a viable 'second way', an alternative to the intolerable dystopia now being inflicted by Bush, Blair, Berlusconi and their horde of pseudo-global termites. Of course, this has to include a global opposition 'from below' to the annual gathering of corporate, financial, institutional and political leaders of the world's main economies at Davos. And there may be more to it than that. Without at least a dose of anarchism, how can the world learn to breathe again?

Those concerned about chattering conventicles and the resurgence of assorted Old Adams might also turn to reassure themselves with the recent thoughts of the singular figure who bridges these two worlds – George Soros. This unimpeachably practical capitalist, who did possibly more than any other individual to usher in the victory of neo-liberalism in the 1990s, has turned against his own progeny. He is still too much of a chatterer (or genuine intellectual) to accept what they have made of his work. His Central European University was meant to foster liberty and democracy – an open society, rather than the termite-mound of manic deregulation and take-all rapacity that grew so monstrously beyond the fallen walls of 1989. By 1998, in *The Crisis of Global Capitalism*, he was already acutely (and of course, knowingly) aware of the contradiction. His more recent *George Soros on Globalization* has carried the argument farther.[7] With typical self-critical candour, Soros wrote near the end of *The Crisis* that he felt disturbed by the sheer abstraction and implausibility of the talk about alternatives then going on. But since then things have become considerably more concrete. Opposition from below has swelled and gained in confidence and sophistication. The proof that a new stage of globalization has arrived is at all levels. It is not so much economic as political and cultural ... and *human*. Neo-liberal economism still deals with what the Marxists used to call 'petty-bourgeois' entities – 'economic men' and women like the dessicated calculators of legend, rational-choice rodents moved exclusively by the short-range and the quantifiable.

At the same time, the real world of initial globalization has been convulsed by a colossal migratory movement in which ever-growing numbers of 'ordinary folk' have globalized themselves in advance (as it were) by climbing into aircraft holds and leaky boats, and making for town – often someone else's town, across any number of frontiers, with defective or non-existent paperwork. Driven largely by unquantifiable desperation and long-range risks, by rage against confinement and hopes for new life-chances and identities, these nomads are a millions-strong repudiation of economists' fantasies. As all serious surveys of the phenomenon admit, this is also a contemporary reprise of one of the oldest constitutive factors of human society. The global countryside deciding to go to town, in such numbers and so unstoppably, is a qualitative shift that in turn alters the parameters and makes return unthinkable. It is terribly poor form, of course, for those to whom 'globalization' meant cosy transnationalism and capital transfers. The governing neo-liberal myopia perceives migration as a contemporary malaise, calling for miserable, short-term therapies of restriction and control, or forced-march assimilation. But the same analyses make the point of how futile such steps are likely to be. There's no use hurrying rolls of razor wire to the border to stop George Cavafy's 'barbarians'. As in his poem, they are 'no longer there' and find ever better and earlier ways to cross – when the sun was still scattering the stars to flight, and 'striking the Sultan's turret with a shaft of light'.

The results are nothing like a homogeneous, uniformly 'global' world. Anthropologists are often far better at observing such changes than political scientists or sociologists. Books such as *The Anthropology of Globalization* show not how omnipresent and inescapable America is in this process, but exactly the opposite. In most new global transactions the US impinges only marginally or partially (where it shows up at all). A similarly disconcerting panorama is provided in the collection *Many Globalizations.*[8] In *The Anthropology of Globalization* a particularly good example is James Ferguson's bitter portrait of today's Zambian 'Copperbelt'. Here, deindustrialization has brought about 'the un-making, rather than the making, of a working class'. The technological advances made by the information explosion have lessened demand for copper wiring, and hence for the main Zambian export. Fibre optics and satellite communication have altered the nature of the 'wired world', disastrously for Zambians. The mining and industrial development that was supposed to make them part of the wider world is suffering severe contraction, and the usual remedies of privatization – lay-offs and 'back to the land' schemes. Most Zambians never made a phone call in their lives, Ferguson points out; but some of them did live in hope of doing so, via the copper wiring they were helping to export to everywhere else. Now they are getting used to the idea they never will. Here, the 'New World Order' means more and more 'poor Africans', unless of course these new 'barbarians' can scrape together enough to emigrate. Ferguson sums up his account powerfully:

A fundamental point is suggested in this small detail. That is that what we have come to call globalization is not simply a process that links together the world but also one that differentiates it. It creates new inequalities even as it brings into being new commonalities and lines of communication. And it creates new, up-to-date ways not only of connecting places but of bypassing and ignoring them.[9]

The former system meant they were supposed to 'catch up' by the right mixture of political nationalism and industrial development (Zambia gained independence in 1964). Failure of this formula has resulted in marginalization and what Ferguson calls 'abjection' – uneven development rendered unassailable and permanent, in a population with an average life expectancy of just over 37 years. Among the factors that stalled Zambian expectations was the rise and rise of the mobile telephone, that indispensable tool of connectedness. Who needs copper wire, when they have ether waves and regular relay-masts? As Ferguson puts it, this is a perfect symbol of the new world order which habitually 'presents itself as a phenomenon of pure connection' and inexorable interaction. Of course the US-led information revolution played an important role here, but its articulation assumes wildly varying, concrete and distant forms, where the first causes disappear from view.

This was brought vividly home to me on the day I happened to read his essay, while in a plane returning home from Australia to Scotland. I landed in the latter's 'industrial belt', which in the 1980s and 1990s had become a significant producer of mobile phones. The news there was that 1,200 producers of mobile phones, including our next-door neighbour, had just lost their jobs. After a steep fall in demand for mobiles over 1999–2001, the Motorola Corporation was pulling out of Scotland and relocating somewhere cheaper (and not in Zambia). Resignedly, I switched on my old-style copper-wire-connected computer to internet news of indignant local protests about marginalization, and the utter failure of both politicians and outworn development formulae. In this zone of once immovable Labour (and even New Labour) voters, local MP Tam Dalyell was instructing his constituents to take it on the chin, preferably lying down. Unseemly protests were unnecessary because the Motorola management (quite decent chaps) were doing simply everything in their power to help them. My object here is not spurious parallels between very different situations, but to underline the same common factor that Ferguson stresses. The 'one world' of globalism is no ectoplasmic sphere from which 'uneven development' will vanish, exorcized by priestly spells of economic correctness. It is much more likely to be one in which unevenness increases – and above all, increases *in consciousness*. Counter-spells invoking the standards of 'cosmopolitanism' will have little purchase upon such differentiation. They will need more robust sources to mobilize their own will to challenge such outcomes.

Here, Paul Hirst's emphasis on the continuing necessity of the national state as the primary hearth of countervailing democratic power is well taken. But this surely implies that nationality politics are needed to mobilize resistance against such outrages, and to formulate on-the-spot alternatives. Far from disappearing, nationalism is changing its skin. The buzz-saws of marketolatry rasp out their habitual comment here: where 'protectionism' is given an inch, can ethnic cleansing be far behind? Thus phony history is added to the dismal apologetics of the moment. The modern nation-state has behind it a phased development, still under way – from the Westphalian kingdoms of the seventeenth century up to the iron-clad Leviathans that came after the Franco-Prussian War in the 1870s. It will evolve differently again under the conditions of globalization, inwardly conditioned by the latter's vast climate shift.

Look around the British-Irish archipelago of today. It used to be considered as the veritable forge of the nation-state, a template of modernity. Liah Greenfeld's *Nationalism*[10] argued that it was the true stem-cell of most later political development. In Northern Ireland, Scotland and Wales, three very distinct models of novel self-government are already visible. The older ethno-nationalism of the Irish Republic is altering so quickly that no one can keep up with it, and still newer versions are surfacing within England itself. Of course consciousness is important in all this, and much more salient since the 9/11 turning point. It is difficult to pin down, but I suggest it may be closer to what the American poet Robert E. Duncan meant 30 years ago when he wrote that the story of our age is that of people 'coming to share one common fate'. 'Fate' has a literary or even a religious resonance, but I think this is not inappropriate. It may be what people 'obscurely feel', but then, in this context, that may be the important thing. 'Feeling' is a mode of thinking too – a way, perhaps, of both seeking out and confirming novel parameters of evolution. Searching to define this, the Welsh novelist and critic Raymond Williams referred to 'structures of feeling'. Originally the parameters of Fate were supposed to be divine. God decreed them, and often decreed that his Chosen Ones were endemically superior to the misbegotten or the leftover rest. Now, the horizons of an uncapitalized fate are simply a cognitively shrinking globe and the knowledge that none are chosen – and hence, none can be second-rate either.

This of course involves a 'climate change', rather than just a crafty reconfiguration of ideas. It has not been beamed down from the Enterprise Institute or from departments of postmodern sociology. Changing metaphors, it is more like a breach birth out of the old world. The first cries suggest something quite different from the traditional ideological projections of universality made by religions, or by the abstract secular Enlightenment of the eighteenth century. Globalizing awareness seems more like 'being in the same boat' than any form of exalted transcendence. In fact the 'boat' may be leaking, unstable, overcrowded and squabbling, with the passengers fighting over the dwindling rations and water, as well as over which direction the craft should take. But none the less, what has come to count for far more is another version of transcendence: the awkward and uneasy recognition of that non-reversible 'common fate', in Duncan's sense.

After the Berlin Wall came down, all particular political borders lost their absolute and dividing certainty. Since 1989, humankind's development is not and never will again be threatened by essential societal (or biosocial) divergence – threatened, I mean, by an Elect of Aryans or White Australians or America-Firsters or Socialist Men (gender stereotypes were essential for essentialism). Without completely losing their old meanings and functions, borders have already acquired a new and less divisive meaning. Quietly, uncelebrated by pageant or ideological transports, like the greyest imaginable break of day, oneness crept in, and has come to stay. New parameters of awareness have started to form, far beneath the histrionics of neo-liberal one-worldism. Though not a by-product of science, it is important to note that this consciousness was almost at once underwritten by the advances made in genetics. Practitioners of 'It was no coincidence that ...' still have much to say about this, I know. But it must be of some importance that the last vestiges of Social Darwinism have finally been put to rest. That elaborate culture of delusion stretching from Robert Knox (1791–1862) down to the Montana Militias and Jean-Marie Le Pen has taken to its death-bed, amid appropriate death-rattles. Which does not mean that *racism* expired. Its '-ism' has lost all credibility, but not the differentiations that it sought in vain to justify. Mind-sets do not vanish just because they are without a civilizational future. At best, they fade away within the advancing common fate. At worst, they pitch themselves, not just against a definable enemy whom they can hope to frustrate, but against a global one whose extent defies their puny influence and may therefore provoke even more extreme measures, imparting a new character to political violence itself.

VIOLENCE AND GLOBALIZATION

One issue in particular now forces reflection on just what this mutation of consciousness from a nation-state to a globalized world means – namely, the altering character of political *violence*. Few more urgent issues confront individuals as well as governments right now. We should not leave the issue to President Bush and his advisors and allies, but need to try and figure it out for ourselves. For this is the question capable of carrying us beyond economics, to the cultural and political heart of what these shifts may portend. Not so long ago 'physical force' like blowing things up (bridges, institutions, supposedly detested symbols like statues, emblems of the state) and occasionally assassinating hated individuals (presidents, governors, traitors to the cause) was a regular aspect of political struggles. Nationalism was the most common single motivation for such old-hat violence. It aimed at liberating a people from oppression by some overarching state, which was of course usually supported by some other people or nationality. The justifying formula was nationalist movements followed by 'nation-building' (or sometimes rebuilding), since the nation-state was accepted as generally right and inevitable.

This recipe was never uncontested or free from disasters, but it was at least *intelligible*, and its more or less tried-and-tested solutions were based upon an approximate global realization of such objectives. Though independent statehood remained the norm, place was in time also contrived for a spectrum of look-alikes and stand-ins: regional self-rule, federal or confederal deals, or – more rarely – joint or consociational modes of government, as historically in the Netherlands and until recently in the Northern Ireland of the Peace Process. Even execrable and generally deplored features of such solutions (population flights or 'exchanges', uncomfortable minority plights, pogroms) were part of the nationalist recipe. The best-remembered and most-quoted example is now post-Communist Yugoslavia (at this moment in its final death-throes, with the Serbia–Montenegro separation). But there were plenty before that, there have been a few since (East Timor), and anyone can see a number of others still on the agenda (West Papua, Aceh, Corsica, Chechnya, and so on). These physical-force activities are unlikely to stop. However, something else is happening as well. In this new trend, both the character and the scale of political and social violence has escalated. The most striking change is that greater and greater numbers of perpetrators now appear willing to kill themselves. This is the opposite of 'war at a distance' discussed by Paul James in Chapters 15 and 17: it is war and mayhem by intimate presence, on an aircraft, in a bus or just in the street, and an indiscriminate and reckless character is part of it. For such combatants there are no 'innocents'. A whole population is supposedly guilty, not just its state, or its tyrants. The peculiar horror inseparable from this has become known to everybody, as is the awfulness of having to 'live with it' in Colombo and Tel Aviv. September 11 was the most sensational episode thus far, followed closely by the Moscow theatre siege and the Grozny explosion.

There had been earlier, rare examples, such as the anarchist campaigns before the First World War. Joseph Conrad's *The Secret Agent* (1907) is a depiction of this in London. Some commentators rediscovered the book after September 11, but for any contemporary reader I suspect the contrast will be more telling than the similarities. At that time self-immolation was a rare, individual phenomenon, whereas it has become quite common since the 1990s – indeed almost an established technique of protest and counter-warfare. In the old days, individuals were often surprisingly willing to 'die for the nation' in battles and struggles where there was a chance they could live for it too. Now they are willing to embrace certain death for the cause or the faith. Youngsters put their names down for martyrdom, and impatiently wait their turn. In Bali the perpetrators did not get themselves killed, since in the circumstances it was easy to escape the scene. But most are now likely to assume that they would have sacrificed themselves, had that not been the case. The much darker shadow of American involvement in Iraq looms over everything, because the Bush government identifies it as the 'heart of darkness' – the main source of capital-T Terrorism in this pervasive new sense. So we are confronting not just altered rules of insurgent violence, but changing procedures of counter-insurgent violence as well. Self-immolating terrorism is bad enough, but the state terrorism it arouses is certain to be far worse.

Not that *this* aspect of the 'New World Order' is so new. In the older perspectives of national-liberation and anti-imperialist struggle too, it was always the case that *most* of the mayhem was perpetrated by states, rather than by the dissidents, agitators, guerrillas and other freedom-fighters. In the same way, one can be sure that most of any eventual body count in the 'War Against Terrorism' will be down to the forces of counter-terrorist revenge. In *The Secret Agent*, one should not forget that the crazy bomb-plot was actually instigated and paid for by the Tsarist state in order to 'teach a lesson' to an over-tolerant, wimpish Great Britain. In her essay 'A World on the Edge' the Chinese-American scholar Amy Chua provides an impressive longer list of the escalating post-1980s violence, from Sri Lanka, Rwanda, the Serb concentration camps of the 1990s, and the Indonesian anti-Chinese pogrom of 1998, down to the murder of her own aunt in Manila. The latter was killed by a Filipino servant in her own affluent household. He was never tracked down by the Filipino police, and their official report gave as the motive simply 'Revenge'. It is worth quoting her concluding attempt at a theorization:

> There is a connection among these episodes apart from their violence. It lies in the relationship – increasingly, the explosive collision – among the three most powerful forces operating in the world today: markets, democracy, and ethnic hatred. There exists today a phenomenon – pervasive outside the West yet rarely acknowledged, indeed often viewed as taboo – that turns free-market democracy into an engine of ethnic conflagration. I'm speaking of the phenomenon of market-dominant minorities, ethnic minorities who … tend to dominate, often to a startling extent, the 'indigenous' majorities around them.[11]

Putting aside for a moment the general validity of this theory, it is important to note that she is stating the contrary of what neo-liberal apologetics gave us as gospel. The latter perceived the end of history as contained in the combination of market conditions with democracy that the engine of enhanced capitalist development would rectify – albeit with delays and hiccups. Conflagrations would become simply unnecessary as nation-states lost their grip and ethnicity could see equality coming its way. Thomas Friedman's verdict is possibly the best known: 'Globalization tends to turn all friends and enemies into "competitors"', erasing 'not just geographical borders but also human ones'.[12] He even proposed a 'Golden Arches Theory of Conflict Prevention', with explicit reference to the spread of McDonald's.

Take another example: Rajeev Bhargava's 'Gujarat: Shades of Black'. This devastating analysis shows vividly of what Friedman's 'competitors' have become capable. Gujarat has gone through very rapid economic development linked to globalization. It has contributed to demolishing traditional hierarchies and has greatly benefited the dominant Hindu community, now finding a voice in the BJP Hindu nationalist government. The 8.8 per cent Muslim minority reacted by burning a train at Ghodra in February 2002, which led in turn to a tidal wave of anti-Muslim hatred with around 2,000 people massacred. Bhargava found that most middle-class Hindus were united in justification of this retribution:

> There were no shades of grey ... the same stereotypes, the same anti-Muslim stories relentlessly ricocheted on us, visit after visit ... Have we all been too complacent about our darker motivations? Do we all have a much greater capacity than we realize to shrug off wrong done to others in pursuit of self-affirmation?[13]

He concludes by suggesting that the weakening or dissolution of traditional boundaries *by economic success* must have something to do with it. Globally assisted growth has engendered 'a generalized egoism – a condition inextricably linked to the current experience of globalization'. In the latter's uncertainty and disorientation, people 'tend to fasten on to material interest and prejudice ... In the midst of a world of evanescence and effervescence, at least *these* provide an anchor.' Ethno-religious borders do not have to be territorial, as was seen in Bosnia, for example. Here they were furnished by caste. But Chua's 'engine of conflagration' works in similar fashion. 'Something else is afoot in India', Bhargava somberly suggests, 'It is wrong to dismiss the violence and its links to terror ... as "evil". The point is: it is human.' He refers back to Alexis de Tocqueville, as well as to the Gandhian tradition, in striving to understand just what it is about human nature that falls foul of such changes. I mentioned earlier how human nature had re-entered the arena of debate, and how social anthropologists have demonstrated more insight into really existing globality than many economists and political scientists. We are again back on the same terrain.

A still wider category may be helpful in grappling with the issue. Official global theorization was founded on 'the decline of the nation-state' and notions of a benignly advancing 'borderless world'. Such concepts are invariably linked to the imagined attenuation of 'old-fashioned' nationalism, a moderate rationality and general welcome for economic advance. One-worldism entails opening frontiers, and a mounting similarity in what will be happening on both sides of them. Hence 'One Market Under God' is bound to foster one human nature as well. We'll get Golden Arches all round – for Muslims as for Hindus in Gujarat, for Filipinos as for better-off Chinese in

Manila and Jakarta – and, according to the dominant ideology discussed in the previous chapter, it must bring conflict prevention quite naturally, as long as they are given time to work their spell. All four cases I have mentioned (Zambia, Scotland, Gujarat and Chua's Chinese minorities) suggest that *exactly the opposite* must be taking place. It has of course been happening *at the same time* as free-trade-led globalization.

These two processes are interrelated even as they are contradictory. One way of understanding this is to say that the post-1989 neo-liberal onrush brought about generalized *boundary loss* – that is, a combination of lowered or even abandoned borders, plus a very powerful ideological conviction of this fact's justice and inevitability. The latter may even have been more important. It has been the veritable *Zeitgeist* of the transitional era, naturally most popular among Atlantic-zone elites and their post-Cold War disciples around the globe. Invisible through the tunnel vision of economic correctness, the boundary-loss process has a human cost. Human nature is also essentially differentiated in *structural* ways – ways that are by no means reducible either to language alone or to aesthetic displays, tastes and 'identity' in a trivial sense. All known forms of human society have been actively configured by various boundaries, ranging from the territorial to the life–death frontier underlying all religious customs and convictions. They were indispensable to kinship formations and collective agency – the capacity of social formations to act meaningfully as one. The origins of what we now call the political domain must have long preceded antiquity. In one sense the 'frontiers' of the contemporary world may date back to the 1648 Treaty of Westphalia; in another they must be rooted in, or attendant upon, the familial or kinship-transmission processes that Emmanuel Todd mapped out in *La diversité du monde* (1999). Political nationalism of the eighteenth- to twentieth-century sort has been one phase of that altering process. But of course it is the nation-state borders of that period that have taken the brunt of globalizing shifts, above all in economic terms.

It does not follow that the deeper effects of the shock were confined to the same terms. Boundary loss must have impacted upon such accreted communal structures, and undone (or at least appeared to threaten) the societal *meanings* through which kinship and other relationships are traditionally reproduced. It is this sort of impact which can then strike into the core of individuals in innumerable ways, bringing about that mutation of the person–society connection that Bhargava found himself observing so acutely in Gujarat.

One aspect of such shifts seems relevant to what I singled out earlier: self-immolation, the growing martyr complex. In one of the founding works of sociology written over a century ago, Emile Durkheim called it 'altruistic suicide'. He argued that killing oneself is a societal phenomenon, rather than just a personal decision; and usually it is related to social isolation and disintegration, or *anomie*. But there is another variant that reflects the contrary – over-close integration, helpless emotional identification with the society or group. Altruistic suicide, he argued,

> is caused by too rudimentary individuation ... [where] the society holds the individual in too strict tutelage, where the ego is not its own property, where it is blended with something not itself. Where the goal of conduct is exterior to itself. That is, in one of the groups in which it participates.[14]

The examples he gave were of Japanese hara-kiri, the Prussian officer corps and Hindu suttee. In the present, however, we need to understand why this has somehow grown in political significance and diffusion – to the point, since September 11, of fostering a climate of general violence and readiness for warfare. If apocalypse is so much in the air, it must arise from a general social change; this must be linked in some way to globalization; and since it fails to figure in the latter's official apologetics it must be found in its unintended consequences or side-effects.

The dogma of neo-liberalism foresaw a shrinkage of the political sphere. As national states grew less important, so would their politicians, and so would mass interest in both nation and state. Individuals were supposed to feel less involved or concerned, and more devoted to material advancement – their own, or that of (at most) their micro-communities such as the extended family or village. If most governments in the neo-liberal world were mediocrities, this only seemed natural. If electorates perceived their self-interested futility, and stopped voting for them, that too was a sign of the globalizing times. 'Global village' was the slogan that summed it up. It originated with Marshall McLuhan in the early days of the information revolution, came into its own after 1989, and is still quite popular. We can now see more clearly that this was never more than a miserable half-truth. And unfortunately, it is the other half that is hitting the world right now. It may have been quite true that globalization diminishes and occasionally abolishes borders, by imposing very general economic constraints upon national aims and expectations. But it is absolutely untrue that the latter then atrophy, or become less emotively significant. In fact, just because 'politics' is in some ways confined by global circumstances, it may grow *more important* – above all, in the vital dimension of collective 'meaning', or identity.

Primarily through American influence, the information revolution has fuelled that dimension in a fashion undreamt of by the older written word. Its technology has fused with lowered borders, increased migratory movements, rising expectations and correspondingly inflamed resentments, to create a militant identity-thirst. People that despair of neo-liberal lackeys and Third Way hypocrites do not lose their wish for meaningful lives and transcendent purposes. They go elsewhere: in the West, religion, reheated xenophobia and

'Reality TV' are evident candidates. But of course elsewhere more violent possibilities abound, as does the chance for more colourful revenge. Going back to Durkheim, individuals in those situations then 'find themselves' under the resultant 'strict tutelage', and emotionally driven to 'blend with something' other than their mere selves. The meaning-nexus undermined by boundary loss is reclaimed by strident affirmation of identity, or even more splendid martyrdom. In other words, what was wrong with free trade mania was not just its economics, but its absurdly parched philosophy of humanity and society. After 1989, right-wing materialism preached the rise of the capitalist individual in a boundary-loss globe, but this 'Capitalist Man' has turned out as much of a delusion as the 'Socialist Man' once projected by left-wing materialism – that already half-forgotten hero of the proletarian *Internationale*. The profounder sources of nationalism and collective agency have outlived both. How can they now find democratic expression, in a globalized world?

CONSERVATIVE APOCALYPSE

America is so accustomed to seeing itself as the edge of modernity that it has failed to perceive its old age coming on. Its revolutionary origins were so influential that it now occludes seeing its own imperialism. In part this is done by abuse of the globalization concept: the globalizing process was launched by the USA, and though nominally independent still carries a 'Made in America' label. Anyone suggesting that the label is a fake, or undeserved – as I did earlier – is quickly reprimanded. The logo somehow belongs to the prime mover, as Enlightenment once did to France, or Catholic Christianity to the King of Spain. Such greater causes belonged to God and humanity, true; but the proof had to be humanity's development into simulacrums of Frenchness or *hispanidad*. In a recent *New York Times* article Michael Ignatieff has underscored the contradiction. The American Republic was always wary of empire and the Old World – 'Yet what word but "empire" describes the awesome thing that America is becoming?'[15] As I noted earlier, first-phase globalization was founded upon the American economy, the force that benefited most from the foundering of communism. But however much it has expanded, that economy remains national, as Bush has demonstrated by the blatant protectionism of the past 18 months. And it belongs not just to a nation-state, but as Ignatieff goes on to say:

> Europeans (in the 1990s) who had once invented the idea of the martial nation-state now looked at American patriotism, the last example of the form, and no longer recognized it as anything but flag-waving extremism. The world's only empire was isolated, not just because it was the biggest power but also because it was the West's last military nation-state.[16]

However, a profound ambiguity attaches to the main term used here: 'nation-state'. Ignatieff wrote a book and TV series many will remember, entitled *Blood and Belonging*.[17] These contrasted ethnic with civic nationalism in the twentieth century, and argued for a transformation of the former into the latter – that is, for a diverse nationality-politics that acknowledged the need to 'belong', yet guided it into civic and constitutional forms which could avoid wars and make international coexistence tolerable. Such a change was impossible as long as the Cold War lasted, with its different models of internationality and constitutional life. Hence its hope is the global-reach vista made possible after 1989: a post-imperial globe enabling more diverse and democratic forms of development. As he points out, this is just what is not taking place: instead, we are living through an afterlife of imperialism, in which two of the former 'martial nation-states', the United States and the United Kingdom, reimpose regimes upon the Middle East. The British Empire set up both Iraq and the Saudi Kingdom from the debris of the Ottoman Sultanate after 1918; now its US successor has embarked on farther 'regime-change', but as part of a far grander struggle against Terrorism.

What is so often labelled as the age of the nation-state, or of nationalism, was in truth that of the Atlantic seaboard state-nation. Nationality-politics is ancient, but it was a novel '-ism' that took the theatrical centre of the political stage only after the 1870s. That is, after France's defeat by Prussia, and the consolidation of Federal America after its Civil War. It happened via the French. '*Le nationalisme*' was forged in reaction to the terrible wounds of Alsace-Lorraine. It was from the outset an instrument for unceasing revenge and reassertion: internal rejuvenation by 'pride', justified through the re-manifestation of destiny. Certainly, modern political culture had worked its way towards this denouement across preceding generations – notably, in reactions to the French Revolution, and the 1848 explosion of smaller nationalities in Europe. But it was the dominant state-nations that rendered it global, through the '-ism'. Almost at once, it entered every tongue and became everyday discourse. Soon it would be 'explained' everywhere by discoveries of blood diversity, inherited cultures and timeless rights, as 'ethnic nationalism'.

In retrospect, the epoch from 1870 up to the Cold War appears as one of imperial contest, and increasingly total wars taking over the globe. But that is the point: empire-ism not only preceded nation-ism, it went on shaping it, right up to 1989. By 1900 the globe was already 'global' enough for such a culture-climate to be inescapable. The dominant or metropolitan intelligentsias commanded the smaller culture-arenas, just as their armed states strove to marshal insignificant polities destined to follow, or else be ignored and left behind. There was an ideological pretence that everything imperial must have grown from and rest upon something national. But in truth the expansive state-nations had adopted and disseminated 'nationalism' as one feature of their own DNA. The world was *actually* made for 'viable', necessarily rather large, armoured and warrior-worthy states capable not just of defending their civilization but also of projecting it. Often defence implied counter-attack – which then in any case entailed projection. Nation-building was one aspect of the latter. After the defeat of Germany, both the Atlantic and the Soviet-Communist domains sought the diffusion of appropriate tame nationalisms, approximately in their own image. This era is mockingly echoed in Ignatieff's title: 'The Burden'. And the implication is that it isn't yet over. Bush and Blair are reviving the White Man's Burden: the former in response to September 11; the latter as part of a long-running campaign of coat-tail redemption summed up in his 'special relationship' with Washington. Imperium-nationalism relies on the drug of exceptionalism; but of course, globalization should be the death of exceptionalism – that is, an end to heaven-hallmarked destiny, the imprimatur of Providence, command-status inscribed by inheritance and executed in Leadership. The response at the moment is characteristically strident: not so quietly into this good night. Afghanistan was not enough. The 'last warrior nation-state' needs a more strategic conception supplied as ideology by the War against Terrorism and as practice by the assault on Iraq. This why the US has slithered back into the ideological world that Ignatieff outlined in *Blood and Belonging* – that is, the world of 'nationalism' in this still prevalent sense, configured essentially by outgoing hegemony, 'influence' and warfare.

There has been much debate about two questions associated with the drive to war. One is, 'Why on earth did not the American government, as a preliminary step, secure some solution to the Palestinian conflict?' Given the evident centrality of this issue for Middle East politics and the *relative* feasibility of setting up a Palestinian state, would it not have been in everyone's interest to attend to that first? However, this question omits the surrender factor inseparable from such a course. It would have meant giving in to political globalization. The two-state formula was a plausible general idea that might well have added Palestine to the growing world-list of national answers – like South Africa, Northern Ireland and East Timor. The latter all owed something to US representations, but in a quite non-imperious sense. In themselves, they stood for diversity, liberation and formal equality. Also, a resolution of the Israel–PLO war would at once have lowered the apocalypse level – the endless envenoming of prejudice and fever-pitch absolutism suffered by both sides, and complained of by so many critics. Unfortunately, recycled and augmented hysteria is exactly what the War Against Terrorism requires.

The second question is simply, 'Why Iraq?' Why a vulgar dictatorship unrelated to the perpetrators of September 11, already largely disarmed, and of course previously supported by America in Cold War times? One shorthand answer has been found in the Iraqi petroleum reserves – as if the USA did not already control enough of the world's oil. But from the angle of political globalization, another suggestion presents itself – it did not matter much which enemy was selected, or where it was, as long as it was presentationally Evil. Iraq did have one further advantage though. It was already 'on the list', in the sense of harking back to George W. Bush's father and the previous Gulf War. It recalled the immediately post-Cold War epoch, when neo-liberalism was at its missionary peak, and all appeared favourable to a one-world market under the American God. It harked back to the dawn, in other words, before the appearance of so many damnable contradictions, abjections, contraflows and howls of resentment. Might not a dizzying subjugation of Iraq somehow restore the odour of such times – as well as 'closing the book', satisfying the dynasty and lowering oil prices?

The resolution of the Cold War ought to have ended such times. As imperialism retreated, as the impasse of Armageddon disappeared and Social Darwinism found its home in museums, a quite different spirit of the age should have moved in and taken the place of militaristic statehood and pseudo-ethnicity – the uniformed 'making of' Frenchmen, Germans, Americans (and all the rest). However, a political revolution would have been required for that, a revolution in which national democracies could emerge, energized by the opening doors and broader horizons of globalization. Instead, an economic revolution usurped the great transition, based on a single berserk notion: the *idée fixe* of marketolatry, unencumbered exploitation, deregulation. It was the general apotheosis of 'civil society'. This was uncomfortably like old-fashioned religion in another way too. In practically Islamicist fashion, it was believed capable of itself structuring and encompassing the new common culture. Democratic nationalism came a long way second – little more in practice, now, than the enabling of capitalism's globalizing domain. Marx's great 'sorcerer of modernity' (1848) had finally won out – and instantly metamorphosed into an economic Nostradamus of gabbling stock exchange forecasts and internet runes.

In the 1960s the Paris students wrote: 'Run faster! The Old World is at your heels!' Ignatieff reminded his readers wryly how, in that preceding phase, 'As Vietnam showed, empire is no match, long-term, for nationalism.' In the short term, alas, unruly dissidence *can* be contained by falling back upon old reflexes and violence. Earlier I tried to describe the climate of enlivened violence and its possible links to other traits of first-stage globalization, and we will extend upon this theme in later chapters. The worst single aspect of the work-up towards the Middle East war has been its revival of fears relating to the one thing thought to have been rendered redundant by 1989 and the big thaw: nuclear weapons have been reinvented and made centre-stage. Unable to achieve this revivification through the UN weapon inspectors, Washington had to bring North Korea back into its sights.

In perhaps the most famous essay of the 1990s on the subject, Donald Mackenzie argued in 'The Uninvention of Nuclear Weapons'[18] that nuclear great-power armouries were vanishing so rapidly because Cold War mythologies had misrepresented them. 'Mutually Assured Destruction' rested on the general conviction that superpowers not only possessed the awesome capacity, but could make it work. In reality, thermonuclear devices in particular had been so colossally expensive, complex and potentially unreliable that no-one knew what might happen in a conflict. Only a few great and ex-great states could afford experimental explosions, and these demanded accretions of 'tacit knowledge' unavailable in war conditions where the Terror was to be unleashed on missiles and planes. It was not surprising that such preparations helped break the back of the Soviet economy, or that both sides seized the chance of phasing them out after 1990. The same did not apply to simpler or old-style fission devices like the 1945 bombs. Re-baptized as 'tactical weapons', these were known to work, and had been reproduced by a number of lesser states over the previous 20 years. Mackenzie made it clear how distant even these were from ideas of backyard or suitcase bombs potentially usable by terrorists. They still demanded a major socio-industrial effort. However, in the 1990s that prospect appeared remote. Such weapons had not been used in Vietnam, or in Britain's war with Argentina in 1982; and there seemed small chance of their use in other regional conflicts or nationalist uprisings.

Now, we can no longer be so sanguine. Early in 2003, William Arkin published an article in the *Los Angeles Times* arguing that current US policy is trying to dismantle the 'firewall' between conventional and nuclear attacks as a prelude to possible use.[19] Bhargava does not mention it in his account of the Gujarat atrocities, but of course recent India–Pakistan relations have also been envenomed by mounting threats on both sides about using nuclear bombs. And the Bush administration has now mounted a parallel campaign on the theme of North Korea's supposed nuclear capability by threatening to suppress its 'weapons of mass destruction' alongside those of Saddam Hussein. Does this mean they would be willing themselves to use nuclear devices, even *in extremis*, if conventional means looked like failing in their object? The former head of the UN Inspection Team in Iraq, Scott Ritter, certainly saw it as a possibility back in October 2002. In an interview in *Le Monde*, he envisaged the stalemate situation in Iraq where, failing a Blitzkrieg success, numbers of US and British troops might be bogged down, in a Middle East aflame with opposition to the assault, and the temptation to use nuclear arms correspondingly increased.[20]

Although such ultimate folly was not committed, we have seen how archaic state-nations can move in this direction. What is left of their former hegemony depends upon the maintenance of political backwardness and atrophy – the shards and scrolls of bygone revolutions, 1776, 1789, 1688 ... It is in this way that early modern, patched up, recycled forms of democracy confront globalization – with the unshakeable conviction of their own leadership. It is not democracy or nationality as such, but their outdated forms, as if the Man o' War and steam propulsion had been decreed the unalterable measure of technology. The state-nation and its state-nationalism have fallen back upon a conservative apocalypse in stages, to restore the Old World, or whatever can be saved of it. It may be that no one can undo globalization, but the prime movers' conceit makes them unable to do other than struggle to control it.

A NEW SEARCH FOR OLD ALTERNATIVES

What should the alternative be? Most of the world wants neither shari'a law nor the neo-liberal rendition of capitalism as blessed by America's Founding Fathers – but is any alternative yet emerging from the tidal turning of 1989 and after? Some estimate of this may be got from looking briefly at two recent sketches of differing vistas, Roberto Unger's 'Boutwood Lectures' and Michael Hardt and Antonio Negri's *Empire*.[21] Unger's title was 'The Second Way: Why We Need an Alternative to the Present Consensus and What the Alternative is'. His 'untimely remarks' began by describing and deploring the ruin of European social democracy, including its Third Way alibis. The latter brought a 'spiritual movement' of privatization that led to 'the abandonment of public life as a proper sphere for advancement of large projects'. Politics became a sphere of mediocrity, while culture responded with escape fantasies expressing 'a sense of entrapment … awareness that the diminished life one lives is the only life one is ever going to have'. Non-fantasy escape requires a root reversal of attitudes, and a reorganization of the production process itself. This will be possible only through 'the creation of a high-energy politics', sustained by 'a high level of political mobilization (which) addresses the creation and the contest of alternative trajectories of cumulative institutional change'. Unger lists the changes that might bring this about, culminating in the surprising idea of 'a public-law framework … making it easier for civil society to organize itself around neighbourhoods, around jobs, and around topics of common interest such as health and education'. Overall, this strategy is designed 'to make us more god-like'. The divinization of humanity rests upon Unger's conception of human nature as a self-transcending source forced to try and 'slowly turn society into a mirror of the imagination'. But this power has been lulled to sleep, as neo-liberal incantations have sectioned society 'into the care of politicians, entertainers and philosophers who taught the poisonous doctrine that politics must be little for individuals to become big'.

In contrast to Unger's low and careful road towards a god-like future, Hardt and Negri's *Empire* took the high road with at times rapturous enthusiasm. Their 'empire' appeared in the year 2000 as an expression of an unstoppable, expansive network that had left the USA behind. It signalled less a mundane oneness than a kind of ontological mutation. We live in the last days of a second Roman Empire that the incursion of the modern barbarians (migrants) is about to transform. A contemporary 'multitude' is under formation – in effect, an alternative 'network' to that of the capitalist sorcerer. Global by instinct and experience, this global neo-proletariat will develop its powers of subversion without Benedict Anderson's 'imagined communities', peoples or nations left over from a discarded past. All the new-style multitude needs is to become cognizant of its own subjectivity – a task (as Emile Durkheim would undoubtedly have thought) of some difficulty, since it requires human society to tear up its own historic roots altogether, and just stop using 'gods' to express what is its own power. Presumably this feat is up to prophets – the book is devoted to Spinoza, the early-modern philosopher who coined the epigram: 'The prophet creates his own people.'

Hardt and Negri's conception of America is odd in the prophetic context. What they perceive is mainly a left-wing, intrinsically experimental republicanism – like a laboratory for the liberated mass future. In other words, they are thinking of precisely the America that was crippled by the weird presidential election of 2000 (as their book was coming out), and then marginalized more profoundly by non-President Bush, after September 2001. They seem to believe that the United States Federation is not really a state-nation, just as it had never been a colonial empire, and could never become a dreary 'Homeland'. The US still figures in *Empire* as a way station towards some dawning golden age. How then has it turned into such a station for the past to regroup and launch a devastating assault upon all the symptoms of awakening that Hardt and Negri discerned? As Gopal Balakrishnan pointed out in his review of this book, what they produced is a far-Left rendition of what Thomas Friedman had done for the Right, with *The Lexus and the Olive Tree* – only, without indication of the institutions, movements and transmission belts that might bring their all-encompassing change about.[22]

Roberto Unger's similar résumé of the process is as follows: 'The network of these advanced networks has now become the driving force in the world economy' – which demands the 'reinvention' of practically everything. But what is a 'network', if not an alliance and co-operation of nodes? And what can these 'nodes' be, except nations – that is, polities *partly* 'invented' but always made in response to nature, both societal and pre-human. The completion or advance of democracy calls for novel constitutional experiments, but such innovation needs vehicles to carry them. What vessels are there, except those made by past collective histories, languages and cultures? Are 'high-energy politics' and 'high-level mobilization' conceivable without 'nations'? Yet the term is conspicuous by its near-absence from both manifestos – as if the authors were above all anxious to steer clear of horrid nationalism. When the idea does force its way in through the back door, however, the effect is rather sobering:

> How can a reform of the world economy ... come about? The first step is for alternatives – real alternatives – to be established *in particular nation-states*, especially in some of the large, marginalized continental countries (China, India, Russia, Indonesia, Brazil) that are now the natural seats of resistance. (emphasis added)[23]

These are the places with 'the spiritual resources to imagine themselves as different worlds, though each of them has recently been inhibited in the achievement of this potential for deviation and rebellion'. Unfortunately, Professor Unger omitted Germany and other parts of the European Union from his miscreants. But at least the list carried listeners back down from the Planet Zylon to filthy old earth, that minefield of identity mania, boundaries, envy, revenge, irrepressible curiosity and other ungodlike traits.

The same cannot be said for *Empire*, although it does strive to touch base by practically unbounded exaltation of migration and pleas for abolishing border controls. They seem to believe this would in itself enable the 'network of networks' that they perceive as inheriting the globe. In reality, surely, population movements are likely to be important determinants of the 'nodes' of futurity – that is, of nationality politics with a different skin, 'civic' rather than 'ethnic', litigious rather than bellicose, identitarian rather than genocidal. Future national identities will be conditioned by the globalizing climate, from the bottom up. In a more mingled world, ethno-nationalism is already near the 'Exit' door. But it is mistaken to confuse necessary with sufficient conditions here. This shift neither embodies nor represents the place of nationality, in either history or human nature. Diversity remains a compelling structure, not a pose or an optional display. Globalization is likely to give it more house-room, not less.

It seems to me that such theoretical sallies end by resoundingly confirming Paul Hirst's position in that original Open Democracy debate I mentioned earlier. There is nothing really surprising or dishonourable about such abstraction and uncertainty. The nerves of political agency were paralysed and mutilated for so long by both sides of the Cold War that they were bound to be at first overtaken by this Old World so implacably on all our heels. On the other hand, it will cross the finishing line only to meet a counter-productive world, in which Hirst's persistent communities reassert themselves. As one unpredictable repercussion succeeds another, and 'natural seats of resistance' find themselves driven to find new voices and agencies, a multipolar world will be that much closer, with growing numbers of sovereign units around each pole: discordant, squabbling, overflowing with imaginative difference and far less inhibited in their potential for deviance. United in relief, however, at common escape from the Invasion of the Body Snatchers that threatened them around the *fin de siècle*. By comic coincidence, the move to war in Iraq was accompanied by a showing in Britain and Ireland of Steven Spielberg's latest, interminable version of this classic tale of American dystopia, *Taken*. It is what Americans have always most feared about themselves.

In his contribution to the Open Democracy arguments about the war, Philip Bobbitt echoes what he calls 'a new resolve, and a new urgency' as the motive force of the military expedition.[24] These elements are certainly present, and I presume do explain why it was felt that 'we must act now', rather than go on dithering as both the USA and the United Nations have done for so long over both Iraqi threats and the Palestinian question. But who *are* 'we'? The urgent determination comes from the government of the USA alone, abetted by the dependent government of the UK. None of the allegations or suggestions made elsewhere in Bobbitt's essay are novel, or imply the need for such a turning. This need has arisen from the dilemma of a feeble and doubtfully legitimate government, aggravated by the repercussions of September 11. American nationalism injected new resolve and urgency into it – which it feels is best harnessed by external deployment. Superpower status then makes it easy to expand 'we' into the international community (maybe ill-served by a foot-shuffling United Nations). Nascent globalizing conditions can of course be interpreted as supporting the extrapolation: the world is not emancipating itself from American control, but returning to the fold and 'recognizing reality'. The hope is that neo-liberalism will also be revived through this conflict – the opiate of that secular fundamentalism which suits a dominant economy.

On this terrain, fake cosmopolitanism comes with the star. Nations don't figure in Bobbitt's plea either, apart from a fairly pious remark about 'restoring Iraq's wealth to its people', which should be 'peoples' of course, unless Kurdistan is again being overlooked. This is not surprising. 'Nation-building' seems to have vanished from the new gendarme's manual. According to a recent issue of the *Washington Quarterly* the idea is in any case quite outdated. Its main section is devoted to 'Nation Building's Successor', which turns out to be 'Postconflict Reconstruction'. Iraq appears to have concentrated the thoughts of reconstructionists wonderfully, and six different articles go on to spell out its principles and aims. The latter stem from a super-principle: 'Not all failed states are created equal.'[25] This disappointing fact naturally entails that, 'Not all will be equally important to the United States and the international community.' The emphasis should thenceforth be upon supporting 'minimally capable states, not building nations'. The woes of this global underclass stem mainly from ethnicity and criminality, and the hegemon's aim must be to restrain (and only occasionally suppress) both. There need be no more Vietnams. Taking nation-building far too seriously brought about that misfortune. Instead, much more distant and institutional means should be used, establishing the general climate and conditions for natives to proceed (eventually) with their DIY business of building up nations.

When such pillars are set out, they look astonishingly like those of the neo-liberal order already in existence. John Keane sketched an outline of the 1989–2001 system in a 2002 lecture called 'Whatever Happened to Democracy?'[26] The political world of neo-liberalism is in truth a 'cosmocracy', one in which boundary loss has been exploited by craven leftovers of the Cold War to restore inequality, electoral indifference, and the 'no alternative' economic rules of competition and deregulation. I touched on the same theme earlier, from a different angle – that of national identity rather than democracy. But successful cosmocracies were not created equal, any more than 'failed states'. Some are distinctly more equal than others, nor does anyone doubt which is the most equal (and powerful) of the lot. The combination of 'an inner decay of representative government' with simultaneous 'communicative abundance' has created a democratic malaise and an atrophy of popular will – as if the very sense of an alternative agency, in Unger's sense, is now threatened.

Western-led cosmocracy was an inchoate and dismal imperium of informality, which after the shock of 2001 felt called upon to acquire some backbone and principles – those of post-conflict reconstruction, precisely, in which capitalism's slipshod *moeurs* are re-garbed as brisk lessons in worthy deportment, slimming down and regime change. The *Washington Quarterly* is published by the Center for Strategic and International Studies (CSIS), a body featuring Walter Laqueur, Zbigniew Brzezinski and Francis Fukuyama on its board. This is no doubt why the message is voiced in a new *langue de bois*, made up of managerial euphemism, postmodern academe and beltway gibberish: 'Indigenous ownership of the process of governance is key'; 'Engaging the local business community is a first step to economic well-being'; 'We know now that development can take place even when parts of a nation are at war' – and so on. Their conclusion is that of Philip Bobbitt's, almost word for word: 'In order to succeed in the future, the United States must act now'[27] (here the voice is that of John J. Hamre, President of the Association of the United States Army). It should not be thought that the USA is exempt from the CSIS's criticisms of the failed-state world. No, two sentences are devoted to the subject, one of which distinctly states that the United States should 'get its own house in order'. But the point is not elaborated farther, and clearly stands low in the order of reconstructional priorities. Today's cosmocrats are beset by matters more urgent than getting Presidents elected by majority votes.

Nor should it be imagined that democracy is entirely absent from their vista. Indeed one of the *Quarterly*'s chapters is on 'Strategic Democracy

Building'. However, a closer scan reveals the real subject to be an operation unknown to everybody outside the USA, and quite probably to most inside it too: the State Partnership Program. This is a curious 'twinning' device through which the father of today's President sought in the early 1990s to 'accelerate the integration of former Eastern bloc nations into NATO', by letting them know about the National Guard, and other exemplary forms of devolved rule. Thus the Slovenes were rewarded by partnership with Colorado (whose Governor, Bill Owens, is one of the authors). But since then, expansion of this successful plan beyond Eastern Europe has meant, for example, that Venezuela is enriched by learning from Florida, and the Estonians by knowledge of appropriately tiny Maryland.

John Keane's demand for a return to democracy has become still more timely. Democratic nationalism is the only possible riposte to 'post-conflict reconstruction' and the other near-incredible alibis of the moment. Over the last year everyone has learned a lot about what he called 'the struggle against blind arrogance and stupidity caused by power', and 'democratic power-sharing as the best human weapon so far invented against the hubris that comes with concentrations of power'. There may have been an old Left that washed its hands in impotent pieties and gloried in impotent moralizing; but I doubt if it will have much to do with the new one being called up by the Sorcerer's tragic mistakes and his windbag excuses. We used to read about such problems in histories and politics textbooks; now they are in the *Daily Mirror* and the six o'clock TV news. Keane said then that E.M. Forster's 'two cheers for democracy' was out of date: three and an encore are needed, as the sole way forward from the 'waning democratic euphoria' inflicted on the purloined and punished world of free-range capitalism.

Democracy is a powerful remedy for hubris. It champions not the rule of the people, but the rule that nobody should rule. It refuses to accept that decision makers can draw their legitimacy from gods and goddesses, or tradition, or brute power. Democracy is a way of life and a way of governing in which power is publicly accountable, in which sitting on thrones and making decisions behind the backs of others – and the intrigues and ambitions that usually accompany arbitrary rule – are deeply problematic.

4
Global Tensions:
A Clash of Social Formations[1]

Paul James

What is the relationship in the contemporary world between the abstract global 'peace' of state-initiated violence from above and the embodied violence of persons hacking into others with machetes as they lay on the ground? Can this be explained simply in terms of the difference between the rationalizing modern nation-state and resurgent tribalism? This chapter explores the contradictions associated with peace and violence in a globalizing-localizing world, both generally and in relation to violence in Rwanda and Bosnia-Kosova. The chapter is intended predominantly as a political essay opening up lines of understanding. It argues that the postmodernists' hopes that postnationalism will offer a way out of the mess is as thoroughly misplaced as the hopes of neo-liberals that pax Americana will bring peace. It is a curious confluence that the Coalition of the Willing now project themselves across the globe with the same new enthusiasm for pax postnationalism as held by the brethren of postmodernism – despite, of course, deep differences on other matters.

We live in confusing times. One of the dominant trends in the present period is the deepening of a set of social contradictions that have only been generalized for a couple of generations. On the one hand, globalization, a process with long historical roots, has been developing at an unprecedented pace through the end of the twentieth century and into the new millennium. A rough, uneven blanketing of capital and commercial culture crosses and connects the world in unprecedented ways. On the other hand, there is an intense fragmenting and reconfiguring of social relations at the level of community and locality. Systemic processes of rationalizing homogenization integrate the globe at one level, while ideologies and practices of difference and radical autonomy frame the popular imaginary at another. On the one hand, globalization carries a structure of disembodied 'peace', tragically defended through strategic defence systems and undeclared technologically mediated wars. On the other hand, the era of globalization is beset by embodied violence in a thousand trouble spots. These are material and lived contradictions rather than simply inexplicable paradoxes. They need to be explained.

It is not that we fail to recognize the surface expressions of these contradictions. In their immediate expression we see them quite dramatically. At the turn of the century it has become commonplace for soothsayers to say that the key trends in the coming period will be globalism, tribalism and individualism. While the naming of those interlocking but contrary formations is helpful in its starkness, the projections of their prominence are often confusingly presented as a paradox of conflicting epochs. The descriptions are utterly value-laden. Social life is presented *as if* we are simultaneously going forward into the technologically driven world of open globalism, e-commerce, Planet Hollywood and abstract 'peace', and back into the ambivalent, anachronistic gloom of neo-national violent tribalisms. Places such as Rwanda, Bosnia, Kosova and Chechnya supposedly stand for the past. They are located in mystical times when social life was ruled by warlords, blood ties and village feuds. They are said to be found in backward settings from where primordial and atavistic sentiments come to seep through the curtain of rational modernity. It is a confusion of times expressed in recent futuristic films and novels. In the West, we are alternatively portrayed romantically as going back to the future in films such as *Pleasantville* and *The Truman Show*,[2] or, more bleakly, shown in cybernetic novels such as *Snow Crash* and *Virtual Light*[3] as going forward into a past world of mega-corporations acting as neo-imperial states, with cyborg outsiders living on the violent edge. Concepts like the 'global village' appear to transcend the tension of past and future but only by leaving the traditional sense of village behind. In the same way that Disney World's Tomorrow Land has been recast as an historical artefact, the concept of 'global village' is now the romantic version of the newer cyberspace term, 'virtual village'.

As an indication of the new sensibility, advertising campaigns in the mid 1990s began to explain how transnational corporations transcend the divide between different senses of locale in the global village. In Australia and New Zealand, the worldwide franchiser of hamburger outlets, McDonald's, began an advertising campaign explaining how each of its franchisees will organize local community noticeboards.[4] In Cambodia, the 'Japanese' car manufacturer Toyota ran a campaign under the banner headline 'This is Our Town'. To the backdrop of a photograph of planet earth spinning in space, the patronizing copy speaks with postcolonial sophistication of the peaceful mutuality of the global project. All the while it slips between different meanings of the 'local' and the 'we':

It's the global village. We live here. You do, too. We're neighbours. And since we're neighbours, we should be friends. It seems that we are all of us – everywhere – slowly coming to this realization. But how do we do it? In a practical sense what steps do we take? We can't speak for others, but for ourselves we can say this: we will do our part to bring the world together by building up the global auto industry ... For the first half of the century we thought of ourselves as a Japanese company ... Now we think of ourselves as a world company. Our responsibility is to everyone.[5]

Despite this self-conscious commercial-political emphasis on the intersecting trends of globalism and community, and despite its embeddedness in everyday life, we still have a poor understanding of the structures, systems and institutions that in the age of disembodied globalism both integrate polity and community and simultaneously threaten to break them apart. Very little work, for example, has been done on the relationship between abstract 'peace' at the global level and continuing embodied violence on the ground. Social theorists over the past decade have made globalization and localism a constant point of reference. However, in turning to ugly concepts such as 'glocalization', defined as the simultaneous globalizing and localizing of social relations, they have named the processes that need to be worked through rather than given us the tools with which to do so. Roland Robertson notes that the concept of 'glocalization' comes from the Japanese word *dochakuka*, originally *dochaku*, which means 'living on one's own land'.[6] However, dragged into the context of global micro-marketing campaigns such as 'This is Our Town', the term came to be instrumentalized as the act of adapting locally to meet global circumstances. This in itself should have given pause for thought, but nevertheless the term quickly became part of the social theory lexicon as an easy shorthand concept for an extraordinarily complicated phenomenon. It is not so different from the way in which the Finnish concept of embodiment, *kännykkä*, 'extension of the hand', used as a Nokia trademark for their mobile telephone, subsequently passed into the generic parlance of Finnish teenagers as the word for phone.[7] It is the process that underlies these etymologies that this chapter is interested in – the stretching between the concrete and the abstract. The embedded and grounded meaning of the terms themselves – living on one's own land, extension of the hand – carry us metaphorically into the contradictions of our time. Expressions of the abstraction of our relationship to others are often carried in the relatively concrete language of the body and of grounded place. These then are the themes of this chapter: globalism and localism, disembodiment and embodiment, abstract peace and embodied violence. While attempting to connect these themes in a way that does not set up related terms as dichotomies, the undercurrent of the chapter is conducted as a critique of those writers who make the *modern* nation-state *per se* the source of the problem, or its demise into postnationalism or *postmodern* cosmopolitanism the source of redemption. In so arguing, I have no intention of defending either modernism or the nation-state. However, in the face of abstract globalism, you'll find hints of a political position that will be followed up in Chapter 7 – one that defends the importance of reflexive, critically negotiated and embodied community.[8] The present

chapter begins with a discussion of the arguments about postnationalism.
It then turns to studies of Rwanda and Kosova as settings through which
to elucidate those problems.

A POSTNATIONAL WORLD?

For many of those writers caught up in the heated discussion of globalism
and localism, the future of nationalism has been reduced to the globally
produced local expressions of individuals experiencing mobile, hybrid and
diasporic identities. This kind of identity formation is increasingly called
'postnationalism'.[9] According to the literature on the subject, postnationalist
individuals-in-mutual-exile may seek 'communal' connection but it is not
on the basis of an underlying attachment to territorial foundations. It
is a loosely configured imagined community that may or may not have
continuing embodied ties. In this view the defence of territorial and blood
ties is seen as the primary source of continuing violence in the modern world.
Postnationalism, they say, thus offers a positive way out of the territorially
bounded and restrictive politics of the bad old nation-state. In fact, most
of these writers go further to announce the imminent irrelevance of the
existing system of modern nation-states. It is blithely presented as a *fait
accompli*: 'the nation-state', says Arjun Appadurai, 'has become obsolete'.[10]
Rather than engaging in a lengthy critique of this position let me just note
three counterpoints.

Counterpoint 1: Postnationalism is presented as a novel development of the
turn of the millennium. In some ways (though with significant qualifications
raised in a moment) we can agree that it does represent a new pressure on
the modern nation-state. However, it has to be recognized that modern
nationalism continues to be expressed at the political-institutional level
through social movements of compatriots acting in concert to achieve a
singular nation-state. Moreover, these nationalisms are ironically often the
response to the same disruptions of globalism that produce postnationalism.
By the same argument, modern nation-states continue to be relevant to
contemporary social relations, despite – indeed sometimes because of –
national responses to modern and postmodern crossings of their borders.
The obvious example is the heightened regulation of embodied movement:
the national regulation of refugees and emigrants.

Counterpoint 2: The kind of postnationalism being described by some
postcolonial writers is only one form of a number of different kinds of
postnationalism. In fact I will go further and suggest that the diasporic
kind of postnationalism highlighted by the postcolonial and postmodern
writers does not represent the most novel form of postnationalism at all.
The postcolonial identity of the person who has moved along the tracks of
globalism has stronger continuities with past forms of hybrid assertions of

identity than do the new postnationalisms of the capitalist West. Reading Benedict Anderson on the creole elites of eighteenth-century Latin America, or Eric Wolf on the mobile Turks of the medieval Silk Road, substantially qualifies any sense that hybridity is a postmodern let alone uniquely recent phenomenon.[11] By contrast, state-based postnationalism has little continuity with past forms of political legitimation. When late-modern states such as the United States of America present themselves as simultaneously national and postnational it suggests that the sensibility of postnationalism needs to be understood in much broader terms than hybridity.

Counterpoint 3: Postnationalism is most often projected normatively as a positive kind of postmodern cosmopolitanism – as multiple or displaced attachments to others in exile. Against this projection I argue that it is done without any obvious exploration of what is a good way of living.[12] In either of these moves – either to advocate postnationalism or postmodern cosmopolitanism – past forms of solidarity such as the modern nation tend to be reduced to clichés, and solidaristic attachment and relatively bounded and embodied placement come to be described as part of the problem. Appadurai writes:

> As I oscillate between the detachment of a postcolonial, diasporic, academic identity (taking advantage of the mood of exile and the space of displacement) and the ugly realities of being racialized, minoritized, and tribalized in my everyday encounters, theory encounters practice.[13]

This appears to treat displacement and exile as a simple opportunity to detach (at least for the privileged), rather than as a vexed dialectic of abstracted insight and more concrete loss.

In order to introduce some of the problems of explanation that haunt the study of nationalism, globalism and violence it is instructive to take a couple of examples of community-polities in flux. In some ways, the two examples chosen could not be more different, but there is much in them that overlaps including the themes of globalism, nation-building and changing forms of identity. One example is the *modern* tribalism of Rwanda caught between traditionalism and modernism as it descended into a postcolonial hell of genocide against the Tutsi. In 1994, about 800,000 people were killed in one of the most horrific periods of concentrated slaughter in recent history.[14] Nearly 2 million people fled as refugees. It was a period with some parallels to the Nazi Holocaust and the attempted genocide of the Jews. The other example is the nationalist violence in the Old Yugoslavia as the postnational war-machines of the United States of America and the United Kingdom attempted to extricate themselves from a war that was never declared. What I hope to open up in these examples is a threefold complication. The first complication is that in contemporary society different ontological formations

– tribalism, traditionalism, modernism, postmodernism – overlay each other in ways that always disturb, and in some cases completely fracture, the kinds of ontological security sustained through their very different forms of social identification and political organization. The second complication is that this violent fracturing of felt-security is bound up with the contradictions generated between embodied ways of experiencing the self and the layers of more materially abstracted processes of social formation. I am not suggesting that the intensification of these contradictions always, or even mostly, leads to social breakdown and violence. At the other extreme, the intensification of contradiction *can* under certain conditions sustain a rationalized indifference to difference.[15] However, indifference, either passive or cold-blooded, was certainly not the outcome in Rwanda. The point of dwelling upon an episode such as the 1990s genocide is that we can see the process of intensifying contradictions most starkly when people's sense of ontological security is so fractured. The third complication is that the violence in Rwanda does not stem from a reversion to traditional tribalism but from the long-term effects of modern globalization. In a parallel argument in the section on Bosnia-Kosova I will suggest that the United States' intervention from above cannot be explained simply in terms of classical nationalism but is related to the emerging contradictions of postnationalism in a globalizing world.

RWANDA: FROM NATION-BUILDING
AND MODERN TRIBALISM TO GENOCIDE

On 6 April 1994, an aeroplane carrying the Rwandan and Burundi presidents was shot down over Kigali. The incident became the apparent trigger for a state of genocide that would see approximately one-tenth of the population murdered over the period of a few intense weeks. Of the victims of the Rwandan genocide, most of them Tutsi, 80 per cent were killed by the third week of May. Apart from a few AK-47 rifles and grenades held by the elite, the predominant killing instruments were those of the hand – machetes or slashing knives, common agricultural tools called *panga*. The use of these instruments entailed that the executioners could face their victims directly, see the blood run from their wounds, watch them die ... and then slash at another living body, again and again and again. The immediate question is why did it happen? How did we get to the point where the intended genocide of the Tutsi population of Rwanda became both thinkable and attempted? A thousand questions follow, some that bear also upon an understanding of the other case to be discussed: the break-up of Yugoslavia and the NATO air war over Kosova.

One question that permeates this chapter concerns the abstracted communities of identity – the 'nation' as a community of strangers, and even the *modern* 'tribe' as analogously abstracted when it too has become a post-kin-related community. How could such abstracted associations generate such powerful embodied personal and social identities as nationalism and tribalism? How do those often-positive identifications intensify to the point that a person is willing to kill a known 'other' for that identification? How, if at all, is globalism relevant to that intensification? More specifically in the cases of Rwanda or Bosnia and Kosova, what impels people to kill other persons with whom, at the level of face-to-face *interaction*, they have been living in an erstwhile fragile and ritualized amity? In the language of the present argument, they entail understanding the relationship between the embodied level of face-to-face relations and layers of more abstract forms of social life, extensions of integration conducted across time and space by institutional and disembodied means. It is important to note that in the precolonial period there was no evidence of *systematic* violence between the Hutu and Tutsi as such. Genocide, I suggest, is a modern phenomenon, with the proviso that, as Tom Nairn argues in Chapter 13, its outbreak needs to be overdetermined by such processes as identity trauma and landslide crises. When the Western media described the genocide as 'tribalism gone mad' they were completely blind to the complexity of the event.

The genocide was clearly under way by the evening of 7 April with the Presidential Guards beginning to work through the death lists of priority targets in the capital, and it quickly spread through the bureaucracy of the (French-trained) Interahamwe and Impuzamugambi militias and out to the countryside. The cold language of 'priority targets', 'bureaucracy' and 'work' is intentionally used here, for there is strong circumstantial evidence that the killing began that way – as a modern, institutionalized and premeditated operation of intentional genocide against the Tutsi and their sympathizers. The killing-machine, the Interahamwe, meaning 'those who work together', may have been haphazard but it was also a state-run volunteer service linked to involvement in a series of earlier massacres. While the carefully targeted killings quickly broadened into mayhem, a layer of institutional efficiency (and 'indifference' to the emotional consequences) remained behind the scenes. Gérard Prunier records that garbage trucks were used in Kigali to help dispose of the dead. To prevent epidemics, some 60,000 bodies were removed from the capital for burial. In short, the genocide was both a modern incident requiring instrumental planning *and* a neo-traditional fugue grounded in embedded differences. It was both an orchestrated single event conducted at a 'distance' by institutionally framed action and, once the slaughter had been initiated, a sporadic series of events spurred on by embodied face-to-face confrontation.

Understanding what happened in Rwanda in 1994 entails looking at much more than the empirical particulars of the event itself. Each of the individual acts of murder in Rwanda in 1994 had its own specificity. For some it was intended as a means of getting rid of the evil Tutsi bodies that beset the land. For others it was under duress as a frightened public act attempting to show overt commitment to the Hutu cause. For yet others it was, as one of the 'innocent murderers' (Jean-Pierre Chrétien's expression), putting one's spouse or child out of his or her misery on the command of a terror squad. However varied the individual's motivations may have been, behind these diverse instances lie more general patterns. The first dimension of patterned change involves the colonial polity and the way in which traditional processes of communal identity were simultaneously institutionalized as modern and legitimized as traditional or customary. In other words, the very nature of tribal difference was reconstituted as part of the global extension of colonialism to Africa in the late nineteenth and early twentieth centuries. Globalism was thus at the heart of the formation of what, as an intentional oxymoron, we can call 'modern tribes'.

Although in relative terms nineteenth-century Rwanda was linguistically and culturally homogeneous – and this makes the explanation harder – it was nevertheless divided into three main 'tribal' groupings: the majority Hutu, the Tutsi (officially, a minority of 9 per cent of the total population before the massacre), and a tiny group called the Tua. Understanding the relevance of this apparently unremarkable constitution of identity for the events of 1994 involves understanding how the nature of cultural division was hardened and thus fundamentally changed by colonial edict long before that year. The precolonial polity, or at least one layer of it, was from the end of the eighteenth century a highly centralized kingdom based upon the semi-sacredness of its leaders – as far as we know, all pastoralists.[16] Only in the nineteenth century through the force of the globalizing intruders, and as the identities of pastoralist and Tutsi became synonymous, did this become a double domination: pastoral aristocracy over agriculturalists and Tutsi over Hutu (and Tua). However, even then a process called *kwihutura* qualified the boundary between Tutsi and Hutu. It allowed the possibility, through accrual of pastoral wealth, of leaving behind Hutuness and becoming a Tutsi. Under German and then Belgian rule, a strict caste-like division separated Tutsi identity, associated with traditional power, and Hutu identity, associated with subjection. Identity cards were issued and the Belgian colonizers used the traditional structure of chiefdom as the apparatus of (brutal) mediated administration. As Mahmood Mamdani brilliantly argues, the colonial state depended on this meshing of the modern and traditional: 'these powers were justified as "customary", and "custom" was proclaimed by the very authority sanctioned by the colonial power as "customary". This tautology was crystallized in the legal institutions.'[17] The European power thus ruled through the Tutsi, now a modern tribe-caste-class[18] who at the same time looked to embodied expressions of their 'essential' difference: greater height, longer noses, and so on – and thus at one level continued to treat themselves as tribes in the old way.[19] As I began to argue earlier, the fixing of tribal identity involved globalizing modernization, as both sides, colonial and indigenous, called for different reasons upon the subjectivity of customary continuity.

The second related point of explanation is simple but important. With independence from the Belgians in 1962 and formal power-sharing, the hierarchy of power was reversed by the weight of numbers of a formal democracy. However, the colonial cultural heritage carried through, with the Hutu still feeling that oppressive weight of history. This resentment was confirmed by an invasion by 200–300 Tutsi refugees from Burundi. It was called the 'invasion of the cockroaches'. Politically driven killings of targeted Tutsi followed, with global bodies such as the United Nations reporting between 1,000 and 14,000 deaths. Thus, as the newly independent polity attempted to achieve what the development theorists of the time called 'nation-building', a run of return pogroms began. In 1988, a Hutu uprising in the north of neighbouring Burundi was followed by mass killings of Hutu; and, in 1990, Tutsi militia from Uganda invaded as the Rwandan Patriotic Front.[20] From this bloody history, some tentative conclusions can be drawn. The months of April and May 1994 were horrific, but 1994 was 'only' the most horrific episode of the many such episodes of violence that arose in the context of globally and locally produced deep uncertainty about the identity of the 'other' Rwandans. The new violence was based in part on a process of ideologically and administratively fixing that identity in an unsustainable modern hierarchy of power based on customary tribalism. This is an example of the overlaying of levels of ontological formation: modernism and tribalism.

Why was the fixing unsustainable? Why, rather than providing for cultural security, as it might have under the ritualized conditions of traditional society, did it set up a history of ressentiment? This leads us to a further dimension of patterned change. Parallel but counter-developments, such as the changing nature of power in a 'democratic' and militarized postcolonial world, rendered that 'fixing' as increasingly fragile and crumbly. This for me has the effect of tempering Tom Nairn's important insistence on modern democracy as the way forward. In this case, democratic proceduralism became part of the problem. Its imposition was effected without thought to the historical constitution of difference. It suggests, as I will argue later in the book, that democracy needs to be reflexively engendered and its modernism qualified by other forms of representation and engagement. This entails much more than saying that forging democracy takes time. The backdrop to the 'reversal' of the hierarchy of Hutu and Tutsi was signalled by formal democratic independence in 1962. However, it had been going on through more than a decade of UN decolonization missions to take apart the fixity of Tutsi dominance. Other modern and globally carried counter-processes to the fixing of identity include the role of school-based modern education and the development of monetary exchange system. These loosened the taken-for-granted certainty of traditional-then-colonial forms of identity without establishing anything workably solid in its place. Thus we have two kinds of tensions. Firstly, there are tensions between the intersecting ontological formations – tribal, traditional and modern. Moreover, there are tensions within modernism itself: tensions between sensitivity and indifference to difference; and tensions between the fixing of identity around reconstituted older forms and processes of its undermining, both incremental and revolutionary. Secondly, there are tensions between localism and globalism – in this case globalism expressed as imperial expansion and administrative extension.

YUGOSLAVIA: FROM MODERN NATIONALISM TO DISEMBODIED VIOLENCE

Just as in precolonial Rwanda where there is no evidence of systematic violence between the Hutu and Tutsi as such, in prewar Bosnia, peoples of different narod and religion lived side by side in relative peace. At least at the level of village life, Catholic Croats, Orthodox Serbs and Bosnian Muslims, later named as the three markers of ethnic cleavage in the Bosnian war, lived together in carefully negotiated criss-crossing civic identity. As Tone Bringa describes, while the kinship networks and rituals of intimacy and religion remained separate, as did the architecture and culture of the household, the social and moral geography of the village provided points of interaction, even social integration for the different groups.[21] The war changed all of this from above, although some patterns of interchange continued. For example, large numbers of Serbs worked underground to support those who were singled out for ethnic cleansing. In Kosova, the situation was similar with the driving force for systematic violence coming from the political leaders and institutionalized military responses as they incited local concerns. Though fuelled by a decade of tension, the first overt grassroots moves towards violence came as late as the mid 1990s.

Just before Christmas 1997 in the village of Llaushe, armed members of the newly formed Kosova Liberation Army appeared for the first time to confront Albanians at a funeral. It closed a circle of determinations. The thousands of Albanians had gathered to mourn the death of a schoolteacher killed by Serb police. Without wanting to suggest that face-to-face community is free of violence, it is galling to read the opposite – namely that it was the subjectivities of face-to-face community and its primordial memories of past grievances that underlay the war. The depictions in newspapers such as the *New York Times* were bad enough, but there were also academic writings attributing the causes of war to tribal divisions – primordial cleavages supposedly restrained by Tito's Yugoslavia, now bursting forth as ethnic nationalism. Tron Gilbert, for example, writes that 'the beginning of nationalism in the Balkans was, in reality, a form of tribalism'.[22] His writing is different only in tone and detail from newspaper articles such as 'Old Tribal Rivalries in Eastern Europe Pose Threat of Infection'.[23] His argument combines all the worst problems of such attributions, though nicely synthesized in an apparently subtle scholarly analysis. The argument is based on the usual ethnocentric claim about the differences between Western and Eastern nationalism: the first, civic and accepting of global diversity: the second, ethnic, culturally homogenizing and bad. 'Cultural nations', he says wrongly, 'lend themselves to tribalism, whereas political nations do not.'[24] From there we follow the well-trodden path to the necessity of Western intervention: 'Tribes in possession of modern weaponry and destructive techniques can only be constrained by counterforce.'[25] This pronouncement tells us more about the dominant political culture of the West during the Bosnian-Kosovan interventions than it does about the complexities of life on the ground in the Balkans. It is to this side of the story – the dominant political culture of the United Kingdom and the United States – that I want to direct the focus of this study, just trying to open up the problems of understanding rather than developing any conclusions at this stage. The discussion will be taken up again in Chapters 15 and 17.

What was the cultural-political context that normalized the necessity of NATO's massive intervention in Kosova? What does it tell us about the changing nature of nationalism that when Bill Clinton and Tony Blair talked about the necessity of the 'humanitarian bombing' of Kosova they invoked the name of globalism rather than national interest? What does it mean that these political leaders were adamant that the war should remain undeclared and strategically mediated by technological military means? What is the basis of the relatively new political obsession about not putting troops on the ground, and having no body-bags return home to mark the tragedy of the conflict? The simple answer to these questions is that NATO did not want to be there in Kosova. They were forced to by a series of contingent blunders and misunderstandings, including a politics of ultimatum against Milošević that was never going to work without either carpet bombing Kosova and Serbia or putting massive numbers of troops into the region. Against the backdrop of inaction during the 1994 Rwandan massacre and the 1992–96 episodes of Bosnian Muslims being ethnically cleansed – both of which gradually became media-broadcast sources of Western guilt – Clinton and Blair felt that they had to find a Third Way. This sensibility and structure of international considerations from outside Yugoslavia, and a modern revival of neo-traditionalism from inside that federation, ended in a postmodern air war of vast destruction from above and a ghastly modern ground war of ethnic cleansing from below. That is the simple answer, but, as with the Rwandan situation, such an explanation takes far too much for granted. It would take masses of background work in order to develop a more satisfactory account. All that I can hope to do here is critically examine aspects of the postnationalist culture in the West that made the abstract violence of dropping bombs from a great height appear defensible as a humanitarian intervention.

A recent tome, *Blood Sacrifice and the Nation: Totem Rituals and the American Flag*, published by one of the world's most respected university presses, provides a fantastic example of a theory that has a snowball's chance in hell of explaining this phenomenon of postnational abstract violence.[26] The book's thesis, that the nation is a tribe founded on a civic religion that demands the blood sacrifice of its children, is made all the more dramatic by taking as its example the United States, a highly differentiated nation without a singular ethnic genealogy, let alone tribal-national roots. Let the authors first set out their approach in their own words:

> What binds the nation together? ... This book argues that violent blood sacrifice makes enduring groups cohere, even though such a claim challenges our most deeply held notions of civilized behaviour.
>
> The sacrificial system that binds American citizens has a sacred flag at its centre. Patriotic rituals revere it as the embodiment of a bloodthirsty totem god who organizes killing energy. This totem god is the foundation of the mythic, religiously constructed American identity. Our notion of the totem comes from Durkheim, for whom it was the emblem of the group's agreement to be a group ... We intend to show totem dynamics vigorously at work in the contemporary United States. We lay out the practices and beliefs that furnish the system without which the nation is in danger of dissolution. Their focus is the magical and primitive use of the flag, the totem object of American civil religion.[27]

As I began to read the book I first thought this writing was merely the metaphoric excess of the introductory page, rhetoric used to draw in the reader before settling down to the serious analysis. However, for all the wealth of empirical description, the book never gets beyond detailed description and methodological mire. The most important insight for our purposes is that the pre-eminent civic nation, the USA, still uses the rhetoric and subjectivity of blood sacrifice. This goes against the classical modernist argument. However, *Blood Sacrifice and the Nation* leaves us with too many questions. How can such a differentiated nation, a nation that does not believe that embodied genealogical kinship is the means of its integration, be considered a tribe? Through its totem system, answer Marvin and Ingle – the kinship form is exogamy. There is no postmodern irony here, only bad theory. Exogamy, they say, actually organizes popular elections and reconciles potentially violent political-clan differences:

Two major clan groups bearing animal identities are descended from the flag, the tribal ancestor, for whom the totem eagle is occasionally substituted. During seasonal festivals called elections, representatives of the elephant and donkey clans form an exogenous mating pair that produces a reincarnated savior king, an embodied totem president who bears a sacrificial charge ... The cross-fertilized membership of the two great non-exclusive electoral clans deflects potentially murderous struggle. It reorganizes the identities of contending groups by focusing away from irreconcilable differences associated with exclusive affiliation by blood and subordinating these differences to blood ties of totem sacrifice.[28]

The tensions in the method abound and show themselves in obvious ways. America is both one large differentiated tribe and a nation of tribes in the plural. The totemic fathers of the nation are those established by sacrifice in war, but Marvin's list singles out as 'the most significant totem avatars for living Americans' the venerated war heroes (not), Franklin D. Roosevelt and John F. Kennedy. Roosevelt did not enter the Second World War until forced to in December 1941; and Kennedy presided over the Bay of Pigs fiasco, the Cuban Missile backdown, and had the 16,000 troops hidden in Vietnam under the guise of being advisors. The evidence is ambiguous as it is for their description of the flag. For Marvin and Ingle, the flag is simultaneously the god of nationalism, the totem emblem, a body, a representative of the violently sacrificed body, and the 'baby' that came from Betsy Ross' body. It is both an artefact based on oral not textual culture and the intimate subject of poems, novels, advertisements, newspaper articles and television programmes. It is the totem 'whose mission it is to organize death', the object that must not be used for commercial purposes, and it is also the motif on everything commercial from table linen to condoms. It is the *male*, transcendent totem that is taboo to touch (even though the Old Glory Condom Company ran advertisements around the slogan 'never flown at half-mast') and the *female*, popular totem that expresses itself in the 'messy, rutting shoving, people' who know the answers to questions about baseball.[29] Such analyses cannot explain the kind of nationalism that fears the return of the body-bags from hot spots of conflict and abhors the death of its own soldiers. When late-modern states such as the United States of America present themselves as postnational, acting violently in the interests of global peace, it suggests that the sensibility of postnationalism needs to be understood in quite different terms, terms that we will develop in Chapter 7.

Despite continuities, the postnational nation is very different from that of the modern imperial nations such as late-nineteenth-century England, Germany or even the frontier-expanding United States. Today's postnations have to carry their pasts with them while simultaneously forgetting/remembering the oppressive practices of that past. They have to commemorate their origins and histories while distancing themselves from previous acts of oppressive violence at the heart of those histories.[30] Rudyard Kipling's England gloriously projected itself as engaged in the 'White Man's Burden' to spread its civilization and power, territorially and globally. The impact of the imperial nations on their colonies was profound and we are still living with its consequences. Rwanda is but one example. However, as Tom Nairn's writing documents, Blair's England is less sure. In this new problem of remembering/forgetting, the new global nations[31] can partially comfort themselves with the new 'reality' that they are no longer interested in extending global territoriality or painting the map the latest version of 'empire red'. The trouble is that they strangely find themselves continually beckoned into wars that ostensively they do not want to fight. The denizens of such countries, including those of Tony Blair's new England and Bill Clinton's America, thus have many competing and contradictory issues to consider: modern ideas of old-fashioned national interest; late-modern concerns about universalistic human rights; and postmodern aversions to the 'ultimate sacrifice' such as dying for a cause, or watching the body-bags return from a place of foreign military intervention. They are caught up in postnational hopes, which under pressure quickly slip back into misremembered national ideals. More dangerously, they are caught in the delusion that most of the violence in the world comes from the contemporary reversions to primordial tribalisms rather than being bound up with the very processes of abstract globalism that they so heartily espouse.

If the unmasking of the contradictions of postnational globalism is at the centre of the political conclusion being drawn here, the need for a new approach to theory and method is crucial to the conceptual conclusion. Understanding the relationship between globalism, nationalism, neo-traditionalism and tribalism will entail developing an approach that takes seriously both their concurrent and intersecting reality, and the way in which they are set within a world of deep ontological contradictions. It is simply unhelpful to say that under conditions of contemporary globalization, primordial tribalism is being revived from near extinction or that nationalism is dying the death of anachronism. An alternative approach can be initiated through two relatively simple steps. The first step involves setting up a method that analyses the intersection of coterminous formations – tribalism, traditionalism, modernism and postmodernism – and does so without collapsing them into each other. The second step involves analytically working across different levels of integration from embodied face-to-face to the disembodied abstracted relations between people. This takes us back to the political point: to uncritically advocate postnationalism, at least when it takes the form of privileging the mobile possibilities of highly abstracted and globalizing relations, is also to find oneself defending new forms of power and cultural legitimation.

Part II

Debating Civic and Post-nationalism

5

Fetishized Nationalism?

Joan Cocks[1]

No student of nations and nationalism should be surprised that a cosmopolitanism of modern intellectual life can flourish side by side with national differences in the intellectual reception of ideas, including ideas about nationalism. A point of wide international currency today, for example, is the notion that national identity matters objectively as a central factor in modern history, and subjectively to individuals who feel themselves to be at least as fundamentally members of peoples as either members of classes or abstract, autonomous selves. Another widely held point is the notion that national communities arise out of historical circumstances rather than from archaic relations or blood ties, draw on mythologies to turn far-flung strangers into political kin, and glorify a rural national past while promoting modern socio-economic conditions.

Such ideas have been especially associated in the United States with a view of national identity as a fiction that hides nothing more pernicious underneath, and with a view of all national identities as equivalent, if distinctive, sets of particularities. These views can be traced to the influence of two theorists of nationalism – Ernest Gellner and Benedict Anderson. Gellner posits the national form as a historically progressive if self-mystifying requirement of industrial society and its universal good of economic growth, and Benedict Anderson portrays the national form as the result of a fruitful 'modelling effect' of 'imagined' – in the sense of 'creative' and 'meaning-generating' – communities, all equivalent multiplications of a good prototype.

In this chapter, I look closely at a thinker who is a prominent 'modernist' theorist of nationalism in his own right.[2] If Tom Nairn is associated, and indeed often associates himself, with Gellner and Anderson, he warrants our attention in part because he takes their ideas in a far more radical direction than they do. Nairn comes to the national question through a hatred of imperial states and a sympathy for small peoples, a partisanship that lends his work real political passion. He sees unequal relations between great states and vulnerable regions as the larger context in which the analysis of national aspirations must be set. By making domination the centrepiece of the national form, he gives a critical edge to 'imagined communities' that undercuts the smarmy, sentimental intimations of the phrase. Nairn also warrants our attention, however, because of the metamorphosis of his ideas from his anticipation of the break-up of Britain in the 1970s to the actual break-up of the Soviet Union in the 1990s. On the one hand, this metamorphosis is rooted in the specificities of Nairn's intellectual and political biography. On the other hand, it mirrors a general shift in international critical thought over the same period, along with the promise and dangers of that shift. Thus we can read the case of Tom Nairn as both a curious and a cautionary tale.

Unfortunately, the three most crucial specificities of Nairn's biography are likely to count as strikes against him. The first strike is Nairn's allegiance to Scottish nationalism.[3] Having enjoyed successful industrialization at the earliest stages of capitalist development, the Scottish intelligentsia and entrepreneurial bourgeoisie were not pressed by economic deprivation to mobilize all Scottish classes as a national mass against England. Hence during the high-point of European nationalism, no heroic people here rebelled against their ethnically alien rulers. For those who find it difficult to support nationalist movements unless they are uprisings of the dispossessed against the dispossessors, this last absence seems especially likely to disappoint.

The second strike against Nairn is that – despite his boundless contempt for all things British – he thinks and writes within the British cultural arena. European-inspired intellectuals in the United States and elsewhere have tended either to follow the lead of the Germans or to fall head over heels for the French. Such national prejudices are unfortunate, especially with respect to questions of political community, for writers from both the metropolis and the peripheries of the old British Empire can offer us what Said has called, in his eulogy to Raymond Williams, a deeply geographical conception of place. Williams fixes his sights on the British Isles, but Said recommends his approach for its power to illuminate 'various structures of feeling involving ... places [like Ireland, Africa, India, the Caribbean and New Zealand], structures fashioned from within Britain as the imperial, metropolitan center'.[4] Almost all of this might equally be said of Nairn, although Nairn is hardly the romantic that Williams is. Nairn focuses not on attachments to land, memories of homelands, or the cultural aesthetics of landscapes but rather on the political economy of geography: the way in which power in certain locations sets the material terms of existence for other locations, so that separate places can be comprehended only if the mind connects them together.

In analysing the geographical place of nineteenth-century Scottish intellectuals, Nairn supplies us with clues to his own intellectual location at once inside and against Great Britain. According to Nairn, Scotland's eminent thinkers and writers, rather than identifying with and activating the Scottish people, emigrated to London, where they 'played a very large part in formulating the new national and imperial culture-community'. In leaving an 'advanced quasi-nation', these Scots differed from other 'hungry and ambitious intellectuals' who flocked from the rural hinterlands of the British Empire to the metropolis. To grasp Nairn's point we need only recall George Lamming's description of the novelists who left the British West Indies for London in the first half of the twentieth century, not out of a refusal to write for a national people but rather in despair over a failure to be read by one, unappreciated as they were by both their own middle and peasant classes.[5]

Nairn differs from the nineteenth-century Scots in his outrage at empire in general and the British Empire in particular. He differs from twentieth-century West Indians in not having been forced to seek his fortune in the imperial capital by a lack of recognition in the hinterland. He joins both Scots and West Indians, however, in treating Great Britain – its hinterlands and metropolis alike – as the broad locale of his working and his work. Even when Nairn writes solely about Scotland, he does so not to champion its national uniqueness but rather to comprehend it, in its British setting, as the exception that proves his general rule about the internal connection between uneven capitalist development and nationalism: Scotland is the case of a nationalist movement that failed to happen when it should have happened, if a shared religion, folklore, hostility to foreign rulers, and the recent memory of an independent state – that is, if almost everything but a relation of economic disadvantage vis-à-vis a centre were sufficient precipitants of nationalist politics. But Nairn concentrates much less on the particularities of Scotland, even in this comparative way, than on Great Britain, on the one hand, and nationalism in general, on the other.[6] Thus his implied audience is not merely Scottish but British, and not merely British but worldwide. More precisely, it is made up of cosmopolitan intellectuals, for, despite his defence of the people against the intellectuals, the popular classes do not read Nairn any more than the peasants read Lamming and his compatriots.

Later on we shall see how Nairn's address to a cosmopolitan readership clashes with his scorn for cosmopolitan social groups, and why he feels that scorn. For now we need only note the global sweep of Nairn's intelligence, as opposed to his localist political sympathies. This sweep is partly a function of an age in which the references and readerships of all intellectuals have become increasingly expansive, but it derives more specifically from Nairn's perspective on modern development, which in turn derives from his Marxism. Nairn served on the editorial board of the British Marxist *New Left Review* from 1962 until a falling out among the board's members in 1983, and he wrote a good many of that journal's pages. This brings us to the third and biggest strike against him, for hardly anyone thinks much of Marxism any more. Even in his earliest and most significant book on nationalism, *The Break-up of Britain*, Nairn is a Marxist merely of sorts. His theoretical and political evolution since then, require us to give the phrase 'of sorts' greater and greater emphasis. I hope to show in the pages that follow how the whole complex of Nairn's commitments to and departures from Marxism makes him the provocative thinker that he is.

In *The Break-up of Britain*, published in 1977, with individual chapters appearing previously as articles, Nairn fundamentally revises Marxism by placing national formation and national conflict at the centre of modern history. While treating capital as a prime mover in that history which transformed the traditional world first in Europe and finally everywhere, Nairn maintains that the most shattering aspects of modern experience are the cultural-political disintegrations and reintegrations that result from this process. The most significant products of capitalism's world invasion are nation-states: 'the relatively mono-cultural, homogeneous, uni-linguistic entities that eventually replace all other forms of cultural and political community'.[7] While echoing Gellner on that last point, Nairn does not share Gellner's view of industrial capitalism as a benign order that gradually radiates out to all parts of the world, providing an economic growth that everyone comes to desire and eventually to attain. Nairn argues instead that the logic of infinite capital accumulation has convulsive effects on the world it invades, and that it gives rise to a world system characterized by deep divisions and inequalities. The most dramatic of these divisions and inequalities are regional and sub-regional, which generally means that the most dramatic antagonisms are experienced between whole peoples. Nationalist movements are responses to these inequalities and expressions of these *antagonisms*. *They* arise to unify and agitate peoples on the periphery or semi-periphery of capitalism against peoples at the core, provoking *nationalist* reactions from the more materially potent core states.

Nairn thereby demotes class conflict from its primary place in the theory of capital. Rather than being the truth that *nationalist politics* obscures, class division leaves its good mark on *nationalism by* dictating the popular form that it must take. To rally the people, *nationalist elites* must speak in the people's language – hence 'the emotionalism, the vulgar populism, the highly coloured romanticism of most *nationalist ideology*'. In contrast to Marxism, with its hyper-rationalistic approach to class *consciousness, nationalism succeeds* at the popular level because it provides 'the masses with something real and important'.[8] Nairn condemns Rosa Luxemburg as the Marxist with the greatest number of wrong answers to the national question. None the less, there is a strong family resemblance between Nairn's analysis of capitalism as a world system divided into cores and peripheries, and Luxemburg's claim that capitalism depends on the exploitation of *non-capitalist economies*. Nairn also follows Luxemburg in *underlining the* catastrophic way in which advanced regions invade and crush peripheral ones. This is why, as Nairn puts it, peripheral regions experience 'progress in the abstract' as '*domination in* the concrete', and 'domination in the concrete' as *national domination:* '*in* the first instance Anglicization or Frenchification', and later, more globally, Westernization or Americanization.

Unlike Luxemburg, Nairn holds that *nationalism is* a necessary response to capitalist penetration, which can be repelled only by a 'militant inter-class community' that conjures up a mythical sense of its own separate identity as the ideological *condition of* a unified political movement to expel foreigners. The upshot of successful national independence, however, is not the triumph of a unique people but rather the independent pursuit by a people of the universal requirements of modernity. Thus capitalism is not transcended but instead extended through a dialectic in which 'capitalism spread[s], and smash[es] the ancient social formations surrounding it', while nationalism arises to resist and then embrace the modernizing process.[9]

While Nairn hints at a socialist future, his dialectic consigns it to a Kafkaesque fate of indefinite postponement, for the contradiction between centre and peripheries is perpetually resolved inside the capitalist world system. Nairn calls internationalism a vast overstatement in the *nineteenth century*, when nationalism flourished side by side with socialism, and an utter delusion after 1914, when socialist internationalism died while capitalism '*continued to* endure and develop, and ... nationalism prospered along with it'. Given Nairn's view of nationalism as a response to uneven development, of uneven development as intrinsic to capitalism, and of capitalism as a fixed part of the modern scenery (in fact, as *the* modern scenery) *internationalism can* never have been anything but suspect: not a dissolution of national barriers, but a pretext for great-power ambitions.[10]

Nairn is equally scornful of universalism as either historical telos or moral ethos. 'In purely economic terms', capitalism 'has always tended towards larger scale, and a utilitarian *rationale* indifferent to pettifogging customs and ethnic colorations'.[11] Yet capital has also had to compromise with local cultures, depends on the nation state, and is incapable of realizing the potential of its 'innate universalism' in a different way than Marxism understood. Its inherently lopsided, uneven *integration of* larger and larger areas into, eventually, a world market and a world productive system means that generality continually begets specificity: defensive activations of the particular are *this* universal's inevitable results. As much as Nairn emphasizes, against classical Marxism, the primary importance of nations and nationalism as the real terrain on which modern domination and subjection are played out, he also insists in *The Break-up of Britain* that nationalism is inherently self-mystifying. Nations are 'imagined communities', perhaps, but their imaginings are necessary distortions of the truth as much as they are creative constructions of national 'truths'.[12]

In Nairn's reading, the explicit principles of nationalism are surface-level symptoms that simultaneously express and mask its deeper reality. For example, nationalism declares that its root cause lies in the uniqueness of nations: 'that human society consists essentially of several hundred different and discrete "nations", each of which has (or ought to have) its own postage-stamps and national soul'. This idea is necessary, Nairn argues, in that Welsh nationalism, for example, must make use of Welsh specificities to mobilize the Welsh people. At the same time, the idea is false, because it 'is not a Welsh fact, but a fact of general developmental history' and, against the spiritualist conceits of nationalism, even 'the most grossly material fact about modern history' that 'at a specific time the Welsh land and people are forced into the historical process in this fashion'.[13]

Then, too, *nationalism invents* the nation as primordial, archaic, antique. Many other theorists in the 1970s and 1980s make a similar point, but Nairn is happy to call the *invention a* kind of false-consciousness, while *insisting that* it responds to real 'latent fracture lines of human society under strain'.[14] The national myth compensates for a lack of modern political, social and economic *institutions that* other nations already have. To understand this is not necessarily to excuse it. Hannah Arendt, for example, scorns the Central and Eastern European pan-movements precisely because they substituted a cooked-up idea for the reality of a *nation-state*. If they wanted to match the national pride of Western nations, they had no country, no state, no historic achievement to show but could only point to themselves, and that meant, at best, to their language – as though language by itself were already an achievement – at worst, to their Slavic, or Germanic, or God-knows-what soul.[15] Nairn is light years away from Arendt here, extending great sympathy to those at the catastrophic end of progress.

Finally, while *nationalism purports* to revive and preserve a people's age-old customs and traditions, it actually looks backward *in order to* look forward. It elicits an *ancient past* to forge an entirely new and modern future, enabling societies 'to propel themselves forward ... *by a certain sort of regression*'.[16] *Nationalism's* regressive/progressive character makes it prone to both chauvinism and democracy, exclusivism and equality, atavism and emancipation. Its moral and political ambiguity eludes nationalists who portray the nation as simply good, as well as scholars who distinguish good varieties of nationalism from bad: patriotic from fascistic, civic from ethnic, anti-imperialist from imperialist. For Nairn, there are no 'black cats' and 'white cats' here: 'The whole family is spotted, without exception.' The spots derive in part from the ferocity of 'energies contained in customary social structures' that nationalist mobilization releases. If the most violent passions of nationalism can be likened to the appearance of the forces of the Id during the breakdown of an established personality, nationalism *per se* can be likened to the whole psychology of a self during a crisis it is forced to weather but does not cause or understand. Alluding to Benjamin's description of that terrible storm we call progress, Nairn states that *nationalism can be* seen as the pathology caused by that storm. He uses the psychoanalytic metaphor against uncomprehending critics of nationalism's irrationalities, but it is bound to irritate nationalists most of all. In Nairn's scheme of things, those nationalists resemble not leaders of glorious peoples but Nietzschean ascetic priests, reinfecting modern suffering and resentment with the germ of nationalism in order to heal those same wounds.

In one sense *The Break-up of Britain* can be read as an epitaph for Marxism, which fails to grasp what Nairn takes to be the most significant lines of conflict of our age. Moreover, it fails as a result of its inherent geographical and epochal limitations. As a theory born in Europe, it was primed to see class conflict in the European nation-states as paramount, rather than the regional conflicts caused by Europe's impact on the rest of the world. As a nineteenth- and early-twentieth-century theory, it could not see those regional conflicts clearly in any case, for the whole story of uneven development had not yet been historically fleshed out. These limitations, Nairn declares, puncture Marxism's view of itself as the science of history, exposing it instead as 'a part of history in a quite uncomplimentary sense ... which has nothing to do with the holy matrimony of theory and practice'.[17]

There are, however, good reasons for reading *The Break-up of Britain* as a neo-Marxist, not anti-Marxist, text. Nairn challenges Marxism because the empirical history of modern capitalism does not accord with it, not because he forsakes historical materialism for some other set of starting principles. He believes Marxism is correct in its understanding of capitalism's Western origins, its absolute pre-eminence as the determining force of the modern world, its character as a contradictory system of domination and development, and its perpetually expansive dynamic. He looks forward to Marxism becoming, 'an authentic world-theory ... founded upon the social development of the whole world'.[18] Finally, he implies that such a development will lead towards socialism, although the precipitants and form of socialism he hopes for are left entirely unclear.[19] In *The Break-up of Britain* Nairn brings nationalism to centre-stage, explains it, defends it, but does not believe it. To see nationalism as intellectually false but historically right has convoluted political implications for the seer; the ability to *be* a nationalist is not one of them.

In the years between the publication of *The Break-up of Britain* and the actual break-up of the Soviet empire, Nairn wrote numerous articles for *The New Statesman & Society* and *New Left Review* on Thatcherism, North–South disparities in Britain, the Scottish Nationalist Party, and the anti-republicanism of British political culture. He also published his anti-British, anti-empire, and very probably anti-English book, *The Enchanted Glass: Britain and its Monarchy*, on the function of monarchy in an age of Britain's advancing decrepitude. In the early 1990s, however, he returned to the question of nationalism in general in a series of articles he wrote for *The New Statesman, Dissent, Daedalus*, the *London Review of Books* and *New Left Review.* Here he responds to the emergence of new nationalist movements in Eastern Europe and the former Soviet Union. More precisely, he responds to what he dubs the 'paranoia' of Western intellectuals in the face of the latest nationalist eruptions, and their characterization of the Balkan conflict as an 'atavistic' and 'Hobbesian' tribal war.[20] Nairn chooses what others would deem a most unpropitious moment – the high-point of ethnic cleansing in Bosnia-Herzegovina – not only to explain and defend nationalism but to come out as a nationalist.

In his commentary on this new age of nationalism, Nairn preserves many key themes from his older book. He still claims, very ardently, that regional inequality is 'the living marrow of actual development', which begins in certain areas of the world that then become ascendant over others. He still understands nationalism as a backward- and forward-looking struggle on the part of the subjected for 'modernization on different, less disadvantageous terms'.[21] With specific respect to the warring ethnic groups in Eastern Europe and the former Soviet Union, he points to the rationality of each group's fears that it will be ruled economically by some other group 'in this new free-but-capitalist world', and so to the sense of its attempts to move the others 'on, or out of the way'.[22] Finally, he still sees capitalism as a globally unifying force that today is pulling even the former Communist zones into its orbit, precipitating in response to its own expansion and centralization 'a previously unimaginable and still escalating number of different ethno-political units'.[23]

However, Nairn sets these familiar elements among other ideas that altogether alter the political character and implications of his earlier position. History itself, according to Nairn, has forced upon him this first change: the erasure of the socialist alternative to capitalism that had at least a hypothetical existence as a distant vanishing point in his older work. This relatively delicate adjustment in Nairn's theory has huge ramifications for the world. Nairn now tells us that capitalist development 'has finally, definitively established itself since 1989 as the sole matrix of future evolution'. Even though it is nationalism that Nairn primarily means to stand up for, he praises nationalism, democracy and capitalism as pillars of modernity 'inseparable from progress' in the straightforward, undialectical sense of the term. He also cites the 'economic revulsion against the anti-capitalist command economies' as a progressive factor in 'the gigantic upheaval against Communism'. In only one essay does Nairn allude to socialism with something of his old affection, but even then he does so in a weird hodge-podge of incompatible sentiments and assertions: 'If market-governed development is the only kind there is, then this implies that there will be [only] different kinds of capitalism' – indeed, an 'immense variety'. Hence 'socialists will have to decide what type of capitalists they will become'.[24] So much for the future possibilities of radical difference in the socio-economic sense!

The second change in Nairn's approach to *nationalism is* more one of mood than of substantive assertion. In *The Break-up of Britain,* Nairn chides internationalism firmly but not too unkindly for being one part metropolitan ideology and one part socialist fantasy. In his new essays, he launches a crueller assault on *internationalism and* cosmopolitanism with ugly undertones. 'There is no doubt about the new spectre *haunting Europe.'* This opening taunt of Nairn's 1990 essay 'Beyond Big Brother' is aimed at leftists and liberals alike, for this time it is nationalism that is the revolutionary force, and metropolitan intellectuals the social group most threatened by it. With a special animus reserved for Eric Hobsbawm and his strongly internationalist *Nations and Nationalism since 1780,* Nairn asserts that internationalism 'originated among the Enlightenment elites, and has been transmitted from one intelligentsia to another ... It has always been the ideology most consonant with their class interests.'[25] The prejudice against 'inherited diversity' parades as a desire to turn 'mere Britons' into 'fully-grown Men' but actually reflects the power of 'the big battalions' to define the requisites of civilized humanity.[26]

In a second essay, Nairn traces internationalism not merely to the class interests of metropolitan elites but also to the characterological antipathy of the European Left for ethnic difference: its 'desperate will ... that social progress should not be so much built on ethnic variety as safely divorced from it'.[27] It is in a third essay, 'Internationalism and the Second Coming', however, that Nairn most avidly exposes internationalists who claim to speak 'from nowhere in particular' and for 'science and civilization as such'. These 'speakers from nowhere' include pre-industrial aristocrats, self-proclaimed cosmopolitans who dabble in foreign cultures, and 'individuals or families from culturally mixed or transplanted backgrounds who genuinely feel that they could choose to settle anywhere', a description, Nairn ominously adds, that leaves them 'open to attack by nativist spokesmen for vices such as rootlessness [and] lack of allegiance'. After 1789 these figures are joined by the 'metropolitan schoolteacher' disseminating civilization 'out and downwards from the appropriate centers', whose cosmopolitanism is 'difficult to distinguish from imperialism; and, finally, the socialist, who hopes to counter both imperialism and nationalism with the ethic of a universal working class'.[28]

Well, not quite finally. Nairn informs us that while post-1789 internationalism lacked 'a social basis in the sense of Burke's educated cross-border caste', it did have a 'composite and shifting foundation'. He lists the three main elements of that foundation as 'metropolitan or Atlantic-left cliques', the working-class movement, and, as he puts it, 'what George Steiner, in a 1987 television lecture on Vienna, called the "Judaic intelligentsia'".[29] One doesn't need a lesson in semiotics to know why Nairn assumes the voice of a Jew in order to conjure up the image of the Jewish carrier of internationalism, given all that that image has stood for in the modern history of right-wing nationalist and fascist thought. Nairn concludes by denouncing the multinational state as the practical foundation of internationalism, proclaiming the collapse of key 'overarching states' in 1989 to be a harbinger of the good collapse of all the rest. In light of his critique of internationalism, however, this collapse can only be disastrous for the motley crew on the other side of the divide from 'the national people': not only the metropolitan elites with their interest in domination, but also intellectuals, socialists, foreigners, Jews, all other diaspora groups, and, if we push the logic of his argument all the way, multi-ethnic local communities and individuals who are ethnic mixtures in and of themselves.

Nairn's onslaught against internationalism forecasts the third change in his position: his new fetishism of ethnicity, locality and nationality. Nairn fetishizes ethnicity partly by modifying the claim that he, Gellner and Anderson once made about the modernity of nationalism and the status of the nation as an invented community. In 1990, he writes that humankind's 'arguably most important natural inheritance is [its] own ethnolinguistic variety' and that 'Nationalism has always been invention after nature'.[30] Two years later, he adds that it is no longer clear that nationalism or regionalism 'derives so totally from the circumstances of modernity'.[31] Nairn speculates that there may be something biological, hereditary and genetic to nationalism and ethnicity after all, which, he assures us, need not imply a natural hierarchy of peoples but does imply an internal species diversity which 'through cultural means has always been "human nature"' in any event.

In an essay snappily entitled 'This Land is My Land, That Land is Your Land', Nairn and his co-author John Osmond add a territorial dimension to the equation. 'All land is somebody's', they admonish, and so modernity must negotiate with the archaic.[32] With these words Nairn not only affirms the primordial nature of national identity claims but also assimilates land rights to those claims, which in turn allows him to highlight the ancient roots as well as modern causes of ethnic and national animosities in shared territories. The ideas of a false internationalism and a true ethnic division feature prominently in Nairn's account of ethnic conflict in Bosnia-Herzegovina. Nairn holds that the situation there of intimate ethnic 'overlay or admixture' is atypical and idiosyncratic, having been 'deliberately maintained' by outside imperial powers which artificially enforced the unity of distinct peoples. In Nairn's view, the real 'curse of this old frontier zone' is that 'it was never allowed to unscramble itself along what became the standard lines of European nation-state evolution'.[33] Given Nairn's detailed delineations elsewhere of ethnic multiplicity in the borderlands of

Europe, and his attacks on European big-state multinationalism, one can
not help but protest against his suggestion here that ethnic singularity has
been Europe's 'standard line'. Nairn infers from this so-called standard
tendency of peoples, the spontaneous and uncoerced preferences of those
peoples. Thus he can attribute the demise of ethnic coexistence in Bosnia not
to nationalist leaders who, in Robert Hayden's quoted words, had to destroy
popular ethnic peace because their own ideology proclaimed such peace
impossible, and not even to a populism which, in *The Break-up of Britain*,
Nairn is careful to distinguish from democratic politics, but to democracy
itself. 'Democracy is people power', he remarks in the 1990s, '[a]nd in this
region people are primarily communities, the democratic impulse is strong
but also collective, ethnic rather than individual or abstract'. While assuring
us that '[n]o endorsement of Great Serb expansionism is implied', Nairn
turns to Radovan Karadzic in support of his case. The old ethnic tolerance
prevailed 'before democracy', he quotes Karadzic: as saying. But '[n]ow
we have democracy ... People no longer have to live that way, we have free
choice ... Why do you wish us punished for that ...?' Here Karadzic suggests
that the situation in Bosnia is the result of the free choices of all the peoples
involved. Nairn seconds him when he asserts that, regardless of Western
metropolitan opinion, a 'crude repartition of Bosnia-Herzegovina' has
already been effected 'on the ground', as if all the peoples involved had
agreed on that repartition. In this way, Nairn redraws the battleline in Bosnia
so that it divides the West on the internationalist side from the Croats, Serbs
and Muslims on the nationalist.[34]

   The break-up of large states is democratic not only because it liberates
ethnic groups, Nairn believes, but because it creates a multiplicity of local
centres of power. His basic argument is that the Cold War stand-off between
the two great empires suppressed 'collective and national ... ferment',
with a consequent 'narrowing and souring of identity and meaning'.[35]
The new age of nationalist disorder may have brought with it dislocation
and doubt, but it also releases new forms of identity and community that
are less rigid and overbearing, more imaginative and diverse, than those
offered by either the superpowers or the large European-style states. Nairn
claims the multiplication of political centres can emancipate the world
epistemologically from 'the metropolitan virtual reality being pumped
out in London, Paris and New York', while the globalizing economic and
cultural force of Big Mac and *L.A. Law* finds its sturdy antidote in '[t]he
nonlogical, untidy, refractory, disintegrative, particularistic truth of [little]
nation-states'.[36] The 'whole tendency of the age', Nairn concludes, 'seems
set against gigantism'.[37]

   Nairn's fetishization of political smallness or locality is not out of tune
with the sensibilities of many metropolitan intellectuals today, but a passing
glance at political theory should make it plain that while the fragmenting

of great states may democratize power internationally, internal democracy and cultural independence cannot be inferred from a polity's small size. A passing glance at economic practice should make it equally plain that economic monoliths and political miniatures can go together hand in hand, instead of opposing one another as point and counterpoint. While Nairn can be accused of overplaying the importance of nationalism in *The Break-up of Britain*, at least he emphasizes its intrinsic ambiguity in that text. In his new essays, he sets nationalism squarely on the side of progress, freedom, diversity and democracy. Nairn does admit that to say that 'nationalism is, very generally, a good thing is not to say that there are no blots, excrescences, or failures'. But even this clashes with his older and more complex insight that the whole family of nationalism is spotted, without exception. Nairn explicitly ascribes his new optimism to an uplifting turn in history rather than to a turnaround in his political point of view:

> Fifteen years ago, I wrote something about 'The Modern Janus', likening nationalism to the two-headed Roman deity ... Since then the whole world has increasingly come to resemble him. But with an important difference ... on the whole, the forward-gazing side of the strange visage may be more prominent than it was in 1977 ... more open and encouraging than it was then.[38]

Against those who demur at the bloody context in which he writes these lines, Nairn harks back to the Cold War order and its threat of species extinction, 'under which humanity cowered' for 40 years. Compared with *that*, the 'new world of liberation chaos' cannot be anything but a step forward. The most impressive fact in Nairn's eyes, given the great scale of ethno-national turbulence, is 'how astoundingly, how unbelievably little damage has been done'. And indeed, he declares, the consequences of even some worst-case nationalist scenario 'would not be, by the standards of 1948–88, all that serious'.[39] In the purely quantitative, body-count sense, Nairn is right: not even genocide can top human annihilation, after all. Still, this line of argument is surely an instance of what Hannah Arendt would call moral stupidity, for human annihilation would not put into perspective, but instead would put an end to, the seriousness of every other human thing. Gazing out on the European landscape in the 40 years before 1948, Arendt far surpasses Nairn in recognizing the calamities that the living human world brings on itself as soon as it makes 'sheer being' the criteria of political belonging and exclusion.

In this chapter, I have emphasized the most unsettling aspects of Nairn's trajectory of thought. In some of his recent essays, Nairn begins to de-emphasize ethnicity as the basis of nations and nationalism in favour of a more eclectic celebration of diverse political forms, including not only the ethno-nation but multi-ethnic cities and city-states. Moreover, in an article written in 1995, he posits ethno-nationalism as a necessary but transitory step on the way to a more tolerant, civic nationalism, based on the principle that, in the words of Michael Ignatieff, 'a nation should be a home to all, and that race, colour, religion and creed should be no bar to belonging'.[40] However, these new proposals are so fragmentary and unsupported by anything that came before that they appear as lapses rather than as a reflective refinement or explicit repudiation of a previous position. Then, too, the last proposal depends on the contrast Nairn had buried earlier between an infantile 'Eastern' nationalism and a mature, more civilized 'Western' one. The conceptualization is inadequate for all the reasons Nairn specified years ago, even if many readers will breathe more easily about his politics as a result of it.[41]

Nairn's latest twists and turns invite a final assessment of his intellectual and political travels thus far. What does this complicated figure offer critical thinkers in the way of virtues to appreciate and vices to avoid? Nairn's sharp tongue and fighting spirit are refreshing in the current intellectual milieu of cultivated irony and world-weariness. His energetic defence of national communities on political and economic grounds, combined with his earlier emphasis on their necessary self-distortions, provides a hard-headed approach to a concept that these days reeks of cloying moralism and romanticism. Nairn's materialism is also welcome in a period dominated by discourse theory, especially as that materialism is not of the 'nothing counts but the mode of production' sort. As much as he is quite definitely a theorist, not a historian, of nationalism, Nairn connects his theoretical ideas to the concrete historical world where the validity of those ideas has its ultimate test, rather than rooting them solely in an ideal world – 'ideal' either in the sense of a wished-for but non-existent reality, or in the sense of a conceptual realm where every idea gains its value primarily from its coherence with other ideas.

Refreshingly, too, Nairn counters truth-claims that he believes to be false (the truths of classical Marxism and, in his early work, of nationalism) with other truth-claims, rather than solving the problem of competing views by deconstructing everything in sight or, worse yet, by celebrating everybody's story. His assertions about modern history may be wrong, but at least they are couched in such a way as to stir up debate. Where Nairn most seriously errs in his sense of authority, it seems to me, is in his obeisance to what Marxists used to call the objective factor in history. While Nairn inherits this tendency from the Marxist tradition, he does so in a highly exaggerated form. Revolutionaries from Marx to Lenin, Luxemburg and Gramsci saw history and capitalism as having an objective logic to them, but they also underscored the importance and open-endedness of subjective will and intentions, even if they never solved the problem of how the objective and the subjective actually meshed. For Nairn, on the contrary, the objective dynamic of modern capitalism is so dictatorial that subjects can only fall into line. Nairn's embrace of the necessity of the real is most evident in his theory of development, which he also inherits from Marxism but turns into something far more merciless and fixed. For Nairn, 'capitalist development' at once determines the entire set of possible *meanings of* development and rules like a natural fact over the world. There is no conceptual *content outside* it, no practical escape from it, and no foreseeable end to it; its traumatic, unevenness notwithstanding, it is all we can hope for now and in the longish run.

In other respects, Nairn anticipates the virtues and vices of post- and anti-Marxist thought today. In his earliest work, he trades in an overemphasis on economics for an appreciation of the cultural and political spheres. He switches from conceiving of politics as the struggle between two internally related opposites – 'a proletariat and a bourgeoisie essentially the same everywhere ... locked in the same battle from Birmingham to Shanghai'[42] – to conceiving politics as multiple struggles between core and periphery, which he also calls fragments, and which today we call margins. In line with other British theorists such as Ernest Gellner, Benedict Anderson and Anthony Smith, and more than a decade before nationalism hit the intellectual headlines in the United States, Nairn revealed the comprehensibility and centrality of a force that many Western intellectuals had considered irrational, inexplicable but luckily passing. While more alert than Gellner, Anderson and Smith to the political effects of unequal regional power, Nairn joins them in his sensitivity to the cultural construction of national communities by means of imagination, fantasy and myth, and also to the good as well as bad effects of such 'fictions'. Most admirably, at least in *The Break-up of Britain*, Nairn has an eye for ambiguity in politics, which he manages to capture in precise analytic terms.

The biggest oddity in Nairn's picture of politics and society is his refusal to recognize nationalism in the core countries as anything other than a reaction to nationalism in the periphery. Rosa Luxemburg was able to do much better than this, simply by noting how European countries used the right to national self-determination in order to justify their colonial adventures in the first place (thereby negating the universality of that same 'right'). Less odd these days, but more troubling, is Nairn's deflation of class as a critical problem. Nairn describes England as a core country that seduces its popular classes into social deference and political quiescence, first with imperial material rewards and then by means of what he will later call a royal, anti-democratic and anti-ethnic 'familial' nationalism.[43] But otherwise, he excises all the right questions a suspicious Luxemburg raised long ago about the national unity of classes whose interests are antagonistic, even if, as Nairn shows us, they are not entirely opposed. Related to his de-emphasis on class division is Nairn's evasion of unsavoury aspects of the division between leaders and led. With respect to nationalism in politics, elite 'manipulation' rather than 'mobilization' of the masses may be the operative phrase. Then, too, that nationalist movements draw on the energy of the people does not guarantee that those movements serve the popular classes at the same time that they serve their masters. Nairn treats such proto-fascist possibilities of nationalism as side issues, but are they?

Nairn's gravest moral-political flaw, however, is his affirmation of the identity principle 'one ethnic people, one state'. He comes to that principle through his support for the liberation of peoples who are the 'done to' in modern history from peoples who are 'the doers'. But given both the intermixture of peoples almost everywhere and the physical power of the state, Nairn's defence of the national self-determination of ethnic groups has its irremediably dark side. To glimpse it, one need only compare Nairn's condemnation of empire as the contrasting political form with Said's much more ambivalent attitude. Said is the master critic of hegemonic centres and imperial oppression, but not necessarily of empire-size political unities. Indeed, he occasionally speaks with real regret of their historical disappearance, for while empires may have been politically undemocratic, they allowed for a social mingling of peoples instead of each people being fortified against the others inside its own nation-state. Said's feeling for the mixing of peoples is reminiscent of Luxemburg's earlier praise, on humanistic as well as class grounds, for the intermingling of peoples in the old Russian and Austro-Hungarian empires, which she urged social democracy to preserve, not destroy, through an international rather than national organization of the working class. Next to both these thinkers, Nairn is deafeningly silent on the idea that cultural heterogeneity within political unity might be, in and of itself, a positive good. Instead, he insists that the ideology of heterogeneity-in-unity has always served to mystify the rule of one people over the rest, and that, regardless of the wishes of cosmopolitan elites, the objective course of history and the subjective will of peoples lead in the nationalist direction.

In conclusion, Nairn's original theory of nationalism as a function of the modern dynamic between peripheries and cores can be said to anticipate the end of the old Eurocentric and bipolar world order. In a duet of style and substance, the systematic character of his thought seems to dissolve as that old order dissolves. On the one hand, his jarring and often contradictory new ideas can be said to reflect the greater space for political thought and action that subsequently has opened up. On the other hand, those ideas also suggest the 'dementia', as Nairn once put it, that develops in situations of tremendous practical confusion. The systematic theory on which Nairn once warily drew had its ultimately damning failures: among them, an overly air-tight conception of the world, and a consequent inability to grasp new actualities and possibilities in the world. It is worth remembering, however, that theory's successes: its rigorous analysis of the strands connecting seemingly distinct and separate elements, and its feeling for the bad impetus but good promise of that, connection. The rigour helped preclude a zig-zagging between disjointed and discordant ideas. The feeling helped prevent a politics bent on dividing humanity into self-contained and self-identical social groups.

Nairn's journey from neo-Marxism to neo-nationalism (and perhaps, in the near future, to some third place) is a special variant of the history of critical thought in our time, with its various dissolutions and reformulations. Unsurprisingly, then, Nairn's traps have also snapped shut on many other social theorists. Although without Nairn's saving acerbity, communitarians applaud cultural homogeneity rather than taking pleasure in the jostling of different peoples inside the same political state. Habermasians accept 'the market' as a necessary, eternal given, turning to non-class social movements as the agents, and an idealized civil society as the locus, of democracy and freedom. Postmodernists jettison 'totalizing' theory for local knowledges and multiple narratives, as if no larger structural forces set the parameters of particularistic existence. Ex-Frankfurt School theorists sympathize with a right-wing repudiation of 'ethnocidal universalism' linked up to a call for the preservation of difference through the separation of different racial and ethnic groups. Finally, identity politicians struggle to make 'being', not 'doing', the centrepiece of social life.

Tom Nairn offers important negative lessons for these disparate groups. His embrace of ethno-nationalism should press all of us to find a way to comprehend political and cultural fragmentation without fetishizing the fragments. His resignation to capitalist reality as the fixed and permanent backdrop for a fluidity and creativity in the political and cultural spheres, should remind us that if we must not reduce politics and culture to economics, neither must we treat these as separated, disconnected realms. Nor should we treat 'capitalist development' as if it were a pseudo-natural process, unaffected by the unpredictability and willed mutability of human affairs. Nairn's insights into the promising tumult of the post-1989 world must be tempered by the recognition that the new is never that new or that singularly good. The current age of nationalism may resemble a forward-gazing phoenix rising out of the ashes of the Cold War, but it also resembles a classic – which is not to say ancient – drama played out on an end-of-the-century stage, with the contradictory themes of populism and persecution, self-determination and tyranny, still very much intact. In the days when he thought on the knife-edge between universalism and particularism, and glared at everything with a half-sympathetic, half-suspicious eye, wouldn't Nairn have seen that problematic mix?

6
Ambiguous Nationalism: A Reply to Joan Cocks

Tom Nairn

> Misshapen Caliban, come in, come in;
> Tell me the secrets of your lost
> Reality, your Pictish origin.
> *White music in the storm is a swan's ghost.*

Douglas Dunn, 'Sketches', in *Dante's Drum-kit* (1993)

IN CALIBAN'S WORLD

In her penetrating critique of my earlier theories about nationalism, Joan Cocks points out that my fatal flaw from the American perspective was probably 'an *engaged* attitude ... unpalatable for liberals and leftists alike'.[1] This deficiency was compounded by other sins as well, like being too confined to the British cultural arena, and remaining over-influenced by Marxist historical materialism. Although Cocks distanced herself from most of these attitudes, she couldn't resist a residual verdict of the same kind. 'Is *The Break-up of Britain* a nationalist manifesto?' she asks, following the question up with another. 'To see nationalism as false but right has tangled logical implications for the seer; the ability to *be* a nationalist is not one of them.' This observation was shrewd, yet mistaken. And my answer today would still be: '*Yes it is*: guilty as charged!' – which is a good place to start from, in order to continue this dialogue. There were tangled implications and contradictions when she was writing in 1997–98, certainly – especially one big one, to which I will return later. But today, there are fewer, and since September 11, 2001 they seem to me far less tangled and confusing than was the case before.

Break-up first appeared 20 years before that, in 1977, when two competing forms of political universalism still seriously contested the earth, amid all the religious and ethical absolutes inherited from earlier ages. Neither nationalism nor ethnicity were well understood, and internationalism even less so, while speculation about human nature remained terribly passé (if not positively wicked) except among social anthropologists and archaeologists, who were of course unconcerned with people like us. They occasionally made

89

jokes about 'we moderns', to which the victims smugly replied with others about their own quaint activities and interests. But that was it: old Adam had been transformed by progress (at least partially) and what *counted* was the bonus of history – the transformed bit, that is, also dubbed 'civilization'.

Now, I'm happy to say, all this seems like another world. Not because of what Cocks, myself or anyone else has written or argued about in the meantime, but because the course of events from 1989 onwards has changed everything. We were living in a world where 'nationalism', as then conceived, was essentially a retrospect. Lapses into it were possible, but with the exception of a few hopeless cases like Yours Truly, that's all they were: returns to a receding and definitely superseded past, symptoms of atavism not yet overcome by the reason of modern times. Fifteen years later, a great process of emancipation has been launched, whose introductory (but no doubt transitional) name is 'globalization'. The misshapen Caliban inside Yours Truly cannot resist ancestral black humour, at this point. There was once a Caledonian sinner who found himself writhing and blistering in the final inferno, and in one last appeal for redemption he cried out: 'Lord, Lord ... *Ah didna' ken!*' At which the Lord himself, between sips of nectar, leaned down from the viewing balcony and casually answered: 'Weel ... *Ye ken noo!*'

What is that we now know? We know that we are all without exception Calibans, and have to live with it. Immanuel Kant's suspicions of over two centuries ago, about the impossibility of making knotted timbers straight, have been verified by the onset of globalization.[2] Such experimental proof was impossible before, as long as there were apparent, semi-credible utopias in competition for the global vote. But this state of affairs passed away around 1989, curiously quietly. Overall, global domination was what the empire business had been about, and here it was, achieved at last. Groups of flat-earth believers may persist, 'fundamentalists' contesting the shift. But of much greater importance is the fact that the largest society on earth did acknowledge the new conditions, over the same period, as 'China rejoined the world' and set about re-establishing the Chinese place, in those terms.

The victor was at first ambiguous. In one sense it was the 'capitalist West', sporting an ostentatious coat of many colours and labels – democracy, liberalism (both traditional and neo-), individualism, freedom, promised prosperity, and so on. The cumulative sense of these was of course a claim to represent History's bonus points, universal values soon to be distributed everywhere. Nationality-politics seemed at first entirely subsumed within this triumphal sales-campaign of Reason. Yet on the other hand, the victory could not help being also that of a single national power, one particular state. However, the USA was in the 1980s not just militarily dominant, but bore a global *authority* built up over the Cold War period. It was what theorists like to call 'hegemony' – cultural and other influences over other governments, peoples, cultures and feelings. It was such *egemonia* that held the two things together. Initially, the American Sales Manager appeared approximately to incarnate the ideals of the broader sales and advertising campaign. Her own nationality-politics did not obtrude upon, or too manifestly divert, the grander cause (or at least, it could be plausibly claimed this was so).

There were always tensions and contradictions inside the performance, which today's critics (both Left and Right) pounce upon with relish. But it didn't fall apart until that fateful hour of September 11, 2001. After that, it disintegrated completely. The completeness of the mutation is what matters most. The curious quietness of the 1989 breakthrough produced its big bang twelve years later, like long-delayed thunder after a premonitory lightning flash.[3] Economic mesmerism at last gave way to politics; and the politics were still those of nationality, albeit upon a vastly extended stage.

The national interests of the USA now subsumed those of *egemonia*. The latter was not *discarded*, but it was firmly and finally put into a secondary and dwindling place. The Sales Manager took over the entire operation, from CEO down to the lobby clerks and sales reps, letting it be known there should be no more wimpish nonsense. American interests and status demanded victory in the War Against Terrorism, and employees, consultants and customers alike had to be for that, or against it. Two Middle Eastern countries were attacked, invaded and regime-changed, to make the intention permanent, and unmistakable. And to the US Boardroom and Upper Management this all appeared reasonable: they were not being imperialists or colonizers. They simply took it for granted that *self-colonization* was the sole possible decision and outlook, for all civilized allies, supporters and friends.

But to most allies and friends (not to mention the already hostile or indifferent) the same switch was perceived as manifesting American nationalism. In other words, political nationalism had moved out of the periphery (Bosnia, Kosova, Rwanda, East Timor, Northern Ireland, Tibet, Kurdistan, and so on) and into the centre – the powerhouse of the new globalizing order. Prospero and Ariel had been sent on indefinite leave. Caliban was in the chair, in the White House. He and his retinue did not of course perceive themselves *as* an overweening nationalist, world-order bully or crypto-imperialist. But this is just the standard blind spot of great-nation nationality-politics, witnessed and recorded in all previous specimens of the condition (Great Britain, Russia, France, Spain, and so on). Only now, following the 1989 takeover of Soviet Socialism Inc., the syndrome had become irreversibly global. We are all 'nationalists' now.

NATIONS AND -ISMS

However, no state of affairs could be more deeply disconcerting for Caliban (and not in the White House alone). If Bush's USA has forced everyone into nationalism – whether of complicity or of opposition – then it logically follows that 'nationalism' is not what it used to be. Once generalized in this terminal way, all nationalists automatically become 'internationalists' too. Citizen Caliban replaces the orang-utan of former times – the barbarians outside the walls, state-of-nature pre-persons waiting to be 'formed'. They are all in the same boat for good; they all know it, or very soon will; and since this lifeboat is an approximately established secular unity, no heavenly rescue ship will now be along to 'save' them. There is in that sense 'no hope' – which of course means that hope lies only 'within us', that is, in what the assorted crooked timbers (or civic-national entities) can do to about their plight. This consciousness is bound to affect the way that *all* nationality politics is conducted. Identity itself has mutated at the root, and group heedlessness has become impossible – or at least, much harder to get away with.

This in turn forces still another reconsideration of just what 'nationalism' was and is about. Cocks makes a very important point here. She reproaches me with 'viewing nationalism in the core countries as a secondary reaction to nationalism in the periphery'. And (she goes on):

> This representation of nationalism as, in its original guise, a politics of the weak against the strong enshrines it as politically left and so as historically 'right'. And yet, by identifying the initial impulse of nationalism as anti-imperialist, Nairn obscures a point Rosa Luxemburg was able to see years ago: European countries had used the right to national self-determination to justify their colonial adventures in the first place.[4]

She is absolutely right about this. Luxemburg's own misuse of that insight, as an instrument for opposing all forms of nationality struggle and liberation, is of far less importance than the understanding itself. She saw where national*ism* had come from. Luxemburg did not think in this philological way, but perhaps some interpretation is possible: the '-ism' had an origin quite distinct from that of nationality itself.

Nationality, human socio-cultural diversity, came from the interminable migrations of the species, over hunting-gathering time – from the African Great Rift Valley to physical occupation of the globe. But national*ism* originated in the generation just before Luxemburg – in the 1870s. It was an ultra-modern phenomenon, unthinkable before the climacteric of that decade. For example, it did not figure in Lord Acton's elaborate anathema against nationality nonsense in 1862.[5] His Lordship may certainly have felt something like that coming on, as in the much-quoted peroration about the course of nationhood being 'marked with material as well as moral ruin, in order that a new invention may prevail over the works of God and the interests of mankind'. But what he sought to excoriate was the political 'principle of nationality' – the heady, romantic brew that had got into peoples' skulls during the short-lived Springtime of Nations, in 1848. Actually, that brew was in the past, and was being distilled into something more potent even the decade that he wrote. It was the decade that began with the American War of Secession and the unification of Italy, and would end with the formation of the modern German state, the Paris Commune and the Franco-Prussian War.

Nationalism began life as *le nationalisme*, part of the reaction of the French state to the frightful double shocks of the Parisian social revolt, and military humiliation by the new, Prussian-led German state. Part of its territory was annexed, bringing on the long-running drama of *La revanche*, a national horizon the next generation of Frenchmen were raised to brood upon – 'Always think of it. Never speak of it.'[6] As I argue later in Chapter 18 this source would be decisive. At least in what was to be the 'commonsense' meaning of most of the following century, nationalism did originate from above, among the great (or would-be great) national states and ruling classes.[7] As Cocks says, it didn't arise from below, or from the rhetoric of the periphery or the colonized. The latter adopted it because they had to – *not* because it was implicit within the older, previously formative ideas of nationhood and national-popular rights. It was of course the 'engaged' stance Cocks criticizes which made me think otherwise: striking a retrospective blow on behalf of 1848, as it were, by claiming far too much for the romantics, for the emergent peoples on the wrong side of the development gap. The idea was that the latter compensated for disadvantage by fostering a climate of counter-claim, which must then have been appropriated by the economically dominant countries (in their own interests, naturally). But however much did get taken up in this way, I see now it could never have conjured up such an overpowering environment. The earlier romantic climate and its politicized nationality awareness were certainly a *necessary condition* of the -ism's formation. But the *sufficient conditions* were different again, and demand attention to other factors. A much greater force was needed, and it could only have emanated from the 'centre', from the power-houses. The evidence here is plain, and requires no speculative mediation or transference.

Once, -isms were just systematic dogmas or doctrines. Then they became popular combative faiths, crusade material, the stuff of meaning-battles, matters of life or death on this earth (rather than over route maps to heaven or hell). They gained a cutting edge, an armoured character corresponding to the forced 'mobilization' of uprooted and urbanized populations. The war-enabled mutation of nationality ideas was (alas) furnished by the great-nation contingent, and built up and diffused in the confrontations that followed the French–German war – the generation of High Imperialism – to culminate in the world wars between 1914 and 1945. Industrialized militarism, 'incidents' in empire marchlands, Social Darwinism, eugenics and the new popular media – such was the crack-cocaine injected into the pre-existing circulatory systems of nationhood. Nor (clearly) are its effects extinct today.

Once such a deep-cultural shift occurs, once communication systems are reconfigured to express it, a totalizing effect is inevitable. It is thought that the world must always have been like that. Stereotypes are inescapable (and were probably even more compelling at that time, in the first flood of urbanization and new mass literacy). So immemorial diversity was reinterpreted as a long drawn out preparation for Bismarck and the *troisième République* (or today, for George W. Bush and Paul Wolfowitz). The discovery of nationhood in the eighteenth and early nineteenth centuries was 'fated' to end in Benjamin Disraeli, Teddy Roosevelt and Benito Mussolini. Because big-nation nationalism conquered, it seemed to follow that its '-ism' must always have been around, at least in latent form – a potentiality of human nature awaiting its chance. Hence it was soon quite natural to lump together what had been in fact discrete, and in their own day somewhat indeterminate, phases or trends. An essence had conquered: shy aspirations for national equality and Aryan-supremacist bellowings had become *the same thing*.

Yet such essentialism too has had its day. 'Nationalism' crystallized within one climacteric, that of the 1870s; but today it is being undone by another – that of September 11 and its aftershocks. However, it can only collapse and mutate into something else, at least partly *in its own terms*. There was no way, no possible means, for such a profound shift to happen 'by agreement', or in negotiated stages, or via the crafty deliberations of think-tanks and professorial committees. 'Epochs' in that sense are blundered out of, or into – as we can now see that 'nationalism' did, from around 1870 onwards. The United Nations organization itself remains an expression of that old international regime (and will presumably now be reconstituted for the new one).

In the 1870s the new imperialist world, whether welcomed or opposed, was felt to be 'inevitable'. And exactly the same feeling has returned to haunt the present decade, after September 11, 2001. Somehow, globalization could assume no other form than this final takeover bid, foiled by a last anti-colonial national-liberation counter-strike (or of course, several of these, depending on the later stages of the Mesopotamian war, above all in Kurdistan). And beyond that point? Well – by forces, personalities, and tendencies still in formation, by the post-nationalist politics of both class and nationality. But the latter will still probably be the more important.

NATIVE SONS, FATHERLESS WORLD

Conceptually speaking, the second climacteric is at least helping to make the first more comprehensible. It helps us to 'locate' nationalism within a broader perspective of nationality and human nature – that is, the actual single-species inter-nationality for which (*tant bien que mal*) 'globalization' has to find new political forms and relations. I mentioned earlier how the first stage of one-worldism remained marked by a vague yet potent American cultural sway – that curious sense in which, during and after the Cold War, and often without open admission or display, the United States remained a sort of second homeland for much of the world. In the context made possible by Joan Cocks' book – a survey of individuals, as well as of ideas – some anecdotal data may deserve a place here. Until round about the year 2000 – I can't recall the precise chronology – I carried a poem with me everywhere, clipped from a forgotten magazine about 25 years earlier. By then, the paper was yellowing and falling apart from confinement in wallets, and from being pinned on so many walls. The verse, by Carl Dennis, is called 'Native Son':

> You try to imagine highways to all men
> But your heart has always loved boundaries.
> The heavy fields in back of your house.[8]

The author admits how he scans death lists for those of his own kind, and only when they are there does he 'board the plane in dreams, and jostle the pilots, and grab the controls'. At parties, his country is like a friend at a loud party:

> Her jokes are no worse than the others
> But they sadden you most.
> You want to take her home before it's too late.

Of course, the enticing but minatory country was America, and Dennis' 'visible streets of America' remained emblematic for someone who at that time, like millions of others, had lived on them without ever seeing them. It was in such obscure yet vital capillary byways that the hegemony of a culture functioned – nowhere more powerfully than through his last verse, which unwittingly glimpsed something of the causes that have borne this great *rayonnement* into the irredeemable ruin of the present:

> It's hard to write letters in your attic study
> When you hear your father downstairs
> Smashing the furniture on his path to a glass.
> He was a wino before you were born:
> You are not to blame;
> You say to yourself as you go down
> To look at the mess.

In retrospect, I'm surprised by two things: the immensity and (as it then appeared) naturalness of US cultural influence, and the completeness with which it vanished, after the year 2000. In this small example, I can faithfully record that the fading paper was put into a small glass clipboard frame in early 2001 – turned into a memento of past feeling and identity, rather than a living companion. But September 11 was not responsible. It was the non-election of President Bush that did the trick, at the close of 2000. No overt 'crisis' was provoked by that family *coup d'état* – only the drugged acceptance of a Supreme Court decision, in order to preserve an absurdly venerated Constitution that had dismally failed its people and nation.[9] At bottom, this was so *like* Britain that no critic of the latter state could at that point feel anything but deep disillusionment. The sons of those wonderful in-back 'heavy fields' had been unable to do anything – they had not risen up, jostled the pilots and grabbed the controls. Instead, the wino had been confirmed in office, and had his mess cleared up so that others could follow: a fatally anachronistic constitution was helped back on to its feet.

The alcoholic father was on his way to unthinkable mayhem, of course, in a very short time. No one knew that in early 2001. But in truth the die had been cast: that is, the die of the state, as distinct from the popular spirit of Dennis' poem, the thing I had always identified with, and which made it possible for so long to imagine Scotland through an American glass. From September onwards, drunken Dad and his cronies seized that spirit, pumped it up into a wounded great-nation passion, and embarked upon a military and state campaign to confirm their domination of the globe. This was national*ism* indeed, as 'radical' and uncompromising as many previous examples of empire – and just as utterly destructive of all gentler, more nuanced forms of cultural and emotional dominion.

I am also surprised by the sensation of loss that accompanied the change. Logical implications had little to with this. At bottom, identity is an emotive force-field. We can't do without it. It's the inherited voice of pastness, enabling both individuality and community – the true 'immemorial' of human society. As Alexander Cockburn has put it, 'the golden age is within us'; but so is the past (and the two can get confused with one another). We 'reinvent' the past all the time too; but doing so is obligatory, not optional. It is inseparable from speaking a language and 'being' a whatever it is: Inuit, Welsh, Jewish, US-American, and so on. Each living being is borne into the world on one bit or another of 'crooked timber'. But for that very reason, we have limited control over it. It is not of course 'destiny' – mythologies of fate are manifestations of *its* power, not the other way round. However, 'choices' of identification are of necessity difficult, deceptive, staged and subject to lapses or reversals. Far too much meaning is compressed into this force-field for anything else to be possible. If we had *control* over it, we would be cyber-creatures, and no longer humans – the constant dread of dystopic science fiction, from *We* and *Invasion of the Body Snatchers* down to Spielberg's *Artificial Intelligence* and the *Matrix* film series.[10]

The great value of *Passion and Paradox* is its unique spectrum of analysis from a similar angle of vision: how theorists of 'the National Question' have wrestled not only with ideas but also with themselves, and why such struggles have been expressed in the resultant philosophies. Nor is the book exempt from its own dilemma: its thread is a profound, lively but anxious preoccupation with the role of Jewishness (and of course, anti-semitism) in the whole story the author unfolds, from Karl Marx to Edward Said, via Luxemburg, Frantz Fanon, Isaiah Berlin (two interrogations), Hannah Arendt and V.S. Naipaul. Important suspects are missing from the line-up, like Ernest Gellner, or only alluded to, like Benedict Anderson. But there's no doubt what the line-up is of: native sons and daughters, hauled in with identity hangovers, their long faces creased with guilty anxiety about possible verdicts of aggravated responsibility for making the world even worse. Jews figure so prominently because of their prolonged diasporic condition and consequent inclination to internationality, or 'cosmopolitanism'. Fear of a fatherless world has become widespread in the post-eighteenth-century world, and any group apparently favouring such a solution can easily be made a scapegoat, or even projected as a conspiratorial force 'behind it all'.[11]

SAINTLY MATTERS

'Is *The Break-up of Britain* an epitaph for Marxism?' asks Professor Cocks, about halfway through her sympathetic hearing. 'Yes and no' was the answer at that time, and I suppose it still is. But her account of Saint Karl in the first chapter of *Passion and Paradox* may have some clues to this puzzle. After reviewing his assorted theoretical views, she points out how in the end

> Marx continues to rely on the category of the nation without a clear analytical basis for that reliance ... He does not see psycho-cultural elements as having the kind of explanatory power that would allow him to ground national identity in collective attachments to a homeland, a shared history, and a familiar way of life.[12]

Explanatory power had to be universal in the Enlightenment sense, owing nothing to religious or idealist fantasies, and also 'material' – related to natural science and its application. Such application was proceeding on the gargantuan scale portrayed by *The Communist Manifesto*, and seemed to override most collective attachments, and consign familiar ways to various waste-bins. Hence the 'material' factor had to be economic, and manifested in the new collective attachments of social class – similar enough in most locations to pass for universal. And as Cocks discerningly shows, the choice must have been influenced by Marx's own identity dilemma. This was at bottom not so different from the one reported in Sir Isaiah Berlin's *New York Times* obituary:

> Of course assimilation might be a quite good thing, but it doesn't work. Never has worked, never will. There isn't a Jew in the world known to me who, somewhere inside him, does not have a tiny drop of uneasiness vis-à-vis *them*, the majority among whom they live...one has to behave particularly well, or *they* won't like us ...[13]

Berlin was the most successfully and prestigiously assimilated incomer imaginable. In contrast, Marx was a systematic forsaker of roots, an exile who had cast off both Jewish and German attachments, and looked to the *Internationale* of a new class for his substitute homeland.

In this situation, the identity stakes were far greater. One would expect the decisive decades of nationalism's formation to make a correspondingly larger impact. And they certainly did. It was in the mid 1970s that the new International working-class movement fell apart in Europe, and was guiltily rehoused in New York, before vanishing altogether in 1876. Only a year or so before another lurid signal of the incoming tide invaded first the music halls, and then the streets, of London: 'Jingoism'.[14] It would be many years (and Marx would be dead) before another *Internationale* was constituted. Both he and his colleague Friedrich Engels could not but be aware of the profound shift, and of its consequences for their carefully elaborated theory, and both sought to compensate by looking in other directions. They did understand that some broader perspective was now needed, going beyond post-Enlightenment history, contemporary politics and economic or 'bourgeois' ambitions.

In other words, 'matter' had to be understood differently. Not capitalist economics and the class struggle alone, but material factors of some deeper and older kind were needed for comprehension of the nationalist world. Yet even by the 1870s this was perilous terrain. In his recent biography of Marx, Francis Wheen attributes the great man's reticence over Darwinism to fear that it might justify Malthus.[15] The latter's 'biological' view of history had made over-population into a motive force of political economy, and led towards eugenics, and the later forms of Social Darwinism. However, there were already more potent visions of that general sort about, derived from the writings of Robert Knox and Arthur de Gobineau – racial readings of history all conducting infallibly to a predestined triumph of North European man. Bismarck's 1971 victory seemed of course to fit such fantasies, which were to culminate half a century later in the Third Reich's 'Aryanism'.

Both men knew that a different, more macro-historical approach was required, and Engels' famous response was *The Origins of the Family, Private Property and the State* (1884), a valiant attempt to re-found historical materialism, basing itself mainly on the researches of the American social anthropologist Lewis Morgan. But Marx himself achieved nothing comparable, and his *Ethnological Notebooks* of 1881–82 do little but (in the words of editor Lawrence Krader) 'pose anew the open questions of control of human development by human intervention, a wholly human teleology, and the natural science of man as its potentiality'.[16] The depth of his despair over the matter was shown by the curious episode that Wheen refers to in his biography. The wrong turning history was taking forced Marx to search for some 'deeper' materialist explanation; and he temporarily found this in, of all places, geology and soil chemistry. In 1865 the French naturalist Pierre Trémaux had published a treatise explaining human social variety in terms of soil characteristics, and as Wheen writes, Marx was for some time transported by the notion. 'It represents a *very significant* advance over Darwin ... (and) ... For certain questions, such as nationality, etc., only here has a basis in nature been found.'[17]

Engels managed to cure Marx of the aberration. But in Cocks' terms it is tempting to interpret this as a symptom of identity under the acutest pressure, looking for any way at all out of an intolerable dilemma. 'Nationality, etc.' was what had gone wrong. But if material nature was somehow responsible, then might there not be in the same direction at least a rational strategy for putting things right, and rebuilding the foundering *Internationale* – the true *Heimat* of workers and cosmopolitan intellectuals alike? The short-cut Marx was seduced by was ridiculous, of course (and compares unfavourably with Engels' enduring labours on the same general front). On the other hand, it was driven by a much greater *Angst*, and the objective problem he was trying to tackle was anything but absurd. It simply could not be taken far *at that time*. Too little was known, genetic science was in its pre-infancy, both social anthropology and sociology were at an early stage, and Freudian analysis lay 30 years ahead. As the whole world (and above all, European Jews) were to discover, fantastic distortions of Darwinism won free rein amid such general ignorance, and in the 1930s and 1940s came close to hijacking the whole development of culture and society. Terminal scientific defeat for such world-views would not come until the 1950s – *80 years on* from the anguish of the 1870s.

So to say that the question of what 'historical materialism' means is unresolved, does not seem to me such an evasion. In the profounder perspectives of thought evoked by Cocks' comparisons, nothing like an epitaph is yet possible. In the short period between her book's publication and this reply, more seismic changes have taken place, and others are certain. These will surely be very important for the Jewish dilemma so crucial to her own approach, as well as for the future shape of nationality politics – and hence for that of the theories we are both concerned with.

'JUST ANOTHER COUNTRY'

In her discussion of the nineteenth century, Cocks makes a very telling side-swipe at a personage unjustly neglected in recent arguments over the US imperium, and its alliance with the Israeli state: Benjamin Disraeli. Like Marx, he was the son of determinedly assimilationist parents; and he also sought personal escape from identity dilemmas through a mixture of literature, ideology and politics. The resulting personal trajectory was extraordinarily successful, and made him a key figure in the British imperial state for a whole generation. He made himself into the embodiment of the new British great-nation ideology, the UK's rejoinder to the post-1860s wave of continental nationalism. And he achieved this partly by *emphasizing his Jewishness* to the utmost extent.

A good deal has been written about the odd relations between ethnic and religious minorities and the majority-run states in which they find themselves. As I describe in Chapter 14, the most common pattern of the nationalist era has been of marginalization, or of outright oppression and (occasionally) of literal suppression or genocide. However, there have been others, common and effective enough to count as much more than exceptions. Minorities have found assorted ways of both resisting and overcoming minority status, and one of the most striking of these has been over-compensation – that is, contribution to the encompassing state 'over and beyond' any mere duty, as a demonstration of active allegiance, or even of indispensability. In United Kingdom history, for example, the post-eighteenth century Scots followed this course with striking success (and some still do to this day). On the contemporary scene the ideology of Northern Irish Protestantism (or 'Orangeism') is another remarkable case.[18]

Cocks points out (quoting Berlin) how Disraeli surmounted the obstacle of his Jewishness 'by inflating it into a tremendous claim to noble birth' – evidence of descent from an ancient Eastern aristocracy, which allowed him to claim equality with the English landed aristocracy he so admired. The implication was complete possession 'by the idea of race', and a glorification of empire, together with contempt for glum equality and democracy – the rule of the mere majority. Popular nationalism – the runaway Technicolor world-view of pepped-up British grandeur, power and inevitable leadership – allowed him to win electoral support for such fantastic notions. Jewish and Anglo-Saxon traditions were fused into a new, composite elitism. It was a 'Lords of human kind' superiority based on economic ascendancy and the supposed invincibility of the British Dreadnought fleet.

Nobody can read of this feat today, whether in Joan Cocks' description or Isaiah Berlin's original essays, without experiencing a jolt. Well over a century after Disraeli's moment of authority, the globe is once more dominated by a 'Jewish-Anglo' alliance that embraces the Israeli and American states, with his own adopted fatherland still in tow. Berlin hoped that Israel would signal the end of the Jewish Question, by turning Jews into a standard-issue, nation-state-centred people. He even hoped that the diaspora would readjust all its attitudes towards those of the citizens of 'just another country', as distinct from the old population *fated* to non-belonging, or God-appointed transience. In fact, the second climacteric of nationalism has re-animated anti-semitism, and even 'globalized' the most nonsensical aspects of the ailment, in a way that Nazism and its precursors never managed.[19]

The point is of course not that Jewishness or the ambiguities of the minority dilemma remain constant: the differences from Disraeli's time are obviously huge. But there is one genuine, persistent and recurrent factor which is recognizably common, and must be the most likely explanation of the surprising similarities: *great-nation nationalism* – or 'imperialism' in what may seem to be a looser or more qualified sense. The -ism of ascendancy no longer aspires to annexation, colonizing occupation and settlement, turning the suborned natives into uniformed or cultural replicas of 'Us', and so forth. It is purer than that. The distilled *Geist* of empire is now neo-liberal economics plus 'democracy' in a mode entailing that the suborned follow 'best practice' – representative election guaranteeing participation in the existing order, civilization as already exemplified. I described this earlier as 'self-colonization'. Failure to volunteer for this is at best backsliding, at worse (and more likely) incipient Terrorism.

After September 11, I was not alone in feeling that the only possible answer (admittedly in an emotive sense) was to treat the USA as 'just another country'. Or putting it in another way, as just one more sample of crooked and knotty timber, rather than as the ruler-bearing hegemon, or straightener-out in chief. This was emotively rather than practically important, I know: its implication was that international relations should rearrange themselves into an extending 'multipolarity' (invariably labelled 'anarchy' by ruler-wielders) in which no great-national contingent would again be in a position to impose order in its own interest.[20] The moral was essentially the same as Emmanuel Todd's in his *Après l'Empire*,[21] although I had not then read the book. This French author of Jewish extraction writes as an anthropologist and demographer, and his previous work was the remarkable *La diversité du monde* (1999), itself also a compilation of previous texts on the same theme. The diversity of the world is indicated also by his subtitle: 'Family and Modernity', the argument being that the inherited differentiation of familial and communal forms and patterns is far too great, and too well entrenched, ever to subside into a homogeneous or conforming identity. In that sense 'diversity' simply *is* (and will remain) human identity – as will nationality, delineating borders, conflicts between 'us' and 'them', and the governing or state forms required to sustain diversity. Cocks accuses me at one point of 'fetishizing ethnicity' in the sense of 'regarding it as an essential truth'.[22] She suggests this is why I slid from Gellner-style modernization theory into a sort of deepening 'primordialism', and came to perceive the secrets of nationalism as deriving from ancestral spirits.

In fact (though there's no reason she should have known this) the transition came primarily from re-reading Gellner himself, and – more important – from delving into his earlier and non-canonical texts. There is an alternative theory about the origins of nationality and social formation in this ampler view, which the anthropologist in him couldn't help working out. But most of that was then sidelined by the brusque (and immensely successful) materialism of his later sociological interpretation of nationalism: the hydra-monster scheme of things created by industrialization and uneven development. This was in fact a partial interpretation, as we can now understand; but it was so right in what it claimed, that other elements were for long overshadowed, or even lost sight of. In truth (as Perry Anderson pointed out in an essay on Gellner and Weber) the theory does tell one everything one needs to know about nationalism, except what one *really* needs to know about it.[23] The elements denied or dismissed may be as, or more, important in a longer and broader perspective. What it leaves out is the causal force enabling entrancement, the roots of identity and both societal and individual *meaning*, without which much of the history of post-1870 politics remains puzzling.

What happened in this century and a bit – from one climacteric to the next, as I put it earlier – is that certain abiding motifs of the diverse societal nexus were hugely amplified and rigidified, with incessant (and now much more homicidal) warfare as both cause and effect. It was the sum of these effects that constituted 'national*ism*' over the period in question: the '-ismic' dimension was undoubtedly 'constructed' and generally imposed at this time. Equally undoubted (as I have conceded earlier) was the main instrument of that creation and its consequences: 'great nation' predominance and its vicissitudes. All societies may be 'ethnocentric'; but it was not ethnocentricity alone that generated the novel field of force, and made of it an irresistible template. It was the 'leaders' (or aspiring leaders) whose *ethnies* required this formidable build-up, for simultaneously domestic and foreign reasons. Industrialization compelled an internal population shift, from rural to urban; and of course all such assertion provoked 'competition' against similar developments, with the inherent possibility of threat, defeat and subjection – typified by the fate of France in the 1870s. Peasants had to be made over into citizens *and* soldiers, and ancestral spirits alone were not up to the task. They needed energetic assistance – an 'ideology' able to amplify and emotionalize the given, an intensification aligning the latter with 'greatness', combative spirit, the defence (or sometimes the extension) of borders.

Why is this so obvious today? Because the whole world has seen it happen again, between September 11, 2001 and the present. Not just the same cycle, naturally: but sufficient of a recapitulation to make a secular blueprint plainer. On the plane of theory, the resulting situation has been very well expressed by Joshua A. Fishman:

> Interestingly enough, the modern world is heir to both of the above traditions: mainstream self-aggrandizement and sidestream insistence on self-determination. They are both very much alive, the one eliciting and confronting the other ... The constructivist view is much more university based, at least in the West, whereas the primordialist view is much more disadvantaged-community based. But there are notable regions of the Western world where the latter view has found university recognition, particularly in tumultuous times.[24]

He goes on to point out Walker Connor has repeatedly urged a rapprochement between these two approaches, for example in *Ethnonationalism: The Quest for Understanding* (1994), and concludes that 'the academy ignores the relevance of this debate and its outcomes "on the ground" at its own peril'. Before Fishman's article was published, it was not the academy alone that was treated to a colossal spectacle, first of aggrandisement and then of 'sidestream insistence on self-determination', in Iraq, Kurdistan and (albeit in non-military mode) all around the globe. Globalization makes this focal argument inescapable, and I believe the present debate between Joan Cocks and myself will be one part of it.

7

Dark Nationalism or Transparent Postnationalism?[1]

Paul James

For the past couple of decades, one of the central and underlying themes addressed in the area of political and social theory has been the deceptively complex question, 'Is nationalism good or bad?' There have been a number of divergent ways of responding. Currently, the dominant intellectual response is to portray the attachment to national community, particularly nationalism in its ethnic manifestation, as a colourfully dressed folkloric harbinger of an abiding series of dark possibilities – from racial vilification and soccer hooliganism to ethnic cleansing and state-sponsored genocide. Radovan Karadžić's Bosnia and Slobodan Milošević's Serbia are listed as part of a calendar of evil going back through Pol Pot's Year Zero to Adolf Hitler's projection of a new millennium.

While the proponents of this position are tragically right that dreadful things have been done in the name of the nation, in attributing an essential evil to ethnic nationalism they take the easy way out. It parallels the way in which modernist neo-liberals and postmodernists alike assume that an unseverable sinew of logic connects Marxism, communism and totalitarianism. The present chapter starts from the proposition that unless we are happy to go with the bland ecstasies and the routinized nightmare-on-wheels of liberal capitalism, and that we are prepared to accept its hyper-rational partner – the minimal civic state – such a dismissal of ethnic nationalism leaves us with more questions than it answers. Most pointedly, we continue to face the question of how we are to live historically in association with others. This is not at all to defend ethnic nationalism in its present and past, or even in its possible future manifestations. It is not to advocate the ethnic nationalist creed of one nation for one state. Rather, it is to argue for social relations grounded in embodied and historically, geographically placed formations of identity. That these foundations are simultaneously mythologized and distorted as the bases of the exclusivist and inwardly turned ethnic nation makes such a task a scary one. Moreover, that this highly qualified emphasis on 'being', depth of association and social boundedness is antithetical to the current dominant alternatives of civic (post)nationalism or cosmopolitan globalism – both espousing radical openness of association – makes the project an intellectually unpopular one.[2]

The publication of Tom Nairn's book, *Faces of Nationalism*[3] and Joan Cocks' powerful critique of Nairn (republished in this volume)[4] provide a thought-provoking starting point for trying to work through the ethics of nationalism and national identity. The other backdrop to the present discussion is the spectre of further ethnic wars around the world. Going back to Chapter 4 and the discussion of Kosova, what we saw was the ethnically Albanian Kosova Liberation Army (KLA) and the dominant Serbian military facing each other in sporadic fighting that threatened to develop into a war of more devastating dimension than that which occurred in neighbouring Bosnia. In Bosnia 600,000 people were said to have died since 1991. Collecting the passions of a crossover of traditional and modern identity formations, ethnic nationalism lies at the heart of the potentially horrific war between neighbours living side by side in apartheid estrangement. Bosnia, Kosova and Rwanda are only a handful of many settings around the world for parallel horror stories. All in all, the period since the fall of the Berlin Wall is not a good time for defending ethnic nationalism. This is the very moment, Joan Cocks argues, that Tom Nairn has chosen to 'come out as a nationalist' and to fetishize ethnicity.

From my reading, Joan Cocks extrapolates her critique a step or two beyond the evidence. Tom can speak for himself, but it seems to me that he has always been a *national*ist of sorts. However reluctant and reflexively critical that sense of nation may be, he has always been a Scottish nationalist with strong internationalist counter-leanings. And his latter-day recognition that nationalism does not derive completely from the circumstances and structures of modernity has always been part of his approach. It is evidenced for example in the distinction he made between '*national*ism' and 'national*ism*' way back in his most famous essay 'The Modern Janus'.[5] There, Nairn links *national*ism to the historical specificity of a people – in effect, their prenational*ist* nationality – while national*ism* refers to the subjective response of an ethnic community to an uneven and generalized developmental necessity based in the structure of a changing capitalist economy – their ideological self-identifying. Thus his discussion of the Janus-faced nature of national identity has a particular referent, national*ism*:

> In short, the substance of national*ism* [note the italics: this is missed by every commentator that I have read] as such is always morally, politically, humanly ambiguous. This is why moralizing perspectives on the phenomenon always fail, whether they praise or berate it. They simply seize upon one face or other of the creature, and will not admit that there is a common head conjoining them. But nationalism can in this sense be pictured as like the old Roman god, Janus, who stood above gateways with one face looking forward and one backwards. Thus does

nationalism stand over the passage to modernity, for human society. As human kind
is forced through its strait doorway, it must look desperately back into the past, to
gather strength wherever it can be found for the ordeal of 'development'.[6]

In short, Nairn is arguing that the good/bad distinction is problematic. Is
not just that it is bad in its fascist manifestations and positive in its counter-
imperialist and liberatory manifestations. Even the most positive form of
nationalism is *potentially* problematic. It is potentially problematic in the
same way that personal expressions of embodied human interconnection
such as romantic love have the potential for the tragic consequences. Most
murders are committed by significant others. This is a central paradox of
the human condition in the period of modernity. If this is right, and I
think it is, the follow-up question needs to be 'Where do we go from here?'
Should we conclude by dismissing nationalism out of hand? Nairn does not
think so; Cocks implies that we should.[7] A second issue, one which runs in
parallel to the question of how we are to respond to nationalism, can be
expressed as follows: 'Has liberal democracy assumed such a dominance in
the present period that any configuration of an alternative politics will, for
the foreseeable future, be necessarily and positively framed by a movement
towards civic nationalism?' Nairn implies 'Yes'; Cocks is not so sure. On the
first question, I tend towards Tom Nairn's position; on the second, I tend
towards Joan Cocks' scepticism.

SHOULD WE DISMISS NATIONALISM OUT OF HAND?

The dominant intellectual response today is to treat nationalism as an
intermediate and passing phase on the way to cosmopolitan universalism
and dispassionate civic responsibility. This echoes, in a more sophisticated
way, the position taken by the development theorists and liberals of the
1960s to 1970s. They posited a series of stages in human history: the
movement from traditional society characterized by rural idiocy and
immobility through a modernizing, industrializing and nation-building
stage to the age of late modern, cosmopolitan global-civic society. The most
sophisticated present-day version says 'No, we cannot dismiss nationalism
completely', but then ends up reducing attachments to nationality to a
residual, privately lived irrelevance. Expressed in such a summary way this
move appears to be intellectually duplicitous, however by following one
of its most prestigious post-structuralist proponents, Julia Kristeva, along
this pathway we can clarify its logic and extend upon the discussion of
postmodernist commentators in Chapter 4. Along the way I will try to
elucidate the strengths of post-structuralism (I think these strengths are
very real) while still questioning its final outcome.

In *Nations Without Nationalism*, Julia Kristeva begins by setting up an opposition between those who worship origins and those who fear them. On the one hand, she perceptively describes the cult of reclaiming origins as the defensive reaction of wounded souls, as 'they withdraw into a sullen, warm private world, unnameable and biological, the impregnable "aloofness" of a weird primal paradise – family, ethnicity, nation, race'. This is the world of France's National Front, the Austrian Freedom Party and, with qualifications given the modernist nature of their xenophobic expressions, the right-wing militia in the United States and the One Nation party in Australia. On the other hand, she criticizes its apparent opposite. 'Those who repress their roots, who don't want to know where they come from, who detest their own,' she says, 'fuel the same hatred of self, but they think they can settle matters by fleeing.'[8] While is it telling that the 'fear of origins' gets only brief mention with the most intense invective reserved for the 'cult of origins', the next move is potentially a good one. We are invited to go back to our origins *in order to* (partly) transcend them. With the addition of the word 'partly' this proposition is central to the positions that both Tom and I take. The political-ontological value of this dialectic depends on what is meant here by 'transcendence'. If it is merely three-step shuffle – one coy step back, to go two flouncing steps forward – then it is not much of a dialectic. If it is based on the hope that the course of history will soon transcend nationalism and ethnic community anyway, and we would therefore be well served by making peace with it in its passing, then I suggest that the position slowly, very slowly, empties out into a sea of surface politics where everything is a matter of autonomous choice. This is what in fact I think happens to Kristeva's position. In her words:

> I maintain that in the contemporary world, shaken up by national fundamentalism on the one hand and the intensive demands of immigration on the other, the fact of belonging to a set is a matter of choice. Beyond the *origins* that have assigned to us biological identity papers and a linguistic, religious, social, political place, the freedom of contemporary individuals may be gauged according to their ability to *choose* their membership, while the democratic capability of a nation and social group is revealed by the right it affords individuals to exercise that choice. Thus when I say that I have chosen cosmopolitanism, this means that I have, against origins and starting from them, chosen a transnational or international position situated at the crossing of boundaries.[9] (emphases in the original)

The freedom to choose undoubtedly has to be placed at the centre of any thoroughgoing alternative politics, but it is only one principle amongst others. Why after all the subtlety of an argument attempting to walk 'the knife-edge between universalism and particularism',[10] does Julia Kristeva chose universalistic cosmopolitanism? The tone of her writing leaves the reader with the following message: *Volksgeist* as spirit of the people (dreadfully bad); the nation as multicultural community with privately lived differences connected by a public *esprit général* (reservedly good); cosmopolitanism in postnationalist communities (very good); and the Europe of Regions (excellent if it allows for the passing of nationalism). Joan Cocks is worried that Tom Nairn launches a 'cruel assault' upon much cruder versions of the kind of position that I have been delineating. However, when Nairn gets stuck into writers such as Eric Hobsbawm for their complacent reductionism in treating nationalism as the unmitigatedly ugly visage of modernity – merely an invented tradition – I am on Nairn's side. I have no problem with Nairn's (self-)critical distancing from romantic or intellectually self-serving versions of internationalism, but I am worried by his new, largely uncritical flirtation with civic nationalism. These are issues of subtle emphasis and tone rather than head-to-head dispute. And so to the second question.

IS CIVIC NATIONALISM THE ANSWER?

Let me enter this area through a more pointed question. Has neo-liberal pseudo-democracy assumed such dominance in the present period that any configuration of an alternative politics conducted in terms of civic nationalism will, for the foreseeable future, be necessarily and problematically framed by ideologies it would wish to escape? Tom Nairn begins his essay from 'Civic Society to Civic Nationalism' with some reflections upon Ernest Gellner's writings on civil society as the instituting precondition of democracy.[11] Gellner, as one of the Marxism-always-succumbs-to-totalitarianism brigade, is writing in the aftermath of the fall of communism. He uses the notion of 'civil society' to set up his ideal new order, one which in his view does not lead either to the restrictions of centralized state despotism or the 'life-pervading' tyranny of identity-based communalism. Despite the development of the concept 'civil society' being in part located within the Hegelian-Marxist tradition,[12] Gellner takes a version of it for his own. It is, for him, not a place of structural inequality protected by a capitalist state (the classical Marxist critique), but an order which, even for the 'timorous, non-vigilant and absent-minded', automatically enhances democratic liberty:

> A society committed to growth and hence to occupational stability [read: capitalism] is thereby also committed to a basic egalitarianism [read: liberal pluralism]: it is debarred from using a device otherwise very widespread among societies, namely the permanent and enforced division of the members of society into sharply separated categories of people with distinct rights and duties, who also deeply internalize their status as members of this or that category [read: tribalism, caste, ethnic nationalism] ...

> This society needs economic pluralism for productive efficiency, and it needs social and political pluralism to counteract excessive tendencies to centralism. But above all, it uses social and political pluralism, but of a particular special, modular, *ad hoc* kind [read: abstracted individuation] which does not stifle individuality.[13]

I have quoted Ernest Gellner at such length here to indicate how he was an ideologue of liberal pluralistic capitalism, but also to introduce his emphasis upon modularity. The modular person lives in a standardized epistemological space – modernism – which allows movement across the hitherto segmented boundaries of traditional culture. In the first historical stage of modernity, according to Gellner, modularism became the basis of both civil society *and* national identity. In the contemporary period, civic society has become abstracted to the point that it makes it harder and harder to sustain older forms of ethnic nationalism. For Gellner this is a wondrous thing. On the 'other side of the Atlantic' – read: 'in the United States of America' – there developed the 'type of society which really produced the kind of freedom which we now treasure, the modularity which lies at the base of Civil Society'.[14] Again, his position is much more sophisticated that the liberal and development theorists of the 1960s and 1970s, but despite himself their political sibling. This is where Tom Nairn's splendidly cutting writing comes into its own. Nairn stops short of accusing Gellner of being a capitalist ideologue as I have just done, but he does point out, for example, that 'in the epitome of Atlantic civilization's civil society, the United States, half of the population doesn't even bother voting'.[15] However, then comes the twist. After criticizing the liberal argument for civil society as an empty politics offering only the market as a guarantor of freedom, Nairn tentatively takes the hand of its cousin, civic nationalism, as offering difference plus civility. And so the essay ends with the most ambiguous of resolutions:

> Differentiated civil identity seems to be what peoples want; its attainment and maintenance demand modern 'identity politics', the same thing as politicised or state-configured nationality ... This too is myth country, which I would not defend in a literal sense, but it may be preferable to the Copernican universe of 'civil society'.[16]

So where have we got to? Yes, we can agree with Nairn, Gellner, Kristeva and Cocks that ethnic nationalism looks bad in the dark. However, in the glare of the day it becomes clear that as alternative projections of politics, civil society, civic nationalism and cosmopolitan post-nationalism are all semi-transparent projections onto the walls of contemporary society. At least in the versions presented here, they do little more than provide a light-show across its dominant structures – autonomous individualism, shallow multiculturalism, globalism and capitalism. Gellner's 'civil society' gets its substance as the hidden hand of individuation in the abstracting machine of liberal capitalism. Against this, Nairn's civic nationalism is far more preferable, attempting to find a balance between cultural depth and the small 'o' open society. Beyond both of these positions, however, there is a desperate need to argue our way through the principles-in-tension that underpin the positive possibilities of living in complex and rich association with others.[17] Pragmatics or sentiment may lead us in the short term to seize on one or other of the expressions of nationalism or postnationalism either for criticism or celebration, but in the long run the only way out of the present mess will be through negotiating over forms of living. This raises a third question.

DOES POSTNATIONALISM OFFER A VIABLE ALTERNATIVE POLITICS?

In an understandable disillusion with the limitations of the national liberation movements, particularly as the movements harden into advocating conventional nation-state politics, critics are beginning to put their faith in the new possibilities of postnationalism. This subjectivity of postnationalism can be defined as a discursive 'attachment' to others who have been lifted out of the boundaries of national identification. The concept 'lifted out' is used here to indicate that transcending the modernist meaning of exclusive territorial attachment can take other forms than just physically crossing national borders. In this definition, postnationalism is a subjectivity abstracted from and therefore only residually beholden to imagined past forms of national identification such as ethnicity, felt common history or bounded territory. It is the subjectivity of the mobile person in a world of traversed spaces. Some theorists go so far as to suggest that it is possible to discern the beginnings of a 'postnational imaginary'. They find it in the messy configurations of migrant ethnic consciousness, transnational religious revivalism and movements of diasporic hybridity. It is treated as an incipient development: both good and bad in the short term, but with positive, almost utopian, possibilities as the nation-state ceases to enthral and enrage. For example, Arjun Appadurai writes that

> These elements for those who wish to hasten the demise of the nation-state, for all their contradictions, require both nurture and critique. In this way, transnational social forms may generate not only postnational yearnings, but also actually existing postnational movements, organizations, and spaces.[18]

For all the sympathy we may instinctively have with such a position,[19] I suggest that without a thoroughgoing exploration of the principles of solidarity and community, advocating postnationalism amounts to little more than a postmodern passion for mobile openness, on the one hand, or an ideologically insensitive support for 'banal' official nationalism and global capitalism, on the other.[20] That is my core argument expressed most bluntly, but it should not be taken to mean that I think postnationalism is damnable. What I will be criticizing across the rest of the chapter is the tendency to look uncritically to postnationalism – much as some nineteenth-century philosophers looked to nationalism – as the way out of the problems of an earlier social formation. In this case it is the problems that we have created through the excesses of modernity, but it does not mean that a postmodern politics provides the answer. One such excess is the increasingly intensified and contradictory use of rationalized violence, projected in the name of either abstract peace or 'traditional' integrity. From above it comes in the form of bombers over Iraq, Afghanistan and Kosova. From below it is clothed in the language of re-traditionalization: including the modernist millenarianism of Saddam Hussein, the modernist neo-traditionalism of the Taliban and the violent nationalism of the UCK, better known by their English acronym the KLA, the Kosova Liberation Army.

It is clear that we need to develop new institutionalized forms of polity and community that go beyond the modern national state, but designating the way of the future as 'postnationalism' does little to achieve that purpose. Neither does emphasizing the virtues of deterritorialized mobility. The chapter takes as its central task the need for a critical exploration of the limits of postnationalism. It concludes by arguing that we need to put back into the centre of politics, deliberations over the principles that frame how we are to live with each. Unless this is given priority, the current debates over postnationalism and cosmopolitanism, globalism and localism, are bound to end up repeating in late modern/postmodern terms the dead-end modernist arguments over the relative merits of nationalism and internationalism.

Whereas modern nationalism was, and continues to be, expressed at the political-institutional level through social movements of compatriots acting in concert to achieve a singular nation-state, postnationalism is expressed as the subjectivity of mobile diasporas of individuals. If these individuals-in-mutual-exile seek 'communal' connection it is not on the basis of an underlying attachment to territorial foundations. It is as loosely configured imagined community.[21] Avant-garde cosmopolitanism has gone through a parallel shift from the modern to the postmodern. Whereas modern cosmopolitanism was problematically projected as a universalistic and singular world community, the advocates of postmodern cosmopolitanism rightly acknowledge the diverse historical and spatial contexts, which they say still residually frame it. However, they go on to defend multiple attachments or displaced attachments without any obvious exploration of what is a good way of living.[22] In either of these moves – advocate either to postnationalism or postmodern cosmopolitanism – past forms of solidarity tend to be reduced to clichés: for example, in Appadurai's words, 'As the ideological alibi of the territorial state, [the nation] is the last refuge of totalitarianism.'[23] Emergent trends are presented as a *fait accompli*: 'the nation-state has become obsolete'.[24] And solidaristic attachment and relatively bounded and embodied placement, both principles that I will be arguing for later in the chapter, come to be described as part of the problem.

One can get a sense of the intellectual fear of boundedness, closure and attributed attachment from Iris Marion Young's claim that racism and ethnic chauvinism derive in part from the desire for community. Appeals to community in settings of xenophobia, she says, 'can validate the impulses that reproduce racist and ethnically chauvinist identification'.[25] Of course, in the narrow sense, she is right. It helps to make sense of what I called earlier the calendar of evil. Similarly, Julia Kristeva is half right when she describes the cult of origins as 'a hate reaction' – defensive hatred: 'so they withdraw into a sullen, warm private world, unnameable and biological, the impregnable "aloofness" of a weird primal paradise – family, ethnicity, nation, race'.[26] It has, as I said earlier, some application to the defensive ethnocentrisms of Pauline Hanson's One Nation or Jean-Marie Le Pen's National Front. However, it is only part of the story, and it certainly does not mean that the ideals of community and its various expressions – tribe, locale, nation, world – should be dismissed forthwith in favour of cosmopolitan cities of contiguous strangers.

Bruce Robbins' introduction to *Cosmopolitics* reveals a parallel discomfort with place:

> To embrace this style of residence on earth (Pablo Neruda's phrase) means repudiating the romantic localism of a certain portion of the left, which feels it must counter capitalist globalization with a strongly rooted and exclusivist sort of belonging ... The devastation covered over by the complacent talk of globalization is of course very real. But precisely because it is real, we cannot be content to set against it only the *childish reassurance* of belonging to 'a' place.[27] (emphasis added)

If attachment to place were actually being conceived as exclusivist by significant sections of the Left then there would be something to criticize, but such examples are so rare or so irrelevant to core debates that it suggests that something else is driving the critique. What Robbins does, despite his sophistication about 'actually existing cosmopolitanism', is engage in misplaced derision. He so concentrates on the definite article 'a', 'a place', that he misses out of the actuality that 'place' is most often lived in practice as a layering of more and less extended relations of interchange and more and less abstract forms of association. It is how we tie those layers together that is the crucial political-ontological question. As he later implicitly acknowledges, 'place' is not the same as specified geographical locale.[28]

It is not the romance of place *per se* which is deeply problematic. The writers of 'romantic' books such as *Rooted in the Land* or *People, Land, and Community*[29] are struggling to counter, even minimally, their mainstream counterparts in the 'community relations' bureaux of Nescafé, McDonald's, Coca-Cola and IBM. Transnational corporate advertising is now dominated by the global-village motif, whether it is Buddhist monks in mountain settings or rural farmers in Tuscany. Television series depicting rural idyll – *Ballykissangel* (Ireland), *Heartbeat* (Yorkshire), *Northern Exposure* (Alaska) or *Seachange* (coastal Victoria) – are indicative of a longing for simple stability that is thoroughly exploited by the global-local style advertising campaigns of the world's largest corporations. Their image-campaigns link the global and the local by simultaneously romanticizing and emptying out the meaning of place. In short, much more than a few souls positing romantic alternatives to the metropolitan polity, it is instrumental management of a continuing and heartfelt desire for placement that has to be challenged – particularly when it is orchestrated by modernist barbarians such as Slobodan Milošević and Saddam Hussein, or postmodern ones such as Bill Clinton and Tony Blair.

CRITICISMS OF THE ADVOCATES OF POSTNATIONALISM

There are many issues to take up, but I just want to mention two. Firstly, the assumption made by postnationalists that national attachment is a bad thing misses out on the social and ethical ambiguity of national community. For me the advocates of postnationalism repeat the mistake of the theorists of nationalism when the latter make the common moral distinction between ethic nationalism (bad) and civic nationalism (good). There is certainly an analytic distinction to be made here, but not an ethical one. In some hands it is turned into a blinkered politics extolling the virtues of the kind of nationalism that the writer happens to hold. For example, Liah Greenfeld reveals her blind belief in Anglo-American versions of the ideology when she advocates 'individualistic-libertarian' nationalism (her term). By contrast, she says 'Collectivist ideologies are inherently authoritarian.'[30] I would not bother to refer to this stupid claim except that an articulate advocate of postnationalism, Richard Kearney, positively takes it up.[31] Should we conclude by dismissing nationalism out of hand and putting postnationalism in its place? Or should we instead focus our attention on principles for underpinning and maintaining complex ethical social relations. I will elaborate this latter option shortly.

Secondly, postnational advocates do not adequately incorporate into their positions an understanding of the paradox that postnationalism (alongside civic nationalism) is now also the refuge of the instrumental state as it also attempts to find its place in a globalizing world. For the advocates of postnationalism is it salutary to remember that it is that very nation-state that is sometimes presented as a post-melting-pot, postnational experiment – the United States of America – that has over the last decade been involved in more systematic violence projected outside its borders than any state since Hitler's Third Reich. In the war against Iraq, filmed as a war without significant casualties, thousands of anonymous soldiers were drowned in sand as NATO tanks with bulldozer-fronted shields filled in Iraqi-held trenches. In the 1999 war against Serbia, the aerial bombing, intended to limit the ethnic cleansing of Kosova, opened the possibility for the Yugoslav militia effecting the mass exodus of hundreds of thousands of Albanian Kosovars. These were the very people supposedly being protected. Although not intended as a totalizing denunciation, these facts make a mockery of Arjun Appadurai's extolling of the 'sheer cultural vitality of this free-trade zone' called America. True, Appadurai does ask for call for the further pursuit of liberty and cultural difference through legal protections, but the full force of his call to America takes the form of going with the flow of postmodern global capitalism:

> For the United States, to play a major role in the cultural politics of a postnational world has very complex domestic entailments ... It may mean a painful break from a fundamentally Fordist, manufacture-centred conception of the American economy, as we learn to be global information brokers, service providers, style doctors. It may mean embracing as part of our livelihood what we have so far confined to the world of Broadway, Hollywood, and Disneyland: the import of experiments, the production of fantasies, the export of styles, the hammering out of pluralities. It may mean distinguishing our attachment to America from our willingness to die for the United States ... America may yet construct another narrative of enduring existence, as narrative about the uses of loyalty after the end of the nation-state.[32]

While lots of good things have come out of America, this argument is bizarre. For too long America has been constructing narratives for others. Three glaring problems with this passage deserve critical noting. Firstly, as many other writers have argued, it is misguided to think that the movement from Fordism to what David Harvey calls 'flexible accumulation',[33] brings about a brave new world of equality-in-difference. One has only to look to the diaspora Chicano community of the Eastern seaboard to see how immigrant cultures can be super-exploited in the information age. Moreover, although separating attachment to America (presumably good) from willingness to die for it (supposedly bad) may be laudable depending upon what it means in practice, it no longer takes us very far into developing a positive form of postnationalism. In the presentation of the technologically sophisticated wars conducted by US-led forces over Iraq and Kosova, much was made of the fact that very few of 'our boys' died. From a position of technological military strength, willingness to kill from a distance has largely surpassed the old-fashioned willingness to die for one's nation as a basis of the call to arms.

The further point concerns the embracing of Hollywood and the style-doctors. For a long time now Hollywood has joined in the postmodern game of presenting America as if it were already postnational and therefore able to stand in for the world at moments of crisis. Postnationalist films such as *Independence Day* (1996) and *Armageddon* (1997) have largely replaced the Cold War nationalism which had Rocky Balboa wearing stars-and-stripes boxing shorts and stepping into the ring to defeat Ivan Drago, the best that Soviet science could create.[34] Hollywood's America now only fights wars over the thin red line of national territory as reruns of old conflicts. With some notable exceptions such as *Wag the Dog* (1997), the American war-machine is uncritically directed globally. However, if you read between the lines, the thrust of the set speeches in these films still assume that the United States sits at the helm of world politics. It is the kind of postnationalism that makes 'humanitarian' interventions into Iraq and Kosova as easily thinkable as leaving the peacekeeping to others in East Timor. In *Independence Day* (1996), Thomas J. Whitmore, President of the United States, speaks of the Fourth of July becoming the rallying point for all mankind:

> Good morning. In less than an hour, aircraft from here will join with others from around the world. And you will be launching the largest aerial battle in the history of mankind. 'Mankind' – that word should have new meaning for all of us. We can't be consumed by petty differences any more. We will be united in our common interest. Perhaps it's faith. Today is the Fourth of July, and you will once more fight for our freedom. Not from tyranny, oppression or persecution, but from alienation. We're fighting for our right to live, to exist. And should we win the day, the Fourth of July will no longer be known as an American holiday, but as the day when the whole world declared in one voice: 'We will not go quietly into the night, we will not vanish without a fight, we are going to survive.' Today we celebrate *our* independence day! (emphasis added)

It is striking how comfortably Hollywood translates fighting for transnational peace back into the heritage of one nation: pax Americana. (The predictable exception to this is in *The Matrix*, which has the City of Zion as the last bastion of transnational peace.) When we get to the last line of the speech in *Independence Day*, 'Today we celebrate our independence day', the ambiguous appellation 'our' has linked modern nationalism and postmodern transnationalism in a comfortable pastiche that challenges nothing. Hollywood even makes it sound as if it is hard work. In *The American President*, the President of the United States, Andrew Shepherd talks about the need to acknowledge the struggle:

America isn't easy. America is advanced citizenship. You've got to want it bad, 'cause it's going to put up a fight. It's going to say 'You want free speech? Let's see you acknowledge a man who makes your blood boil, who's standing centre-stage and advocating at the top of his lungs that which you would spend a life-time opposing at the top of yours. You want to claim this land as the land of the free? Then the symbol of your country cannot just be the flag. The symbol has also to be one of its citizens exercising his right to burn that flag in protest.'

In one very particular way, for the banal postnationalists the transnational nation is hard work. There are so many contradictory issues to consider: modern ideas of old-fashioned national interest; modern concerns about human rights; postmodern aversions to the 'ultimate sacrifice' such as dying for a cause, or watching the body-bags return from a place of foreign military intervention; postnational criticisms of half-remembered national ideals. In this sense it is hard being part of the American establishment. Their late-twentieth-century morality has an immediacy that is occasioned by televised instances of graphic human rights abuse: the tortured face of a young child, news of the murder of a journalist, images of an bombed-out embassy. However, it is constrained by parallel horror of the death of a single US soldier or the downturn of a single day on Wall Street. In films from John Wayne's *The Green Berets* (1968) to Steven Spielberg's *Saving Private Ryan* (1998) the same message is conveyed, albeit in different guises: if we look after our private morality, the big ethical questions will take care of themselves.

In last scene of *The Green Berets*, a beret-wearing Vietnamese boy asks John Wayne, 'What will happen to me now?' and the soldier replies: 'You let me worry about that Green Beret. You're what this is all about.' John Wayne rises from his knees and takes the child by the hand. Suddenly afternoon blue light turns to golden sunset and a male military choir sings:

> Back at home a young wife waits.
> A Green Beret has met his fate.
> He has died for those oppressed.
> He deserves his last request.

In the last scene of *Saving Private Ryan*, the private, who has been saved by a company of men who nearly all die to that end, stands over the last fatally wounded all-American, Tom Hanks. Before dying, Tom rasps out the words, 'Just, earn it.' As Private Ryan stands there he cinematically shades into his older self, now standing over a headstone. A voiceover intones the 'mature' sentiments of private morality:

To be honest with you, I wasn't sure how I'd feel about coming back here. Everyday I think of what you said to me that day on the bridge. I've tried to live my life the best I could. I hope that was enough. I hope at least in your eyes I've earned what all of you have done for me.

As the old man stands there reflecting on an ethics of self, it is a good moment to turn to a broader focus on a social ethics of community, an ethics which puts forward principles for living with others rather than just asks for liberal goodness.

PRINCIPLES FOR AN ALTERNATIVE APPROACH TO POLITICAL COMMUNITY

I started the chapter by saying that without a thoroughgoing exploration of the principles of solidarity and community, postnationalism amounts to little more than a postmodern yearning for openness on the one hand, and an ideological compatriot of globalism on the other. The postmodernist critics do have principles assumed in their politics, but in my view they do not go deep enough. They can be summarized as assuming the virtue of the following interrelated ways of being in the world and relating to others:

1. radicalized choosing – this involves emphasizing the ethic of autonomy, where the individual chooses and rechooses the constituents of life from amongst the pastiche of possibilities, past, present and future. It is usually associated with a critique of the search for roots or a place to belong. This is where postmodernism repeats at a more radical level the politics of modern liberalism;
2. boundary crossing – presented as if being on the margin is always better than stabilizing one's place; as if being related to territory is always a root cause of conflict. This involves an emphasis on 'the transnational [domestic] dimension of cultural translation – migration, diaspora, displacement, relocation';[35]
3. fragmented subjectification – involving emphasis on identity-as-hybridity, and a particular process of hybridity at that. This is hybridity-always-in-process;
4. ambivalence – of identity, authority, power, etc.;
5. difference – as a form of alterity which at its most radical is anti-communitarian;
6. cosmopolitanism – as a non-universalizing universalism. It can take various forms including postnationalism and post-liberal multiculturalism;
7. deconstruction – as a method of viewing the world around. This is relevant to the themes of this chapter insofar as it involves deconstructing the 'totalization' of national culture without putting anything in its place.

I don't want to dismiss these principles entirely but to question them as one-sided. The following discussion provides only a schematic beginning.[36] Rather than arguing for nationalism or cosmopolitanism, transnationalism or internationalism, postnationalism or postmodern hybridity, it suggests that social relations should be based ethically and practically on positive principles of interrelationship – pragmatic and contradictory ideals considered as principles-in-tension. These principles need to be argued about, negotiated and worked through the various modes of practice and over varying levels of space-time extension and social integration. They include principles such as the importance of reciprocity in co-operation and an emphasis upon equality, not held as discrete liberal rights but as an interwoven tapestry of 'ways of being'. In addition, social relations should be based upon and therefore qualified by our relationship to nature. Two ideals stand out here: firstly, treating nature as ecologically limited and therefore economically limiting; and secondly, treating nature as ontologically foundational and therefore culturally limiting. Importantly, this last principle has the effect of undermining the primacy of 'the cultural' in the so-called culture/nature divide or 'the intellect' in the so-called mind/ body divide. For present purposes it has the effect of questioning the easy mobility of one's social arrangements as valorized by the postmodernists. It is dangerous to begin by listing principles and leaving them undefined, but we have to start somewhere. They are set up here in three layers of increasing ontological depth:

1. principles conceived at the level of rights and procedures
   • democracy-justice (used as a shorthand for the usual clustering of principles around liberal-participatory or socialist democracy)

2. principles conceived at the level of integrative forms and practices
   • reciprocity-co-operation
   • autonomy-freedom
   • equality-empathy
   • solidarity-authority
   • identity-difference

3. principles conceived at the level of ontological foundations
   • ecology-ontology (used as shorthand for a clustering of principles relevant to nature-place, temporality and embodied life-mortality)

Individual principles in this list have a long history of being embedded within various traditions, Western and Eastern, recent and traditional. However, these principles are usually set negatively against each other as discursive formations such as socialism and liberalism battle it out for the ascendant moral ground. Social practices, it is suggested here, should be set within the social context of these negotiated principles-in-tension, conducted across intersecting levels of social relations and qualified by ecological-cultural limits. The overriding complication is that each of these principles are contradictory or at least in tension with each other. For example, if we take the principle of equality it clearly has to go much deeper than the liberal notion of equality of opportunity or the social-democratic ideal of distribution of wealth as it might be expressed at the level of procedural rights. However, that is not to turn equality into an ontological absolute. Proclaiming equality for indigenous peoples in settings where they are dominated by integrative modernisms (in countries as diverse as Australia, the United States, Indonesia) should not for example involve overriding the identity-difference principle. It is by the latter principle that we can defend the possibility of different forms of living and therefore of layered forms of governance even within a postcolonial setting (for example, the Inuit in Canada or the Zapatistas in Chiapas). In advocating an alternative politics of layered community – including national community – we need not aim to annul these tensions, but instead productively to open them up to transparent and self-reflexive regimes of negotiation.

The tensions have to be worked out in practice between people across the various levels of association – local community, region, nation, world – rather than through setting up *a priori* formulations which tend to privilege the particularized local or the global-universal. Instead, for example, of arguing as Offe and Heinze do for the abstract market as a means of limiting the obligatory implications of reciprocal community[37] – and thus supposedly enhancing autonomy[38] – the principles of reciprocity and autonomy (expressed superficially in liberal terms as contractual obligation and liberty) have to be considered as pertaining to all realms of social life including the market and the state. The market and the state are not spheres of autonomous activity. The nature of the abstract market and the abstract state themselves need to be fundamentally qualified by practical and more embodied expressions of reciprocity across the various levels of extension from the local to the global.

All of this needs considerable theoretical elaboration and real-world illustration. Let me take these tentative beginnings a couple of steps further by focusing upon one of the primary principles of social reproduction – reciprocity.[39] I will follow its pathway through what were described earlier as levels of extension from the local to the global, and levels of integration from the more embodied settings of face-to-face integration to the more abstracted settings of disembodied, technologically mediated sociality. Advocating relations of reciprocity importantly names one of the principles-in-tension to be negotiated in the broad canvas of human relations. However, without some sense of the levels of abstraction across which reciprocity can be lived (and given the contemporary pressures of globalization), we too easily find ourselves taking the more comfortable path of institutionally abstracted forms of reciprocity and solidarity. We allow institutionalized exchange relations conducted by nation-states, corporations, aid agencies and the like to mediate our relations to others. It thus reduces the layered possibilities of public reciprocity to national tax redistribution regimes, regional balance-of-trade agreements and global aid programmes.

There is nothing wrong with these kinds of abstract reciprocity as such: quite the opposite. However, we need to keep in mind the proviso that the way in which they are handled is often instrumental, self-serving and oriented to the extension of institutional power. Abstract and universalizing reciprocity, especially if based upon a modified version of the old Marxist maxim 'between each according to their means ...' would be integral to a manifold of levels of reciprocity. Relying on the nation-state for managing this exchange is to flatten out the principle completely.

The possibilities of abstract reciprocity range across the various levels of time-space extension from local exchanges between acquaintances and strangers to global regimes of exchange, co-operation and support. The overriding problem is that in contemporary market-driven cultures, abstract rather than embodied reciprocity dominates the public sphere, while more concrete, embodied and particularized forms of reciprocity have retreated to the private realm of family and immediate friends. In the context of communications, the problem is that disembodied communication through the media and internet are more likely to be the source of sentimental solidarity with far-flung liberation movements than the much more demanding kinds of communication entailed in a relationship of embodied reciprocity.

The contrast being made here is not simply between instances of mediated and face-to-face communication, that is, communication as mere interaction. We are talking about the nature of the relationship in terms of how it is bound by deeper levels of integration. By contrast with abstract reciprocity, embodied reciprocity or reciprocity at the level of the face-to-face involves producing, exchanging and communicating with, and for, known others. It is where the act of co-operation is part of a long-term, relatively unmediated relationship of mutuality and interdependence. For obvious reasons embodied reciprocity is more easily conducted the closer one gets to home, but in theory (and practice) it is possible across the reaches of social extension from the immediate locale to the other side of the globe. In the case of the recent struggle in East Timor, for example, it meant being more than part of a solidarity group that writes notes of support or puts pressure on politicians. Here it ideally entailed working with East Timorese people both in Australia and in East Timor across a range of activities – political, cultural and economic.

Expressed more generally, enriching the depth and range of such a co-operative's relations of reciprocity would, on the one hand, entail the individuals who participate choosing to make the activities of the interconnected activities of the interconnected face-to-face groups more central to their rounds of everyday life (under the qualified and qualifying principle of autonomy-freedom). On the other hand, it would involve setting up specific solidaristic relations for the interchange of goods and visitors with groups from other places, particular places in which people can be supported in working projects of participatory self-help. This kind of reciprocity, drawing lines of connection within the region or across the globe, all too obviously involves confronting the obscenity that the abstract state system does little to alleviate the deaths by malnutrition and bad water of one-tenth of the children born on this planet. By contrast, billions of dollars can too easily be spent on a war over Kosova or Iraq when one's principles are based on the abstract notions of transnational sovereignty and 'humanitarian' intervention. The optimal aim would be develop lines of co-operation based upon ongoing negotiation, reflexively conducted in awareness of the tensions between the principles of reciprocity, equality, solidarity and autonomy. Rather than facilitating autonomous hybrid individuals touching down in exotic moments of superficial reciprocity and solidarity, the kind of politics being advocated here embraces long-term solidarity with particular others, conducted as a way of life.

CONCLUSION

The twentieth century, more than any before it, was marked by the horrors of mass wars over territory and cultural integrity. It is understandable then in this new century that the postmodern response is to put the burden of blame upon attempts to stabilize relations to place and community. It is just as understandable that the avant-garde late-modernist response is to call for new forms of universalism based on non-exclusionary cosmopolitan citizenship. Advocating a discussion of the principles of community – reciprocity, autonomy, equality, solidarity and ecology – and critically assessing how they are lived across extensions of space from the local to the global, is intended to take us beyond those responses, linking the particularities and differences of place to the generalities and universalities of ethical debate.

Part III

Reflecting on Old and New Nations

8
Ukania:
The Rise of the 'Annual Report' Society

Tom Nairn

Without a more decisive rupture at the level of basic grammar rather than rhetoric – of form rather than content – New Labour's political renaissance could only be undertaken 'the wrong way round'. It was fated by its own history to move periphery-first. Authority had to be conceded outwards without the prior establishment of a new central framework capable of encompassing all the new energies and demands. When General de Gaulle decided it was time that France 'married its own century', he set up a new republican constitution to consummate the wedding. In Germany and Italy, new federal or regional patterns of government were imposed after fascism, in order to modulate and confine the unitary state. In Spain the post-Franco democracy designed and enabled the Catalan, Basque and other autonomous governments, by first of all erecting a radically novel political and juridical mainframe. But in the United Kingdom the mainframe itself has remained sacrosanct. Behind a firework-display of fizzling rhetoric about change and modernization, it has simply been carried forward, and trusted to go on evolving. Trust it, and therefore us.

Things will settle down and generally sort themselves out, while in the meantime (which could mean a lifetime) things can go on in the circular kind of way people (that is, England's people) are used to, albeit with some changes round the edges. In France and Spain new state constitutions were seen as the necessary condition of a political break with the past. But after Thatcher, only a new politics was demanded, not a new framework for political living – and that in order to redeem and continue the past, not to break with it. Recent episodes of UK history may have come to be despised and rejected; but not the longer perspective of Britishness, within which success and world leadership had been for so long celebrated. Only on the periphery had 'radical' changes become unavoidable, in the more European sense of ruptures or definite new departures. For 'Middle England' itself, these were reckoned to be superfluous – or at least able to be indefinitely postponed.

There were in fact interesting poll and survey indications in the later 1990s that English opinion may have been a lot more open to new departures than party political leaders assumed. Unfortunately, it was the assumptions of the latter that counted. They continued to believe that dramatic departures of style and communication accompanied by minimal, adaptive changes to the constitution were most in accord with the subjacent mood. Hence some departures from the stick-insect rigidity of Thatcherism were in order – but not of such a kind as to frighten the horses. Socialism had been exorcized in accordance with the same supposed mood. After which, it would have seemed damnably un-British to start imposing a Hispanic-style revolution up top: surely some modernization touches would do instead? Enhanced (only cynics would say 'disguised') by brilliant new ideas? Might not some thoroughly intelligent bricolage, plus a strong dose of accelerationism, and technicism restore the basis of Anglo-British statehood for long enough? And keep the restorers in governmental business for long enough, too?

VECTORS OF ARCHAISM

The past does not simply 'survive'. To be reproduced effectively within modernity it requires vehicles, social devices and intentions. Through these devices what would otherwise be fossils become allied to new interests and passions, acquiring the style, even the fashionability, demanded by what the Situationists originally called *la société du spectacle*. One of the key vectors for this is economics. It is still a common error to believe that the Habsburg Empire so wonderfully captured in Robert Musil's *The Man Without Qualities* was economically hopeless or doomed. In fact it did fairly well until killed off by war and defeat. David Good and other historians have shown how notably it was advancing by 1914, after a period in which Austria-Hungary had indeed lagged behind industrially. Society there may have been unviable, and particularly the contradiction-riven state, but this was not for reasons rooted in economic development alone. Like other deplorable truisms of the time to come, 'It's the economy, stupid!' was quite familiar in Vienna.

'Was the Habsburg Empire an economic failure in the sense that it could not engineer modern economic growth prior to its collapse?' asks Good. His answer is 'an unequivocal "no"'.[1] The empire grew at a significantly faster rate than the United Kingdom over the period between 1570 and 1914, and its GNP per capita was by then equivalent to that of France. Of course it straddled the ancient socio-economic gap between West and East, and hence contained within its own borders a steep 'development gradient'. Yet the latter, Good points out, was less steep than the one between the North and the South of the United States. The latter's 'impeccable credentials' as a model of successful capitalist evolution have been largely the result of backward projection from the post-Second World War period.

Although it had not caught up with Belgium, the English Midlands or the Ruhr, Franz-Joseph's empire stood comparison with Mediterranean and peripheral Western Europe (which meant, with most of it). The implication is plain, if disagreeable to economics worshippers: there was no straightforward relationship between development and political success or stability. 'Modernization' never fails to create contradictions and stir things up. It provided Vienna (today, London) with greater resources to buy off opposition, dangle bribes and be terribly broad-minded; but at the same time, it made the unbribable, and the resentful and the contrary far more aware of their unequal, left-behind status. Not everyone can be bought off equally. Any measure of success – like the arrival of a railway, the opening of the first supermarket, sudden access to college education – generates an irascible appetite for more, and more quickly. The broad-minded, blueprint in hand perceive this as unreasonable: impatient narrowness, egotism, jumping the queue. Thus a grander, encompassing, controlling sort of identity comes to oppose more particular, self-assertive, 'I'm as good as you' identities. The sharper the impact of socio-economic change, the more this clash turns towards nationalism – the sense that life or death may be at stake here, unless control of development is made to lie where it should (with us, not them).

Success in statistical tables and growth leagues does not automatically favour a grateful, conserving philosophy of evensong, egotism and familial values. The British Conservatives discovered this in the late 1980s, not long before they fell helplessly through the floor. Neither does stagnation and the sense of retreat or confinement encourage either revolution or nationalism (except among tiny minorities who know in the abstract that what people tolerate is actually 'intolerable', and inform them of this). There may have been some formative periods of industrialization when such combinations were possible – times when modernity existed only in pockets, as the privileged accident of one nation or another. But its generalization has swept this away. Along with the debris has gone what Emmanuel Todd has recently baptized as *L'Illusion économique*, the notion that economic development itself is the sufficient condition of any specific political or state pattern, or of the triumph of any particular ideology. The universal necessary condition of all advance ceases to be the special explanation of any one forward movement.

Modernity required – and in its later evolution goes on requiring – certain new economic and social circumstances. It does not follow that these circumstances determine modernity in the concrete sense of its lived and acculturized evolution. However one-sided, the socio-economic renaissance of Thatcherism had more strongly undermined the class basis of a traditionalist state than anything before it. Its deregulation and attacks on corporatism corroded the familial sense of a societal order which, like that of the Habsburgs, had evolved over time an arm's-length rapprochement with an earlier phase of capitalism. After the demolition of this structure, nation and state no longer retained their long-established fit. Yet at the same time Thatcherism worshipped and propped up the state. On that level it was utterly philistine. Exaggerated loyalism and hysteria over timelessness became a kind of compensation for the regime's self-conscious economic radicalism – as if only endorsement of monarchic and other rituals, and of the state's untouchable unity, could prevent *everything* that was solid from melting into the air.

Much did melt, of course. But by no means everything. It was probably the successful or half-successful side of Conservative economic renovation that helped to carry forward the archaisms of Britishness into a new age. Although at a heavy cost, that aspect of it furnished a comparative advantage and stability, which the 1997 change of political regime then inherited and exploited. In striking contrast to all previous Labour governments, Blair was able to undertake his devolutionary measures against the background of an over-strong currency and significant business support. His pro-European stance and agreement (albeit mainly 'in principle') to the common currency ensured a new level of City and big-business tolerance – or even approval – reflected in the climate of a famously Moosbruggerish British press. Yet that same good fortune was bound also to rehabilitate some of the anachronism carried forward with it. A half-revolution must constantly insure itself against whatever has not been destroyed – against the past still there, against an identity discountenanced, even humiliated, yet not really broken up and cast into the tail-race of history. Huge New Labour efforts had gone into presenting this insurance policy between 1995 and 1997. It seemed the only way to win the kind of electoral victory which the British system prescribed. Over-adaptation to the economics of Thatcherism and deregulated liberalism, extreme canniness over all matters fiscal and financial, and a convert-like disavowal of socialist money-throwing antics: these now became the surprising preconditions of renewal and change. Yet it would obviously be quite hard to avoid a general or blatant conservatism from arising around foundations like these. Hence there was the absolute necessity for an ostentatious, perfectly sincere and fireproof form of 'radicalism' to balance that tendency. The Tories had counterposed a mummified statism against their radical economic upheavals. The Labourites now had to offset their mummified economics with an ostentatious display of verbosely political radicalism. We have seen something of what this meant: 'youthism', high-technicism, millennial and style-mania, and the accumulation of think-tanks and divining rods in appropriate official, quasi-official and entirely spontaneous polyhedron.

Rather than from plutocratic plotting and self-interest, it is important to observe how this arose out of an objective dilemma. It derives from the structural fate of a decrepit multinational polity whose inherited nature renders it incapable of either solving its problems or dissolving them. It can only pretend to do both, with a kind of mounting insouciance and braggadocio. Ultra-prudent and custodial economics could not help favouring an equivalent conservation of the state – and so the prolongation of 1688–1707 anachronism. But at the same time, real changes of state had become unavoidable on the periphery, as had a distinctly unconservative style of ideas and public policy. Thus the Scots were given back their parliament, the Welsh were awarded a political voice, and the Northern Irish were reconciled to a new and only half-British Protectorate – all amid a clamorous fanfare of radicalism suggesting that these were but early instalments of a gathering revolution.

At the centre of affairs, however, the 'revolution' was meant from the start to be far more decorous, indeed not revolutionary at all. Some changes to Europe's most grotesque political relic, the House of Lords; a mild form of proportional representation (if approved by referendum); a half Freedom of Information Act; an upgraded style of monarchy, affected (but not carried away) by Princess Diana's example; a proper place at Europe's heart (when economics permit, again via referendum) – all these decorous shifts were to occur within a comfortably indeterminate timeframe, implying further long cadences of stable British existence. From its first day in office, Blairism has planned to last longer than Thatcherism did. Thus what counts most in the 'gathering revolution' is clearly the gathering part; execution will come later, as and when opportunity allows (or quite possibly, fails to allow). And what if it gathers only to clear away again, or to be politely refused in referenda? Well, the deep assumption remains that Britain and 'Middle England' – the imaginary repository of the national life-force, nowadays usually assigned to southern suburbia – will survive that. Deeper down, in the central processing unit (or as would once have been said, the controlling instinct) of Britishness, this continuity is what matters most. Survival: in whatever grandeur remains possible.

A PROPHECY OF END-TIME

About the contradictions of Blairism one thing will never be said: 'They could not have known.' In fact the *responsables* of the New Order were told, and it is already revealing to see how clearly they were told, that this time survival, continuity and grandeur would no longer be enough, however ably modulated and publicized. Political revolution was required. Only six months after Blair's electoral triumph, a study appeared with precisely that title: Anthony Barnett's *This Time: Our Constitutional Revolution.*[2] It had a cover picture showing the Union Jack at half-mast over Buckingham Palace in a nostalgic September light. This was appropriate, for the book's story is like Musil's, only much more amazing: the foundering of a crown state recounted day by day, sometimes word by word, in contrast to the long ironic retrospect of *The Man Without Qualities*.[3]

The British flag had only been raised over the royal London residence by popular demand. Previously the royal standard had only ever flown there when the monarch was physically present, a demonstration that regality was of greater importance than mere nationality. Kingdom was the important half of 'United Kingdom', even if Parliament had made inroads on the rest of it. However, the bare flagpole now looked offensive to the huge crowds mourning the death of the Princess of Wales. Its indifferent nakedness seemed to accuse their grief, and their caring – as if Queen Elizabeth and her household, then on their annual holiday at Balmoral, were also indifferent. Did they not seem to care about the loss of their outcast daughter? In death the latter had acquired a title: 'the People's Princess'. Prime Minister Blair confirmed this after the fatal crash in Paris, in what was immediately seen as a stroke of public relations genius. It was as if he scented from extremely far off the odour of a revolution from below.

There was a lot of gooey sentiment and romanticism mixed up with the resentment, of course, as both left- and right-wing critics of the mood insisted. But what did they expect? A century and a half of patient effort had gone into the formation of romantic-popular monarchism. It was a broader elite project pursued by governments of both the Left and Right, which had long since cast national identity into this specific mould. That mould had been a form of control. Yet now, briefly, the same force was out of control and in the streets, as a mass idolization of somebody both 'inappropriate' and dead. Yet there were both Socialists and Reactionaries who found nothing to say but: 'This is a bit much!' In truth, nothing could have indicated more clearly the malaise of the electorate who had voted so resoundingly for radical change four months previously. Barnett was surely right to devote so much space to analysing the incident. It showed the availability of public opinion for a sort of change previously unthinkable. For all its sentimentality, he observes, the Diana cult none the less 'expressed a form of the contemporary that connects to the landslide of May 1st', and implied the possible 'normalization' of British political life. Under Thatcherism, society had in an almost literal sense become 'divorced' from the old state, including its petrified monarchy. In the September days of 1997 the divorce had been spontaneously completed, in

a vast movement of people who by their very existence demonstrated that the premise of the 300-year-old British Constitution had been swept away. The people are now independent-minded and capable ... The question now is whether the political elite will allow the constitutional transformation to proceed.[4]

Barnett's argument is of course that the renovated elite must not just allow but compel it to proceed: 'this time' is the only time likely to be available for a widely popular reconstruction of the state, a genuine revolution from above. Hence we get the urgency of tone in the book, and its sometimes hectoring manner. Behind it lies the sense (also the fear) of there being no other time coming. Even if launched from above, a revolution can only be 'genuine' when it meets and is modified by some positive response from below. The moments when such conjunction is possible are rare. To let one go would be folly.

There was only one way of realizing that moment – the route described in some detail over a number of years by Charter 88, the vigorous reform group that Barnett helped to found in the 1980s, and for some time led in the 1990s. It is not as if 'This Time' were a lonely or eccentric cry from somewhere beneath the stones. The message came right out of the most significant non-party campaign of the 1990s, and many Labour Party leaders had professed warm sympathy with its aims. Since the somewhat miserable 300th anniversary commemorations of 1688's original revolutionary imposition, the Charter had pleaded passionately that enough was enough. Even a standard-issue off-the-shelf constitution would (some now thought) be better than William and Mary's quaint palimpsest of cod-feudal shards, early modern scratchings and bipartisan 'traditions' reinvented so often that no one had the slightest idea what purpose they originally served. And surely, with some imagination and national pride, wouldn't the unthinkable become possible? A new British Constitution meriting its capital letter, inspired by the approaching century rather than the one before the one before last?

Barnett's indictment of the *ancien régime* takes up all the first part of his book, 'The Meaning of 1997', and overflows constantly into the second, 'Voicing the Constitution'. The reader is left by it in a kind of trance, like the suspension of belief that used to attack Ethiopian intellectuals of the 1970s when they returned home from studying abroad to confront the court of Lion King Haile Selassie: *How is all this still possible?* At the end of the twentieth century? With the democratization of the globe in full spate, and Nelson Mandela running South Africa? *How dare it endure one day longer on earth?*

The least that could be expected after May 1997 was surely a statement of some exit plans, and a sketch of the replacement. This need not be a *pronunciamento* accompanied by a detailed blueprint: instead, what the author recommended was something like Anthony Giddens' 'utopian realism'. What this meant was 'articulating clear, principled goals and then setting about them with practical measures that are given the space necessary to be assessed in a context of consent'.[5] On the other hand, such a programme does have to be uttered. With all the respect due to Karl Popper and George Soros (both suitably endorsed in *This Time*) even a pragmatic, anti-grand-theory prospectus must at least be adumbrated, since without that 'the country has no clear idea what "the greatest constitutional change for a century" means and where it is supposed to lead'.[6]

By the end of the year that Blair took office, however, there was still no such idea in place. As Barnett worriedly pointed out in December 1997, the statement had been promised before the election, and then simply never delivered. Now the democratic revival, which had been so strongly in the air of both May and early September, needed its momentum to be kept going. The practical measures undertaken (like devolution) demanded 'a sense of larger purpose ... In terms of the constitution, a clear statement of principles and purpose. The sooner the better.'[7]

METHODONE KINGDOM

Alas, 'the sooner the better' implies the later the worse. As winter turned into spring, the government's first anniversary was celebrated, and Mr Blair's first Cabinet 'reshuffle' of July 1998 ensconced New Labour's authority more firmly, it became steadily clearer that the first instalment might well be the last. The maximal and daring might already have collapsed into the minimal and safeguarding. No statement of grand constitutional renewal was ever to come. Instead, there would be another long-lived regime of decline-management – a generational reign, as it were, comparable to that of Mrs Thatcher in 1979–97. Once more, radicalism would boil down to staying afloat, albeit in an interestingly different way. As with the early concessions to Scotland, Wales and Ireland, some constitutional changes were still needed to secure that way. One was a form of proportionality in political elections, to qualify the desperate lurches and 'landslide' turnarounds of the past. The second was some change to Great Britain's revising chamber. Alongside the modernized monarchy, rendered critical by the Diana affair, a more acceptable House of Lords was also needed. These vectors of continuity had themselves to be upgraded, simply to pursue the time-honoured role assigned them.

They certainly represented overdue episodes of modernization. But in the hardening context of Blair's 2000 regime they could also be stability reforms. Thus the 'radical' would be a realignment of the archaic, rather than the straightforward replacement which Charter 88 and *This Time* pleaded for. Electoral change was the more important of the two. The fantastic lurches of 1979 and 1997 had become too dangerous for an antique creaking across the threshold of the Third Millennium. In a Europe and (soon) an archipelago regulated by proportional electoralism, the boxing-ring pantomime of 'first past the post' was no longer easily sustainable. True, Blair's party had benefited from the old mechanisms in May 1997, but only in the wake of prolonged adversity, during which both the Left and the Centre of UK politics had been under-represented for nearly two decades. If the system was left intact, nothing could be surer than an eventual surge in the other direction. The instinct of Labourism, even the New sort, was that in Britain, and particularly in England, this reversal action would happen sooner rather than later, and was more liable to affect the Left than the Right.

The ancient theory had been that knockouts ensured 'strong government'. This might have been all very well when the British Empire possessed a fundamentally strong ruling class – the old patriciate, culturally at one although ruling via different parties. But things had altered fundamentally. The combination of decline and Mrs Thatcher had ruined that elite. She started off her reign with a Cabinet of grandees and great acreage, and ended with one of journalists, estate agents and sleaze merchants. These put her out of business, then revealed themselves as incapable of setting up on their own account. So 'the system' now came to mean nothing but inebriate parliamentary majorities based on a minority of the votes cast, generating machismo power, think-tank mania, mediaeval staggering fits like the Poll Tax, unrestrained petty-bourgeois opportunism, and sovereignty delusions which the rest of the world now sniggered at. New Labour was second-born into this post-patrician world. Which meant that its 1997 majority bore the wounds of four successive KOs, and the scars from a prolonged agony of internal modernization. Was it not due some compensation? That meant not just obtaining but staying in office. On his first day in power, Tony Blair launched an electoral campaign for the post-millennium ballots of 2002 and 2007. What was most new about reformed Labourism was this hardened and reoriented will – the determination to construct not merely a stand-in government, but a different and more stably based British elite order.

RAPID ASSEMBLAGE OF A NEW RULING CLASS

This meant in turn that New Labourism, unlike the Thatcherites, was directly confronting what one must call the sociological problem of Great Britain *in extremis*. That is, how to replace the former ruling class by a plausible substitute. 'Britain', the empire's rump-state, can only be kept going by some new regulating and stabilizing cadre, one really capable of taking over from the gentlemen. Hostile critics claimed from the outset that Blairite 'radicalism' is mere conservatism; but actually it is more like conservatism. One should not judge it solely in terms of the former Left–Right spectrum. Seen rather in terms of curatorship, as a form of state survival-kit, it becomes more comprehensible. The Conservative first-born 'natural party of government' had been smashed into pitiful wreckage by the farce of Thatcher's last days and the May 1997 landslide. It would be in a life raft for years to come. To the second-in-line now fell the spoils, but also the onerous duty, of preserving and renewing one of history's outstanding polities – the oldest existing state in the world with any claim to modernity.

From 1997 onwards, much effort would be expended around a single question. 'Just what is Tony Blair's project?' asked many sceptical minds, particularly on the Left. The replies have been curiously sparse and unconvincing. But that may be because these enquirers have generally been searching for a socialism substitute – some novel formula for social-policy redemption and advance. Accompanying this quest went a perfectly logical idea: the new government may as yet be professing no such formula, but at least some Cabinet craniums (preferably those in charge) must surely have one? Surely they must know what they're doing, if only they would tell us (and meanwhile, listen to our advice, and engage in dialogue).

However, what if the logic itself were erroneous, in the sense of misdirected? What if, that is, there is neither a 'project' of that kind, nor the smallest chance of one being concealed in private ruminations anywhere round the Cabinet table? Would it not then follow that the only effective 'project' of end-Britain is *diminuendo* survival-transition from the management of decline into the management of disintegration, leading eventually to a suitable testament and funeral arrangements? Both countering economic decline ('Thatcherism') and re-engineering the political control-system ('Blairism') have naturally presented their aims as 'radical modernization'. But both these words have become terms of bluster, especially the term 'radical'. After the 18 years of Mrs Thatcher and Blair's 1997 election campaign, it has come to signify little more than 'Have a nice day!' in the United States.

The problems addressed may indeed be 'radical' (basic, through and through, fundamental, and so on) but the available or short-term answers are really of a theme-park nature. There is no conceivable radical solution, in the sense so much bruited about by Mr Blair's thinkies and cultural gospellers. The unwritten goal of 'youthism' is death, even though – as in Mexican ritual commemorations – its processions and exhibitions may be filled with exuberant, even hysterical, life. The stage management and scripting of the interval can (naturally) only be the work of the party in power. But the existential dilemma structuring its parade means that the party must be (or anyway try to be) the Party. That is, it must be a class substitute, a permanent-seeming elite which makes the end-time bearable. New Labourism had to justify its '-ism' by both being and showing that it was much more than a movement in Tony Benn's or Michael Foot's sense – an ethical crusade occasionally permitted into office. It had now mutated into a replacement patriciate, the armature of a further phase of British statehood, indelibly Great in both name and nature. While manoeuvring towards election-worthiness in the period 1994–97 it had been in reality transforming itself into such a cadre, an elite surrogate. So state-worthiness turned out to be the winged creature inside the dull chrysalis of Old Labour, still so fatally encrusted by Clause Four and the socialist old-stagers of the historic Left.

Thus in the early Blairite cultural atmosphere there was a deadly mixture of toxic influences, all already hostile to plain Painite radicalism. On one hand a wing of nostalgics, voicing elegiac regret for past socialist achievement, which they considered betrayed by the new administration. But their factional answer was self-evidently useless: resuscitation of the world now lost, or else invention of a new-model doctrine that could hardly help smelling and feeling awfully like the old one. Or, on the other hand, there was public relations postmodernism: smart devices and conceptual ways around 'outmoded' problems or attitudes. The latter could, all too easily, be made to include dreary old nation-state constitutionalism. If everything solid is melting into the air in that sense, why bother trying to pin it down again into an old-fangled constitution.

The prophetic admonition of *This Time* fell exactly between these current streams of thought. It clearly despised the tomb-cults of nostalgic leftism, yet insisted that real novelty depended upon pushing through a few plain-talking, 'old-fashioned' reforms, the sort eschewed historically by the Britishness of both Left and Right. As if by slide-rule design, therefore, Barnett managed to utter what almost nobody at that moment of time wanted to hear. The most significant political diagnosis of Ukania's *fin de siècle* passed practically unnoticed amid the court gossip, the hand wringing of defunct socialism, and the deranged sentimentality of William Hague's refugee Toryism.

One gets the sense from reading *This Time* that it will be small consolation to the author to have his prophecies fulfilled. While exhorting a new regime to get it right, he could not help cataloguing the ways it could go wrong. As he was writing, those ways piled up around him. By December 1997, when the book appeared, they loomed over him: the spectre of a less-than-half revolution, already contracting into its own compromises and conceits. Thatcher also had brought about a less-than-half redemption, which had ruined both her and her party. But this was even more serious. If, as I have argued, Blairism is really a last-ditch attempt at maintaining the United Kingdom by the formation of a pot-noodle ruling class, then nothing much can be visible beyond it. In different ways the nations of the old composite state are likely to end by throwing it off, and afterwards they will evolve into differing selves – the identities for so long occluded by the superimposition of Britishness. The fall from such an apotheosis can only be into depths as yet unplumbed. Whether or not the great renewal prospected in *This Time* was possible, its failure must leave us 'after Britain', in a genuinely post-imperial condition.

CORPORATE POPULISM

In the summer of 1998, Blair's government submitted an Annual Report to the people. The business-style title was deliberate. It began with a ten-point contract, and a full-page portrait of the Leader in his boardroom, the Cabinet Room at 10 Downing Street. 'Changing a government is like sweeping away the entire senior management of a company', he announced. In spite of critics saying 'this Government is more concerned with style than substance', he insisted it had made a good start. To underline boardroom confidence the Annual Report was full of full-colour illustrations of customers, with improbable messages scrawled over them: for example, a girl sitting in front of the Bank of England saying: 'I am pleased with changes that have been made and am looking forward to the improvements in the transport system.'

Barnett followed up *This Time* with an incisive account of the Report's assumptions. Unable to implement a new conception of the state, Blairism had defaulted to the model of a business company. Great Britain had in all earnest become what journalists had so often dubbed it in the past – Great Britain plc, 'the image of agency provided by big companies'. So socialism had lapsed finally into corporate populism. This is neither ancient subjecthood nor modern constitutional citizenship. It is more like a weak identity-hybrid, at a curious tangent to both. Voters are seen as customers (like the girl at the Bank of England), while the Party Executive 'manages party, cabinet and civil service as if they were parts of a single giant company whose aim is to persuade voters that they are happy customers who want to return Labour to office'.[8]

This is certainly better than mere deference. After all, customers are expected to object and criticize a bit (even if most don't, most of the time). But then, by taking their protests into account, the management normally expects to reinforce its own market share. It is 'the modernization of subjecthood', rather than a replacement for it. The sovereign crown gives way to the managing director and his unanimous executive board, devoted at once to profitability and (again in the Annual Report language) to Britain 'regaining its pride and ambition, at home and abroad' and telling the right story at all times: 'we are a great nation, filled with creative, innovative, compassionate people'. A great nation, but much more emphatically a capitalist one. Where the Poll Tax had failed, an Annual Report now appeared to be signalling success.

Since the national factor cannot really be costed, it is easily caricatured as a question of soulful romanticism or delusion. However, such commonsense is itself philistine. It fails to recognize something crucial. When Marks & Spencer betrays its customers the result is an annoyance; for a nation-state to let its citizens down can be a question of life or death, and not in war-time alone. Peoples have not 'imagined' such communities by chance, or out of irrational impulsions from the soul. Identities are not aesthetic choices but ways of existing, or of trying to exist better. This is the nation which has counted in modern, nationalist times, and it is not very like the portraits in Blair's Annual Report. The national-popular has generally been not so great, hard done by, struggling, threatened, at war, filled with not always 'creative' and sometimes angry people who think they can't afford so much compassion and look around for redemptive leadership. They turn to the nation of war memorials, oaths, poetry, sacrifice and mythic blood. It is the coiner of the phrase 'imagined community', Benedict Anderson, who has himself underlined the contrast between these two worlds in a recent essay, 'The Goodness of Nations'.[9] Democracies must feel themselves more than the data of annual reports, even euphoric ones. He uses an odd selection of things to make the point: the war memorial at New Haven, Connecticut; an episode of *The Simpsons*; the North Indian 'celibacy movement' – however, since he wrote, post-1997 Britain may already have supplied a more telling one.

The exemplification lay in the contrast mentioned earlier, between the popular reaction to the death of the Princess of Wales and New Labour's response – the reaction typified, about a year later, by this Annual Report. In late August to September 1997 the living (in Anderson's terminology) were in the streets and trying, however sentimentally and confusedly, to 'secure the Rightness of the country' and reorient it away from the shame of a rotten decade. A year later, they had become ridiculous illustrations in a kind of annual sales report. Populism had been recuperated and rendered respectable, and also given this small-minded and neo-liberal cast. Somehow business as usual had resumed, and normalcy been enhanced as never before, carrying forward much of Mrs Thatcher's *Geist* but with the added panache and excitement of a new sales drive. 'Britain' was buzzing once more, but the sound was a reassuring one: safety-first *redressement* rather than the unsettling music of republican constitutionalism.

ENGLAND AND ...

Just how safe the Annual Report country is meant to become was convincingly shown in early 1999. Although Scotland is the biggest problem for Blairland, Wales remains its closest neighbour. As well as the physical intimacy of a long north–south marchland, the two countries were historically united by early conquest and absorption. In the modern era that union of unequals has normally been awarded a strange name of its own, which appears in all legal documents where it is necessary to treat Scotland, Northern Ireland or other dependencies separately: 'England-and-Wales'. The term conveys a bare modicum of recognition with an associated stress on functional unity.

Whatever gestures may be needed elsewhere, here we have two who are truly as one.

The post-imperial return of Wales has therefore been very distinct from that of Scotland. It has resembled much more closely the typical ethno-linguistic trajectory of repressed nationhood – cultural mobilization directed towards nation-building and the eventual formation of a state. After Blair's electoral victory of 1997 a first Welsh Parliament was part of the pay-off. This was conceived quite differently from the Edinburgh one – as a first instalment, non-legislative body with executive control over the existing Welsh Office budget but otherwise limited to debating and offering advice. When it came to power, the Cardiff National Assembly members were to be consumers indeed.

But six months before the National Assembly met, the New England-and-Wales was already in trouble. The Assembly was conceived as a voice. But the trouble with allowing a national voice to speak up is that it may say something. Alas, speech can indeed be a form of action. It may even say (do) something disagreeable or (as in this case) something vexingly Welsh. Blair's reading of the old Austro-Marxist runes made cultural Welshness a blessing, naturally. But only provided it did not impinge upon the deeper peace signalled by the 'and' of England-and-Wales, whereby England will go on conducting the orchestra to which choir and harp would continue to make their traditional contribution.

In 1997 and early 1998, the Welsh Assembly plan was guided by the Welsh Secretary of State and leader of the Welsh Labour Party, Ron Davies. He led the successful cross-party campaign for a 'Yes' vote that reversed the decision of a previous referendum in 1979. Critics commented on the narrowness of the victory, compared to Scotland, but usually overlooked the huge shift in opinion it represented. Mr Davies himself never made this mistake. He frequently emphasized the continuing trend, as distinct from the arrangements of any one moment. 'Devolution is a process, not an event', was his way of putting this. Such an attitude might in time have boded ill for London but we shall never know, for Davies was prematurely struck down in the summer of 1998. It was not a London omnibus or a fatal illness that did for him, but scandal. The after-effects of an ill-understood fracas on Clapham Common forced his resignation as government minister, party leader, and almost certainly first Prime Minister of the new Assembly in 1999. This accident of history cast a revealing light on how devolution was regarded at Westminster.

For Blair and his Cabinet, devolution is emphatically an event, not a process. Nothing could have been done about Ron Davies. He came with the territory and had been responsible for the referendum success. But after his disgrace they were determined no other process-merchant would take his place: only the safest and most pliable of leaders would do – preferably someone impeccably British, and not too keen on the whole autonomy project. They had already had to change the British Constitution in Northern Ireland for the sake of a peace process, and were extremely disinclined to do so again to placate a new form of local government in England's oldest internal colony. A line had now to be drawn.

Once more, the actual phenomenon of Blairism at work pre-empts any conceivable satire. Suppose a hostile Tory commentator had written something like this, for example: 'Power-freak Blair, like the tin pot dictator he actually is, has chosen the most notoriously supine, cardboard figure in the Welsh Party to do his bidding, using every rotten trick in the old Party rulebook to get his own way while continuing to rant about reform and third-way democracy, just the way Eastern Europe used to be!' The writer would, alas, only have been saying in tabloid-speak what every other journalist was then to write in his or her own fashion. In *The Times* William Rees-Mogg put it this way:

> Wales has been insulted ... by the way in which the choice of Leader for the Assembly has been manipulated. When Tony Blair was chosen as Leader of the Labour Party, the trade union section of the electoral college operated 'one man, one vote'. When Alun Michael was chosen Labour Leader for Wales, the majority of the trade unions returned to the old block vote principle. Three trade union leaders were sufficient to cast the votes which gave Alun Michael his victory.[10]

Thus in the end a resounding majority of actual Welsh members voted for Rhodri Morgan, a well-educated dissident with trouble written all over him; and Mr Michael was wheeled on to centre-stage by traditional Old Corruption amid a tropical downpour of Radical and New Life protestations. As Rees-Mogg concluded, a great number of those whose vote was scorned in this way were likely to think 'devolution to Wales is a sham, a cover for the maintenance of English supremacy, enforced by the Blairite rigging of the leadership election', and turn to Plaid Cymru. Six months later, at the first elections, they did so turn.

It was not as if the government's attitude was confined to Wales. Although less crassly, analogous pressures were being applied in Scotland as well, and also in London, around the selection of Labour's candidate for the new Mayor. At the same time, a BBC *Panorama* documentary was broadcast on just this wider theme, and gave a convincing picture of a regime back-pedalling furiously to undo, or at least restrain, some of the awkward political consequences of devolution. A general counter-revolution was under way designed to preserve 'England-and- ...' everywhere else too, in approximately their traditional roles within the mystery play of Britishness.

ENGLAND'S ENGLAND

The core of the problem is that behind England's Britain there lies England's England, the country which has largely refrained from speaking, in large part because a British-imperial class and ethos have been in possession for so long of its vocal cords. A class has spoken for it. This is the evident sense in which England has been *even more* affected and deformed by imperial globalization than other parts of the archipelago. What might come 'after England'? In Julian Barnes' fantasy novel *England, England*, the whole sclerotic culture is transplanted in theme-park form to the Isle of Wight. Sir Jack Pitman, a business and media tycoon reminiscent of Robert Maxwell, 'reconstructs' Englishness on the island, complete with a downsized Westminster, Windsor, Manchester United, White Cliffs, imperialism, Harrods, whingeing, and so on. Invented tradition is everywhere, like 'the old English custom of downing a pint of Old Skullsplitter with a twiglet up each nostril'. 'We are not talking heritage centre,' he rumbles, 'we are offering *the thing itself.*'[11] This project is disastrously successful, and declares independence as a micro-state of truly corporate populism. Meanwhile, the real 'real England', a mainland thus deprived of its essence, sinks slowly backwards into time. 'Anglia' takes over from Britain. 'Quaintness, diminution, failure' create a different landscape, possessed by a new-old innocence and goodness:

Chemicals drained from the land, the colours grew gentler, and the light untainted; the moon, with less competition, now rose more dominantly. In the enlarged countryside, wildlife bred freely. Hares multiplied; deer and boar were released into the woods from game farms; the urban fox returned to a healthier diet of bloodied, pulsing flesh. Common land was re-established; fields and farms grew smaller; hedgerows were replanted. Martha Cochrane, who has abandoned Isle-of-Wight England for this arcadia, asks herself 'if a nation could reverse its course and its habits', but of course the answer is her own life in this country isolated from Europe and the world, in which items are again 'sold by the hundredweight, stone and pound for amounts expressed in pounds, shillings and pence', where 'four-lane motorways peter out into woodland, with a gypsy caravan titupping over the lurched, volcanic tarmac', and thunder has regained its divinity.

In *This Time* Anthony Barnett acknowledged the necessity of English reaffirmation as part of the new constitutional process. It has to be more than the rebranding advocated by Mark Leonard's Demos pamphlet *Britain*™ (1997), which would amount to acquiescing in Jack Pitman's featurescape. Such modernization of the theme park will not do, even given the *rayonnement* of the Millennium Dome. Nor is mongrelization a solution – that is, a self-conscious embracing of multicultural diversity in preference to ethnic majority nativism. That was argued for in Philip

Dodd's *The Battle Over Britain* (1996), where ethnic minorities and regional identities capture the dissolved essence of the nation and remanifest it as an inherently variegated democracy. But such a 'preference' has to be expressed. How can it be shown, without a constitutional mode of expression, and a prior redefinition of sovereignty? Democracy is not popular instinct or the simple prevalence of a majority: it is a constitution, or nothing, If this is not put first, then it will come last – and quite possibly too late.

In *The Times* of 12 February 1998 (coinciding with the devolutionary debacle in Wales) political editor Philip Webster announced something else. It was like a cloud the size of man's hand, in a diminutive box on page 10. But behind lies a great storm, gathering below the horizon: 'Beckett to give England a Voice'. Mrs Beckett's ministerial plan is to 'give England a distinct voice in Parliament after Scottish and Welsh devolution' by setting up a committee of English MPs. Although humbly named the 'Standing Committee on Regional Affairs', there is no one in Scotland, Wales or Ireland who will be deceived for a second by this: it was intended as the *de facto* English Parliament, convened on its own for the first time since 1546 (when Wales was formally incorporated). Since no provision was made for the majority in Blair's radical project, it will be forced to make its own, erupting bit by bit, using disguise and alias, proceeding through an obstacle course of tactical accidents and afterthoughts. The government's Modernization Select Committee was supposed to agree to Mrs Beckett's scheme and (the report concluded) 'will almost certainly back the idea'. Whether it became important does not matter for the purpose of our argument – evolution in that sense is unavoidable.

Populism like this finds its own way to nationalism, and there is nothing new or inherently harmful in that. However, it would have been better to plan for it, by putting a coherent, overall constitutional change first, rather than leaving it in this way to the uncertain and possibly uncontrollable last. An intelligible *Grundgesetz* would at least have paved part of the way towards equality of representation and treatment. In Austria-Hungary the Germans may not have wanted such equality, but at least they had the choice: nobody pretended they were not there, or 'took them for granted' in that curious sense which has dogged Englishness throughout the long decline of Britain. It is from this occlusion that the dominant scenarios of English futurity seem to have come. On one hand, we see the idea of reversion to an irrecoverable rurality, the natural wilderness or village condition of a post-British culture. On the other, we see the more advanced (but also more negative) longing for a virtual dissolution of identity into multiculturalism or 'Europe' – meaning here a broader identity-formation within which nations somehow disperse or painlessly cease to matter.

Blair's project makes it likely that England will reform on the street corner, rather than via a maternity room with appropriate care and facilities. Croaking tabloids, saloon-bar resentment and backbench populism are likely to attend the birth and to have their say. Democracy is constitutional or nothing. Without a systematic form, its ugly cousins will be tempted to move in and demand their rights, *their* nation, the one always sat upon and then at last betrayed by an elite of faint-hearts, half-breeds and alien interests.

9

Australia:
Anti-Politics for a Passive Federation[1]

Paul James and Ben Wellings

How did it come to pass that a public relations slogan became the oft-repeated 'truth' of the 2001 Australian Federation celebrations – 'with a vote, not a war, Australia became a nation'? This question goes to the heart of the problem of understanding the meld of official fervour and public passivity, and it carries through our theme of globalism, civic nationalism and war. Our argument is simple. The proponents of the celebrations were too insecure about the cultural legitimacy of the Federation, let alone the public passion for the institutions of the nation-state of Australia, to treat the year as an important period of necessary debate and reflection on core issues. A few public lectures aside, it became a year of parades and dubious slogans. One double-page advertisement in metropolitan weekend magazines asked the self-congratulatory question: 'What kind of country has always known the value of a vote?' The positive answer comes first: Australia, a nation formed not by revolution, but by an evolving democracy. The embarrassment comes later in the small print: 'The 1902 Commonwealth Franchise Act specifically withheld the right to vote in federal elections from Indigenous Australians and people of Asian, African, and Pacific Islander backgrounds.'[2] Thus there was a passing acknowledgement of problems in Australia's past, but it was always overridden by public relations messages. Why is it that most politicians and commentators so fervently defended the 2001 Federation celebrations in Australia against civic apathy? More importantly, why is it that they sought uncritically to gloss the past and embrace a shallow form of civic nationalism? 'Civic nationalism' is a form of nationalism that emphasizes the civic relationship of citizens to the state rather than that of embodied ties and passionate support for an ethnic or national community. It is often taken to be the most positive form of nationalism – and indeed it can be – however, as Tom Nairn attests in this volume it has its own ambiguities and contradictions. This chapter explores the strange year of the celebrations, a year of top-down organizational fervour and relatively passive public interest. Public spectacles occasionally drew huge crowds. However, the crowds were mostly there for the pageantry and colour, rather than because of a foundational attachment to the political process.

This issue of the managing and flattening out the deep tensions of national politics can be put in a larger setting. Before we discuss the Federation celebrations in detail it is worth relating two contextualizing developments. Both have their roots in the decades of the latter part of the twentieth century and earlier, but are being acutely felt now. The first concerns the impact of globalization. In the context of globalization, the *modern* nation-state faces a series of shearing tensions between state (polity) and nation (community), between the divided polity-community and the economy, and between sections of the 'community'. With globalization has come new kinds of movement of people – mass tourism and systematizing multiculturalism – as well as an accentuation of old kinds of movement – people attempting to escape disintegrating homelands. Moreover, the pressures of the postmodern layer of the economy, with its flows of capital and influence, flows that transcend the old regulatory boundaries of the nation-state, have meant that the government has moved to deregulate the economic sphere while reasserting the connectedness of the nation in the cultural sphere. Taken together, this means that the multicultural community called 'Australia' is fundamentally different from the Australia of a generation ago, and that sections of that community no longer trust the state to protect their way of life despite the government spending more on self-promotion than any commercial advertiser in Australia, including Coca-Cola.

The second contextualizing development that helps us understand the Federation celebrations concerns the slow crisis of liberal governance. Despite the naturalization of liberal democracy as the dominant form of governance across the Western capitalist world, politics has taken a further turn of the screw. In countries as diverse as the United Kingdom, Japan, Italy and Australia, an unnamed crisis now pierces deep into the variable formations of political life. It affects political cultures ranging from those of archaic stability and paternal authority to those of predicable volatility or civic passivity. In short, the realm of politics is increasingly treated with cynical suspicion. More and more, the standing of politicians has become dependent on two sources: the day-to-day routinized tidings from the stock exchange and occasional good cheer through massive public spectacles. In the United Kingdom, Tony Blair had a brief moment of return to public confidence with the birth of his son, but it only took a couple of weeks for political life to return to the slough of staged passion. And as it did, it even became common public sentiment that, in Blair's Britain, politicians and their spin-doctors were intent on colonizing public-private moments such as births, weddings and deaths. Voters still vote for him as, in other places, they vote for an Italian media-magnate indicted for mafia connections, or an American millionaire with a born-to-rule vacancy of mind. However, electoral choice is based increasingly on the feeling that the alternative candidate is worse, and electoral activity increasingly on the feeling that one should at least participate minimally in the political process. Yes, the liberal-democratic state continues to be sustained by an unassailable shadow-legitimacy. However, it survives in part because nobody can think of anything better. In other words, even though neo-liberal *state* continues to be afforded a passive meta-legitimacy, we face a legitimation crisis of *governance*.

In Australia, despite the 'success' of the Bicentenary celebrations, the faltering glory on the cricket field, and a couple of spectacular weeks during the 2000 Sydney Olympics, the loss of faith in conventional governance has been evident in the bathetic celebrations of the centennial of Federation. Of all the liberal-democratic states, perhaps only in the United States – paradoxically, a country, since Watergate, used to the chronic crises of state legitimacy – has the nation remained firmly tied to the Constitution. In Australia, by contrast to the US, however, Australians neither trust the documents that hold them together nor have the courage to enact constitutional change. This was beginning to be picked up by commentators nearly a decade ago. Hugh MacKay writes: 'The cynicism of the mid-1990s, however, is much more than a simple extension of what has gone before. Today Australians are trying to come to terms with the fact that the nature of politics itself has been redefined.'[3] In the cultural sphere it no longer even causes Australians comfort to know that it was the former hero of *Gallipoli*, Mel Gibson, who patriotically starred on the battlefields of North Carolina as the new *Patriot*. It is easy to see then how inadequate is the mainstream cultural-political response to this disenchantment. In the centenary year of Federation the film industry has given Australians reruns of *Crocodile Dundee* and the state has been featuring all-new advertisements for Australians' black-and-white past.

This chapter sets out to examine the selling of the spectacle of Australian Federation as part of an attempt to legitimize a nation-state that is increasingly perceived to have lost its way. The internal loss of faith in liberal governance and scepticism about the effects of the projected 'inevitable' rush to globalism is now being addressed, we argue, through an enhanced reflexivity about how to deliver civic education to national citizens. We are not suggesting that there is something essentially wrong with the renewed emphasis on civics or civic nationalism in itself – that is, apart from the blinding superficiality of this particular version. Be that as it may, we are arguing that the mainstream proponents of the celebration have entered a different and much more dangerous territory. Firstly, they have allowed it to be associated with a defensive white-blindfold attitude towards the darker side of Federation and a history of instrumental nation-building. Secondly, this pressure to re-legitimate the nation is not far removed from an associated market-driven imperative to sell the national image as an attractive brand name, both locally and globally. Thirdly, under conditions of scepticism about the state, civic learning is now being used as a form of civic management without putting in place the accompanying reform that would make that civic learning meaningful in the first place. Such reform would have to go far beyond tinkering with the Constitution, and it would have to eschew the current public relations-style approach. As we will argue, there are a number of conflicting themes that permeate this turn to civic management: the desire in a globalizing world to give the impression that Australia is reconciling multicultural diversity with a national identity; the pragmatic need to comfort the non-immigrant, older, white population and other potential One Nation supporters with the thought that they are important; and the vainglorious hope of addressing with mere words the sensibility of those who hold to the high ideal of reconciliation with Australia's Indigenous population. These themes are being addressed in the language of 'banal nationalism' – a nationalism that is reluctant to proclaim itself as nationalistic.[4] In the United States this issue is handled by slipping sideways to use the term 'patriotism'. In Australia, the official languages of 'multiculturalism' and 'nation-building' uneasily mix together, smoothing over real issues that divide Australia. The chapter begins by addressing the themes of civic management and ends by looking at the politics of the white blindfold.

MANAGING CIVIC EDUCATION

The slow crisis of politics in Australia became especially clear during the 1999 referendum on the republic. Most pro-republic campaigners were so concerned about being uncontroversial – and taking advantage of the continuing shadow-legitimacy of the state – that their proposals for constitutional 'change' sought to maintain the current system without more than a change of symbolic wording. In response, voters not only rejected the republican model on offer, but did so in part because it was perceived that politicians were going to run it. The outgoing secretary of the Australian Labor Party acknowledged this in a speech to party members in Canberra. Referring to the pre-referendum deliberative poll held in Canberra, he argued that, 'it took two days of fact and debate to convince citizens in overwhelming numbers to vote "Yes", but it took only two words to undo the good work. That's two days of education versus those two words – "politician's republic".'[5] This notion that the republican model on offer to the electorate was divorced from people's concerns was popularized by other politicians, including a senior member of the Coalition Cabinet.

The liberal political commentator Paul Kelly gave further expression to this general and enduring anti-politician sentiment when he claimed that both the Coalition and the Labor parties were a 'national disgrace'. This mainstream journalist went on to argue that the Australian people were the 'victims of a conspiracy – a betrayal by the political class against the best interests of the nation'.[6] 'Conspiracy' is a strange word in this context, because politicians rarely have time to connect systematically with others beyond the usual cabals of party politics. Nevertheless, the hype that permeates the centenary year of Federation has assumed a cultural commonsense, and the response to it can be seen as continuous with the uneven cynicism about Australian republicanism. Celebrating Federation thus presses on as an attempt by the political elites to reconnect a sceptical populace with the political processes and structures of governance.

During a speech at Corowa in 1993, then Prime Minister Paul Keating argued that:

> The Constitution was the foundation of a new national entity. Read in 1993, it is an uninspired and uninspiring document: complex, legalistic and virtually impossible to relate to contemporary Australian life. It was framed as a routine piece of nineteenth-century British imperial legislation ... We want Australians to consider the strength and weaknesses of their Constitution. We want them to debate the advantages and disadvantages of making our constitution more closely reflect Australian reality, Australian values, Australian hopes. In the end we want an Australian constitution in which Australians believe.[7]

Rhetoric aside, for Keating the republican push was not so much about enabling the people to reclaim the Constitution as contradictorily about teaching them to be good (postnationalist) citizens. Now, in the wake of the 1999 republican failure, what we are seeing is the desire to press on with this pedagogic agenda in the absence of actual constitutional reform.

Preparations for the Centenary of Federation were influenced by the Report of the Civics Expert Group, *Whereas the People*, published in 1994. The writers of the Report were struggling with very real issues. One of its main concerns was just this lack of connection between people and the structures of governance. The Report warned that 'a civic capacity depends on informed and active citizens and there is disturbing evidence that many Australians lack the knowledge and confidence to exercise their civic role. As we move towards the centenary of Federation, it is timely to reconsider and revive our civic inheritance.'[8] This push for increased citizen participation can be seen as a response to a declining sense of national cohesiveness and a fear of 'fragmentation'. It is hinted at in the Report through passages such as those that quote from Bryan Turner on the effects of post-industrialism and postmodernism on society:

> With the development of mass consumption and mass systems of information, social styles and cultural practices become mixed into an indefinite mass of tastes and outlooks. With this fragmentation of culture there also goes a fragmentation of cultural sensibilities, a mixing of lifestyles and the erosion of any sense of cogent

political project or coherent political programme, as the lives of individuals become increasingly merely a collection of discontinuous happenings.[9]

The sense of a cultural-political crisis is acutely portrayed here. However, in line with an assumption commonly held in the globalizing nation-states of the West, the Report argues that increased civic awareness offers the best method of reconciling the contradictions of diversity and collective identity. This then begins the slide from civic participation (an important issue) to our first theme of managed political integration: the later tendency by the Howard government to treat multicultural difference as a problem to be reconciled with words. It is a message repeated by the Department of Immigration in their report *A New Agenda for Multicultural Australia* (1999). This document lays particular emphasis on notions of civic duty and allegiance to the state. According to the Report, civic duty 'obliges all Australians to support those basic structures and principles of Australian society which guarantee us our freedom and equality and enable diversity to flourish'.[10] It sounds fine on the face of it – civic integration at one level that allows for continuing cultural difference at another is a positive principle – however, keep in mind that this Report came out within a setting that tends to treat the only sustainable differences as those that are emptied of politics or passion. This context can be illustrated by a government that became policy-paranoid about the incursions of illegal immigrants; an immigrant museum in Melbourne that reduced the immigrant experience to a series of individualized stories without political content; and an Olympic Games opening ceremony that reduced multicultural difference to a series of globalizing clichéd dances marked by different-coloured clothing.

The second theme of political integration concerns our suggestion that the Centenary of Federation is simultaneously an attempt to reintegrate Australia's Anglo population back into the system. The Australian Citizenship Council noted that 1999 was the 50th anniversary of Australian citizenship, an event, it argued, which is most closely associated with the naturalization of over 3 million immigrants since the end of the war. 'In this sense,' says the Council, as if words will make it so, 'the inclusive nature of Australian citizenship has been spectacularly successful.'[11] However, later on the same page it refers to another aspect to Australian citizenship, that 'in the consciousness of Australian-born people it has been somewhat less important as it has come to them automatically rather than by choice and has not in itself always been seen as a prominent national symbol'. In contrast to fears that it is the migrant population which will not fit into established 'Australian values', it now appears that it is the Australian-born community who is in need of integration into the Australian system. This is the very sentiment that was first forcefully expressed by She Who Cannot Be Named in her maiden speech in parliament in 1996: 'I am fed up of being told, "This is our land". Where the Hell do I go? I was born here and so were my parents and children … Like most Australians I worked for my land; no one gave it to me.'[12] The Australian Citizenship Council cannot refer to Pauline Hanson. In an oblique reference to the backlash in the bush, the Civics Expert Group suggest that the formal education system is not providing young citizens with the required amount of civics training, adding that the unskilled and those living outside the cities were amongst those particularly poorly served by the formal system. An ANOP study into civics education cited by the Report confirms that 'this lack of knowledge is widespread and thus the education target is essentially the whole community'. It is here that the civic nationalism of the centenary year of Federation plays a key role, although as we will see later it is this very ideology of overt nationalism that groups such as the Australian Citizenship Council want to disavow.

What then were the bases for the celebration preparations to proceed? According to the guidelines published for the Endorsement of National Centenary of Federation Projects, Events and Activities, the act of Federation was an event that 'not only changed the political landscape within Australia, but united its people and fostered economic, social and cultural stability'.[13] From this standpoint, with the state as the guarantor of the nation and its stability and prosperity, the National Council of the Centenary of Federation (NCCF) saw the anniversary as an 'occasion to reflect on the past, to appreciate our democracy, to acknowledge our history and experiences, to take pride in our achievements and look with confidence to the future'.[14] If it were all so simple, if it were all so much an already-achieved condition, then we might well ask what all the fuss is about. Why was so much money being poured into the celebration? Why was it spread over a year of interminable spectacles? And why was so much of the money spent on media advertising rather than on supporting grassroots-initiated activities?

The NCCF was created by the Council of Australia Governments (COAG) and received considerable financial and bureaucratic support from the federal government. The sum of $1 billion, designated the Federation Fund, was allocated to the commemoration of the Centenary of Federation. This is supposed to snowball. Much of the publicity was designed to attract corporate sponsors to augment the Commonwealth funding. Coles-Myer was the first major corporate sponsor of the Centenary, contributing $3 million to the funding of anniversary events and programmes. Coles-Myer CEO Dennis Eck said that the company, on behalf of its 157,000 employees was proud to support Australia's Centenary of Federation. He continued: 'the political stability and growth which has stemmed from Federation has provided a solid foundation for the Australian corporate sector to build on'.[15] A joint Federal Government and Australian Tourist Council initiative entitled 'New Century, New World, Australia 2001' was designed to assist

Australian business and government to invite their colleagues to Australia during the Centenary celebrations. This campaign was designed to lure the 'lucrative' business travel market and was intended to 'assist corporate Australia build international presence and influence partner, affiliates and clients'. All in all, the Centenary is supposedly 'great news for our tourism industry'.[16] In order to finance itself the government licensed its trademark Australia insignia to Australian manufacturers, including t-shirt makers and manufacturers of 'souvenirs, stationery, toys collectables, homewares and much much more'.[17]

In order to promote the aims of the Centenary, the NCCF co-ordinated a series of events and activities that began in 1999 with advertising campaigns and publicity stunts such as an around-Australia run by Pat Farmer, and continued throughout the entirety of 2001. Other national events for the year 2001 included:

- a parade in Sydney on 1 January from the central business district to Centennial Park. In Melbourne, the day began with a flag-raising ceremony 'proudly presented' by Australia Post™ and a march to the Tattersals™ federation arch followed by 'the great Australia day BBQ... proudly presented' by Carlton and United Breweries™. A total of $7.8 million was spent on Federation day;
- a service from Darwin on 19 February commemorating the first time that the Commonwealth's territory was attacked;
- a Federation Cultural Festival in Melbourne in May to celebrate the opening of the first federal Parliament (the AMP corporation's 'Journey of a Nation' travelling interactive expo had already passed through Melbourne by that stage);
- a National Flag Day in September celebrating the design of the official Australian flag;
- a steam-rail journey between Port Augusta and Perth 'to provide a reminder of the unity achieved through federation';
- a year-long international symposium entitled 'Holding Together', which was concerned with 'the question of the coherence of nation-states at a time when some countries – and Australia is a notable example – hold together, while others fall, tragically, apart'.

Not all the events were on a national scale, and there was a putative emphasis placed on 'participation' at a local level. State governments also played a role in the celebrations. However, despite the part to be played by the individual state governments in such activities, the encouraged consciousness was a Commonwealth-wide one. The official guidelines emphasized that in order to receive endorsement and funding, any activities needed to be 'national in nature'; a criterion that they asked should be 'considered carefully'. It must contribute 'to an enhanced sense of nationhood'.[18]

Inclusion is described as 'a priority' by the NCCF, with the programme being designed to embrace 'the first Australians, older Australians and new Australians'.[19] Here, linked to our first two themes as if they work as a chronological flow, enters our third theme: the need to address the issue of black and white reconciliation. Early in 1999, Deputy Chairman of the Council Rodney Cavalier and CEO Tony Eggleton went to the Northern Territory and met with Indigenous representatives from the media and business and community organizations. The possibility of 'original Australians' playing host to 'all Australians' at an 'inclusive arts and cultural festival in Central Australia' was discussed. This was part of the NCCF's commitment to 'examining ways Indigenous Australians can make a significant contribution to the centenary year'.[20] According to Mr Eggleton, 'Unlike the Bicentenary, which was not seen by many indigenous Australians as a cause for celebration, the Centenary of Federation commemorates the establishment of institutions to protect and promote the rights of all Australians.'[21] His words evidence the rhetorical papering over of structural problems and historical grievances. The notion of the Federal institutions as 'protector' of Aboriginal rights sounds lame in the context of the controversy still surrounding the *Bringing Them Home* report (1997), but for those with longer memories the term 'protector' conjures up a history of brutal control in state- and church-administered enclaves of pain.

WHO IS EDMUND BARTON?

These three themes, embracing first Australians, One Nation Australians and new Australians, are brought together around three activities: education, spectacle and advertising. It is the national projection of historical verities that was the greatest area of concern for the organizers. In the public sphere, civic education was reduced to learning a few facts and reinventing a few political hacks, with the focus divided between television advertising and developing the school curriculum. It is in this area that the concerns of the Civics Expert Group and later the Civics Education Group were most directly addressed. The History and Education Program was launched by the Council in July 1999 and was allocated $10 million from the Federation Fund. The aim of the Program was again to support 'activities which contribute to an enhanced sense of nationhood, and raise awareness of the 100-year journey of Australia's Federation'.[22] Council Deputy Chairman Rodney Cavalier stated that

Our research suggests that within the community there is a limited understanding of the significance of Federation and its centenary. More importantly, it does tell us that

when people are better informed about Federation and how it affected our way of
life in Australia, their interest in celebrating the centenary increases significantly.[23]

As with the Republic Referendum of 1999, education thus emerged as the
missing link for popular endorsement or participation in such projects.
From the beginning of 1999, a series of advertisements were released as
Community Service Announcements, the first of which focused upon the
community ignorance of the first Australian Prime Minister, Sir Edmund
Barton. The second advertisement continued in the pseudo-pedagogic vein,
filling in more gaps in popular Australian history by focusing on the role
of Indigenous sports people in Australia's early cricketing history. Overall,
the History and Education Program aimed to create histories for a popular
audience, especially young children and those living in remote communities.[24]
However, more 'expert' analyses of the Federation and its Centenary were
also encouraged in the fields of broadcasting, exhibitions, performances,
publications, multimedia/online productions, seminars, conferences and
research. A selective list of History and Education projects included the
following:[25]

- a multimedia/online production from the Australian Multicultural
  Foundation aimed at Australians from 'linguistically and culturally
  diverse backgrounds who may have little knowledge of key elements
  of the Federation story' ($250,000);
- 'Why Australians Matter', a three-part television production that
  commemorated 'the ingenuity and enterprise, environment and sense of
  humour that have helped forge the Australian character' ($200,000);
- a book and CD-ROM from the Office of the Status of Women that
  examined the economic and social history of women and their role in
  the formation of Australian nationhood ($105,300).

The prospect of research grants to cash-strapped academics also drew
the academy into the Centenary celebrations as part of the History and
Education Program. A lot of the work was concerned to make the history
exciting to contemporary jaded readers. For example, on the back cover of
a book entitled *Makers of Miracles*, containing essays on the 'Federation
Fathers', Di Langmore recalls:

When I studied Australian History at School and university, the 'Federation Fathers'
seemed to have none of the fascination of glamour of some other figures in Australian
history ... [they] looked old, bearded and often corpulent. They did not seem to
do much except sit around arguing and writing. If I had been told that Alfred Deakin
wrote passionate sonnets to his wife, that Edmund Barton was an affectionate father

to his six children, or that fat George Reid married a Tasmanian farmer's beautiful daughter ... I might have found them more interesting.[26]

A PECULIAR KIND OF NATIONAL BIRTH: THE WHITE-BLINDFOLD VERSION

Through this education process, a romantic-bland historical narrative of Federation begins to emerge which can be summarized as follows: prior to 1901 there was no Australian government, but rather six self-governing colonies peopled by British subjects. Although there were practical reasons for the six colonies to form a Federation, such as defence co-ordination, free trade and the central administration of immigration, there was by the later part of the nineteenth century 'a growing feeling of national pride'.[27] This growing sense of pride meant that 'almost everyone agreed that joining together in some way would be a good thing'.[28] In some countries, such unification required a war or revolution to be achieved, but in Australia, unification was a peaceful process, initiated by the people. On 1 January 1901, Australia became a nation via a ceremony in Centennial Park and Edmund Barton became Australia's first Prime Minister. Women soon gained the vote after Federation (proudly ahead of most countries) and even though Aboriginal people lost the federal vote in 1902 they still contributed much to the nation in terms of art, culture and human resources. Although most Australians at the time of Federation were from Britain, now Australia is much more diverse, which is one of its strengths and defining characteristics. Overall, the story is a 1950s schoolbook version of history – mythological in the worst rather than the best sense of the word.

Historical interpretations, particularly their contested debate, are vital to any national community. However, as Anthony Smith points out, whilst historians have often been some of nationalism's most trenchant critics, they often play a prominent role in the uncritical spread of the ideology itself. 'The history of nationalism,' writes Smith, 'is as much a history of its interlocutors as of the ideology and movement itself.'[29] The concern is to link the past with the present in a way acceptable to the demands and constraints of current political society. The existence of 'the nation' in the past is used as an attempt to justify its existence in the present, as well as projecting the nationalist vision forward into the future whilst mobilizing the population for certain economic or political ends. In the case of the Federation celebrations it was done through the misuse of history – pure and simple.

Aspects of Australian history since 1901 were enhanced or downplayed according to their usefulness to the pedagogic, integrative project of the Centenary organizers. The White Australia policy was barely mentioned, even though the Immigration Restriction Act was one of the first acts of the new Parliament in 1901. Neither were the assimilation practices carried out against the Aboriginal populations given more than a glancing acknowledgement. As noted above, the NCCF's official 'Federation Story' maintained that by 1901 'almost everyone' agreed that Federation was a good thing, despite the self-interest of the different states threatening to scupper the project, and the fact that an earlier referendum had failed. Unsurprisingly, the official story cannot be sustained consistently even across the various official sites. The Queensland government's version of the Federation Story is slightly different to the national website version. It emphasizes that support for federation in Queensland came most vocally for those in the north who hoped the whole idea might prove so unpalatable to the politicians in Brisbane that separation might ensue.[30] The 'growing sense of national pride' referred to in the NCCF's version of events also needs to be qualified. National pride in 1901, argues Luke Trainor, was intimately bound up with imperial grandeur, to which the events in Centennial Park gave ostentatious expression. Being part of the British Empire was seen as the best way to guarantee Australian trade links and provide defence from attack from rival imperial forces. For many nationalists in Australia the loyalty was to Empire, the Crown or the 'British race' as much as to Australia itself.[31]

The Centenary's supporters make much of the popular foundations of the Commonwealth of Australia. Donald Horne, board member of the New South Wales Centenary of Federation Committee and co-author of the Australian Citizenship Council's *Australian Citizenship in a New Century*, was irked by the 'Australia Week' celebrations in London during the summer of 2000. He feared that these celebrations in the former imperial metropole would send out the wrong signals, namely that 'Australia became a nation as a by-product of British generosity'.[32] Similarly, historians such as Helen Irving argued that 'the people' were 'an essential part' of Federation, and John Hirst suggested forcefully and dubiously that Federation was a process of the people all along.[33] It is not hard to find evidence to counter their positions. Stuart Macintyre, for example, shows convincingly that Federation was not a hugely popular event. 'Australians,' he says, 'can hardly be accused of rushing into Federation'.[34] He is sceptical of the principle, advanced at Cowra in 1893, that 'the cause should be advocated by the citizen and not merely politicians'. The author of this principle was himself a politician and the make-up of the subsequent Constitutional Conventions leading to Federation were overwhelmingly drawn from the political elites. Macintyre continues: 'the politicians, having impugned their own calling, called forth a voice that could restore its legitimacy, they reinstated the people as a disembodied presence, capable of an altruism that they themselves could not achieve'.[35] Even *The Bulletin* noted popular apathy to the outcome of the Federation negotiations:

The fact has slowly dawned on [*The Bulletin*] that nine-tenths of the population takes no real interest in the future Australian nation, in the alleged glorious destiny of this continent, in the marble metropolis which is to be the political centre of the Commonwealth, or in any of the other abstract glories of a united Australia.[36]

The contemporary evidence, particularly outside of Sydney, was equivocal. Roslyn Russell and Philip Chubb note that, despite the 'stupendous culminating occasion' in Sydney's Centennial Park, enthusiasm elsewhere was more muted. In Hobart the crowd was 'not a large one [and] neither was it very demonstrative'. In Brisbane, 'maybe it was the heat' that meant that 'there was a lack of enthusiasm on the part of the public', whilst in Melbourne 'everybody felt happy, but nobody felt inclined to make a noise about it'.[37] However, in writing this apathy for the official story, little noise is taken to be an indication of true Australianness. Present-day enthusiasts use the pre-Federation plebiscites of 1898 and 1899 as indications of popular support for Federation. These events are used as evidence that 'Australia was created with a vote, not a war – in peace, not in anger'.[38] Russell and Chubb's history of Federation, *One Destiny!*, repeats the same theme of a 'nation brought into being peacefully'.

It is the apparently peaceful nature of Australian unification that is said to mark it out from other nations' experience of nationalism, notably the violent revolutions or wars of unification that brought Italy, Germany and the United States into being. In the Centenary happy narrative, this peaceful evolution into nationhood is something that characterizes Australian nationalism today, thus making Australia a 'tolerant' society. The Australian Citizenship Council also picks up this theme about the special character of Australian nationalism. However, the Council goes further, arguing that Australian nationalism is not nationalism really at all – it is what we have throughout the book been calling 'postnationalism'. Thanks to increased civic awareness Australia is supposedly about to leave such an ideology as (classical modern) blood-and-flag nationalism behind. Australia is compared with the United States:

Right from its birth in the Declaration of Independence, the United States defined itself not through the new form of nationalism, but in its political beliefs and institutions ... Australians have not gone that way. Instead they have made 'national' claims – about the kinds of people they are, even about the physical land Australia is ... Now, even at times of celebration, Australians do not characterize themselves by their political system primarily, or at all. They have shown almost a complete lack of interest in looking for the distinctiveness and the comparative success of the civics institutions that frame their citizenship ... The result is a strange situation in which one of the greatest elements of Australian potential – its 'polity' – is one of those that is least spoken about.[39]

The Council was quick to point out that their promotion of Australia's polity as a focus of allegiance and source of pride is not nationalism because it is underpinned by civic values:

> The values are not nationalistic. They are the very opposite. They proclaim that Australians can live together in peace and have a strong sense of community within their country even though they are different from each other in many ways. In this we could still set something of an example to the world.[40]

The Council argued that Australia can transcend nationalism and national identity and move onto something nobler, which in turn will become a source of Australian pride. However, to do this it must rely on the promotion of nationalism in the Centenary of Federation.

Despite a year-long advertising campaign reminding viewers that 'Australia was created in peace and not in war', it is also relatively easy to show that this was not necessarily the case. For example, somebody forgot to tell the Department of Veterans' Affairs what the official line was on the matter. Its own publication notes that 'from its very inception the Australian nation was involved in war'.[41] At the time of Federation, the Australian colonies were involved in the war in South Africa. Ultimately, the colonies and Commonwealth would send an official number of 16,124 men and women across the Indian Ocean, of whom 518 would die – more than the total number of Australians who died in Vietnam.[42] Referring to the South African war, Lord Tennyson, the Governor of South Australia, stated at his Federation address in Adelaide that 'the Empire had been federated on the battlefield, and the charter of Federation had been sealed by the blood of many heroes'.[43] Defence considerations had been an important catalyst for federation, with Australia having a single military commandant since the 1890s. It was believed that a united Australia would be better and more efficiently able to defend itself, and the empire. Indeed, one of the first acts of the Commonwealth was to dispatch troops to South Africa. In March 1901, Whitehall cabled Melbourne stating that the 'patriotic action' of the New Zealand government in sending 1,000 men to fight had strengthened the imperial government's hand in bringing the war to a swift conclusion. The cable continued: 'His Majesty's Government do not desire to press for further offers, but if your government should wish to follow the example of New Zealand, we should gratefully accept reinforcements of 2000 men on the same terms and conditions as last.'[44] Edmund Barton cabled back two days later: 'Mr Barton presents his humble duty [to] gladly send reinforcement of 2000 men to South Africa, as desired ... .'[45]

Furthermore, the entire European settlement of Australia rests upon an unspoken internal colonial war that supported the appropriation of

Aboriginal lands. The Commonwealth of Australia inherited control over lands won from the original owners during more than a hundred years of conflict, resulting in 2,000 settler deaths and an estimated 20,000 Aboriginal deaths.[46] Such statistics make it harder to argue that Australia was indeed founded in peace and not in anger. If, as the Centenary narrative implied, there had been no internal war, then there are more problems for the Commonwealth's legitimacy. If Australia had not been won by conquest then neither had a treaty with the original inhabitants been enacted, nor had the original inhabitants invited the Commonwealth onto their lands. If this is the case, then the very legitimacy of the Australian state is called into question in international law – that is, unless we still hold to a doctrine of *terra nullius*.

CONCLUSION

Through the centenary year of Australian Federation, we saw the popularizing of a distorted version of history and politics. Intentional or otherwise, this official story sustains the shadow legitimation of the liberal state by conflating its creation with the birth of 'the Australian nation'. According to the emerging Federation narrative, it is the Commonwealth that gives the Australian nation its full expression and guarantees its prosperity and continuity, framing Australian citizenship and multiculturalism. Unfortunately, the terms and style taken in reinforcing this message of Australian nationalism are shallow and unsustainable. Writing a decade years ago, John Hutchinson looked to assess possibilities of developing a forward-looking kind of nation-state, critically aware of its past and actively working through contemporary realities of deep multicultural and indigenous differences. The last chapter of his book *Modern Nationalism* described Eastern and Western Europe as a lost cause in this respect and turned to the New World immigrant societies of Australia, Canada and the United States to ask the question, are they 'pioneers of postnationalism or insecure parvenus?'[47] We will ask that question of the United States in Chapter 17, but at the moment a judgement of Australia leaves us feeling pretty depressed. On the evidence of the Centenary of Federation celebrations, Australia has gone backwards since 1988. Despite important counter-trends, it remains an insecure island-nation of bland defensiveness – the insecure parvenu. Now this defensiveness is caught between a posturing concern for spectacle, continuous with nineteenth-century 'official nationalism' and an awkward defensiveness. Australia under the Howard government has developed a new awkward-looking self-consciousness, a certain kind of postnationalism that now feels comfortable in using the images of everyone from encomiasts, creative consultants to war correspondents – in fact anyone who'll take a snapshot – to project an image of itself to itself. John Howard's embarrassing early morning walks in baggy shorts have come to signify a new strutting on the world-stage. The period since 2001 has confirmed this assessment. Having become excited about its peacekeeping role in East Timor, Australia is now caught in a web of intrigue and counter-intrigue as it follows two other insecure nations into the Third World War – otherwise known as the War on Terror. With a war, not a vote, Australia has entered the twenty-first century.

10
Late Britain:
Disorientations from Down Under[1]

Tom Nairn

Down, down, down. Would the fall never come to an end? 'I wonder how many miles I've fallen by this time?' she said aloud ... 'I wonder if I shall fall right through the earth! How funny it'll seem to come out among the people that walk with their heads downwards! The Antipathies, I think.'

Lewis Carroll, *Alice's Adventures in Wonderland* (1865)

Everyone arriving in Australia from over the equator knows the seasons are different – leaving spring to discover autumn, and so on. That much is discounted in advance, and is actually quite easy to get used to. But there are deeper levels of disturbance as well, often left unmentioned, perhaps because they are harder to pin down. Regular jet-plane travel has made East–West 'lag' familiar, and accustomed travellers to the idea of the body clock. However, what is far harder to accept is the upset of the body compass. The sun tells you each morning that south has become north and (therefore) that the felt east has turned into the west, and vice versa. As if this were not enough, another sort of disorientation sets in as you leave the airport. Reading the newspapers in the taxi into town, well-known labels show up, like the 'Labor Party', 'the Liberals', 'asylum-seekers' and bothersome swinging voters in 'marginal constituencies'.[2] The trouble is, they mean something intensely different, and surface familiarity merely renders that difference all the greater; it is a quite alien state and social fabric that is deploying such counters (though frequently beneath a camouflage of mythic affiliation or descent).

Another unexpected side-effect of this *dépaysement* can be disruption of retrospect. One's own past suddenly feels odd as well. Whole tracts of it seem questionable, even amazing. This effect is particularly powerful in looking back at the United Kingdom general election of 2001, held a few months before the Australian election.[3] From Melbourne, the entire episode now feels like a Lewis Carroll dream. Were such events possible? I mean, can there actually *be* in that other world such a country as the one variously billed as 'Britain', 'Great Britain' or 'The United Kingdom of this and that', where around 20–25 per cent of the population restored sovereign power to the White Rabbit Anthony Blair with an overwhelming majority? It is where Her Majesty's Opposition then did him the favour of scuttling away down three different rabbit-holes simultaneously, thus awarding him the possibility of a decade or so of office *after* his present one expires – that is, until the Weapons of Mass Destruction sexing-up scandal took hold. It is a place where history has fallen down from tragedy, and passed far beyond farce into realms of previously unknown abasement.

THE VANISHING CONSTITUTION

The place to begin a journey to explore these mysteries is the election results map, as published by the BBC on 8 June 2001. This dramatic document followed on from its main webpage: 'Vote 2001', headed 'The Vote That Never Was: A Labour Landslide and the Tory Leader Resigns'. So, *no change there then.* That same page bore no less than four images of the toothily grinning Blair, in one of which he is kissing a baby (his own), alongside the astonishing statistics of triumphalism: 'Lab 413; Con 166; LibDem 52; others scarcely visible'. The results map that followed had the conventional colours, red for New Labour, blue for the Conservatives, and assorted shades of green or yellow for the Liberal-Democrats and Sinn Fein. But a glance at this showed a picture wildly at variance with the BBC's official complacency – in fact, it showed a picture nobody would have dreamed of ten years ago.

There is just one Tory-blue patch outside England, in the area of southwest Scotland (the constituency of Galloway and Upper Nithsdale). This was described by the BBC as 'the most agricultural constituency in the British Isles', and also the one worst affected by the foot-and-mouth epidemic that accompanied the election campaign like a howling Greek chorus. Resentment at government mishandling of the crisis, plus some feuding in the ranks of the Scottish National Party, gave Peter Duncan a 74-vote Conservative majority over his SNP opponent. This was universally viewed as an unrepeatable accident, even by Conservatives.[4] It was that rare event, an exception which actually proved a rule – the rule here being that British Conservatism has abandoned (or been abandoned by) the peripheral countries of the United Kingdom. The initial desertion took place in 1997, and 2001 simply confirmed it.

The former 'natural ruling party' of Great Britain has given up, in other words. Toryism in that old sense is extinct in Scotland and Wales, as well as being on the retreat in England.[5] (Of course it was never present in Northern Ireland, but I will come back to that later.) What's more, I cannot resist drawing attention to another overlooked internal frontier of the Old Country: the Tamar River separating Devon from Cornwall. This part of the UK is now also 'Tory-free', and thus part of the Celtic-affiliated common trend.

However, the 'red' of New Labour still pervades throughout the country (except in Ulster). This is what now holds the United Kingdom together. The land of the White Rabbit depends upon the Crown and a single political party – that manic grin again and its *overwhelming* majority. But what of the British Constitution? Surely the indestructible fabric still stands, unaffected by the eddies and the accidents of mere parties? Well ... no, it does not. What fabric there was has quietly gone into the dark, for reasons I will go on to explain. All that remains of it is the toothy smile of Lewis Carroll's Cheshire Cat, the grin which hung round in the air long after the actual animal had vanished. 'The Cat vanished quite slowly, beginning with the tail, and ending with the grin', wrote Carroll, '... wasn't that a curious thing, a Grin without any Cat? Would you like to see one?' British voters see one all the time now – it appeared, for instance, in an extraordinary war dance at the 2001 Labour Party Annual Conference shortly after a declaration of war on Afghanistan, and in Blair's 2001 conference speech on world hunger, hardship and general badness.

The British Constitution was only a virtual Rock of Ages. Its true being consisted in the belief of its worshippers, and the way they acted out such convictions. Its chief boast was that it did not need to exist in any vulgar, modern sense – written down for the rabble to peruse. No, it was simply the agreed power structure, carried forward by 'conventions' and the profoundly shared attitudes of a class-structured system. It was carried forward, and then, in the nineteenth century, crystallized as world empire.[6] These shared assumptions covered all the territories involved, and were consecrated by the Crown – enabling different parties and policies to succeed one another by tacit agreement rather than formal 'holy writ'.

But there is a downside to this system, heavily underlined by the last UK election. Once the shared psyche and conventions evaporate, *there is nothing left.* From that bourne, no traveller will return indeed. The cat can never come back to retrieve his smile. All that the great repositories of statehood then do is *pretend* that he has not really gone – 'put on a show', as it were. That is what 'Blairism' mostly is. Its British 'Third Way' is pantomime smoke and strobe lights, designed to bolster audience conviction and keep them in their seats for as many repeat performances as may yet be possible. The non-written system depended upon *the system:* in truth, that is, an actually working two-or-more party and policy continuum capable of alternation, and embracing the whole turf. Without that embrace, the sole remaining continuum is just New Labour's increasingly hysterical one-party performance, with the Crown wobbling uneasily on top of it.

As time passes, this performance has to be constantly intensified – it demands ever more primary colours and tabloid decibels. Reckless populism becomes its substitute for both democracy and reform. Thus the Millennium Dome 'tent' at Greenwich was a mega-circus meant to hammer home all-British rejuvenation and conviction. However, it proved the most expensive flop in entertainment history, largely because (as most commentators agreed) it was impossible to think up suitable 'content' for the display. The wellspring of Britishness was exhausted, and nothing worthy could be found to install under the great common roof. Such a failure should have brought the common government down. But instead, the guilty party was awarded a landslide election victory. How was this possible?

THE NON-VOTING PARTY

It was possible because the non-will of the people prevailed. Society had, in the interval, resigned from the political state. There had already been ominous signs of growing indifference in the 1997 election, when only 28.6 per cent of the enfranchised had supported New Labour. This was a mere two points behind what *Guardian* journalist David Mackie has called 'the Non-Voting Party'.[7] But as the 2001 election approached, Mackie was predicting that the Non-Voting Party might be set for its best result ever. Never was prophecy so quickly borne out. The NVP won a sensational 15 per cent victory over its New Labour opponents: 40 per cent as against 25 per cent. It had been widely feared that participation might slump down from the seventies into the lower sixties; in fact it fell to 59 per cent – clearly within sight of current US norms.[8] By 2005, if present trends continue, the UK will quite clearly be leading the West in apathy.[9]

I will spare readers any references to postmodern and other *Zeitgeist* alibis about this phenomenon. It goes without saying that the profound conceit of New Labourism found no culprit other than the universal decay of Western culture, and the shifting sands of globalization. It was simply inconceivable that such a lapse might be due to the blinkered, parochial ineptitude of one particular out-of-date state struggling to survive – to remain its grand and integral self, as it were, with the maximum of flourishes and a minimum of changes. Blairite blabbering about their 'revolution' has been a way of avoiding the constitutional changes that could have had the effect of normalizing Great Britain, of making changes that acknowledged contemporary realities; these would not have constituted a 'revolution' exactly, but would have involved a number of quite mundane modernizing reforms. But this is what no true Westminster junkie can stand: being reduced to the ranks of the ordinary, the unexceptional, those abandoned by a deity whose attention has been unfairly (but permanently) distracted elsewhere.

Historically, United Kingdom identity has rested upon a purloined Hebraic confidence in 'Providence', that sense of occupying a central throne as heaven's chosen ones. The subsequent passage from the ranks of Elect to those of the un-Chosen has been, subjectively speaking, a terrible experience. Divine meaning snatched away is the bitterest of medicines – in some ways possibly worse than military and political defeat. The losers of the Second World War reinvented themselves as the non-imperial principals of a great recovery. But for a state elite facing cosmic demotion such ruptures have no appeal: better to hang on to the greatness one has, or to try and refloat it by association with a successor Elect like the USA.

FOR WORSE, FOR BETTER: THE SELLING OF BRITAIN

Surely, some will object, Great Britain cannot be doing all *that* badly? Government PR regularly offers glowing tableaux of a prospering and forward-looking country. Beset by problems, of course – like the rural apocalypse of foot-and-mouth, the failures of the National Health Service, the near-collapse of the national rail network, the intelligence crisis over Iraq – yet simultaneously striving to improve things, and not wholly without success? The objection is quite justified. The publicists of Britland should be accused of exaggeration, rather than outright mendacity. The real trouble is that they are talking about something quite different. What they normally choose to depict is the progress of United Kingdom *society*, rather than the downfall of its *state*. The latter goes on being 'taken for granted', and is deemed immutable. However, the stories of society and state have now become not simply different, but widely divergent. British 'civil society' (a convenient shorthand) has indeed been prospering in the circumstances of post-Cold War globalization – albeit very unevenly, chaotically and with pathological side-effects.

But then, such contradictions are standard. Free trade capitalism was ever thus. It was immortally described that way in a great poem of 1848, *The Communist Manifesto*. Thus a southeast England survey in 2001 showed people on the whole rather cheerful about their prospects and looking forward to better times 'for me and my family'.[10] But the survey also indicated that the same people were quite indifferent to politics in any broader or ideological sense, and if anything hostile to, or cynical about, leadership and state. It depicted a population severed from the ruling class of former times, rather than 'liberated' from it – if liberation is taken to mean a new start, or a more representative or democratic replacement. 'They' had disappeared and, as with Mrs Thatcher, nobody wanted them back. The controlling caste has vanished. Yet only self-serving poltroons and chancers seem to have stepped into their shoes – and somehow nothing could be done about this. New Labour self-servers were merely less corrupt (as yet) than their predecessors, the implication being that such was the way of all political flesh, curable only by some future popular mutiny, or rejection shock (that is, not by political reform, let alone 'revolution').

Thus, things getting better at an individual or atomized level serves to reinforce their getting steadily worse – I would argue, incurably worse – at the *Alice in Wonderland* level of Her Majesty, Black Rod, the House of Lords and the Mother of Parliaments. The 2001 election was a new low in this disintegrative process. The existing electoral system, a first-past-the-post conjuring trick, now functions like a wedge splitting off the social order from a genuinely decadent state elite. The latter's decadence comes not simply from failure, or from the series of disasters that have shaken the British realm over the last decade. It is rooted in the impossibility of that realm's embedded will and enduring purpose. However, do not take my word for this. Take Tony Blair's. When he got back to London from the Nice Conference of the European Union at the end of 2000, he reported to Parliament:

> It is possible, in our judgement, to fight Britain's corner, get the best out of Europe for Britain and exercise real authority and influence in Europe. That is as it should be. Britain is a world power. To stand aside from the key alliance – the EU – right on our doorstep, is not advancing Britain's interests; it is betraying British interests ...[11]

Greatness is all. For a world-power, making use of Europe is a necessity, but remains one tool among others. There is no question of joining in the sense of merging, or identifying the national interest with such a wider project. No question (that is) of being like the Danes, the Irish, the Portuguese, the Italians or the Scots (forever whingeing about 'Scotland in Europe'). Different standards apply. But, again, do not take my analysis for it. *The Economist*, that most unbending critic of Blairism, commented two days after the July 2001 vote:

> Mr Blair is no 'declinist'. He believes that Britain can lead in Europe, not just take its place as a loyal member ... He does not accept that leading in Europe implies weakening Britain's bond with America. He argues that Britain has a 'pivotal' role in world politics (and) Mr Blair relishes cutting a dash on the world scene.[12]

'Declinism' is old hat – the long period of ill-managed retreat and graceless withdrawal from the 1950s to the late 1970s. Mrs Thatcher put a stop to that in 1979. The 'Great' was drummed back into Britain again, by a combination of neo-liberal economics and iron determination: decline gave way to outright redemption. Soon the formula appeared to be confirmed by the foundering of the Soviet imperium and the misfortunes of social democracy in the West. British 'redemptionism' gained impetus in the early years of globalization, and won over Labour completely when Tony Blair became leader in 1994.

The problem is that decline management was a possible strategy, though profoundly uninspiring; and making a political break, building a reformed

UK system, federal or confederal, might also have been possible, albeit difficult. But redemption is not possible at all – or at least, it is possible solely on a basis of pretence and increasingly absurd assertiveness, or of self-important servility towards a helpful outside force. There is no real way in which 'Great' can be re-enacted or maintained, or even convincingly displayed (as the Dome farce revealed). On the other hand, the inherited institutional structures of the state can still *prevent* changes from taking place. This is what Westminster politics is now about, and what the 2001 election was about. Triumphalist immobilism is the leitmotif of end-game Britain.

IMMOBILISM AT WORK: LIVING IN LATE BRITAIN

The laws of redemptory immobilism work like this. (Here I am merely recapitulating long and sobering analyses made by academics such as Jim Bulpitt and others.[13]) The 1688–1832 state was an aristocratic creation devoted, like the Venetian oligarchy of early modern times, to the exploitation and supervision of a sprawling commercial empire. It evolved a two-party 'electoral dictatorship' that valued centralized stability above all else. There was no other way of controlling the disparate, sometimes centrifugal, elements of such a ragbag enterprise. The home archipelago was disparate enough, and as the maritime imperium swelled in the nineteenth century a formidable institutional core became both consort and controller – the world conceit of the Imperial Crown, and of Blair's present-day determination to preserve its 'pivotal' role.

As Paul Kennedy's chronicle *The Rise and Fall of the Great Powers* shows, no other former world power has ever been able to withstand defeat or revolution (or both).[14] But Great Britain was spared this standard fate by its 'finest hour' in 1940.[15] However, escaping that fate has invited another and less spectacular one, which Kennedy does not encompass. It has produced the tragi-comic parameters of a sole survivor, an albatross-state forever unwilling to settle for life as a coastal seagull. One should also keep in mind how strong are the self-reproducing traditions of such an institutional or 'civic' nationalism. It may be that in some sense such traditions are always 'compensating' for the absence of British ethnicity; but in that case, the implication must be that civic-political identity, at least in some places and over important periods of time, may be understood as being more powerful than the ethnic variety.

Post-1979 Britain shows a power system bent on remodelling society in order to preserve or reconstruct such an inherited 'identity'. This project, which of course became Blair's self-conscious 'Project' in 1997 discussed previously in Chapter 8, may be hopeless in the longer term, but it still keeps going today for a number of important reasons. One of these is economic. Most arguments about late Britain have concentrated on neo-liberal economics, and the acceptance by New Labour of Mrs Thatcher's deregulatory programmes of the 1980s. Though justified in its own right, this focus has also served to divert attention from the *national* conjuncture involved. One particular, indeed genuinely unique, state problem was at least temporarily resolved by Thatcher's resolve to swim so strongly with the tide of resurgent post-Cold War capitalism. She was quite right to see 'there was no alternative' to this – and Blair in his turn had to accept and even hype up the only show in town. The only show (that is) for this threatened polity. The initial decade of contemporary globalization generated plenty of alternatives elsewhere: in Scandinavia, for example, or in Ireland. Smaller democratic countries almost immediately benefited from the great thaw, and their souls as well as their budgets were the better for it. At the same time, the European Union, essentially a co-operative of such nobodies, prepared for longer-term advance with a common currency. But not Great Britain. The latter retained the main economic armature of its former imperium, in the form of the City of London, whose institutions of trade and exchange had in the 1970s managed a somewhat lumpy transition from the Keynesian welfare state to globalization. The umbilical cord had been strained but not broken. And then, in the 1980s and 1990s, the City found new prosperity in a recreated free trade universe. The United Kingdom state had never depended upon industrial leadership, let alone 'supremacy'. Its continuity lay with the pre-existent 'globalism' of finance and trans-oceanic exchange, a fabric, which, of course, was now flourishing as never before, and has provided the lifeline for British state continuity.

Certainly, a transition of elites took place within that development, from aristocracy to the present stratum of exchange billionaires, mediocrats, ennobled pundits and duly rewarded civil servants and generals. But this change was largely favourable to the preservation of the archaic state and all its trappings. Only industrial capitalism had ever been guilty of democracy and conspiracy with the plebs. By contrast, financial capital was either tolerant of or positively favourable to the pomp and circumstance of monarchy, populist pantomimes and pageantry politics. It was awfully keen on the Millennium Dome, for example, and cruelly disappointed by its unexpected failure and abandonment. It is 'outward-looking', since this is where its business interests lie, and hence quite well disposed to outward-posturing and to all-purpose busybody governments pretending to be pivots. For an exchange nexus, 'Great' just means being everywhere at once, and having a right to have its finger in every pie. Occasionally attired these days as 'cosmopolitanism', the essence of Britishness lies in being far too big for tiresomely national boots. But that has suited the new, globally adapted southeastern England quite well. The City always detested 'little England'; now its hegemony has acquired the splendid post-imperial costumes of globalization, as well as a New party of political servitors.

SOVEREIGNTY: THE IRON LUNG

The preservation of 'sovereignty' is crucial for the servicing of this system. And this implies reliably vast majorities, which entails, despite earlier hints to the contrary, keeping the lethal 'first past the post' election system. This alone can conjure crushing majorities from shrinking minorities of voters, and thereby guarantee decisive authority: no fudging and fumbling coalition would have a hope of redeeming the British day and securing Greatness. Democracy would have it by the throat in no time. This is why the object of late-British constitutional reform is to prevent constitutional reform. Blairite 'modernization' has aimed at tidying up the inherited anachronisms of both government and state, the better to conserve them. It aims to replace the old blue-blood House of Lords with a new 'appointed' House of Lords: aristocracy reborn as cronyism. New Labour is also keen to see Prince Charles installed as the new-century monarch, one capable of finally dispelling republicanism. Thus the ancient unwritten customary order will continue indefinitely, without tiresome disturbance of the British identity ('all we hold dear', and so on). The 2001 election was an outstanding victory for this campaign of systemic obfuscation and reaction.

Twenty-five years ago, the late Lord Hailsham suggested that Britain was becoming an 'elective dictatorship'.[16] Party rule had turned into Cabinet rule, which then mutated into dominance by the leader. Elections would be transformed into referendums, staged by leadership whim, at which the people would periodically renew its prostration – whether eagerly or sullenly did not matter very much. The *effective* electorate would shrink to the small number of 'floating voters' who had to be cajoled or bullied into casting their ballots, thus maintaining the credentials of the Mother of Democracy. If most voters abstained from that honour, it would be a pity, but not fatal. If people were not bothered about 'politics', it could only be because they were content with their lot. And this was, in fact, the most widely pronounced verdict on Britain's non-voters of June 2001: a perverted idea of 'the politics of contentment'.

These rules of the redemption polity are of course self-perpetuating. Simple majority voting supports a two-party order, which makes it practically impossible for new or third movements to muscle in, which in turn reinforces the two-party order. Voter fatalism intensifies, as does acceptance of the regime and its stay-as-we-are political identity. Elections become periodic reaffirmations of the faith, and proofs of the futility of constitutional reform. In this quaint Ukanian version of the 'end of history', only egg-headed fanatics fail to see that Britishness is forever, in the best of all possible worlds. *Society will* go on changing, naturally, and this is why think-tanks have replaced stately homes as the shrines of British *mentalité*. Mrs Thatcher discovered the things, and Blair has elevated them into a clerisy. Their task is to generate smart *policies* that will ensure painless change (painless to the state, naturally). Who would deny that politics has to be about policies? However, what the politics of immobilism encourages is the *fetishization* of policy making, as utterly brilliant ways of going round in neo-liberal circles and 'delivering' the minimum of alteration needed to stay out of trouble, with the maximum of profit for whoever assists 'the Project'.[17] Westminster has a practically bottomless wardrobe of stuff to help with these charades: David Hume's waistcoat, Edmund Burke's breeches, W.E. Gladstone's old watch, Churchill's finest-hour hat – all regularly deployed whenever the New falters or starts to rub off.

GREAT STATE, TROUBLESOME PEOPLE

If we return once more to the 2001 election results map, a somewhat broader interpretation now seems in order. The old Westminster system has effectively withdrawn from the periphery of devolved government, in Scotland, Wales and Northern Ireland. But the hidden third dimension of the map is that, simultaneously, its multinational state order has become 'hollowed out' in England as well. Less than a quarter of the electorate supported the winning party and government. Now add on a fourth dimension: by these indications, in 2005 or 2010, landslide-style victories could result from the ballots of a fifth or even less of eligible voters, with results even more like the Mad Hatter's tea party in *Alice.*

Closer scrutiny of the results map will also show that the still-serried ranks of English blue are not what they seem. They increasingly represent EU-subsidized fields, not people. Surveys like Anthony Seldon's *The Blair Effect* have made clear how strongly the existing system now favours urban constituencies.[18] Demographic movements mean that it takes fewer votes to put in a New Labourite than a Conservative.[19] At the same time, suburbs formerly 'staunchly Tory' have gravitated over to Blairism, above all in the resurgent south. The abysmal performance of the Conservative Party in the 2001 election expressed a tidal movement pushing Toryism back into the shires – a patchwork of depleted rural provinces, smaller towns and half-ruined industries. It would be serious enough if Conservatism had become 'an English party', as so many have said since 1997. The fact is, it shows signs of becoming the party of non-metropolitan England – a far more serious fate.

Just how serious this was is demonstrated by the election aftermath. The standard reaction would have been for Tories to 'rally round' a successor leader who looked capable of bearing Mrs Thatcher's redemptionist mantle – that is, somebody who could be ready by 2005 or 2010 with a plausible alternative scenario, appropriate think-tank artillery, new European alibis, ingratiating visits to court in Washington, and a reasonable number of new money-bags in tow. There was even a plausible candidate to hand in Michael Portillo. But it all went hopelessly wrong. Feeling the rug being tugged from beneath their feet, the Shire Tories insisted on having one of their own sort, a ramrod-backed military gent.[20] As the American republican journalist Hans Nichols noted:

> At a Duncan Smith meeting in Harrogate, a former MP joked: 'If you spot anyone under the age of 40, you'll know they've come to the wrong place.' Of course, he wasn't really joking, because the average age of a dues-paying Tory is 65. Like most of its members, the Tories are on the brink of extinction.[21]

Probably nobody in Scotland or Wales would have supported any new Tory leader, whoever he was; but it is now plain that almost nobody south of Watford or east of Reading will support this character either. The 'middle ground' in the Tory Party has been not so much lost as fled from, in pursuit of yesterday. Thus Middle England is no longer what it was – and again, in ways not visible on the Westminster results diagram.

The dilemma of 'non-metropolitan' England lies in the way that the metropolis has itself changed. Since Mrs Thatcher won office a generation ago, London has evolved into a cosmopolis. The 2001 census will probably show around a third of its population as comparatively recent immigrants. A veritable deluge of incomers overtook both it and its adjacent area in the 1990s, generating the largest 'black economy' in Europe alongside the City's refashioned prosperity. The successes of Thatcherism had reconfigured England, in fact, at the same time as they completed the destruction of the old ruling elite. Both of these big changes were quite unintended, and completely irreversible – and largely explain both the force and the probable longevity of Blairism.

'England' has become the place you have to get across, in order to reach London. It is DuncanSmith-land, as it were, where time has stopped and the clocks now run backwards.[22] In her *Nationalism: Five Roads to Modernity*, Liah Greenfeld sees England as the original forge of the nation-state, the template of modernity.[23] But fate is now turning heroic origins into a zone of indeterminacy, the *terrain vague* of an identity partly lost to Empire and now further drained by the southeastern city polity – possessed by its own 'great wen'. Again, no one should read condemnation into this judgement: I remember London as it still was in the 1960s, the capital of England, and theatre of the mercifully brief efflorescence of Powellite Anglo-nationalism. Each time I disembark these days on the way back from Melbourne, I feel grateful for the transformation. But at the same time, the structural dilemmas posed by such a shift must be recognized. Referring to the recent work of the great Canadian urbanologist Jane Jacobs, Kevin Pask points out how theory has 'Increasingly turned to the idea of the nation as defined by a single metropole', with the accompanying presumption that

> the nation is a unit of metropole and periphery, the former now thoroughly dominating the latter. Each great city requires its own hinterland (already a stunning demotion of the 'heartland' of classical nationalism) and the nation becomes the city-state writ large ...[24]

Post-1989 globalization has undoubtedly reinforced this trend, just as it has promoted the emergence of nations, and the formation of regional alliances or groupings of states. Capitalist expansion in the nineteenth and twentieth centuries resulted in the creation of protective breakwaters – primarily, as Pask suggests, those of ethnic or 'heartland' nationalism. Today, the breakwaters are more varied, and even less predictable in their effects.

For nations to become 'city-states writ large' may work in a few cases, but there are some nations incapable of following this route, and England is one of them. There was never the smallest chance of Britain becoming a 'hinterland' of the southeast; but we must remember that 'England' represents about 85 per cent of Britain, and contains several other vast conurbations, like Manchester, Merseyside and, above all, the post-industrial valleys of the Tyne and the Wear, around Newcastle. These are in the long run more likely to become European competitors than appendages of any southern city-state. But they are currently prevented from finding political voice by the Westminster counter-revolution: the mummy case of the Windsor Monarchy, and the ceaseless parade of Great Power pretensions. In typically sleekit style, the Blairite bauble-bearers have taken to half-advocating 'regional assemblies' for these left-behind indigenes of the North, secure in the knowledge of how weak 'popular demand' for such bodies is likely to be. As they smugly point out, strong regional government 'has never been a feature' of historic England. Well, of course demand for this, as for other, constitutional changes is weak. It is kept weak by the system, and its metropolitan media carpet-bombers. This is the essence of the Britannic palsy: a system just democratic enough to prevent farther democratization, while laying it on thick about its own superiority. The Unwritten Constitution remains sacrosanct to prevent or constrain the release of new voices – both class and territorial – that should be the normal accompaniment of a rapidly developing civil society. But here the whole point is to keep 'normal' at bay. Like the Thatcherites who pioneered the Redemptionist Way, Blairites believe that Britain already has as much democracy as is good for it. We have already seen how the fact that over half the population had given up on politics was presented after the 2001 election as a proof of this wisdom. The people were too happy to be bothered voting. Furthermore, repoliticizing them is seen as simply leading to trouble – as it did in Wales and then in London.

The growing divide between society and state that I referred to earlier in Chapter 8 has this consequence. State-fostered populism generates a society that abstains from voting responsibly, and becomes capable only of mutiny. Mutiny against the Poll Tax destroyed Thatcher. The Welsh would not have a perfectly sound (but Centre-inspired) candidate imposed upon them. Londoners rebelled against New Labour and clamoured for an actually popular candidate who then had to leave the party to get elected. In the 2000 'fuel protests', the regime was twice paralysed by inexplicably popular movements against properly sanctioned tax increases. The 2001 election campaign itself was shaken by ugly 'race riots' in non-metropolitan badlands, where natives and incomers alike demonstrated total mistrust of state intentions and parties. The people are a bad lot: in fact, many of them may soon be as deserving of transportation to Australia as they were back in 1788.

A POLYGRAPH OF DISINTEGRATION

It follows that the break-up process is more many-sided and unforeseeable than appears from the election results map. Devolution is only the most visible part of it. It is widely believed abroad that New Labour 'gave' Home Rule to Scotland, Home representation to Wales, and then a new consociational government to Northern Ireland. Well, this is correct; but the term 'gave' hides an unusual number of ambiguities. Extensive regime blarney was devoted at that time to the virtues of wise decentralization and healthy local government – as if British socialism had always longed for these things, but (alas) had been unable to do anything about them when previously in power. But a more accurate reading of the 1997 runes would be that by 1997 it was no longer possible to escape from doing *something* about all three parts of its domain. Blair's incoming administration owed important debts to the Scottish and Welsh battalions of his party.[25] Mafias take debts seriously. It was those soldiers who had enabled it to survive the humiliating defeats of the 1980s. But the same provincial cadres had simultaneously been battling against advancing nationalist movements in their own countries. They understood that some concessions were now needed to help them (as they hoped) win such wars. And movement in a Home Rule direction was the very least they would settle for. This was both aided and complicated by the figure and persona of Gordon Brown, co-architect with Blair of New Labour, and head chieftain of the clan known as the 'Brownites'. The Scottish part of this saw Scottish Labour as its own fiefdom, promoted devolution from a very Westminster world-view and articulated a narrow, antagonistic idea of British unionism.[26]

In Ireland the situation was simpler: Blair was pursuing a strategy begun even before Thatcher's time, and continued by the Conservatives over the 1980s and 1990s. This was for an agreement with the Irish Republic on cautious disengagement, accompanied by a consociational (or cross-community) government in Ulster. Quite reasonably, all Westminster governments have calculated that a successful and peaceful withdrawal would enhance Britain's international standing, while a civil war and forced retreat would seriously damage it. Blair and his then Foreign Secretary Robin Cook thought that a new drive was needed to implement this strategy. And the result was the Belfast Agreement of 1998: Northern Ireland's 'peace process'.

These 'devolutionary' initiatives are now, however, in wild disarray – a disarray which has been justified on the grounds that discrete policies were made to measure for each different situation. But this is only the David Hume's waistcoat rationalization of the Mad Hatter's party (where, it will be recalled, the clocks all misbehaved themselves and the argument ended up down a treacle well). There has been no constitutional plan that might risk making sense. There has been no question whatever, for Blair, of the United Kingdom Constitution being reformed, as distinct from having some new bits tacked on to it. Ukania is terribly flexible about such add-ons and plug-ins, but completely rigid about sovereignty, the unswerving essence supposed to preside over the Centre of Things. A constitutional plan which made sense would thus be little better than a suicide note: the anguished farewell from his bed of rags of a wretch doomed to normalcy – proportional representation, plurality of powers, democracy, creeping republicanism, the dank humiliation of being 'quite important', but pivotal no more.

This is not to deny for a moment the value of such initiatives in themselves. Of course, Scotland is better off advancing towards recovery of statehood, as is Wales with its own representative voice. The Northern Ireland constitution and assembly is arguably the most important achievement of the 1997–2001 New Labour government, voted for (we should remember) by decisive majorities in both the Republic and the North itself. However, 'in themselves' is another deceptive phrase. None of these changes are as yet 'in themselves', or self-standing. All continue to depend upon the United Kingdom's non-constitution, upon a collapsing structure of authority that rests on a dwindling basis of real allegiance, and yet persists in identifying all its incorrigible weaknesses as wondrous strengths. David Hume's waistcoat has turned into the straitjacket of terminal Britishness. The inmate has given up figuring a way out and settled for just being himself: 'British through and through'.

During the last general election campaign, quite different campaigns were fought in the devolved and Tory-free countries of Her Majesty's state. The Ulster contest was about the future of power-sharing government there. The Scottish and Welsh votes were rehearsals for the next elections to their own parliaments, marked by further advances for the SNP and Plaid Cymru respectively, increased resentment in the English hinterland, and a beefing-up of the Save Britain campaign.[27] In other words, the UK will be moving on from the Hatter's tea party of 2001 to the insane croquet competition of 2005 to 2007 (the latter date being the third centenary of the Treaty of Union with Scotland, the architrave of the existing state).

There is an old blueprint for the post-British Isles, which runs like this: four nationalities simultaneously recover from the colonial addiction and resume their separate, or partly separate, ways. Scotland, Ireland, Wales and England will in the end agree amicably on forms of independence, and the big new population of incomers to the archipelago (who are mostly in England) will swap 'British' for 'English', and before long hardly notice the difference (aided by the near certainty that a reconstructed England would be more democratic than Britain ever was). 'British' would then become a loosely ethnic label in something like the old Greek sense, denoting certain cultural traits common to the archipelagic tribes. Though politically independent, the latter would be most unlikely to abandon such traits overnight – any more (for example) than the Irish Republic did in 1922 or 1947. Civil society would remain (so to speak) mainly 'British-Irish', at least until someone thinks up a smarter term than 'archipelago'.

Unfortunately, this is a formula for an intelligible or standard game of croquet, played on more or less level ground by the contemporary rules of nation-statehood. In *Alice in Wonderland* things unfold differently. They are much more like what seems presaged by Her Majesty's general election of 2001:

> Alice thought she had never seen such a curious croquet ground in all her life; it was all ridges and furrows; the balls were live hedgehogs and the mallets live flamingos, and the soldiers had to double themselves up and stand upon their hands and feet, to make the arches ...[28]

All the players play at once, 'quarrelling all the while' and fighting for the hedgehogs, who constantly unroll themselves and crawl away, while the soldiers get tired of waiting and wander off, and the Queen works herself into a furious passion, stamping about and shouting 'Off with his head!' or 'Off with her head!' Alice confides in the Cheshire Cat that she has understood the real point of the confusion: 'The Queen is so extremely likely to win that it's hardly worth while finishing the game.' Hearing her, 'The Queen smiled and passed on'.

It will be clear that there must be something else wrong with that tidy old blueprint. The assumption it encourages is that all the problems of devolution and fragmentation must arise from peripheral nationalism. They do not. It was of course a necessary condition of the collapse that national movements and claims assert themselves; but the sufficient condition of Britain's end lies within the core itself.[29] The underlying motor of disintegration is in the contradictions of a state that has now grossly outlived its historic day, but would rather fall apart than cease being itself through reform. The finest hour gave it a new lease of life; but when that lease ended in the 1970s, nothing would persuade the title-holders to relinquish their tenure and make an honest end to the grandeur of a departed age. Thatcherism and Blairism have been at bottom strategies of state salvation, in which their own societies are ceasing daily to believe. Loyalty survives solely in the Protestant last ditches of Ulster, or the blatant self-interest of the neo-British managers who now squat in the abandoned mansions of the former ruling class. Willy-nilly, all the *societies* of this heirloom state find themselves driven towards the true salvation of exit.

Under such conditions, exit will naturally assume different forms, and there has been prolonged debate about this in the echo chambers of postmodernism. The one that concerns me most, however, is distinctly pre-postmodern. The Scots really know what has to be done to the Treaty of Union. When asked whether they want independence *now*, a majority of them still haver about putting it off or hanging around in case some ineffably better offer turns up. On the other hand, one survey after another has also shown that most of them think independence is inevitable. If something is inevitable in a reasonably foreseeable future, would it not be best to anticipate it now, or as soon as possible? But the ghostly persona of Britishness still appears to walk abroad, even in Scotland, defying democracy, outliving genuine loyalty and conviction, with the 'Exit' door near at hand. Let Britain soon be laid to rest.

11
North America:
The Misfortunes and 'Death' of Ethnicity

Tom Nairn

The concept of 'cultural diversity' comes with many interpretative problems. A good example comes from Canada, more specifically from the writings of Scottish-Gaelic loner Alistair MacLeod. What do these stories tell us of the dilemmas of the ethnic, the counter-ethnic, and the supra-ethnic? Like 'nationalism', ethnicity was invented for deep-political reasons, as part of a great-nation 'strategy' that became global discourse, and to some extent political reality. But examination of its origins also suggests that its utility may be lessening today under the pressures of post-1989 globalization. Consideration of Alistair MacLeod's remarkable stories serve to illustrate the theory. The stories are depictions of ethnic life, and death, and can be read as a great elegy, not only for the community, but for a certain way of understanding communal society itself. They depict ethnicity pushed to a logical limit, and (in effect) condemning itself to disappearance, or dissolution within some great whole. The concept of 'ethnicity' (c.1970–c.2003) was never what it appeared to be. It never depicted the essential – human nature in the raw, a commanding inheritance from past social time – but rather a politics of transition meant to humanize the racial nationalism that had preceded it (c.1870–c.1970). Its limits and erosion (also conveyed in MacLeod's writing) now suggest that diversity will have to find alternative expression in the era of globalization. The 'post-ethnic' is on the agenda, as much as the 'postnationalist'. Advances in democratization and constitutional systems now offer the most plausible way forward.

THE LIFE OF GHOSTS

In Alistair MacLeod's short story 'As Birds Bring Forth the Sun', the narrator's father takes in a wounded puppy and brings it up 'as one of the family' in Cape Breton, Nova Scotia, Canada. Later the pup – *cù mòr glas*, the big grey dog – has six pups of her own, as huge and grey as their mother. But these end by attacking and killing the human father who made them possible, on a remote small island off the Nova Scotian coast. After which, the dog pack mysteriously vanishes. No traces of it are found on the island,

and from then on it reappears only in dreams and visions. The implication is that these were actually ghost-dogs, symbolizing something of abiding importance to the family, and to the remote Gaelic-speaking community of which it was a part. At the end the family sit around the dying father's bedside, 'taking turns holding the hands of the man who gave us life, afraid for him and for ourselves':

> We are afraid of what he may see and we are afraid to hear the phrase born of that vision ... Bound here in our own peculiar mortality, we do not wish to see or see others see that which signifies life's demise ... We would shut our eyes and plug our ears, even as we know such actions to be of no avail. Open still and fearful to the grey hair rising on our necks if and when we hear the scrabble of the paws and the scratching at the door.[1]

This is the stuff that has riveted thousands of readers – like all MacLeod's short stories, and his one great novel, *No Great Mischief* (2000). The scratching at the door may remind some of that other great modern ghost story, W.W. Jacobs' 'The Monkey's Paw'. An elderly couple is granted just three wishes, and one of them is to bring their only son back from his grave. But when they hear the scrabbling at the door, they realize he has come back as a mangled cadaver, so their very last wish must be to put him back again, at peace in his grave. MacLeod's version is the stronger, however, because it so powerfully conveys the message of a death beyond that of the one man – a death that somehow concerns and matters to every reader. This is what I'll call here the death of 'ethnicity' – the wider group, the extended family or (in this case) the clan, Clan Donald (or one bit of it, exiled to Cape Breton). The wider group by implication is all of us, or some important part of all of us. MacLeod's particular group descended from Donalds who had fought for Prince Charles Edward Stewart at Culloden in 1746, and subsequently switched sides to join the British, Hanoverian armies of the later eighteenth century. Some of these in turn fought in the army that defeated the French colonizers of Canada, at Quebec City in 1759. The commander, General James Wolfe, had previously written a letter about his Highlanders saying: 'They are hardy, intrepid, accustomed to a rough country, and no great mischief if they fall.' The tale is retold several times by MacLeod, and is of course the source of his novel's title.

I would argue that all MacLeod's fiction is an extended rumination upon this death, a prolonged litany or elegy – not just for those killed at Quebec, but for the fate of the entire community he comes from. The world is full of comparable communities, in Ireland as well. However, one is immediately forced to say, this is an elegy that has been widely misunderstood and often misrepresented. That is, depicted as a form of romantic nostalgia, the comforting recall of great communal virtues and principles that have, somehow inevitably, succumbed to the pressures and temptations of shallow modernity. So it can appear safe to wallow in it, shedding the occasional tear over the recollection of an 'imagined community' on its way through history's exit door. Ought one to donate a few dollars to language revivalists and culture enthusiasts – the equivalent of respectful prayers round the death-bed, or flowers on the grave?

Frankly, it is nothing of the kind: and MacLeod deserves far better than this. I think the real nerve of his fiction – above all in *No Great Mischief* – is a subtle yet bone-piercing *critique* of those very things romance addicts have so solemnly and systematically wished to see. His writing is certainly elegiac; indeed, every part of it is a reflection upon death and disappearance. But what counts in this – and also makes it so moving – is a fine degree of authorial distance from the scenes and memories so vividly recounted. MacLeod isn't a theorist; he absolutely avoids spelling anything like that out, and tries always to 'let the facts speak for themselves', with great success. But this doesn't mean that there *is* no theory in these descriptions, or that no broader social or political message can be discerned in them. I suppose it does mean that readers have to be more careful, to capture the creative balance. Adherence to this writer's astonishing subtlety may be needed, in order to avoid seeing what many readers are somehow predisposed to see in such tales of ethnic life and manners.

THE COINING OF ETHNICITY

The 16 tales and one novel are possibly the most comprehensive literary portrait of 'an ethnic group' anywhere in the world. But anyone trying to tackle them in a more theoretical or analytical way should ask, first of all, just what 'ethnic' and 'ethnicity' mean. These have become almost over-familiar terms: every evening news programme bears items on 'ethnic Albanians' in Kosova, or 'ethnic Kurds' in Iraq or Turkey. They constitute a fixed point of reference in today's political world: the obligatory backward perspective on constants of custom, speech or communal inheritance. In this process we have come to assume that ethnicity has always been with us. If this is so, it took an amazingly long time for discourse to register the fact. Etymology indicates that until around the year 1970 'ethnic' remained a resolutely abstruse and academic word. The term certainly had an earlier prehistory in English, denoting something like 'heathen' or alien. And we do find it in fairly regular use from the later nineteenth century, for example in the sociology of Max Weber and in anthropological texts in English – but always on a rarefied, rather scholarly plane. No popular commentator or tabloid journalist would have dreamt of using it. Then relatively suddenly it appeared everywhere. Such shifts are very important, and seem to take place when a new wider situation or problem emerges – something passionately affecting most people, but for which existing language and theory is unequipped.

In Chapter 18, I put forward a similar argument about 'nationalism', and suggest that while plenty of people had got worked up about nationhood, nationality rights, national oppression, and so on, from the later eighteenth century onwards, the '-ism' did not impose itself *until the 1870s*. We don't find it as popular usage, registered in dictionaries, until then – that is, after the Franco-Prussian War, the emergence of an all-Italian state in 1870, the concurrent rise of Wilhelmine Germany, and (of course) the difficult reunification of the USA after the Civil War of the 1860s. It surfaced first in French, '*le nationalisme*', most evidently signalling the inflamed mass sentiments of a country that had suffered defeat, and the annexation of part of its territory (Alsace and Lorraine), as well as the Paris Commune's uprising in 1870. A more potent ideological medicine was required by those who succeeded Napoleon III in power. And this was supplied in part by the mutation of 'Frenchness' into a more combative and authoritarian '-ism', a creed admitting less compromise or underlying dissent.

In a very short time the terminology thus generated spread to everyone else, as *das Nazionalismus*, *il nazionalismo*, and so on. The world of mounting imperial strife, as well as of Social Darwinism and the 'yellow press' (as they used to call the tabloids) needed such an emphatic idea. Industrialization and urbanization were by that time transforming the fate of millions, and new stereotypes and shared feelings were a part of it. The masses were not just 'invited in' to history: they had to make themselves at home there, and an aspect of this *entrée* was colourful ideas like class and nation. Such terms denoted strings of attitudes and emotions, communal memes that played a functional part in the new European and global stage drama of militarized, high-pressure nationality politics. The fuller implications of this were soon spelt out in the Dreyfus Affair of the 1890s, including the disastrous 'modernization' of anti-semitism. The culmination was to be the 30 years of mayhem between 1914 and 1945.

The deeper cultural mutation entailed by such affairs of state and empire has endless examples. In the space of this chapter, I can do no more than literally mention one of these, because it's of such obvious relevance to MacLeod. This is the intensifying, or orchestration of *nostalgia* as a keynote of the human condition – the sense that originary sentiments, the 'blue remembered hills' of early experience are, and somehow should be, definitive, even commanding, both for the individual and the community. Modernization theories about nationalism have stressed factories, offices and trade, but there was an 'industrialization' of nostalgia and comparable sentiments proceeding contemporaneously, a mutation of sensed connectedness or 'belonging' that found voice in gutter press and high-brow poetry alike. Nor has the process stopped since then. Indeed, we see something analogous to the discourse-ascent and generalization of 'nationalism' happening to 'ethnicity' from the 1960s onwards. All accounts I have found link its rise to the appearance of two books: Nathan Glazer and Daniel P. Moynihan's *Beyond the Melting Pot* in 1963, and the same authors' *Ethnicity: Theory and Experience* in 1975. A shift seems then to have occurred in 'Anglophone terminology concerning the nature of the social units we study', so that 'Quite suddenly, with little comment or ceremony, ethnicity is an ubiquitous presence.'[2]

Naturally, the 'Anglophone' tongue in question was of course United States' English. It was *American* identity that actually and urgently needed this change. Just as France's injured great-nation persona had demanded a more hard-edged, armoured version of nationality and nationhood in the 1870s, so the great-American identity now urgently required a replacement for 'race'. Why was this? By the 1960s, America was confronting a number of profound challenges, both domestically and in international relations. In practice these were often inseparable, since the undisputed leader of the capitalist Free World was now exposed to non-stop reproach or recrimination for its internal racism. How could US governments argue seriously for national liberation from communism, while the hypocritical repression of Jim Crow racism persisted at home? The USA had played a leading part in destroying the ideological world of Social Darwinism, of justified genocide, and Aryan hierarchy – but only to furtively keep it all going at home, under disintegrating wraps. The world of gas chambers and forcibly imposed eugenics had been demolished; yet every bus and diner in Alabama still bore excruciating and painful reminders of what all that had meant. A phoney solution to the greatest war of the nineteenth century had survived into the second half of the twentieth, profoundly dishonouring to the American Constitution – and even to 'the West' as a whole.

As the Southern civil rights movement gathered momentum, the dilemma was getting even more painful. And simultaneously another challenge was appearing – large-scale Hispanic immigration, mainly from Mexico but then from all over Latin America. All at once, both the old 'melting pot' theory of assimilation and the post-Civil-War-cultivated 'blind spot' towards anti-black discrimination became intolerable. A new theory of Americanness was urgently needed. The 'American dream' had to be not just kept running, but somehow given new wheels and a different direction.

That was what was required, and it was duly supplied by the idea of the 'ethnic', as refurbished and popularized by Moynihan, Glazer and their many followers. The role of Daniel P. Moynihan was particularly important here: an academic turned politician, later the Senator for New York, and a key figure in Democratic Party affairs. He was also a celebrated stage Irishman, in other words himself an 'ethnic' and (as everyone would soon be saying) an outstanding specimen of 'Irish-American' humanity.[3] When he died in 2003, no obituary omitted some account of the frequently flushed face, riotous pub evenings and great Hibernian collapses. But this was part of the point of 'ethnicity'. Since Afro-Americans and Hispanic-Americans were now inevitable, and proving relatively unmeltable, all other Americans (including the Anglos, the Greeks, the Irish and the Scots) had to claim (or initially, to award themselves) equivalent status and credentials. The ex-rulers too now had to have their 'roots', alongside the newly emancipated, and the tidal wave of newcomers. In France of the 1870s, nation-ism (national-ism) had been the formula for maintaining and renewing the state; in the USA of the 1970s, I suppose it could have been 'ethnic-ism' – the term is occasionally employed – but in practice 'ethnicity' sounded better. Multiculturalism, the rapidly theorized consequence, was both repair to and rejuvenation of an ailing constitutional order.

From the outset, the point of ethnicity was profoundly political. It was a reimagining of society's fabric, intended to dispel evil habits and shades, and to project a better alternative. And it was a great success in just those things. To lay emphasis on the deeper political strategy at work is in no way to deny it was a step forward. *Of course*, 'ethnic' was preferable to 'racial', and culture – the posited vehicle of ethnicity – was a huge advance on 'blood', or physical appearances, or thoughtless conjectures that an inscrutable 'immemorial' must prevail. The will towards multicultural equivalence and forms of respect did stand for a civilization superior to the demeaning mythology of Social Darwinism and genetic superiority. It emerged as a sign of the vitality, of the continuing powers of self-regeneration and creative dominance in the United States in that era. It was also in line with a more general shift going on at the same time, reflecting the emancipatory movement of the 1960s (especially the student movement), and also the accumulating real knowledge of genetics itself. 'Ethnicity' could only have gathered such confidence, and imposed itself so totally, in the generation after the DNA discoveries of the decade before. There was a long way ahead to the charting of human genome; however, science was moving rapidly in that direction, and perceived as discrediting the old mythologies of descent.

The new and expansive concept of ethnicity added a certain equality of *communal* rights (not without much reluctance) to the older philosophy of individual rights. In theory at least, none should now have 'roots' disbarring them from office or from wealth. All roots were construed as equal, and as transcendable – that is, surpassable into the more exalted spheres of the civic-constitutional and the economic (for example, the sacredness of capitalist enterprise for all). Indeed, all such origins *must be* transcended, without being denied or simply lost. However, 'transcendence' in that crucial sense also implied conservation. The point of the new ethnic-political distinction was exactly that: it sought the *salvation* of the existing wider state, in a new and more acceptable way, as opposed to threatened separation and internecine squabbling. However important the emancipatory side of 'ethnicity' was, we must recall that it remained only one part of a larger state-national enterprise. It was a vital modification of nationalism, not a replacement for it. After all, 'nationalism' too had been a sort of emancipation in its inception. It allowed new space and justification to popular identity, and to the new literacy and assertiveness of a humanity being rapidly urbanized – of people denuded of traditional meaning-supports, and forced to search for others. Without that liberating side, it could not have won such resounding primacy over the industrializing world. And just as French prestige had once easily enabled the diffusion of 'nationalism', now American cultural and media hegemony carried 'ethnicity' into other Western and then global tongues. Hence what had once signified 'heathen', or outside the walls – a designation of barbarians – now came to mean 'good' or natural. But – one must always remind oneself – *conservative* good, natural and right within certain limits. These limits remain those of state, or *the political*, the higher realms where more universal and abstract standards apply.

THE DEVIL'S PURITY

Among the articles marking Daniel Moynihan's passing in the year 2003, I was amused to find one that identified him with Satan's second coming on earth.[4] In later life he produced a book on the post-1989 strife in Eastern Europe called *Pandaemonium*, in which he argued that all these troubles arose from misinterpretation of his and Glazer's earlier work. Such misreadings led to the wrong sort of ethnicity, the kind that thought ethnic nature *alone* justified separation or independence, as well as ethnic cleansing (and so on) to get it. Far from discrediting it, Bosnia and other calamities of the 1990s therefore underlined the wisdom of his 1970s' theorization about ethnicity as wholesome, inevitable (etc.) *in its place*.

But this brings me back to MacLeod, Nova Scotia and Canada. Just what is that 'place'? Alistair MacLeod's stories are a marvellous and comprehensive description of the same thing. Written between 1968 ('The Boat') and 1999 ('Clearances') they portray the 'blue remembered hills' of the Gaelic-speaking Scottish Highlanders of Cape Breton, Nova Scotia, in Eastern Canada. Cape Breton is the eastern bit of Nova Scotia Province, and so the most easterly edge of Canada. These places are separated from Ontario and the great western mass of Canada by the French-speaking Province (or more exactly the near-state) of Quebec. They were settled largely by Scots, including a large number of Gaelic-speaking, Highland Scots, some of whom (like the Donalds figuring in MacLeod's prose) had been cleared from North or Western Scotland by the capitalist agrarian reforms of the nineteenth century – that is, the 'Clearances' to which the last part of MacLeod's collected volume returns.

It is important to note how odd, even unique, these circumstances are. This was a community both isolated and deprived in many different ways at once. Partly driven into exile for economic, rather than political, reasons, it arrived in the territory of the Eastern seaboard Mi'kmaq people, long after a much larger French colonization of the St Lawrence valley – present-day Quebec and 'Acadie' in New Brunswick Province. As MacLeod relates, they went on 'conducting all their lives in Gaelic' well into the twentieth century. Only in the 1930s does the father in 'Clearances' reluctantly acquire some English in order to do business with new customers from Ontario and the USA. In order to be no longer 'trapped in the beautiful prison of the language he loved', he grunts testily, 'We will have to do better than this ... We will have to learn English. We will have to go forward.'[5]

If they had remained in that sense so 'backward', this was partly provoked by another barrier: they found themselves separated from the rest of Anglo-Canada by the vast country of Quebec, not just a 'settlement' like their own but an ex-colony with a political as well as a social (or 'ethnic') mind of its own. Not too surprisingly, this location tended to make them turn inwards. And such inwardness in turn encouraged a degree of obsession with the past – their own history in pre-industrial or even in pre-Hanoverian times, in the clannic social inheritance of the preceding Kingdom of Scotland. That was part of what continuing to 'conduct their lives in Gaelic' meant, or implied. It implied lapsing back in the right, congenial company to the eighteenth or even the seventeenth century, when Highlanders had occasionally won battles and wars, or at least seemed to count for something in a wider world.

But no longer. All MacLeod's stories depict an extended, clannic-type family going round in circles, in a hard landscape and coastline that knocks almost everything out of them. Individuals escape (like MacLeod himself), westwards to Ontario and Toronto, or southwards to the USA, but remain psychically tied to this homeland. Many of the stories are about returns, but all the returnees ever find is slow run-down, disintegration, a replacement of farming and fishing by tourism, and well-to-do incomers quite ignorant of the Clearances – convinced indeed that they're simply bestowing some overdue prosperity upon a hard-up, if picturesque, environment. So what draws them back? It is the nostalgia of formative belonging, the fact that 'blood is thicker than water'. This is the most common phrase in MacLeod's prose. On the last page but one of 'Clearances', the father-figure reflects upon the strange relationship between Cape Breton and Ardnamurchan in Scotland:

He was at the edge of one continent ... facing the invisible edge of another. He saw himself as a man in a historical documentary, probably, he thought, filmed in black and white ...[6]

THE TRAGEDY OF THE ETHNIC

This is of course a perfect characterization of Macleod's writing itself. So much of it is obtrusively earthy and gut-wrenching that it's tempting to think of it as 'realistic'. But in any humdrum sense, it is not. Anyone interested in a realistic portrayal of Scots in Canada would do well to turn to the memoir of another distinguished Canadian intellectual of the late twentieth century, John Kenneth Galbraith. In 1966 the celebrated economist published *The Non-potable Scotch: A Memoir on the Clansmen in Canada* (Penguin, London). Written in a laconic, often humorous style as different as it could be from MacLeod's, this account (now out of print, unfortunately) deals with the same umbilical-cord and extended-family theatre, but presents it in quite a different light. The assumption there is that an immigrant community has arrived to create a new life for itself, both collectively and individually, and that this is incompatible with imported, unaltering circles of existence. In the same figurative sense, 'new blood' is simply part of that, even it proves less 'thick' and coagulating. So is new politics – Galbraith, like Daniel Moynihan, was an academic turned liberal-American politico, and as far as I know nobody has yet bracketed him alongside Beelzebub.

In his 'Foreword' to MacLeod's collected stories, John McGahern says these 'gradually acquire the richness and unity of an epic poem', and 'through that high art that conceals itself' present the reader with 'a complete representation of existence'. Fair enough, but what the epic poem also represents is a cruelly *incomplete* existence – that of a clannic remnant, unable either to integrate and move on, or to reconstitute itself politically (as the French eventually did in the St Lawrence valley, after their defeat of 1759) and forge a state or a region of its own. The tragedy and final self-destruction of a society too bound into, and in the end strangled by, 'ethnicity' – this, surely, is the cutting edge of MacLeod's prose (the message of that black-and-white 'historical documentary'). Wallowers in romance – to whom I shall return in a minute – find MacLeod terribly 'colourful'. This is because he focuses so exclusively on the irreproachably 'ethnic' – on what in Edinburgh they used to call (and doubtless still do) 'hatch, match and despatch'. In MacLeodese this reads something like: birth-pangs, blue-remembr'd hills, non-stop screwing (sometimes exogamous, but largely endogamous), family feuds, back-breaking toil, and then lights out. In all the actual Scottish migrant communities one knows of (Highland or Lowland) *religion* played a very important role, whether Catholic or Protestant, or involving feuds between the two. But faith is absent from the Cape Breton heathens depicted in this particular movie. One suspects it may be deliberately left out, in order to emphasize the supposedly more basic traits of 'ethnicity'. In other words, while dispersed clans or tribes have usually carried a form of self-transcendence with them, convictions about a deity and another world, the MacLeod-landers depicted here aren't so lucky.

All they have is ethnicity, and ghosts, as conveyed in the story I began by mentioning, 'As Birds Bring Forth the Sun'. The murderous canine shades evoked there can only be those of the extended-family community itself. MacLeod makes the point in the story, and indeed rubs it in a bit. And the terrible dread consuming those around the father's death-bed is that of acknowledgement – recognition that this style of insular self-sufficiency bears only death at its heart. 'Ethnicity' can only lead on to profounder questions of meaning – questions to which the world conjured up in *Island* and *No Great Mischief* by definition contains no answer.

ETHNICITY'S END

MacLeod's novel *No Great Mischief* retells the story again, but in a more sustained and artful way than the shorter tales. Its compass is much wider, and its reverberations that much deeper. I will not attempt to summarize the whole narrative, but I feel it is important to draw your attention to the climax and conclusion of the book. These are immensely compelling: among the greatest achievements of recent writing in English. However, the power at work here also seems designed to utterly confound romantic or nostalgic indulgence in the very themes so richly expounded.

The narrator's extended family finds employment in a uranium mine in Ontario. This is hard, dangerous, but relatively well-paid work, and the Scots form an effective work team to cope with the conditions, partly because of their ethnolinguistic solidarity. The mine management ably exploits this, and employs other 'ethnic' work-squads for the same reason. And yes, there is an Irish one among them, briefly described, with an exchange of courtesies about them being 'but different branches of the same tree' (and so on).[7] But the most important teams are the Highlanders and the Québecois, and a state of wary rivalry exists between them. Then at a certain point this degenerates into outright hostility. The MacDonalds suspect a Frenchman of having killed one of theirs in the mine shaft, though they can't prove it, while the Quebeckers fear the Scots are manoeuvring to get them out and take over their jobs. However, these tensions are tolerable, and the values of coexistence are stressed in a very beautiful, extended passage in chapter 22.[8] This is prose that seems to capture and extol everything positive about romantic ethnicity – about a past relived and reverberating into the present, in a kind of creative dissonance with other such traditions – reciprocal rather than competitive. If any more heart-breaking threnody to 'ethnic culture' exists in modern writing, I haven't come across it. It deals with music, and the real closeness of the folk traditions that remained alive, on both the sides of the dispute at the mine. A mysterious itinerant fiddler is smuggled into the mine by the Scots, there is something legendary about him. And he plays so well that the French come out of their huts and join in.

> The sun moved higher and heatedly across the sky, yet no one seemed to think of sleep. It was as if we had missed the train to sleep and there was nothing we could do about it in our present state ... The music dipped and soared ... At other times the titles seemed lost or perhaps never known, although the tunes themselves would be recognisable after the first few bars ... 'La bastringue'; 'an old hornpipe'; 'la guigue'; 'a wedding reel'; 'un reel sans nom' ...[9]

Then this is abruptly noticed, and stopped, by the management. What the mine-owners want is to see ethnicity returned to, and firmly kept in, its 'proper place'. They sling out the Pied Piper, and things go back to normal. Until, suddenly, they take a terrible plunge for the worse. The leader of the Québecois, Fern Picard, suddenly accuses the Scots of being thieves and liars: '*Vous êtes des voleurs et des menteurs. Vous êtes des trous de cul...* '[10] A terrible fight follows in the mine-waste lot. It's as if the battle of Quebec was being fought over again. Pipes and wrenches are used, and finally Fern Picard is killed – killed by Calum, the narrator's older brother, and current top man of the 'Clan', or at least its Cape Breton remains. Another Calum had led the first immigrants from Moidart and reconstituted them in Canada; and this is one of his direct descendants.

The twentieth-century Calum is found guilty of second-degree murder and given life imprisonment. Then the Highlanders make an appalling discovery. Picard had been quite right: a thief and liar must have been among them, and he had indeed stolen the Frenchman's wallet, with a thousand dollars in it. They decide to pay the money back to his family. But as if that wasn't bad enough, they all know who did it: he was indeed 'one of theirs', but from over the border in the USA – a draft-dodger MacDonald cousin from San Francisco. Why had they taken in this bad apple, and found him work in the mine? Naturally because, in their world, blood remained thicker than water, regardless of differences between Canada and America, and of attitudes towards the Vietnam War. Such are the joys of ethnicity, and such its fearful quicksands. From this low point, things can only get lower, and the conclusion of *No Great Mischief* is the figurative demise of the Cape Breton community. It is represented by a long drive back from Toronto to the island, ending in a raging storm that renders the causeway from Nova Scotia to Cape Breton almost impassible. Calum, murderer and Clan Chief, has by this time been released from prison and turned into an alcoholic in the Toronto backstreets. When he knows he is dying, he asks the narrator to drive him home to die. They only just make it, and he passes away just over the causeway: 'I turn to Calum once again. I reach for his cooling hand which lies on the seat beside him. I touch the Celtic ring ... .'[11]

However, the ring has by this time no consolation to impart. The fearful ghost-dogs have caught up with them both, and this time nothing will be left behind. The 'great mischief' was the whole thing, not just what happened in 1759. It was an historical experience which, whatever its nobility, its redeeming and humane aspects, remained haunted by and doomed to perdition. As the grandmother says in the story 'The Return': 'It seems we can only stay forever if we stay right here. As we have stayed to the seventh generation. Because in the end that is all there is – just staying ... .'[12]

LE PAYS DES HAUTES TERRES?

As I said earlier, MacLeod is no schoolmaster handing out points or places to his characters. In the confrontation between the Highlanders and the Québecois he doesn't say that the latter 'win', or come out best. *But they do*. And in a number of subtle ways the author indicates why this is so. I won't test your patience by relating just how it's done. *En bref*, it involves the sub-plot of a friendship between the writer and a French-speaking mineworker, Maurice Gingras, who refers often to what keeps him personally going: '*Le pays des Laurentides*' – the country of the Laurentians, the land of Saint Laurent. This is a visionary country that for a time featured in populist politics, not exactly the existing state of Quebec, but something close to it.

The point is that the Cape Bretoners have nothing corresponding to that vision of country, no idea or will towards self-government. Their meaning-fund lies all in the retreating past. It has neither will nor realizable hope, to carry it into an altering future. The deadly finality of nostalgia and re-evocation is all they possess. MacLeod's prose is a superb portrayal of both the richness and the inexorable limits of such an expiring world – the world of a single national remnant, of course, but also (I would argue) that of 'ethnicity' as such, taken as a separate or essentialized category. In the penultimate chapter of *No Great Mischief*, just before the death-ride, the writer accidentally finds a message from Gingras, scribbled down years before in a phone-book page. It says just '*Le pays des Laurentides*' plus an added note that 'you will understand'. It proves too late to contact him again: he has left for the USA, but the bell has been rung (for the reader, as for the narrator).

I mentioned earlier how MacLeod has suffered at the hands of nostalgia addicts. It may be useful to end with some words on one outstanding interpretation of that sort. It has been provided by Professor Emeritus Karl Miller, in the Rutgers University literary review *Raritan*.[13] 'MacLeod's books are elemental and ancient, they go back to the world of Odysseus, to Homer's Ithaca ...', begins Miller, who then frankly explains how strongly he favours such elemental ethnicity over the complicated, modern world of nationality politics. He is dead against the politicization of the ancient and elemental, particularly in Scotland. Some Scots are for going it alone, and some descendants of Clan Donald now have a parliament that may let them do so:

> That would, in my view, be a wrong move rooted in a phobic tribalism, an atavistic and ahistorical tribalism, moreover ... Scotland, Wales and England share an island and have run as a not intractable union, e *pluribus*, for three hundred years. Ireland is another story.[14]

I suppose this is kinder than saying the Irish got it all wrong. Note the adjectives here: 'phobic', 'tribal', 'atavistic' and 'ahistorical', an awful bunch. Miller notes with satisfaction that 'There seems no likelihood of a Nova Scotia *libre*, of a tribal state there of the kind that continues to come about'.[15] He is recognizably a spiritual cousin of the late Senator Moynihan in all this. Homeric elementality is very admirable, and well worth describing in this contemporary version ... just as long as it stays *in its place*. Just as long as it remains honestly 'ethnic', that is, comfortably Homeric rather then dishonestly political. The mine-owners have no objection to Homer; it's politics that bothers them. 'Ethnicity' has become like the officially designated limbo or waiting room of modernity. The heathens can no longer be kept in outer darkness, but by God they have to go on waiting their turn; and if some should pass away in the meantime (like MacLeod's *clann Chalum Ruaidh*), well, that's better than running the risk of phobic atavism, and so on.

The MacDonald's are better without a 'Cape Breton *libre*' therefore – better without any equivalent of the *Pays des Laurentides*. In effect, Miller is making General Wolfe's point over again: *some* mischief if they fall, sure, as described in the nightmare ending of MacLeod's book – but nothing like as much as might ensue if they did not, if they stood up to be counted politically. The actual end beyond the fall is to be *nostalgically* remembered, in poetry and song. And this is in fact how Miller ends his rumination. He comes across some folk-singers in Brittany, two Jewish girls doing numbers from all over the Celtic diaspora, and is moved by them. This is how a civilization should survive, in lively and affectionate remembrance: 'Alistair MacLeod is doing this too', he ends, 'I hope he would see them as sisters.'[16]

It will be obvious, I believe, Macleod is doing nothing of the kind. The Professor is merely projecting his own prejudices on to the texts studied. But to steady our nerves further, let's go back to a MacLeod story I mentioned before, 'Clearances'. This is about the big changes going on now in Cape Breton, and how the local people feel helpless in the face of outside profiteers, foreign improvers and speculators. Why? It is because they have no political power. A distant government is always on the side of the incomers and the rationalizers. The father reflects that in truth they were always at the mercy of 'the Government'.[17] Things have just got a bit worse, and they're still without local means of resistance, in the sense of democracy. He will just have to give in and sell out – this is the same man who suddenly felt he was like a character in a black-and-white documentary film – and he does so in Gaelic: '*Seo nis. Sin e ged tha*' – there you are, that's the way it goes.

In the old country, back in Ardnamurchan, things have started to go a bit differently. Part of the reason why Highlanders (and many Lowlanders) left was the impossibility of buying the land they had traditionally worked. The tractable, *e pluribus* Union was opposed to such moves. It favoured a Scotland carved up into giant estates run by a few hundred landlord-capitalists. Canada, Australia and New Zealand had such a pull on the Highlanders because they thought they could get or acquire their own property there. But last year the new Scottish Parliament passed legislation to delimit and even counteract some of the evils of landlordism: not enough to please everyone, but a long way better than the conditions that once drove *clann Chalum Ruaidh* to Cape Breton. Atavistic tribalism has nothing to do with this, and democracy quite a lot.

THE USES OF ESSENTIALISM

In conclusion, the ideology of ethnicity was a modification of nationalism, whose story has in many ways echoed and humanized that of the nineteenth-century ancestor. It appears to be characteristic of such large shifts that they present their direction as 'essential' – as new discoveries of something that must always have been there, and hence of truths that will configure the future as well. However, 'essentialism' is not just an academic aberration to be pettily censored in classroom 'deconstruction' sessions. It manifests life-and-death attitudes, and the deepest emotions – the passions of millions attempting to make the best of the forms of anomie imposed upon them by socio-economic development. Unless individuals felt that their essences were involved, neither 'nationalism' nor 'ethnicity' would ever have functioned. That is, it would never have functioned *politically*, where 'politics' denotes a basic level of meaning, and not simply the institutional forms or the personalities and parties of a given moment.

It was upon that level that ethnicity represented a liberation, and a rejection of the earlier crudities of race and blood that had so fatally circumscribed 'nationalism'. However, this emancipatory movement would quickly discover its own limits. The new meaning-world was in turn circumscribed and rendered conservative, by the convulsions linked to the end of the Cold War, and to the great further expansion (and population movements) of 'globalization' following 1989. A partial and compromising emancipation was then overwhelmed by the flood-tide of capitalist economic expansion, with its neo-liberal ideology of individual and entrepreneurial ascendancy: the imperium of *Homo economicus*.

In response to this, diversity is being forced towards greater politicization. MacLeod's prose is a stark portrayal of ethnicity deprived of political meaning; of an essence marooned in time and space, incapable of collective will or assertion. He depicts a civil society 'locked out' from the consolations of other-worldly faith as well as active being in this world. At the mercy of outside forces and events, its fate is death by nostalgia – a process of practically bodily dissolution and loss. The contrary is of course political self-assertion, but one itself emancipated from the essentialist mythologies of race, ethnic *Geist* and religion. Possible formulae for such an advance are hard to find, but it may be relevant to cite one suggestive example. In the conclusion to *The Human Web: A Bird's-Eye View of World History*, historian William H. McNeill focuses upon the 'heightened sense of insecurity' derived from recent developments. His 'personal hunch' is that as well as the new parameters of globalization 'we also need face-to-face, primary communities for long-range survival':

> Communities, like those our predecessors belonged to, within which shared meanings, shared values and shared goals made life worth living for everyone, even the humblest and least fortunate ... [hence] the most critical question for the human future is how cell-like primary communities can survive and flourish within the global cosmopolitan flows that sustain our present numbers, wealth and power.[18]

This leads him to suggest 'a new symbiosis' will be needed, between human diversity and the more compelling 'web' of sameness or homogeneity threatened by post-1989: neo-liberal globalism. However, like 'cell-like', the very term 'symbiosis' seems to imply a quasi-biological interpretation of the dilemma. It allows that diversity is nature – but naturally selective rather than societal nature. The 'rules' of the latter (which take up most of the book in question) do not lend themselves to such a reading, nowadays any more than in the receding age of Social Darwinism. Politics, in contrast, can be perceived as rooted in 'second' or social nature – far more deeply and indispensably than those cultural and customary bundles awarded priority by the world-view of ethnicity. Though originally generated out of biological selection (how could this fail to be so?), boundaries and the resultant collective configurations are the foundation of that diversity – communal *and* individual. These alone account for 'human nature' in any sense that now has to be reimagined in the circumstances of globalization.

12
Central Asia:
Continuities and Discontinuities[1]

Paul James and Andrew Phillips

The sudden collapse of the old Soviet Union in late 1991 marked the near-end of 'East European' colonialism and the advent of independence for the 15 constituent republics of the USSR. In the wake of the upheaval, the focus of attention was dragged across the Balkans to Chechnya and back to Kosova, trying to understand the blood passions affecting neighbours and apparatchiks alike. This chapter discusses the largely forgotten, newly independent states of Central Asia, and aims to assess the nature of nation formation in these states given the multiplicity of sub-national and transnational identities. Whilst it is useful to recognize that a common epistemological layer of modernism has been developing since the forced modernization of Central Asia in the 1920s and 1930s, the chapter sets out to argue against notion that nation formation involves the necessary dissolution of traditional ties. Rather, we suggest that a layering of subjectivities and ontologies is likely to persist, leaving the 'identity maps' of Central Asia caught in a series of tensions between traditionalism, modernism and an emergent late-modern reflexivity. This is a very different case study from others in this book on Scotland, England, the United States and Australia, but in it we find the same themes of uneven change and overlaying social formations.

In assessing a given polity's prospects for nation-building, one's conclusions are to a large degree determined by the meaning ascribed to the term 'nation'. If nations are regarded as essential communities, then the notion of the nation-state as a recently constituted polity-community is anathema – the self-consciousness of national community in the nineteenth century and its political expression in the formation of nation-states are seen as part of a natural progression. While this conception of primordial national formation has become increasingly marginalized in academic circles, a different version of primordialism has recently emerged in popular writing, this time in relation to the rise of neo-nationalism at a time of global change. It is smuggled back inside an argument about those *fragmenting states* such as the Soviet Union or Yugoslavia that contain more than one nation. The argument assumes that as these nation-states fragmented, the 'nations within' inevitably again become self-aware, and sleeping nationalist movements were reawakened. It is a new version of the oft-quoted misapprehension that the modernist Ernest Gellner called the myth of the sleeping-beauty nations.[2] Against this primordialist myth, it is our assumption that national identity is borne upon changing and contradictory subjectivities and related to changes in the dominant structures and subjectivities of the society. This is not to challenge Tom's argument in other chapters to the extent that his return to a kind of neo-primordial position is based on the very defensible claim that 'the nation' is formed *out of* a deep history of social formational change. Nevertheless, what we want to do is to emphasize the discontinuous history of any one 'nation' and the discontinuous history of the forms of society-building. However, it does suggest that he overplays his hand in Chapter 16 when he suggests that the 'sorcerer of modernity' will sweep away religious fervour.

By the same methodological approach, we are very critical of the modernists. Against a structural modernist such as Gellner we are concerned there is the risk of setting up a new myth – the myth that in the first stage of nation formation modernity sweeps all before it, turning traditional ways of life into fragments to be instrumentally used by the 'awakeners' as carriers and agitators for cultural nation-building. A more recent version of the modernizing myth has gained *post facto* credibility in the period of the War on Terror as commentators have attempted to come to grips with the number of nation-states that never became fully modern. States such as Afghanistan are said to be *failed states*, those that began the modernizing process and failed to proceed to the next stage of national democratic take-off because of some intervening force such as the Soviet invasion or the Taliban counter-revolution.

Even the best of the general approaches that conceptualize the nation as a collective identity responding unevenly to the pressures of modernization, risk reducing the nation-state to being merely a formation within an all-embracing and globalizing modernity. The uneven development thesis has a way of turning into an argument about eventually catching the tidal wave of history. Whether one grants causal primacy to changes attendant upon industrialization,[3] to the uneven diffusion of modernization across different *ethnies*,[4] or to the emergence of 'imagined communities' through the mechanism of print capitalism,[5] such approaches tend to implicitly rest on the sharp discontinuities asserted between *Gemeinschaft* societies grounded in traditional structure and modern *Gesellschaft* societies unified by 'culture'.[6] This dichotomous outlook ignores the multi-layered nature of societal integration and thus has difficulty accounting for the qualitative differences between nations.

Moreover, regardless of whether or not one thinks that the national subjectivity has premodern roots (as, for example, from very different perspectives, do Tom Nairn or Anthony Smith), or alternatively that nationalism is constructed self-consciously by elites (as does Eric Hobsbawm[7]), the task of explaining the process of nation formation all too quickly becomes reduced to tracking a people's exposure to the facets of modernity, facets that are afforded causal status in a way that blankets out tribal and traditional identity formation. Thus growing exposure to an industrial division of labour and exo-social education (Gellner), the experience of an imagined community via the mechanism of print capitalism (Anderson), a heightened awareness of the uneven diffusion of the fruits of modernization between different *ethnies* (Smith) or an increasing incorporation into the world capitalist system (Wallerstein[8]) are said to engender a corresponding growth in national subjectivity which carries the 'past' with it as merely the content of a modernizing social form.

In this chapter we attempt to walk a methodological tightrope, drawing appreciatively but critically upon the insights of the modernist writers while emphasizing, in a way that they do not, the contradictory effects of modernization. On the one hand, in Central Asia as elsewhere the processes of modernization have been essential requisites of nation formation. Whilst the 'nation' can be experienced prior to the onset of modernization by certain individuals, usually by intellectuals who work in the media of disembodied extension such as writing, it is the structural processes of modernization that generalize this subjectivity across the minds and bodies of the populace. The incorporation of the mass of the population into Gellner's culturally homogeneous space of modernity nevertheless represents at best one measure of nation formation. In addition to this horizontal yardstick, one must also consider the 'depth' of the nation, that is, the extent to which the national subjectivity shapes an individual's identity.

Given our argument that social integration occurs simultaneously at different levels, the presence of multiple layers of identity within the same individual is to be expected. In order to determine the depth of the nation, and by implication its durability in the face of attempts to redefine the high culture of a society, it is thus necessary to speculate on the nature of the constitutive space that the nation occupies for an individual. For this to occur, it is critical that the researcher studies the *specific* quality of the intersections of levels of integration within the society under scrutiny. For the purposes of the following analysis we distinguish three levels or modes of social integration: (i) relations of face-to-face integration, usually the dominant mode of integration in tribal societies, where embodied presence defines the form of the social ties; (ii) relations of agency integration where agents of institutions such as the state mediate and abstract the relations between persons, an important level of association during the formation of empires and nation-states; and (iii) relations of disembodied integration where disembodied media, technologies and techniques of communication and exchange such as mass communications come to link strangers across increasing expanses of space and time. These are related to different ways of being-in-the-world: tribalism, traditionalism, modernism and, of least relevance in this case, postmodernism.[9] Instead of taking time now to explain the approach, for the purposes of our critique it is sufficient to say that if we can show the deep historical and continuing relevance of face-to-face integration and formations of tribalism and traditionalism at the heart of contemporary Central Asian nationalism then we have fundamentally called into question the one-dimensional modernist approaches of theorists such as Ernest Gellner. This is not just a theoretical question. It has crucial consequences for understanding the nature of social life in places where Islam is deepening its hold. Sometimes, in the case of the Taliban, the *return* to fundamentalism (in other words, as *neo*-traditional fundamentalism) occurs as scholars, clerics and students, intellectually trained across the boundaries of modern techniques of pedagogy and neo-traditional reassertions of 'Truth', find themselves becoming unreflexively modern in form and reflexively traditional in content. This kind of Islam tends to be hard-line and oppressive. Alternatively, sometimes, such as in the case of the tribes that crossed the border to fight with the Taliban, Islam is a traditional *truth* that merges with tribal cosmologies. This kind of Islam needs no epistemological defence, only practical action against those who would attack it.

NATION FORMATION IN CENTRAL ASIA

To the extent that Central Asia is referred to at all in the popular press and electronic media, depictions of the area infer that it has remained largely cosseted from the forces of globalism and modernization, that is, except for the obvious 'exception' of Afghanistan as it was caught up with successive wars from the British to the War on Terror. 'Logically' on this basis, nation formation would be impossible in Central Asia given the continued salience of traditional loyalties and the inability of the peoples to undergo the ontological shift necessary to 'think the nation'. The *Sixty Minutes* current affairs version of this is that the accordion effect of squeezing hundreds of years of European development into 20 or 30 years in Central Asia (development referring not just to modernization but to the shifts that had been occurring from the Reformation onwards) would foreclose the possibility of national subjectivities emerging without the tensions that would tear people apart. Ernest Gellner's version of this is no more subtle. It subsumes Central Asia within a homogenized post-Soviet experience:

> The situation was quite different in the lands of the Tsar of All the Russias. Within a few years of shattering military defeat, the empire was re-established under new

management ... The strength of the ideology and of the institutions that it engendered did, however, prevent the lands of the tsar from following, for seventy years, the same path as that followed by the erstwhile lands of the Habsburgs and the Ottomans ... [With the collapse of the Soviet Union] the societies caught within this system resumed the development which had been frozen seventy (or, in some areas, forty) years earlier.[10]

Thus we have, on the one hand, the popular press version of the once-frozen uniqueness of Central Asia and, on the other hand, the disappearance of the particularities of Central Asia in a modernist attempt to universalize the process in a new myth of cryogenics. As the following historical overview reveals, the experience of colonialism and the consequent development of nascent pan-national movements amongst the indigenous intelligentsia, together with the imposition of largely fictitious 'national' ethnonyms by a 'European' power and the exposure to rapid but partial modernization, render the Central Asian experience far from unique, and rather invite comparison with both Africa and the Middle East. Paradoxically, if we are to adequately understand the particularities of contemporary nation formation in Central Asia, it is essential that they be placed in a wider historical context.

CENTRAL ASIA PRIOR TO RUSSIAN COLONIALISM

The territory of Central Asia has one of the longest recorded histories of human settlement, and has been both the subject of innumerable invasions and the seat of glorious civilizations at different times.[11] The experience of repeated invasions together with exposure to manifold cultural influences via the Silk Route, which for a time represented the safest passage for commercial traffic between Europe and China, led inevitably to the formation of a highly heterogeneous local population, albeit one in which Turkic peoples predominated.[12] The population was further fragmented in the sixteenth century when the Uzbeks and Tajiks adopted sedentary lifestyles whilst the tribes in southwest Central Asia (Turkmen) and the inhabitants of the Asian steppe (Kazakhs/Kyrgyz) remained nomadic.[13] In saying this it is crucial not to retroject the contemporary meanings that have been ascribed to terms such as Uzbek and Turkmen – that is, as ethnonyms denoting separate nations – when such terms originated to distinguish between different tribes who, with the exception of the Persian Tajiks, were all of Turkic origin. Indeed, the very fact that the term 'Uzbek' originated to denote a group of tribes who traced their genealogy back to Uzbek Khan, grandson of Ghenghis Khan, is indicative of the social formation that existed at this time, one in which predominantly face-to-face and agency-extended forms of integration connected peoples, and in which loyalties to family, tribe and clan were central. The social formations necessary to enable the nation to be imagined were still centuries away.

The social space between sedentary and nomadic peoples grew until, by the eighteenth century, it became possible to distinguish between two separate ways of life. On the one hand there existed a sedentary core of three Uzbek feudal khanates, namely, Khiva, Kokand and Bukhara.[14] Each khanate was ruled by a leader who claimed, and was largely granted, authority as a supra-tribal and therefore *traditional* leader. (Uzbek tribal autonomy had been subordinated to the rule of traditional forms of authority under Tamerlane as early as the fifteenth century.[15]) The khanates incorporated all of the major ancient cities of Central Asia, and also contained within their borders the peoples of Central Asia who had experienced the most enduring contact with Islam. Whilst Uzbeks dominated the khanates, the presence of large numbers of Persian Tajiks meant that bilingualism was widespread even amongst commoners.[16]

Conversely, the nomadic periphery by definition contained no great cities and was inhabited by tribes that had either been introduced to Islam late in history (the inhabitants of the steppe) or who had been converted by Sufis who practised an eclectic form of Islam incorporating many purely shamanistic rituals (for example, the Turkmen).[17] Islam was thus less institutionalized amongst the nomads and more strongly syncretized with pre-Islamic beliefs than in the core.[18] Tribal loyalties were correspondingly stronger in the periphery than in the core. Whilst the core and peripheral societies interacted, with the nomads of the periphery alternately invading the khanates and serving as mercenaries for the khans, two *qualitatively* different social formations none the less existed in Central Asia on the eve of the Russian conquest.

IMPERIALISM AND THE FIRST STIRRINGS OF IMAGINED NATIONS

The Russian conquest of Central Asia can be divided into two periods. The first spans the period 1731–1854, during which time the Kazakh/Kyrgyz steppes were absorbed into the Russian Empire.[19] The fact that the Russians negotiated separately with each of the three tribes on the steppe, thereby reinforcing the power of existing subjectivities, together with the incremental pace of Russian expansion during this period, whilst presaging what was to follow, had no direct bearing on the formation of national identities in Central Asia.[20] Thus it need not detain us further.

The second period of Russian expansion in Central Asia roughly coincides with what Roland Robertson has dubbed the 'take-off phase' of globalization.[21] Between 1865 and 1881, Russia absorbed the three khanates (although they survived as self-governing protectorates) and what would later become Turkmenistan into the newly named region of Turkestan.

A hunger for raw materials (principally cotton), competition with other imperial powers (principally Britain) for control of the area and the age-old justification of needing to impart the fruits of civilization on more 'backward' peoples all played a part in driving Russia south.[22]

The necessity of responding to Russian hegemony together with the introduction of European ideas via Russian immigrants provided the requisites for proto-nationalist sentiments to emerge amongst elites. Moreover, and in keeping with the rise of nationalist movements in both Europe and the periphery, such sentiments were first evinced by individuals used to working in the abstract/disembodied medium of writing, namely, intellectuals. From the late 1890s onwards, the vision of a pan-Turkic nation encompassing all Turkic speakers 'from the Balkans to China' (the Tajiks, being bilingual, were included in this category) gained increasing currency amongst Central Asian intellectuals.[23] Significantly, just as the first advocates of Pan-Africanism and Pan-Arabism were deracinated intellectuals (many of whom were Western educated *and* Christian),[24] so too the Pan-Turkists contained within their ranks disproportionate numbers of Tartars,[25] an ethnic minority that had no tribal attachments and whose modernizing intellectuals were thus doubly removed from the grasp of traditional subjectivities.

Attempts were made to propagate Pan-Turkism through the dissemination of pamphlets and through the production of a short-lived newspaper written in a purified Turkic script purged of Arabic and Persian elements.[26] Nevertheless, the first attempt at nation-building in Central Asia failed. We suggest that this failure can be attributed to two distinct factors. Firstly, whilst the professional and ethnic/social background of the Pan-Turkists allowed them to 'think' the nation, the majority of the population were relatively unaffected by the changing modes of practice that would otherwise have enabled them to accommodate a national subjectivity. The amirs of the three khanates discouraged the kind of exo-social education (Gellner's term) required to establish a single epistemological space throughout the populace. This conservatism was supported by the Tsarist authorities who, in any case, relied on skilled Russian immigrants to support the fairly limited industrialization that was taking place in Central Asia at the time.[27] The result was that by the turn of the century the vast majority of Central Asians remained illiterate and, with the exception of those dispossessed by the Russian immigrants, largely isolated from the processes of modernization.

If one employs the horizontal measure of nation formation established earlier, it can be effectively argued that national subjectivities did not exist outside a fraction of the intelligentsia in the early 1900s, thus 'nation formation' had yet to occur. However, as established in the introduction to this book, the absence of a broadly based national subjectivity did not preclude the establishment in Europe of nascent official state-nations by nationally minded elites.[28] The failure of elites to mobilize anti-colonial sentiment and thereby forge an enduring state-nation when the opportunity arose with the implosion of the metropole in 1917 (as an extension of Tom Nairn's theory would presume) must therefore be attributed to the second inhibitor of nation formation during this period, namely, the prevalence of competing visions amongst elites. The division between Pan-Turkists, Pan-Islamists (including both the fundamentalist Qadims and the Westernizing Jadid (reform) movement) and the tribal separatists of the steppes (the Alash Orda) can in turn be attributed to the persistence of traditional identities among large sections of the elite.

Prima facie, the persistence of traditional identities amongst the educated elite seems incongruous. Whilst it could be argued that many Pan-Islamists and tribal separatists were merely fighting to preserve their prestigious positions in society, such a stance underestimates the degree to which traditional mores were internalized even by elites; the capacity to operate within abstract media does not automatically grant one the capacity to step out of one's skin, as it were, and to assess all situations from a purely dispassionate and self-interested perspective. The persistence of tradition amongst members of the elite can be attributed to a notion that forms a recurrent motif in our analysis – whereas in metropolitan Europe modernity gradually emerged from the ashes of tradition, the conflicting ontologies of modernity and tradition collided even more violently and unevenly in the periphery as they were diffused by the imperialist activities of the core.

The implications of this are profound. In Europe, changes from the Reformation onwards – such as the decline in the power of the papacy and a growing sense of human beings as autonomous individuals, the rise of centralized absolutist states, the efflorescence of Enlightenment rationalism and the identification of the people as the source of state sovereignty in the works of writers such as Locke – laid the groundwork for the emergence of national subjectivities amongst elites. Thus elites were able to imagine the nation from the mid eighteenth century onwards even if the ontological shifts necessary to turn 'peasants into Frenchmen'[29] required the advent of industrial capitalism and the introduction of state-run education systems, the last which can be dated to the latter half of the nineteenth century. In Central Asia the collision of modernity and tradition led all but the most deracinated of the intellectuals-clerics to seek salvation in reconstituted variants of traditional identities rather than succumb to the modern European idea of nationalism. (One can already see the early parallels to the situation today.) The inability of the elites to form a unified front, as demonstrated in the numerous declarations of autonomy by different authorities during the Russian Civil War paved the way for the Soviet re-conquest of Central Asia in the early 1920s.

THE INVENTION OF NATIONS AND ACCELERATED MODERNIZATION

The persistence of tradition amongst sections of the elite together with the isolation of the masses from the processes of modernization have been shown to be mutually reinforcing factors militating against nation formation. Such barriers were substantively confronted with the national delimitation of Central Asia, which was initiated in 1924 by the triumphant Soviets and which had led by 1936 to the consolidation of the national borders extant in contemporary Central Asia.[30] Whilst the delimitation was motivated in part by the principle of *divide et impera* (the Islamic *basmachi* rebellion throughout Central Asia was not completely quashed until the late 1920s), and was also a concession to the different socio-economic conditions both between and within the sedentary core and the nomadic periphery, ideology also exerted considerable influence.[31] Stalin's nationalities policy had at its core a notion commonly found in discourses on the nation – namely, that whilst heightened national awareness was an inevitable by-product of modernization, it was none the less transient and would eventually give way to cosmopolitanism. The belief that the formation of nations would mollify indigenes' demands for autonomy and the conviction that the transition to a socialist mode of production would eventually dissolve national loyalties as a 'new Soviet man' came into being thus led (*pace* Gellner) to the self-conscious construction of nations 'from above' from the 1920s onwards.[32] This is what might be called reflexive modernism.

The gap between Stalin's Eurocentric conception of national identities and the reality of multivariate traditional identities in Central Asia necessitated a self-conscious process of cultural invention of the kind described by Eric Hobsbawm in his writings on nationalism, but it is our argument that these inventions were only lived at one level of social being: the public abstracted level. This is also not to suggest that these inventions were superficial – to the contrary, as we will see, invented languages became the means of articulating national sentiment – rather it is to argue that the layers of identity did not collapse into an undifferentiated plane of modern meaning.[33] Whilst the peoples of Central Asia spoke different dialects in different regions, these dialects were derived from a common Turkic heritage. The use of Arabic script, heretofore the sole means of common communication across Central Asia, was forcibly discontinued, whilst Soviet linguists accentuated the differences between regional dialects and elevated them to the status of 'national' languages. Soviet historians painstakingly fabricated 'national' histories and the new nations were delimited on the basis of allegedly objective measures that had no subjective significance for the peoples involved. When citizens in the sedentary core were asked to nominate their nationality on their identity cards they frequently had difficulty deciding whether or not they were Tajik or Uzbek, given that many were a mixture of both.[34]

The invention of nations must be considered in the context of a much broader process of accelerated modernization forced upon Central Asians from above. In their determination to drag the peoples of Central Asia into modernity, the Soviets attempted to stamp out expressions of traditional identity. Mosques were closed, the Sufi orders were suppressed and holy sites in the nomadic periphery such as the tombs of tribal leaders and Muslim mystics were desecrated.[35] The assault continued into the 1930s as collectivization of agriculture led to forced denomadization in the periphery, whilst the diffusion of a 'historical materialist' outlook through the introduction of compulsory exo-social education sought to further undermine tradition in the minds of the populace.[36]

The significance of this period in relation to the development of national subjectivities cannot be underestimated. The common view, predicated as it is on the incorrect belief that Central Asia had yet to experience the effects of modernization, posited that when such processes were eventually experienced, the 'accordion effect' of compressing such change into a short temporal frame would preclude the development of national subjectivities. The period of accelerated modernization presents us with an opportunity to test whether or not the ontological shifts necessary to 'think' the nation can be affected within a relatively short space of time. There can be no doubt that the period of accelerated modernization inflicted immense trauma on the peoples of Central Asia. The mass migrations of the 1930s, not only from the nomadic periphery but also from the sedentary core, into neighbouring countries parallels the mass migrations from Europe to the New World during the modernization of the late nineteenth century.[37] Both cases involved large numbers of people translocating themselves physically over large distances in order that they might remain psychologically in the same place. Conversely, in Central Asia, as in Europe, those that remained were immersed in an exo-social education that provided the skills such as literacy deemed necessary to conceive of abstract communities such as the nation. Whilst such exposure did not guarantee that national subjectivities would take root, it nonetheless made the prospect of broad-based nation formation possible for the first time.

At the same time, the period of accelerated modernization in Central Asia was characterized by the durability of tradition. Despite the best efforts of Stalin, premodern loyalties retained considerable power. The *mahallah*, the locality in which one was raised and which was typically based on familial networks and linked by genealogical principles,[38] remained the focus of social interaction for most Central Asians. It provided a ready-made identity map of steadily expanding concentric circles of loyalty (from locality to clan to region) within which one could locate oneself. Significantly, this identity map retained considerable hold not only over those individuals primarily used to dealing at the face-to-face and agency-extended levels of integration, but also over the supposedly Russified nomenklatura, who were accustomed to operating within the disembodied medium and who thus should have been immune to such a parochial outlook.

Whilst one could argue that the tendency of the nomenklatura to set up networks of patronage amongst those from their native *mahallah* was merely a manifestation of realpolitik, this is an oversimplification. Specifically, it imputes a rationalist, individualist and pre-eminently modern outlook to persons who in spite of their exposure to a modern ontology were nevertheless embedded in a social milieu in which premodern values and loyalties remained deeply entrenched. The Soviets' continuation of tsarist preferences for importing Russian proletarians to facilitate Central Asian industrialization together with the adoption of a more conciliatory attitude towards Islam from 1941 onwards (an acknowledgement of the continuing hold of Islam over the populace by a regime anxious to retain Central Asian loyalty in the Second World War) no doubt reinforced the bifurcated consciousness evolving amongst the people of Central Asia.[39]

The sudden reframing of the life-world of the general population and its attendant traumas is probably not unique to Central Asia or even to the developing world but rather a malady inextricably associated with modernization. However, what distinguishes the rest of the world from metropolitan Europe is the fact that the gradual modernizing in Europe over several hundred years infused elites with a modern *Weltanschauung* from the mid eighteenth century onwards whilst eroding the material bases for a continuation of traditional lifestyles by the masses.[40] In the developing world, by contrast, modernity collided with tradition more dramatically and across all classes. The persistence of traditional social formations created a hybrid traditionalized modernity in which the emergence of a common epistemological space inscribed in the language of nations coexisted with rather than displaced traditional identities. This explanation adequately accounts for the changing conceptions of identity from the 1920s onwards. However, given the subjective nature of identity and the totalitarian character of the Soviet state, macroscopic evidence in support of this interpretation only manifests itself from the period of glasnost onwards.

GLASNOST, INDEPENDENCE AND AN UNCERTAIN FUTURE

With the advent of glasnost the first overt evidence that national subjectivities had established a foothold in Central Asia emerged. Intellectuals began to agitate for the adoption of the language of the titular ethnic group as the language of state in each republic; this in spite of the fact that such languages had been largely constructed by Russians merely two generations earlier.[41] In 1986, the replacement of the Kazakh First Secretary of the Kyrgyz Communist Party by a Russian provoked serious riots in the Kazakh capital of Alma-Ata, whilst in 1988 the first avowedly nationalist political grouping came into being with the establishment of the Birlik Popular Front in Uzbekistan. These events, and the extent of popular involvement in both the riots in Alma-Ata and protests pushing for changes in the language policy,[42] indicate that national subjectivities now exist in Central Asia not only within elites but amongst the masses as well. Nevertheless, the evidence of a nascent national subjectivity must be counterposed against the even stronger revival of traditional identities in recent times. A resurgence of Islam assisted by both glasnost and the international Islamic revival[43] has seen a proliferation in the number of mosques being built in Central Asia and a dramatic increase in the number of young people attending *madrasahs*, most notably in Uzbekistan.[44] Meanwhile, in the states comprising the once nomadic periphery, many of the holy places desecrated by the Soviets are being restored at the initiative of local citizens' committees and pilgrimages to these areas are on the rise.[45]

Attempts to reconcile these two seemingly discrepant trends must begin with an acknowledgement that life is experienced at distinct and yet overlapping levels of integration and that as such one's identity, far from being unitary and fixed over time, is rather multiple, contextual and relational.[46] Thus, it is entirely possible for an individual to be a member of the Middle Horde, a Kazakh and a Muslim depending on the social context. It should not be inferred that this process is necessarily self-conscious – far from it. Rather, by (practically) separating out the realms of identity, a young Turkmen is able to reconcile her pilgrimage to an ancestral tomb for the purposes of enhancing her fertility with the atheistic exo-social education in biology that she would have received under the Soviets.[47] What this example, and evidence of a more general renaissance of tradition amongst the young demonstrates is that it is possible for not only different subjectivities to exist within one individual, but for different ontologies (mystical, sacred, on the one hand, and historical, materialist, on the other) to operate across different social contexts. In the words of Yaacov Ro'i:

> The collective consciousness of the Central Asian peoples seems to be simultaneously subnational, national, and supranational. In other words, they identify themselves at one and the same time as, although apparently in different contexts and on different levels, as Tekke, Laqay, or Manghyt (just to mention some of the region's ethnic groups and tribes); as Uzbeks, Kirgiz and Turkemen; as Central Asians or (with the exception of Tajiks) as 'Turks'... [moreover] the Islamic component has become a fundamental facet of all Central Asian nationalisms or national consciousnesses – as part of the national heritage – without it necessarily signifying religious practice.[48]

If one employs the measures of nation formation described earlier, it is apparent that the nations of Central Asia, whilst broad, are not comprehensively embedded in citizens' conception of themselves. The nature of these nations invites the possibility that the terms by which the high culture is defined may be subject to challenge. This has indeed been the case in Central Asia, but the challenges have not gone very far. The Pan-Islamic IRP (Islamic Revival Party) has established cells in all five republics, and has been particularly active in the traditionally devout Ferghana valley, which lies within the borders of Uzbekistan, Tajikistan and Kyrgyzstan, but these groups have faltered or tended to operate as national bodies. In short, pan-Islamism adds another tension to the layering of national subjectivities in the sedentary core rather than an alternative form of exclusive identity. Meanwhile, in the periphery, traditional cleavages remain salient though they have rarely led to inter-clan conflict.[49] In addition to these 'potential' challenges to 'classical' nation-building, the ethnic heterogeneity of the populations, especially in Kazakhstan where Russians outnumber Kazakhs, has hampered the development of a homogenizing national outlook, as demonstrated by sporadic outbreaks of inter-ethnic violence.[50] The elites of Central Asia remain haunted in particular by the civil war in Tajikistan between an unreformed Communist nomenklatura and an Islamic-led opposition.[51] However, we would argue that Tajikistan is anomalous,[52] and that the chaos can be attributed to the presence of compounded social cleavages of tribe, religiosity, ethnic community and level of economic development that are not representative of Central Asia as a whole. Just as their nomadic ancestors were able to syncretize Islam with shamanistic practices, so too it is possible that contemporary Central Asians will be able to retain a layered sense of national identity in conjunction with traditional identities. Conversely, it is doubtful that further industrialization will simply dilute traditional identities – the qualitative shift that enabled national subjectivity to emerge has already been made. If parallels in Africa and Southeast Asia are anything to go by, elites will continue to manage and manipulate the political expression of traditional identities, either through reflexive syncretic association or by manipulative cultural management rather than by vainly hoping that further modernization will dissolve these identities. And they will do so because the layering of identity is a lived reality rather than simply based on invented traditions.

Part IV

Confronting Terror and Violence

13
Democracy and the Shadow of Genocide[1]

Tom Nairn

Genocide has become another spectre of our times. It is repeatedly voiced in novels, films and 'harrowing' journalistic or TV accounts, and is now calling forth distinguished academic studies like Michael Mann's *The Dark Side of Democracy*.[2] Events from Tibet and East Timor to Kosova and Macedonia constantly feed the tendency, which is almost invariably underpinned by a deeply gloomy vision of human nature. 'Is *this* what we are really like?' The ray-of-hope people then tend to clutch at is the thought that this is what we *would be like*, were we not at least part of the time prevented from being ourselves by reason, religion or at least reluctant calculation of the probable costs of 'being ourselves'. Another very typical example comes from the great Polish journalist Ryszard Kapuscinski in his recent article 'On the Nature of Genocide' in *Le Monde Diplomatique*.[3] His subtitle, 'A Century of Barbarism', indicates a line of argument that follows Hannah Arendt, Walter Laqueur, and Zygmunt Bauman's *Modernity and the Holocaust*.[4] In Kapuscinski's terms, 'Contemporary civilization has as part of its essence and dynamic certain features capable ... of producing acts of genocide.' Far from receding in importance, these may be on the increase. Rwanda, Bosnia and East Timor have all occurred in the 1990s, and yet reproduced many traits of, for example, the Nazi Judeocide and the massacre of the Armenians earlier in the century.

Kapuscinski gives a left-Catholic version of this dismal story. He believes that 'the eclipse of religious conscience, and the atrophy of feelings and of the distinction between good and evil' have contributed to so many disasters. 'Love thy neighbour' has lost its conviction, he argues, and opened the door to more deeply embedded traits of human nature – a distrust of the Other and of the Unknown easily exploitable by 'contemporary ideologies of hatred, like nationalism, fascism, Stalinism, racism ... .' The only answer lies in 'raising the moral level' of both individuals and societies – a more lively spiritual awareness and a greater will to do good, and 'treat thy neighbour as thyself'. Shortly before this interpretation there appeared another, by Québecois-British theorist Michael Ignatieff.[5] His left-Protestant view of the subject is if anything gloomier than Kapuscinski's. He claims that inherited moral principles have a 'tribal' origin that puts difference above the common

205

features of the species. Thus 'moral universalism is a late and vulnerable addition to the moral vocabulary of mankind', and is always liable to collapse under pressure. Human nature craves above all homogeneity and a 'world without enemies'. In situations of breakdown it will usually be this desire that (suitably orchestrated) appears to offer salvation. *We* will only be ourselves once *they* are out of the way – once and for all.

Ignatieff goes on to give a very interesting account of the origins of the term 'genocide'. In fact he provides a potted biography of the man who coined it, Polish lawyer Raphael Lemkin. The term dates from 1943, and was founded upon the latter's book *Axis Rule in Occupied Europe*, a juridical analysis of what the Nazis were doing in the territories of the New Order. Lemkin realized that 'Aryanism' was in fact a project to permanently divide the human species, a goal which involved 'inverting the equality provisions of all the European legal traditions' and – where necessary – 'putting down' all those who either would or could not conform. Once that division was achieved, eugenic control would cause the elite or super-species and the assorted sub-species to develop separately, and cease to contend over rights and spoils. Democracy would be dead. This was the true 'Final Solution', for which the Jews and Rom of Europe were being used as guinea pigs. In its awesome context 'genocide' was a rational way of putting peoples on one side or the other: up with the lords of humankind or down among the long-term losers (whose complete disappearance would, in the famous phrase, represent 'no great mischief').[6]

Lemkin's solution was to reinforce the ideal oneness of *Homo sapiens* by providing a firmer legal foundation for it. Jurisprudence had to take over from religious or moral aspiration. That idea underlay the Nuremberg trials and the constitution of the United Nations. 'Late and vulnerable' it may be, but it has persisted through one disaster after another, and seems likely to be enhanced under the conditions of post-1989 globalization. One fruit of this strange era of transition is the recurrent liberal idea that 'we' – the world community, or would-be community – have already assumed a kind of putative responsibility for things like post-Yugoslav 'ethnic cleansing' or the Rwandan massacre of 1994. This is the theme, for example, of Linda Melvern's *A People Betrayed: The Role of the West in Rwanda's Genocide*.[7] In such accounts the world is often contracted to mean 'we in the West'. This elision implies that the Atlantic area (or even NATO) still pursues the 1945 victory by (so to speak) standing in for a non-existent world authority. Hence it can be judged culpable whenever outside intervention fails to forestall or arrest atrocities. In a world still stubbornly divided – maybe more so than during the Cold War – raising the moral decibels appears the only tolerable response.

DEMOCRACY'S ROLE

However, such exhortation would benefit from a more realistic assessment of the 'nature of genocide'. There is a contradiction at the heart of all these analyses, which emerges most strikingly from Kapuscinski's. The strongest point he makes there is to point out that 'no genocide has been perpetrated in the twentieth century in a country *where democracy reigned.* Thus far, the latter seems to be the only effective obstacle to the genocidal temptation ... .'[8] True, but the judgement requires two qualifications, one minor and another of the greatest importance. The lesser caveat is that 'democracy' cannot here be confused with sociological majority or with a single referendal vote or empowerment. Most Germans did vote for the Third Reich, and most Rwandans (the Hutus) for the government that ended (as Melvern describes) by sponsoring an extermination programme. However, if *democracy* had persisted in those countries it is unlikely that the atrocities would have followed. Democracy is a constitutional *system*, not a vote. In fact, it is a system or it is nothing. It has to be a juridical order that permits both minorities and head-counted majorities to persist, to change their positions, and to confront one another in more than a life-or-death endgame. But the purpose of the German and Rwandan-Hutu regimes was precisely to bring such an endgame about, discarding constitutional democracy in the process.

The second and much more significant limitation to Kapuscinski's verdict is that he does not perceive how democracy *has also been a cause* of the genocidal explosions which make him despair. Michael Mann puts it very well in his forthcoming book: 'Genocide was the first consequence in modern times of rule by "we, the people" – the first truly dark side of democracy.'[9] There could never have been the hopeful, progressive side *without* this shadow. No person, no people exists without its shadow, and no real development has ever occurred on the plane of angels. Unless we appreciate this seminal role, there is little chance of awarding democracy a therapeutic one. It becomes simply an 'obstacle', a way of reining in destructive impulses which would otherwise prevail. Democracy must reinforce 'Love Thy Neighbour' – not the other way round.

In fact it was invariably the advent of democratic equality, or at least the inchoate fertilizing hope of democracy's coming, that triggered both mass insufferance and utopian desires. This was what engendered, in Ignatieff's words, the sense of 'a world without discord ... free of the enemy without or the enemy within'.[10] That in turn gave leaders and intelligentsias a new means of mobilization – the captains of reaction, as well as those of democracy and civic empowerment. Sometimes, in the short run, the captains of reaction have been more effective. In the former Yugoslavia, for example, where democracy had been non-existent, creatures like Ratko

Mladic and Slobodan Milošević found it all too easy to turn utopian desires in the authoritarian direction of 'Greater Serbia'. However, ten years on, we must also acknowledge that these are war criminals on the run. Pol Pot is a vile but fading memory. During 1994–95 the executioners from Rwanda's Interahamwe dissolved into what Melvern vividly describes as a great African horizon black with people, 'the fastest and largest exodus ever recorded'.[11] So, do the transient 'achievements' of deluded scoundrels really justify so much prophetic gloom? By contrast, 'democracy' is the name of the long, difficult and ascending game of modern times. Yes, it has brought devastating storms with it; but also, it alone bears the possibility of eventual climate control and so of a world with (at least) less discord and indurate hostility. There is nothing utopian about *democratic* nationalism. And contrary to religious and secular hypochondria, there is *in the longer term* nothing fragile or vulnerable about it either. The 'century of genocide' Kapuscinski bewails is also the one that decisively defeated fascism and authoritarian communism, and has relegated Social Darwinism to the pathology museum.

DEMOCRATIC NATURE

The underlying cause of the inherited hypochondria in these accounts is an idea of fallen human nature. Not mass killings alone, therefore, but the queasy conviction that this sort of thing must be somehow endemic to humans. Old-time religion and strained moral universalism then appear as unsteady safeguards against such congenital weakness. Unable to escape ethnocentrism and bloodlust, *Homo sapiens* will have to be forever preached at, and occasionally charged in the dock to follow its better self. Is there not a suspect changelessness about all this? After all, fifty or a hundred years ago, before Himmler, the Khmer Rouge and the End of History, the same verdict was reached in much the same tone of voice. Has nothing at all changed except (as clerics and schoolmasters seem always to think) for the worse?

The mass killing of others is of course part of 'human nature' like everything else, in a banal sense. The trouble is, no one knows enough about our authentically inherited societal nature to be anything but banal. A great deal is now known about genetic nature. But notoriously, this tells us extraordinarily little about the socio-cultural or communicative 'nature' that humans have grown on the foundation of natural selection. Most of what we really *know* here comes from the story of modernity itself – that is, the time between the eighteenth century and the present. But this is yesterday in humanity's terms: the epoch of the conjoined convulsions of democracy, industrialization and nationalism, from which it remains very hard to draw grand conclusions about human (as distinct from modern) nature.[12]

It is this difficulty that allows time-honoured nonsense to reproduce itself unchanged. Knowledge of genes has far outpaced that of society. Speculative capitalized abstractions about the Group and the Other are little more than flimsy shortcuts to despondency. Evolutionary psychology may be gradually changing this, but it will take a long time to shift 'commonsense' out of its ruts. In the meantime, it may make more sense to try and view modern democracy as analogous to modern technology. The application of science to industry and commerce (and now everything else as well) has, in Walter Benjamin's celebrated phrase, been like a storm of progress and created 'piles of debris growing skyward' at the same time as it has bestowed new horizons on humankind. Yet the sole available answer to such threats lies *in its further advance*. It is through more humane or 'green' technology, the information revolution, the exploitation of new sources of energy, that the debris can be removed, or at least lessened. It will never be found by pretending to stand still, or by pining for the lost idyll of pre-industrial times.

Surely the same is true of democracy? Overcoming catastrophes like the modern genocides entails a great development of democracy, rather than falling back upon religious precepts, or a fake psychology of doomed human nature. As with inoculation, the cure can only arise from within the 'ailment' itself. Civic nationalism is the sole remedy for ethnic nationalism: that is, an identity-politics capable of coming to terms with the 'shadows', and accepting the clay of human existence rather than fleeing from it into abstractions or realms of disembodiment. It is in this sense that democracy can be likened to the political technology of modernity: simultaneously destructive and creative in accelerating growth, self-repairing, and looking forward (presumably) to fuller realization in 'postmodernity'.

A SUCCESSFUL GENOCIDE

At the last mid century, democratic governments were in a minority. Today they are an overwhelming majority: including, admittedly, pretend democracies like Florida and pre-Fox Mexico, or the bath-chair parliamentarianism of the United Kingdom. One interesting pointer to imminent change comes from looking back at the mid century before last – the 1850s. During that decade the most successful genocide in recorded history was nearing its end, in Van Diemen's Land. It was carried out by British colonialists.[13]

When HMS *Beagle* brought the young Charles Darwin there in 1835, he was surprised to be invited to an evening of Italian chamber music in Hobart. No shadow upon later triumphs is cast by observing that at that point Darwin was also a young imperial ass. He saw around him chiefly 'testimony to the power of the British nation ...Visiting Australia has given me a grand idea of the power and efficiency of the English nation' (and so on, to his sister Catherine).[14] Twenty years before the island was re-baptized after another great Dutch explorer as 'Tasmania', its previous population had been reduced from around 20,000 to 210, 'concentrated' in an 'improvement camp' on Flinders Island in Bass Strait. The very last one was to perish in 1877. 'It was unfortunate', comments an earlier biographer, Sir Gavin de Beer, 'that Darwin never had an opportunity to see these living fossil specimens in an Old Stone Age of culture, with a skull capacity of only 1200 cubic centimeters.'[15]

The dreadful story was retold in a new and arresting way last year, in Matthew Kneale's *English Passengers*.[16] Most readers know that Michael Ondaatje's *The English Patient* was actually a double-dealing Hungarian Count, so charred by flames that everyone was taken in by his public school accent. It may also be recalled that the Count's prized possession was a tattered edition of Herodotus, the early Greek travel writer who recounted the astounding diversity of human customs. His spiritual home was a hunter-gatherers' cave covered with mysterious rock paintings, somewhere in the south Libyan desert. Kneale's characters and locations are no less disconcerting, and in the end the book encompasses an equally vast panorama. The 'English passengers' are a pair of unsavoury lunatics: the Reverend Wilson, unshakeably convinced that Van Diemen's Land must have been the site of the Garden of Eden, and Dr Potter, an early racist who travelled everywhere equipped with calipers for measuring the capacity of people's skulls. Potter is modelled on the Scottish anatomist Robert Knox, the one associated with the infamous 'body snatchers', Burke and Hare, before narrowly escaping being lynched by the Edinburgh mob. In London he went on to pen a 'classic' of ethnic science: *The Races of Men: A Philosophical Inquiry into the Influence of Race over the Destinies of Nations*. This work served empire well, and gained some influence in the ante-bellum Southern states of America.

In a fit of absence of mind, these 'cretchy fritlags'[17] hire a Manx ship and crew to sail them round the world. Captain Illiam Quillian Kewley (Ulysses) and his band of rogues turn out to be the kind of coastal-trade chancers that Herodotus would have at once recognized, liked and distrusted. They start by pinching an Admiral's silver dinner service, then get themselves thrown out of every port from London to Melbourne and back. Yet they still return with a decent swag to 'Peel City' (Ithaca). Van Diemen's Land fills them with a horror far greater than the monsters of Antique legend. In this Hades of the new Romans, chamber music and hymns accompany forced labour and annihilation of the unworthy. They (and the reader) perceive not the power and efficiency of British Empire but its mixture of fierce commercialism and do-gooding pomposity, the subjugation of the world by a vile combination of righteousness and fire-power.

Kneale is also following the example of William Golding 40 years ago, in his novel *The Inheritors*. Golding tried to see the war at the beginning of human time through the eyes of the losers, the Neanderthals. Similarly, *English Passengers* presents genocide through the eyes of 'Peevay' and his family, Tasmanian natives trying to resist the choice forced on them by 'the ghosts': extermination or Improvement. Reverend Wilson almost dies while failing to locate Eden, then decides it was probably back in England all along. Dr Potter wanders about the Underworld with his deadly calipers and notebook, before concluding that the Manx are only slightly above Aboriginals on the evolutionary tree. They survive by being such crawlers, filled with proper awe of 'the mightier and cleverer fellows' around them. In the coming Great Conflagration of Nations, there can be no doubt that the Black Type is fated to go first: 'And while it is in the heart of men to find sadness in any such occurrence, it may be considered that such an outcome is not without justice ...'.[18]

THE DEMOCRACY OF DEATH

English Passengers is among other things a salute from one near-obliterated culture to those on another and less lucky island. I suspect that Philistine politicos like Australia's John Howard and Britain's Tony Blair might learn something from Kneale's emblematic narrative. It helps us understand what 'atonement' and reconciliation are truly about. Most would agree that after genocide, in one sense real justice is none. Once a population is gone, what might have been its contribution to the alchemy of human culture can only be guessed at. And yet, astonishingly, the vanished do speak again in this new Odyssey, though inevitably through imagined mirrors, and in somebody else's voice. What kind of rediscovery is this? And why is it being made now?

We are living through the still thawing permafrost of both imperial and cold-war culture. After 1989 neither politicians nor business leaders wasted their time imagining what would happen if the entire glacier were to melt away under them. But just as the great freeze had to congeal things not directly connected with state and military preoccupations, so its end must release ideas and emotions far removed from the cramped stereotypes of neo-liberalism and the shards of Atlanticism. Such liberated meanings may be like birds in the air, and find expression first in cultural forms. Happily, earth-shifts do not depend on management consultants and political parties. They are unacknowledged legislation, from the country beyond the Pale.

The legislation implicit in *English Passengers* may be something like this: we are now all in the same boat, democracy is the only tolerable ship-board regime – but its positive functionality demands a far-reaching renegotiation with the past, as well as with those sharing the present. This is why ancestry matters in a new sense, quite distinct from the constricting mythology of ethnic nationalism – and also from the 'timeless' templates of religion. Whatever the new or third nature of 'globalization' is, it cannot be constituted without a new retrospect, and a new and much vaster framework of justification and memory. In another shrewd observation, Kapuscinski notes how rare it has been for states and leaders to admit their guilt over genocide: 'Germany here constitutes the exception which proves the rule. In most other cases, power either rejects the accusation or remains obstinately silent on the subject …'.[19] But may it not be that German exceptionalism also stands for an emergent new rule? And that this is related both to Germany's exceptional democracy, and to its present leadership in Europe? Philistines think that historical revisionism means tut-tutting over the errors of Bill Clinton and Mrs Thatcher, or (stretching things a bit) Roosevelt and Churchill. But the creative imagination works in more unruly and fertile ways.

On Tynwald Day every July the new laws of the Manx Parliament are read out to whoever cares to turn up and listen, from a mound at the end of a field at St John's (not far from Peel City, near the centre of the island). They are declaimed first in the language of Captain Kewley and his men, then in English. It's mainly a fun day. People turn up with children and picnics, and wander in and out of the pubs and tents. There are a few individuals around dressed as Viking warriors, terrifying nobody (Norse invaders are credited with bearing the seeds of democracy to Man before the Norman Conquest). A brash loudspeaker commentary tells people what's going on; there are hundreds of three-legged flags, a brass band, uniforms and prayers. To see events like these after reading Matthew Kneale's book brings a deep perturbation of the heart. The thought is irresistible: had 'Peevay' and the people of that other island been spared, then in time, in an antipodean summer never to come, they also might have celebrated democracy in a similar way; and been most fortunate to do so. Instead, they were buried in Benjamin's storm of history, vanishing beneath the 'piles of debris'. Archive and imagination alone conserve their memory. The admission of guilt can in itself change nothing of this. Yet that is only a key, the way to a much greater change in the *meaning* of such recollection today, for all the parties still concerned. And all *are* concerned. The human present never escapes from the past, nor is any episode of that history really 'particular' in the sense of an island on its own. How it 'reads' the story of the main reconstitutes a sense of itself, and of all future time.

But look out: there are always fritlags about. One can only hope a few of them turn to *English Passengers* and re-read the odyssey of humankind: how important and difficult it is to return home, how monsters and customs officials can be outwitted, and how lunatics like the Reverend Wilson and Dr Potter can, in the end, be disposed of to make the human voyage safer.

14
Nationalism and the Crucible of Modern Totalitarianism[1]

Tom Nairn

Eighty-one years ago there occurred an event, obscure at the time, from whose terrible consequences the world of 2004 CE has not yet completely recovered. The place was Munich, capital of the historic Kingdom of Bavaria and now the second city of the recently formed all-German Reich or Commonwealth. The time was five years after the end of the First World War, when this new would-be imperial state had been defeated, and then both punished and humiliated by the victors. What was to become the most extreme currency inflation in history had begun, fuelling the strangely inebriate climate described in the words of a contemporary economist: 'Things political and economical here are in a bigger mess than ever, the future wrapped in Egyptian darkness ... .'[2] By the autumn of the same year the Reichsbank would be issuing 100-trillion-mark notes, and it took a pocketful of them to buy a single US dollar.

In the darkness, reckless and despairing forces multiplied. Munich was their favoured venue, combining as it did relative economic backwardness, cultural vivacity and a particularism as yet incompletely reconciled to German unity. Many Bavarians still perceived the latter as domination by Prussia and Berlin. They distrusted the centralism of the Weimar Republic as much as its supposed leftism and openness to 'Jewish influences'. One consequence of this was that all-German nationalism assumed an especially shrill and raucous form there. Immediately after the war an independent Bavarian Republic had been proclaimed under the leadership of the socialist Kurt Eisner, deposing the native Wittelsbach monarchy and calling on the other German states to follow its revolutionary lead. The call was not answered, and Eisner's regime endured only a few months. What it did succeed in doing was to arouse the fear of death among the predominantly conservative cadres of the stately old capital on the Isar, as well as in Bavaria's 80 per cent Catholic countryside.

The significance of that milieu for the rise of German fascism has been underlined in a remarkable study by David Large: *Where Ghosts Walked: Munich's Road to the Third Reich.*[3] His title comes from Stephan George's poem on the city, evoking the *Frauenkirche* or Kirk of Our Lady, in sight of whose spires alone the true Münchner feels at home on a 'soil as yet untouched by bane, in the town of folk and youth'. Within its charmed walls amiable ghosts from the past still walked in broad daylight, and blessed or consecrated the present. Later on, the greatest of Munich writers, Thomas Mann, was to give a bitterly different picture of those same ghosts. Are they not also the darkly mediaeval spirit of 'Kaisersaschern' in *Doktor Faustus* – the well of the Devil himself, whose waters flow through Adrian Leverkuhn's hypnotic music before driving him to madness and death?

THE BIRTH OF A WOLF

'How is it ... that everything rotten and unable to maintain itself elsewhere was magically pulled towards Munich?',[4] asked novelist Leon Feuchtwanger, driven from the city by anti-semitic persecution. While Berlin was becoming one of the world's most cosmopolitan cities, he mused, Munich slid irresistibly into provincialism and bloody-minded racism. Among those drawn to the Bavarian capital was would-be architect Adolf Hitler. Originally a draft-dodger from the Habsburg Empire, he joined the Bavarian army instead and became a trench-messenger during the war. We know why he liked Munich. 'A heartfelt love seized me for this city', he wrote in the 1920s,

> what a difference from Vienna! I grew sick to my stomach when I even thought back on that Babylon of races ... Most of all I was attracted by this wonderful marriage of primordial power and fine artistic mood ... [that] remains inseparably bound up with the development of my own life.[5]

The terms are interesting. Much later on the term 'primordial' became the customary concept for theories ascribing an ethnic or premodern foundation to nineteenth- and twentieth-century nation-states. The artistic mood was that of a mind capable, in something like Benedict Anderson's contemporary sense, of imagining national community along just such lines through the hypnotic rearview mirror of feigned retrospect and mythology.[6]

He returned from the Bavarian army in 1919 as a 'political education agent' – in effect a political snitch paid to infiltrate new political organizations and report back to the Bavarian government. One of these was a small gang of (mainly) war-veterans calling itself the Deutsche Arbeiterpartei or Workers Party. It numbered only a few dozen but was seen as having anti-Bolshevik 'potential'. The bosses encouraged their agent to join and help fund and then lead it; and a few months later it was able to stage a successful mass meeting in the Hofbräuhaus, a city-centre beer cellar. There something astounding happened.

The sickly looking Austrian spoke for the first time before a large audience, announcing the movement's new 25-point radical programme while his fellow members held opponents at bay with truncheons and well-aimed beer mugs. The platform included nationalization of trusts and the confiscation of war profits, but that was not what gripped the listeners. It was the voice itself – a raucous, snarling furnace-blast from some scarcely human region, sounding indeed like the echo of primordial will, overriding every doubt and liberal scruple. The Workers Party (later the National Socialist Party, or 'Nazis' for short in the Munich vernacular) had made its mark. Its leader wrote afterwards: 'When I finally closed the meeting, I was not alone in thinking that a wolf had been born that was destined to break into the herd of deceivers and misleaders of the people.'[7]

THE TRUE WOLF'S LAIR

In time, that wolf was to enslave the people of all Germany, slaughter much of European Jewry and come within measurable distance of world domination. But as David Large argues, its womb lay in Munich, and it was with good reason that Hitler insisted this city was the spiritual home of the Third Reich. After its monstrous birth, the NSDAP grew into a mass movement capable of taking over the whole city centre for its first party rally in January 1923. Some months previously, Mussolini's Italian Fascist Party had leapt into power following the march on Rome, and pressure mounted for a comparable coup in Bavaria. Now supported by significant parts of the Munich establishment, the Nazis planned a three-day political carnival to culminate on Sunday 28 January. Conservative historian Karl Alexander von Müller attended its main event, and published a memoir about it. He recalled how 'the hot breath of hypnotic mass enthusiasm' attained its unexampled climax as Hitler led his entourage through the shouting masses:

> He passed very close to me and I saw this was a different person from the one I had met here and there in private houses: his narrow, pale features were concentrated in wrath, cold flames leapt from his piercing eyes, which seemed to search left and right for possible enemies, as if to cast them down. Was it the mass audience that gave him this uncanny power? Or did he empower the audience with his own inner strength?[8]

This was the first of the Party Days, which, after 1933, were turned into great state and media occasions. The best known is that of 1934, filmed by regime cinematographer Leni Riefenstahl as *Triumph of the Will*. But the triumphalist path was laid eleven years before, when the party occupied and defended its original lair against rivals and opponents, with the connivance of a local elite more afraid of 'Jewish Bolshevism' and heartless capitalism than of those claiming to voice ancestral blood and instinct.

What was the source of Hitler's hypnotic power? On a personal level the physical voice was obviously important. Innumerable commentators would remark, like Müller, on Hitler's insignificance and ordinariness. But part of his authority must have lain in the sheer contrast between these features and his vocal cords. When he projected his voice in public it was as if the 'wolf' was released, its power bizarrely amplified by the banality of the source. Chaplin's mocking film *The Great Dictator* concentrated on the latter, but could not of course reproduce the former. As Marshall McLuhan observed in the 1960s, the voice was coincidentally appropriate to the new communication age just then being inaugurated by radio. *Where Ghosts Walked* throws more light upon a more specific and important factor in the equation. Large's emphasis on Bavaria suggests how the specific toxins of German nationalism arose partly out of a fierce, sometimes almost irresolvable, tension between locality and centralized power. Detestation of Berlin and Prussia was endemic among Bavarians, and heartily reciprocated in the Prussian counter-myth of Munich as a Hicksville of beer-swilling cretins, second-rate painters and slaves to the crucifix. In fact there were Nazis who despaired of Hitler's obsession with the South – at one point Goebbels even proposed expelling 'the petit bourgeois Hitler' from the movement unless he shook off its pernicious influence.

But what the Austrian 'outsider' may have instinctively grasped was the fruitfulness of that very tension. The wide disparities of Germany – a loose collection of smaller kingdoms until only one generation previously – could only be fused effectively together by a violently addictive ideology, through beliefs imbued with the force of traditional religion, plus the most modern media techniques (like radio). And the materials for this forging process were most conspicuously present in Munich.

The Wilhelmine Reich had been a hastily assembled and ramshackle structure, still haunted by the shades of mediaevalism. Its defeat in 1918 and the subsequent crazy economic landslides of 1922–23 and 1929 fostered a special sort of disorientation, where these ghosts were at once reanimated, quite unreconciled to the new Republic, and yet had nowhere to retreat to. In Large's account, Bavarian separatism haunted every moment of Munich politics – yet almost no one really wanted to risk a return to the Wittelsbach monarchy. But at the same time the Nazis dangled a heady escape route before those caught in this dilemma: they suggested that Bayern could become the font of true 'Germanness', within which rural backwardness would be magically changed into universal mission – into a redemptive crusade to fuse province with Reich, then Germany with the world. The biological science of the period supposedly guaranteed the deal. And now the contract was enunciated by a voice unleashed from some outer (or was it inner?) exultant darkness, the clamorous shriek of Beelzebub himself.

THE BROADER PICTURE

A wider historical and theoretical problem is also implicitly addressed by David Large's argument. In most accounts of the development of nationalism, the processes of Italian and German unification have figured in a highly favourable light. Even liberal or left-leaning histories generally stern about 'narrow nationalism' have viewed the late-nineteenth-century Italian and German states with approval – indisputably progressive victories over 'feudalism', the bringing together of unviable petty statelets. Does not such 'modernization' in some way prefigure present-day demands, when (again) nation-states ought to be joining up rather than breaking up?[9] But there was always an awkward downside to the bland vision, and it is here that *Where Ghosts Walked* has most relevance. Regrettably, both these great and exemplary unification projects ended in fascism. Indeed, they invented the beast. Was this just bad luck? Anything but, if one reinterprets the rise of Hitlerism more circumspectly, with more careful attention to its regional/ national roots. After he got out of Munich, Thomas Mann denounced the degeneration of his city's culture into 'high-flown, wishy-washy cant, full of mystical euphoria with hyphenated prefixes like race- and folk- and fellowship-',[10] but he failed to underline sufficiently how the cant responded to the profound moral failure of the Wilhelmine state. Similarly, Italian fascism – with equally strong regional roots, a comparable charismatic chieftain and quasi-military organization – demolished Risorgimento liberalism and the Savoy monarchy by 'marching on Rome' (or more exactly, by threatening to).

In both situations, hastily created state-unions had dissolved a host of older countries – city and princely states, early modern or even mediaeval kingdoms – in a way intended to be final, and which indeed still appeared so in the circumstances of the 1920s. In that imperialist or big-state world very few thought seriously of returning to the Dukedom of Tuscany, Piedmont, Hanover, to Bremen city-state or Bavaria. And yet liberal-progressive unity, the grandly proclaimed wider identity, had clearly foundered. What way out was there but a drastic reformulation of that identity along illiberal populist lines, emphasizing the things either denied or sidelined by the former unity regimes? But such emphasis demanded an oneiric or even inebriate style, since in conditions of crisis only the headiest concoction had a hope of transcending the gross regional/national contrasts still alive over both territories.

It should also be remembered that high-flown mystical euphoria about *Volk* and race gained an added electrical charge *from the conversion process itself*. This is what Hitler and Mussolini counted on, and it becomes much more visible on the smaller scale. A Lombard or a Sicilian, a Rhinelander or a Bavarian who bought into being 'Italian' or 'German' in their new fantasized sense would almost certainly do so to excess. Repression of one identity format is best achieved by fanatical embrace of another – something quite familiar in Britain, in both Welsh and Scottish conditions. In the post-First World War era the available formula for such non-democratic 'rebirth' was provided by Social Darwinism and the mythology of pre-scientific genetics – ideas then quite widely held (we should not forget) in the UK, France and America as well. In fact they were pretty influential in the British Labour Party, as shown in the early career of Harold Laski. The Kramnick–Sheerman biography showed to what an astonishing extent the early life of both Laski and his wife Frida Kerry was dominated by the eugenics movement.[11]

However, another lesson in David Large's story is the sheer complexity of the conditions needed to generate disaster on that scale. In other circumstances the same ideas led to quite different consequences – or, as in Britain, just evaporated in the face of new challenges. Blaming such catastrophes on 'nationalism' alone is as much use as blaming a violent storm on the weather. If one looks comparatively at some twentieth-century cataclysms, then a tentative diagram of their causation might look something like Figure 14.1.

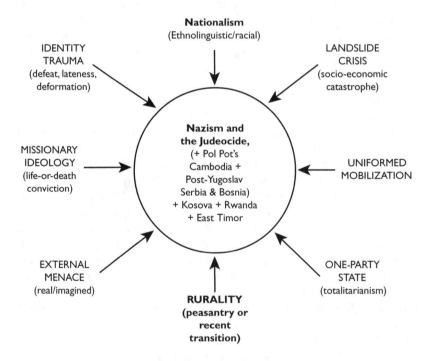

Figure 14.1   Great nationalist disasters: the fusion effect

The analogy used for this model is that of a thermonuclear fusion process (with apologies to Donald McKenzie).[12] Sometimes thought to be achievable in shorthand – as in the myth (if that is what it is) of the 'suitcase bomb' – such reactions depend in fact upon a wide range of necessary conditions. These can only be assembled (fortunately) only by exceptional means, and even then temporarily. While no precise social or historical analogy is possible, I think one can say that a similarly wide range of precipitating factors is needed for the disastrous societal 'explosions' which have brought about genocidal or ethnic-cleansing pandemonium, and closer-range studies like *Where Ghosts Walked* or Ben Kiernan's *The Pol Pot Regime* make this a lot more obvious.[13]

In a more distant or superficial perspective, 'nationalism' – in the sense of ethnic or racial nationalism – has often been made the main, or even the sole, cause of such disasters. Argument then goes round in inescapable circles. If ethno-nationalist politics is responsible for the horror, *and* (as most broad-brush analysts tend also to believe) is 'inescapable' and recurrent, then history settles down into the sad business of waiting for 'the next time', and doing one's (probably futile) best to exorcise fate in advance. But actually this is little more than headline history, in the service of a deeply conservative world-view.

The most salient ideological feature of such crises is some form of nationalist belief, which is presumably why it gets seized on as the culprit. However, its critical impact has been inseparable from two accompanying conditions (left and right from the top, in Figure 14.1): a structural 'identity' cramp or developmental antagonism, and a recent or ongoing 'landslide' instilling deep personal fears – a sense of the societal earth actually giving way. David Large gives a vivid idea of how these functioned in 1920s Bavaria. In the more recent examples, we know what the equivalents were: for Cambodians, an historical dread of disappearance, followed closely by being carpet-bombed 'into the Stone Age'; for the ex-Yugoslavs, the repressed inheritance of Greater-Serb identity, reanimated in circumstances of both state and economic collapse; and for the Rwandans, as Paul James discussed in Chapter 4, the long history of colonial and postcolonial reconstruction. Yet even these conditions might not have generated catastrophes without some or all of the other factors indicated in the graphic as the 'missionary' or crusading mentality capable of turning national aspiration into a version of imperialism, and an associated 'foreign foe' used to foster such paranoia. Psychologically, the two things have usually been linked together by the fixed idea of 'life or death': that is, the communal and threatened existence (in which individuals feel a personal stake) will be sustainable only by an external drive against those bent on the people's death.

Looking to the right of Figure 14.1: it is also significant that *uniforms* figure prominently in most situations of this kind: they are a way of both legitimating and advertising violently radical aims. Hence either military or paramilitary formations have canalized and taken over most ethnic violence, and the biggest offenders have been, not surprisingly, those of the state – with Indian 'communalist' violence as the most important exception. But 'the state' in most cases has meant 'the Party': all such cataclysms have *also* been struggles either to obtain one-party autocracy (Germany) or to reinforce and preserve it (Cambodia, Serbia-Yugoslavia and Rwanda). The Party in turn can function only through an autocratic leader.

Finally, it should not be forgotten that this complex reconfiguration of ethno-nationalism has normally had a powerfully *rural* or small-town foundation. This has often tended to be overlooked, partly through misunderstanding of the all-powerful German example. It is easy for modern commentators to forget just how rural the Germany of Hitler and Heidegger was, above all the south Germany portrayed in Large's book. He depicts what today cannot help seeming a largely different and lost Central-European world. As he is careful to underline in the epilogue, the wolf's lair of Nazism was far removed indeed from today's Munich, one of the greatest industrial conurbations in Europe. Back in the 1920s it was still the overgrown, easygoing 'county town' of a largely peasant culture. Cambodia of the 1970s and Rwanda of the 1990s were overwhelmingly peasant nations. At the moment of Yugoslav collapse, both Bosnia and Serbia remained far less touched by a process of halting industrialization than many outside observers realized – is this not why they were able to produce a 'village war' unconcluded in the present decade?

This element may also help us towards a tentative general chronology of ethno-nationalist disaster. Such explosions have been intimately linked to the moment of rural–urban transition – 'moment' here meaning not 'instant' but a world-historical phase, possibly multi-generational in duration and yet with a determinable beginning and end. In it wolves like Mussolini, Hitler, Milošević, Pol Pot and General Habyarimana were born. They were products less of the countryside and peasant culture than of the new lairs of forced passage, in which ancient attitudes and reflexes conducted a survival battle against modernity, of necessity emotionally violent and rooted in an idealized past time. These were also among the 'ghosts' of Large's book, and sometimes they won, for a time. But if some of them are still around, or pending, at least we can see they are not inscribed in human nature or history. All their baleful presence implies is that the 'moment', in the complex sense I have tried to indicate – modernization, urbanization and their updated descendant 'globalization' – is itself far from over.

15

Control and the Projection of a Totalizing War-Machine[1]

Paul James

Photographs of dead children regularly appear in the world press. The killing of Anas bin Nazir in 2003, shot in the back by the Indonesian military as he ran through a rice paddy in Aceh, is a recent example. However, there is one syndicated photograph that I cannot get out of my mind. Taken in 2001 after an exchange of gunfire at a checkpoint near Jerusalem, the photo stands out as carrying something beyond the usual image of simple tragic death. It is poised at a moment of contradictory truth. It depicts a Palestinian youth lying prone and half naked in the middle of a dusty street. A dog-sized robot – camera-eyed and remote-controlled – checks to see whether or not the boy terrorist is dead or still dangerous. To one side of the photograph a woman carrying a shopping bag begins to cross the street. The human moment is frozen at the point of a technical question. The woman, and the body politic of an imposed nation, waits as the necroscopic machine checks on a technicality: is the potential risk neutralized, or does it still present a threat?

Certainly this act of technological mediation ameliorates risk for the unseen soldiers. However, at the same time it also dehumanizes the threat and safely objectifies the 'enemy'. No one mourns the dead person – not even the bystander. There is no rite of passage to mark the passing of life from his body. The emotional power of the photograph works off that very contradictory abstraction, contrasting the post-human intervention with the banal humanity of an old woman engaged in one of the necessary transactions of everyday life. It just so happens that she wants to cross a street where someone has been killed. The photograph thus subjectively counterposes instrumental mediation, human mortality and quotidian necessity, even as it carries this condensed moment of tragedy to us, the newspaper readers thousands of kilometres away – mediated tragedy, breakfast toast and momentary effect. To the extent that the photograph still works emotionally, we do not live in a post-human world. Nevertheless, I want to argue that the lines between the human and means of technical mediation are being blurred. Every time that instruments of the abstract war-machine are used – even if ostensibly to protect us – or every time we glance at yet another image of violence and the emotional effect is diminished by even a shade, we are allowing our world to be overlaid by a strengthening level of the post-human.

Just as the image invokes a tension between the technologized post-human and the mortal human, the present chapter works across the same field of concern. It addresses in particular the tension between the rationalized deployment of technologies of death and the putative motivation of their use to project the 'humanitarian' values of liberty and security. The chapter argues three main points. Firstly, it suggests that the hope of 'freedom from fear', defined in its broadest sense, has been drawn into a tragic association with a new kind of war-machine.[2] Secondly, it suggests that the techniques and technologies of the war-machine are built upon a generalizing practice of increasingly abstract engagement, both physically in terms of nature of the delivery of force and emotionally in terms of how we relate to those against whom the force is being directed. The widening War on Terror threatens to carry us towards a condition where we are dangerously abstracted from those defined as 'Other' – terrorists, warlords, mullahs, and children overboard. This process of abstracting the Other has long been with us ideologically, but it has become qualitatively more dangerous as the processes of technical mediation have compounded the possibilities of controlling, killing and knowing from a distance. This is compounded by the way in which we vacillate between active paranoid fear of the Other and passive acceptance of the machine that promises to moderate that fear. The third main thrust of the discussion is to suggest that in the context of the War on Terror the abstract war-machine is being developed with the intention of projecting a *totalizing effect*. While total control is by definition impossible and the unwieldy machines of 'totalizing effect' have a tendency to generate chaos rather than calm, the resources of the war-machine are being generalized across both the international and domestic spheres with the goal of total control – this is the other side of the promise to win the War on Terror.

THE MULTIPLIER EFFECT OF TERROR AND THE FACE OF THE 'OTHER'

We now fear potentially threatening strangers in ways that lead us to consent compliantly to the deployment of a permanent war-machine across an undefined theatre of war. We now countenance technologies of violence that kill from high in the sky, and special forces that operate secretly across the ground – forces from above and below specially trained to operate in those undefined zones where no war has been declared, and civilians and social infrastructure are targeted as often as are combatants. Although this process has historical roots in the twentieth century going back to Dresden, Hiroshima and Nagasaki, under the cover of this War on Terror a new stage of 'humanitarian' state terror has been extended with a devastating multiplier effect. How has this consent taken hold? Alongside the image of the necroscopic robot, let me present another image, an image that we are supposed to recognize as dehumanized evil: the pudgy face of the Serbian politician Slobodan Milošević. Along with Saddam Hussein and Osama bin Laden, he is presented as one of the reasons that the new totalizing military machine is necessary.

I recently sat in the International Criminal Tribunal in The Hague and watched the section of the trial of Slobodan Milošević pertaining to a little village in Kosova called Račak.[3] In that village a massacre of 45 persons occurred, and, as I will discuss later, part of its importance lies in the fact that NATO seized upon the massacre as a turning point in its decision to bomb Serbia and Kosova.[4] Slobodan Milošević sits to one side of the Court Room No. 1, acting as his own defence. He sits alone, except for a surprisingly alert armed guard, changed at regular intervals. The courtroom is surprisingly small, divided in half by bulletproof glass with the public gallery on one side and the proceedings occurring on the other. What struck me about the trial were some strange crossovers with the situation that Hannah Arendt describes in the trial of the convicted Nazi war criminal Otto Adolf Eichmann. Eichmann's trial was held in Jerusalem in April 1961. (It incidentally takes us back to the city where our discussion started, where the Israeli government and its soldiers have now become new oppressors in their ill-fated attempt to totalize freedom from fear.) Back in the postwar years, Jews were trying to come to grips with the horror of their own oppression by the most brutally efficient totalitarian regime the world has yet seen.

Otto Adolf Eichmann was rightly found guilty of crimes against humanity, but not for the right reasons.[5] He was in charge of efficiently transporting persons across the countryside – mostly Jews and Gypsies. The only indication of an order to kill that the prosecution were able to produce in that trial was a scribbled note written in 1941 by a 'Jewish expert' in the German Foreign Office after a telephone conversation. It says 'Eichmann proposes shooting', but it has little status as evidence. (By chilling coincidence, this note was written in relation to a state-organized massacre in German-occupied Serbia in the very year, and country, that Slobodan Milošević was born.) Eichmann claimed that he 'never gave an order to kill either a Jew or a non-Jew; I just did not do it', and he probably didn't. He did however admit to 'aiding and abetting' the commission of crimes through organizing the transport of Jews to concentration camps, and it is on this basis that he should have been indicted. The problem is that because the victors were searching for a personalized explanation of the systematic horror, the court was reduced to a Star Chamber. If the question had been posed in terms of taking responsibility for the effects of a war-machine – including the effective use of its rail system – the Allies would have logically also had to interrogate their decision to extend their machinery of war into fire-bombing and dropping nuclear bombs on civilians. The evidence shows that British and American policy makers effectively employed state terror against civilians in Dresden, Hiroshima and Nagasaki, using their mass deaths as a form of exemplary accountancy to show the military power of the Allied forces to the Axis powers. Churchill, in his letter to Lord Beaverbrook about the area-bombing strategy, was clear that the strategy was directed at civilians, confronting the Nazi homeland with 'an absolutely devastating exterminating attack'. As W.G. Sebald argues, the bombing continued long after it was clear, firstly, that the morale of the German people was not being broken, and, secondly, that it had little military impact. Sir Arthur Harris, Commander-in-Chief of Bomber Command, remained uncompromising to the end because of a simple logic: 'the war in the air was war pure and undisguised'. The joint RAF-US Eighth Army Air Force 'Operation Gomorrah' in the summer of 1943 over Hamburg was simply intended to end the life of the city. The firestorm reached 2,000 metres into the air and raced through the streets at 150 kilometres an hour leaving behind melting windows, bubbling asphalt and lumps of reduced human flesh with flickering bluish phosphorescent flames. In the 131 cities and towns that were attacked, 600,000 civilians were killed and 3.5 million homes were destroyed.[6]

The circumstantial testified evidence is similarly overwhelming that during the period that Milošević was President of the Federal Republic of Yugoslavia, *his* forces were involved in widespread mass killings, but it is not even as clear cut as it was in the case of Allied bombing during the Second World War that he directly ordered the attacks against civilians.[7] The tragedy is that given the nature of his trial the process is certain to remain more a mediated spectacle of personality politics than an elaborator of the complex truths of contemporary war. Upholding the principle of individual culpability continues to be important, but here unfortunately it is being tethered to the desire of the winners to explain away the horror as the machinations of criminality. Milošević protests that all he was doing was directing his war-machine to counter terrorism in his own country. Like Eichmann, it seems that he will rightly be found guilty of crimes against humanity, but not for the right reasons. If we admit to ourselves that what Milošević is guilty of is letting loose a war-machine in an attempt to totalize state security against a putative threat of terrorism, then Henry Kissinger, Ariel Sharon, George Bush, Bill Clinton and George W. Bush are similarly indictable.[8] And, on these grounds, so they should be. In all these cases, crimes against humanity were perpetrated while these leaders had both *de jure* and *de facto* responsibility for questionable military operations. Let them face the words of one of the wiser judges in the Eichmann trial:

these crimes were committed en masse, not only in regard to the number of victims, but also in regard to the numbers of those who perpetrated the crime, and the extent to which any one of the many criminals was close to or remote from the actual killer of the victim means nothing, as far as the measure of responsibility is concerned. On the contrary, in general the degree of responsibility increases as we draw further away from the man who uses the fatal instrument with his own hands.[9]

This particular judgment relates to one side of my second argument. However, the lines of the technocracy of command have been so stretched that the perpetrators of ill-conceived 'humanitarian intervention' can no longer even countenance the idea of being brought to account, even for bad-faith decisions that lead to countless deaths. The only war criminals on our side can be the occasional (non-American) foot soldier caught in an act of unwarranted embodied violence. Despite the number of civilians killed in the Second Iraqi War, now conservatively estimated to be between 5,000 and 7,000 persons, the fact that the ostensible purpose of the war has proved to be dubious – weapons of mass destruction have yet to be found – will not see George W. Bush brought to trial.

The other side of that argument is that when we dehumanize the perpetrators of obvious horror – from Milošević and Eichmann to Saddam Hussein and Osama bin Laden – we mask the all-too-human possibility that ordinary persons such as George W. Bush are equally as capable as psychopaths of presiding over campaigns of terror from a distance. In demonizing the 'Other' we lose any capacity to understand why *all* perpetrators of systematic violence, whether in good or bad faith, might act as they do. In the case of Milošević, when none of the NATO policy makers felt compelled to think through the consequences of the Serbian attachment to the heartland of Kosova, they assumed wrongly that a brief period of aerial bombardment would bring 'peace'. In the case of the Palestinian martyrs, when strategists continue to explain away suicide-bombing as the result of extensive religious brainwashing, they assume, again probably wrongly, that heavy and unremitting military retaliation will bend the will of the 'arsenal of believers'.

THE ANTIMONIES OF TOTALIZING CONTROL AND THE POST-HUMAN

I want now to link this discussion to the issue of *totalizing control*, introduced in Chapter 2. It is a process with contradictory outcomes. Even in the case of totalitarian Germany it was always either a pretension or an uneven effect, rather than an actual possibility. Nevertheless, either way, the current form of global totalization, I suggest, has Strangelovian consequences that *at one level* are taking us towards a postmodern and post-human condition.

Michael Hardt and Antonio Negri call it 'Empire', a single power or logic of rule that manages messiness and destroys fixed boundaries. They write:

> In contrast to imperialism, Empire establishes no territorial centre of power and does not rely on fixed boundaries or barriers. Empire manages hybrid identities, flexible hierarchies and plural exchanges through modulating networks of command.[10]

However, I find their metaphor of a society of control presiding over a new plurality unconvincing. It misses out both on the different structural levels of sovereignty and the different formations that in one setting throw up, for example, the traditionally conceived notion of martyring one's body for a sacred cause, and in another setting engender the postmodern confidence that a National Missile Defense System will bring freedom from rogue states.

While the contemporary projection of control continues to carry with it modern techniques of efficiency and organization conceived decades ago, it is now overlaid by various postmodern guises: totalizing organizational security (funding a massive war-machine and security apparatus so that we can be supposedly free from fear of attack upon our bodies); totalizing capital (advocating that the commodity run completely unregulated so that we can be 'free' to fetishize our deepest desires); and totalizing techno-science (granting scientists the unfettered freedom to reconstitute nature so that we can dream of being free of want or disease). It is the first guise that is most relevant to the present chapter, and here we find an apparent paradox. Firstly, as I argued in Chapter 2, the only way potentially to enhance the totalizing control is to totalize the freedom of 'us, the good guys' and to objectify the others as abstract strangers and a potential threat. Moreover, as David Lyon documents, the effect, for example, of attempting to develop a 'totalizing' surveillance system is to turn the gaze of the system upon ourselves, to merge normalized surveillance and the special circumstances of terrorism:

> Early forms of surveillance picked up only specific data, watched only particular activities. Today's assumes increasingly, that all monitoring will produce searchable records. The surveillance situation altered once it became possible to extend the 'gaze' from national state and capitalist corporation record-keeping and monitoring to include all kinds of everyday transactions. The records of Mohammed Atta, on CCTV tapes and digital logs, were collected not because he was doing anything unusual or deviant. Just the opposite. Data-gathering is routine, generalized, and distributed across almost every sphere of daily life. Once these records are examined, however, it may become incumbent on 'data-subjects' to account for their activities. All data-subjects lose their innocence and we all enter a more 'fish-bowl'-like world ...[11]

In other words, the Pentagon's programme of Total Information Awareness (the TIA Office), by striving to integrate the databases of everyday life from medical records and school transcripts to credit-card transactions and web cookies, ends up catching us all. Just as it is counterproductive to dehumanize the perpetrators of crimes against humanity because it ends up objectifying everybody, so too it is counterproductive to develop techniques and technologies of totalizing military control. Every technology that has been developed has become part of an escalation of the need for new techniques of 'totalizing' control. The technologies either fall into the 'wrong hands' or set up the conditions for a counter-technology that renders them less totalizing, with the subsequent rationalization that we need a new level of protection. For example, after the invention of the atomic bomb, the politics of the abstracting war-machine went through a number of overlapping stages:

1. an atomic bomb named 'Little Boy'[12] was used pre-emptively to free us from an evil war-maker, Japan, subsequently spurring the Soviet Union to develop a comparable capacity;
2. the hydrogen bomb and an intercontinental ballistic missile system was developed to free the West from the Soviet threat, leading to the doctrine and untenable reality of mutually assured totalizing destruction, and thus making the technology at least potentially unusable;
3. nuclear weapons were subsequently further developed technologically, on the one hand, to make limited battlefield use possible (giving way to the fear of other states using the weapons in theatres of war as they also acquired nuclear capacity); and on the other hand to project a totalizing missile defence system – Star Wars and Star Wars II;
4. finally, with the new technological possibilities, we have been overcome by the image of terrorists carrying suitcase bombs, denoting 'dirty bombs' or flying domestic aeroplanes into buildings, thus getting underneath any potential missile shield by putting their own bodies on the line. This has prompted the development of the most active and engaged peace-time military machine that the world has ever seen.

The latest development announced in the aftermath of the first stage of the Second Gulf War is a programme called Falcon (Force Application and Launch from Continental US) aimed at fulfilling 'the government's vision of an ultimate global reach capability'.[13] The aim of the Falcon technology is to develop reusable, unmanned, hypersonic cruise vehicles that can deliver warheads without depending on forward bases, and enable almost immediate military responses to crises across the world. Used in conjunction with the missile shield, this is intended to allow for totalizing flexibility and overcome the unusable intercontinental nuclear missile system.

CONCLUSION

War, or more technically, 'militarized peace', continues to prevail in Iraq, Afghanistan and Israel–Palestine. In Kosova they are still rebuilding their devastated social infrastructure with limited support and in North Korea new tensions are developing. In short, the application of massive force has not brought about a positive peace anywhere, and long simmering conflicts such as Kashmir are intensifying as two more states develop weapons of totalizing defence. Despite this the headlines point to the United States simultaneously preparing for new zones of military engagement: the accompanying war of words has again been ratcheted up as the self-designated 'allies' continue the cultural legitimation of further acts of state terror. It is fitting that Australia's foolish Foreign Affairs Minister, Alexander Downer, gets the penultimate word. Attempting to find an explanation for the extension of war to Iraq, Mr Downer likened the situation to the choice the Allies had in the Second World War in response to the totalitarian regime of Nazi Germany: appeasement of the bad guys or deployment of the good war-machine. The problem as I have been concerned to argue is that world politics and the consequences of military action are rarely that simple. Even the evidence from the tiny Kosovan village of Račak leaves more questions than it answers. Račak, the site of a massacre of 45 people, was presented as a trigger for the NATO intervention. As it turns out, of the massive list of offences listed against Milošević by the International Criminal Tribunal, Račak provides the only indictable evidence of a massacre in Kosova prior to that fateful day on 24 March 1999 when from far away some NATO generals and politicians decided that the only answer to the military activities of the Federal Republic of Yugoslavia was a deluge of bombs. As time goes on, it seems less and less likely that the advocates of total security will deliver positive peace. The answer to all of this is much more likely to come from politically engaged people, living locally in a diversity of places from Jerusalem, Belgrade and Kabul to New York and Melbourne, and working across all levels of the social from the regional to the global.

16
Terrorism and the Opening of Black Pluto's Door

Tom Nairn

Aeneas was praying and holding on the altar
When the prophetess started to speak: 'Blood relations of Gods,
Trojan, son of Anchises, the way down to Avernus is easy.
Day and night black Pluto's door stands open.
But to retrace your steps and get back to upper air,
This is the real task and the real undertaking.'

Seamus Heaney, *The Golden Bough*, from Virgil's *Aeneid*,
in *Opened Ground: Poems 1966–96* (1998)

One of the key things about September 11 is that no one claimed responsibility for the atrocities. They were an ontological statement, rather than propaganda of a deed for a particular nation or oppressed class. The world was meant to stand revealed by them. Reality was God's ultimate struggle against Satan, exemplified by the martyr-hijackers. In such a cosmic phantasmagoria, a new world war is nothing. The bigger the Satan, the harder he will eventually fall. The perpetrators, attacking a society already so strongly inclined towards belief in UFOs, moral absolutes and the Christian version of fundamentalism, must have calculated that they could hardly fail. Yet fail they will, for perfectly mundane and profane reasons having little to do with the atavistic theology of either side. Brendan O'Leary was surely right in the aftermath of September 11 to call for normality: '*Be normal* ... think about being normal as a way of standing up for yourself and your values.'[1] In other words, keep your head. The object of the criminals was socio-cultural decapitation. In the long run of history they will not be allowed to get away with it. But one might also observe how the silence that O'Leary underlines was connected to another absentee from the excitable post-September 11 cacophonies – nationalism. In my view the two silences are intimately related. In fact, it is possible to argue that one explains the other. The atrocities can also be seen as standing for a new strain of nationalism: an 'ethno-cosmic' liberation movement, as it were, so grandiloquent in its goal as to require no apology or explanation. No responsibility need be claimed for the Creator's will: it has simply to be made manifest. However, overreach also implies futility. Blood relations '*of Gods*' do not exist, and no actual nation is either divine or chosen.

Less than a decade ago, most ills of humanity and of the coming century were being laid at the door of a more conventional nationalism. Bosnias were seen coming everywhere, unless the Atlantic-Trademark sense of Reason prevailed. Rationality was then thought to be taking up a new logo – globalization. Selfish ethnicity was perceived as getting in its way. Throughout the benighted 1990s, no op-ed page was complete without this daily dose of spectral anarchy and pandemonium. Now the tune has abruptly altered. I suspect most people would be quite happy to have the demons of yesteryear back, rather than these Horsemen of the Apocalypse. There was, of course, plenty of real anarchy and pandemonium in the 1990s as the post-Cold War thaw got under way. It would be shameful to excuse or exonerate any of the ensuing disasters. However, a decade later, it should be acknowledged that many of these disasters have either been resolved, or are on the way towards an answer. The fact is that, to give just some examples, at the end of an awful ten years, Milošević is in jail in The Hague, while Mladic and Karadzic are on the run; democratic peace of a sort is at least holding in Northern Ireland; East Timor is independent; democratic South Africa may be on the way to becoming the continent's first great success story; Iran is evolving steadily away from the post-1980 theocracy – and so on.

EXIT TO THE UNDERWORLD

Actual civic nationalism, as I've argued throughout the book, leads to actual solutions, even if these are clumsy, painful and approximate. Ethnic cleansing was a particularly noxious side-effect of that kind. Terroristic actions were often involved, and the cumulative body-count far exceeded that of September 11. But none of it meant 'the end of the world'. An abyss separates it from September 11, which was intended to signal just that. Humanity was being called through Black Pluto's door into an antique underworld of theocratic absolutes and paranoid finality. The saintly criminals were seeking to provoke a War Against Terrorism that would inevitably employ counter-terrorism as one of its tactics, thus setting up an indefinite spiral of outrages. God's will can then emerge from the ruins. It is a pity, but the subsequent years suggest that we have actively obliged them.

As Virgil's prophetess said, strip-cartoon apocalypse is the easy bit: for that, her dark door does indeed stand ever open. The information technology linked to globalization makes it more visible, and even more inviting (at least in the sense of imaginable). It encourages an inebriation of the collective soul, much in evidence right after the events. The harder part is finding one's way back into the upper air of normality, where the majority can reassert their non-apocalyptic visions of the future. Yet I doubt if this will prove so difficult. It is simply not the case that any mysterious Clash of Civilizations is at work behind this crisis, rooted in immemorially divergent values or world-views. I suspect that something more like the exact opposite may be true. These hooligans of the Absolute were compelled to act because they (or those behind them) know that there is, in the globalizing world, a steadily advancing majority *against* fundamentalist or spirit-world politics. Unless they strike now, it will soon be too late. The genesis of September 11 lay in mounting despair, rather than conviction of real political or social victory.

The crux of their dilemma lies in the Middle East. This is the zone in which secular nationalism has worked least well, for a particular combination of social and longer-range historical reasons. The inverse of that failure has been the promotion of a premodern religious world-view into the breach. Islam, linked in collective recollection to a distant era of Arab conquest and supremacy, became the stand-in for both democracy and nationalism. The fall-back upon this *ersatz* concoction has been a misfortune for the Muslim faith as well as the rest of us, the infidels. It promised earthly heaven to the former and humiliating defeat for the latter. Neither delusion has the slightest chance of realization. But they have already generated vast mayhem on their way to failure.

A WORLD OF ONE'S OWN

In his moving account of *The Arab Predicament*, Fouad Ajami concludes bitterly that

> It is easy to judge but hard to understand the ghosts with which people and societies battle, the wounds and memories that drive them to do what they do ... The renaissance of civilizations is used as a weapon because so many in the Muslim world and the Third World as a whole feel they live in a world constructed and maintained by others ...[2]

Nation-states have been the main instrument of the real battle, and in the last quarter of the twentieth century *democratic* nationalism has become its commanding credo. These are the effective means by which people and societies are coming to live in a world 'constructed and maintained' by themselves. Globalization stands for the achievement and consolidation of that movement, not for its dissolution. By far the best overview of its impact upon the Middle East is the one given by Roger Owen in *State, Power and Politics in the Making of the Middle East*.[3] Owen's study originally came out in 1992, but his second edition, published in 2000, contains a new closing section on 'The Remaking of the Middle Eastern Environment after the Gulf War'. This makes it startlingly clear why the Wahhabites and al-Qa'eda had to undertake some highly visible counter-action: they are on the retreat everywhere even in their Afghan redoubt and Saudi Arabian citadel. Owen observes that

> In a global economy with a well-educated middle class and virtually open access to information from abroad, it does not seem likely that (the region's) stick and carrot approach to political management can be maintained indefinitely. Sooner or later, issues which have always been implicit in both religious and secular discourse will be made increasingly explicit. These include notions of citizenship, the rule of law, religious toleration and a regime legitimacy that comes not from appeals to security, ideology or achievement but from popular representation and a consensus among the nation at large.[4]

All this is death and anathema to God-struck super-nationalists like Osama bin Laden. However, the influence of such ideas might be stayed, or even turned, if a suitably aggressive Western crusade could be provoked – a palpably Satanic onslaught which might drive the emergent middle class back into the fundamentalist fold. I agree with Fred Halliday's account of US imperialism. In the twenty-first century we have seen a remarkable change, but in the decades at the end of the twentieth century, and compared to its European predecessors, rather than the Captain America portrayed in so many diatribes, its keynote has been muddled and sometimes well-meaning hesitancy.[5] This must have worried the Islamicists too. Their foe was falling down on the job, and needed some stiffening. Would a few thousand deaths in the heartland do the trick? In short, the murderous onslaught of September 11 was aimed most significantly *at the people of the Middle East themselves*. This is well described by Murat Belge.[6] The American and other victims in New York and Washington were made sacrificial lambs for a re-conquest of Muslim opinion. From Nigeria to Indonesia, the latter accounts for something like a third of the world.

Across the European Union, people are familiar with the concept of 'democratic deficit', but there is also such a thing as 'nationalism deficit', and the Islamic part of the world has suffered from a devastating combination of both. Mundane if mistaken calculation suggested to the perpetrators that big numbers could compensate for these structural failings. Properly led, might they not still bring down Godless capitalism, via prolonged and brutal struggle? After all, Muslim insurgency had witnessed Godless communism collapsing in the 1980s (and played a minor part in its fall). It beats me why anyone should expect anything better from a character like Osama bin Laden. He may look like old images of Jesus Christ, but is the seventeenth son of a crooked construction tycoon. No one who has encountered him saw a hawk of the desert – rather, a soft-handed fixer and couch ideologist. His slaughter funds flowed from an odious version of Arabian state-fostered capitalism, not from heaven's will. Presumably the unfortunates who committed suicide on September 11 believed in the heavenly vision; whether their backers and organizers did, only time will show – and this would be best shown in a courtroom, before the steady gaze of humanity at large. Dubious acts of vengeance in remote corners of Asia will not achieve it. What we do know is that the 'counter-crusaders' want to restore or impose conservative theocracy, male-authoritarian hierarchy, the supposed warrior-virtues of antiquity, and shari'a law.

RETRACING THE STEPS

The great, liberating thaw of modernity will never be turned back by such acts of despair. Another interesting contribution to debate described the affirmation of American nationalism that has followed September 11.[7] John Down drove from San Francisco to Los Angeles, reflecting as he travelled on the 'civic religion' of a stricken country, and its response to 'violation by an unseen evil'. I am ashamed to see how bargain-basement anti-Americanism has surfaced in some analyses; what accounts like Down's reveal is surely a kind of grandeur – a solidity and humanity of outraged reaction, made up of new vulnerability, determination and a sense of everyday sacredness. He does end up fearful of the immense power behind such displays, in case it 'leads the US further down the path of retribution that may well sow the seeds of a future terrorism'. Of course vengeance was seemingly in order after September 11. However, very many voices have insisted, in the USA itself as well as amongst its allies, that justice is the only true revenge. To strike back instantaneously is a natural impulse. But it is surely more important that justice should be inexorable, final and public. No preposterous War Against Terrorism could achieve anything like this. It will do little but cast all the proverbial black cats into one indiscriminate bag in a darkened room, and (as Down dreads) provoke further atrocities.

What the extra-American world should fear is not US *nationalism* but the debility of the American *state* – what Paul James in Chapter 17 calls the plight of the 'insecure nation'. The constitution linked to their 'civic religion' is a crumbling anachronism, as the last presidential election demonstrated. Some sense of proportion must be retained here, I agree: Old Glory is less of an archaism than the United Kingdom, for instance, or the nostalgic debris of Saudi fundamentalism. Still, both George W. Bush's position and his Texan machismo depend upon it, and might in the event of further disasters attempt to prop themselves up by mobilizing appeals to the holy-smoke Christian conservatism which it also embodies. This is another reason why defence of the positive side of globalization should not be an American prerogative. In an early contribution to the Open Democracy forum, David Held called for a new international body dealing with terrorist outrages, modelled on the Nuremberg and Tokyo tribunals and under United Nations control.[8] The idea has been amplified by his joint essay with Mary Kaldor, 'New War, New Justice'.[9] Writing before the International Criminal Court came into existence, they argue that this new body should be 'an International Court [where] the terrorists must be treated as criminals and not military adversaries'. In one sense, few would dissent while thinking of *this* example of terrorism. The trouble is that any sweeping new formula takes us straight back to the black cats in the dark room. For instance, would the US Air Force's mistaken strike at a Sudanese medical laboratory have qualified for a Court appearance? Should the Real IRA bombers of Omagh go there, rather than to courts in Dublin or Belfast? What about the Palestinian human bombs who continue to go to their deaths? And the Israeli counter-terror meted out in retaliation?

Tempting as the concept of a single new institutional riposte undoubtedly is, it may be over-influenced by the climate of the moment – the feeling that September 11 is a defining moment for humankind, as Held originally wrote. But it was not. A miserable old world near the end of its tether was hitting back, using new technology to amplify a brazenly antediluvian message. The new world – currently paraphrased as Held and Kaldor's 'globalization' – should not think in terms of short-cuts and overpowering ripostes. Time is on its side, recession or not. The combined forces of development, democracy and secular nationhood are on its side, much more evidently than over the decades of the Cold War concluded in the 1980s. For example, as far as the mundane configuration behind these bombings are concerned, every newsreader and TV viewer over the entire globe has known for decades what the real problem is: Palestine. As I introduced in Chapter 3, the general malaise of the Middle East, and by extension of other Muslim-majority polities, has been consistently focused on and envenomed by the incurable abscess of the Israeli-PLO conflict. The Arab failures that Ajami mourns, and the 'general tone of bitterness and despair' described by Owen, have in practice constantly returned to and fed off this particularly disgraceful stalemate. There have been of course plenty of other big regional problems as well: the Iran–Iraq War, Kuwait, Kurdistan, the Sudanese civil war, and now the downfall of the Afghan state. But none has the staying power and sheer ideological resonance of the Palestinian war.

BACK TO THE UPPER AIR

The Israeli-Palestinian war represents an *impasse* of nationalisms, to which the sole solution will be the formation of a viable, secular and democratic Palestinian state. American power has both imposed and fuelled the conflict, and yet has shrunk from imposing the solution (out of the motives that Fred Halliday has described). Yet such an advance was *overwhelmingly* in its own long-term interest, as well as that of Palestinian Arabs and everyone else – except the Holy Warriors. Had it been achieved sooner, it is doubtful whether the September assaults would ever have happened. Nobody wants a new world order regulated by a US gendarme; but what is at issue here is a poisonous remnant of the old world order, festering on into the more liberal age of globalization. An acceptable nation-state remains the only way forward. Perry Anderson's 'Scurrying Towards Bethlehem' provides still another overview and set of proposals for Palestinian nationhood.[10] Writing not long before the September 11 attacks, Anderson concluded that 'The dismal political history of the Arab world over the last half century gives little reason for thinking (a solution) is likely in the short-run.' He saw small chance then of the Bush Presidency shifting its stance, or of 'the larger submission of the Middle East' ceasing to prolong the West Bank paralysis. Since September 11, something of a new start has been forced. Colin Powell's State Department has found it intolerable to preside over another round of the interminable feud, while simultaneously struggling to concert its new anti-terrorist strategy. Does the Bush government Road Map policy in favour of a Palestinian state give us hope of a more permanent answer? Not in the short term, particularly given the complications of the long Iraq war. Nevertheless, the general point here is that a meaningful response to Holy Terror lies upon this plane: real undertakings in the upper air of a nation-state world, which is still striving for classical goals within the more fluid and liberating medium of the global marketplace. As for the latter, the solid will go on melting into air, and bear the most heavenly ecstasies of religious fervour away with it. Its single unconscionable freedom – free trade, however naked and shameless – will continue to nestle, settle and establish connections everywhere, creating still more massive and colossal productive forces than have all preceding generations together, and enforcing the social and political constitutions required by the new empire of civil society. The true 'sorcerer of modernity', it conjures up the power of future worlds, not the netherworlds of antique faith and superstition.

17
Meta-War and the Insecurity of the United States

Paul James

The 'War on Terrorism' has opened the possibility of a globally continuous state-of-war where the enemy is both abstract entity (terrorism) and particularized 'evil' other – Osama bin Laden, Saddam Hussein, with new figures of evil inevitably and continually named as the situation unfolds. It is a condition of meta-war with many new characteristics: where the enemy no longer necessarily carries the status of national sovereign nor controls national territory; where the targets are defined on the run and the theatre of operation can be named without justifying evidence; where the state-at-war can rename the terms and conditions of a post-liberal society of hyper-surveillance; and where fine calibrations of risk assessment and gross increases of social insecurity are two sides of the same coin. Despite this real possibility of a horrific new kind of continuous postnational state-of-war, it has supposedly become unpatriotic to doubt that American military action is both necessary and just. The rubbish that has been reported in the press is extraordinary. Why at a time when war seems to be going beyond old-fashioned nation-state conflict is criticism defined in nationalist terms as un-American or un-Australian? Understanding the mainstream response to the attacks takes us deep into the heart of Middle America and to the insecurity of nation-states in the West as they undergo massive change. This chapter begins with a discussion of the nationalism-from-within before going on to examine the nature of the new condition of meta-war.

SEPTEMBER 11: A PREFATORY NOTE

We all struggled with how to respond to the terrorist attacks on New York and Washington. At least in the first few days after the attacks it was understandable that the recorders of this 'day of infamy' resorted to iconic images, nationalistic clichés and apocalyptic prose. It was an awful day. Surpassing the images of *Independence Day* and *Armageddon*, and going beyond the 'reality' of Hollywood special effects and cinematic thrill-rides, mass death moved onto the streets where actual people work. It was nothing less than an act of shocking terror. Writing in the days after September

236

11, one *New York Times* journalist talked epochally of prior times when normality, security and freedom were found in the small rhythms of routine. Now, being at home does not automatically bring freedom or security.

> Although the wound is obviously deepest here, it isn't only this country that has been altered. America is not only a place. America is an idea. The knowledge of this secure elsewhere was what kept freedom and hope alive for millions around the globe for two centuries. It was the force that broke the stalemate in the first Great War, the place from which the world dared to hope for peace after 1918. It was the beacon toward which countless immigrants travelled, in order to leave their somewhere behind. It was the rock upon which Churchill summoned the will from his people's terrified hearts to go on and win against the darkest forces that freedom had ever encountered. It was the symbol that ultimately brought down the Berlin Wall and faced terror in Tiananmen Square.[1]

In this account, America *is* freedom. Hence for the sake of the world, totalizing security has to be projected both outward through going to war and inward as 'homeland security'. And here is also the crucible of the problem (to use Nairn's phrase). Americans have long watched from a distance as living persons have been terror-bombed in towns such as Beirut, Belfast and Nairobi, or in Hiroshima (1945), Hanoi and Haiphong (1972), Tripoli (1986), Bagdad (1991), Basra (1999) and Belgrade (1999). This time with the attack on the Twin Towers, it came home with a vengeance. Just by listing a few of the cases brings home the issue in a second way. All of the instances, apart from the first three listed, involved United States forces conducting acts of terror from a distance against American-defined evil others. In all cases the US government knew that civilians would probably die, and in all cases they argued that it was simply necessary. If news commentary and letters to the paper are anything to go by, even by mentioning the fact that the United States has itself acted as purveyor of terror, I will be immediately taken out of context and wrongly assumed to be saying that the attacks of September 11 was the deserved outcome of a history that goes back for decades. Not so. Nobody deserves to be terrorized. Rather, the position stands with the thousands of demonstrators who marched through places such as New York City after the terror, concerned about the plans of the US government.

What I *am* saying firstly is that nothing excuses acts of barbarism, but secondly that barbarism knows no boundaries of proclaimed good and evil. As the good George W. Bush prosecutes a war on a network that nobody yet has proven to be involved beyond reasonable doubt, and as commentators talk of a Third World War, it is possible that the apocalypse that we have already experienced will be repeated and repeated across the globe. Afghanistan and Iraq may be only the beginning. The obscenely named 'Operation Infinite Justice' opens the possibility of self-confirming and escalating hostilities of desperation from both sides. The fact that the war in Afghanistan was hastily renamed 'Operation Enduring Freedom' underscores the *1984* Ministry of Love-style use of masked words. This is not a comic-tragic naming in the way that the strategic invasion in 1983 of peaceful little Grenada by a handful of Ronald Reagan's crack troops was called 'Operation Urgent Fury'. This time, unless the direction pursued changes radically, it will mostly involve the tragic undermining of that very freedom, both within the nation-state as rule of law is distorted and across the globe as the pursuit of postnational terrorism is used to rationalize acts of state terror from above.

THE CONTRADICTIONS OF TRANSCENDENTAL NATIONALISM AND POSTMODERN UNIVERSALISM

Understanding the mainstream American response to the September 11 attacks takes us deep into the heart of Middle America. One week after the attack, on the Saturday night, the world watched as the actors and singers from Hollywood and MTV mourned the tragic loss of life that occurred in attacks on the World Trade Center and the Pentagon. The programme, a telethon fundraiser entitled *America: A Tribute to Heroes*, was broadcast to 210 countries. Tom Hanks, boy-next-door and star of Steven Spielberg's blockbuster war movie, *Saving Private Ryan*, opened the evening in a low-key manner. He named the brave souls who reacted to the hijacking of Flight 93 and intoned their last words, 'We're going to have to do something.' Celine Dion sang 'God Bless America'. The evening ended with the now iconic video-image of the US flag flying silently over the debris of the collapsed towers. No commentary. No introductions. No credits. None were necessary. It was a transcendental moment, at least for those for whom the flag lives.

Throughout the entire programme there was not an off-key note, not an unscripted moment that called for self-reflection about the consequences of massing a war-machine to strike at an unverified enemy. Clint Eastwood, affecting the same expression that he wore in his film *In the Line of Fire* (1993), spoke with gravel-voiced intensity about 'ultimate triumph':

> It was the twenty-first century's day of infamy. It was a day that will live in the annals of courage and patriotism. Tonight we pay tribute to those who were lost and those who survived the fire and the fate that rained down upon them, and the heroes at Ground Zero who had life and death wear an indelible badge of honour. We celebrate not only them, but all our fellow Americans, for the intended victims of this attack were not just on the planes, and at the Pentagon, the World Trade Center. They were wherever else they roam the sky. The targets were not just the symbols of America but they were the spirit of America. And the intended victims were all 300 million of us. The terrorists foresaw a nation fearful, doubtful, ready to

retreat. Oh, they left us wounded, but renewed in strength. And we'll stand and will not yield. The terrorists who wanted 300 million victims, instead are going to get 300 million heroes, 300 million Americans with broken hearts, unbreakable hopes for our country and our future. In the conflict that's come upon us, we're determined as our parents and our grandparents were before us to win through the ultimate triumph – so help us God.

By a generalizing shift, expressed first in the words of politicians in the United States, it thus became an attack on all of us, an attack upon all civilization. Doubt became unpatriotic because the nation-of-America felt that any disloyalty begets social disintegration. This is the response of an insecure nation undergoing change. In this context, only clichéd reversions to the Manichean Cold War rhetoric of the kind 'If you're not for us, you're against us' seem adequate to the momentousness of the new. *America: A Tribute to Heroes*, Clint Eastwood's set-piece and Celine Dion's rousing and sentimental rendition of 'God Bless America' takes us deep into the fears of mainstream American culture. It also takes us back to an earlier filmic attempt to understand a different war – the film was *The Deer Hunter* (1978), the war, Vietnam. The last scene of Michael Cimino's film closes on a few friends in a small Pennsylvania town pub trying to make sense of their ravaged lives. In wan unison, but growing in volume, they sing 'God Bless America'. The final scene is stopped in freeze-frame as they raise their glasses in hope. As the video cover says, 'it's more than a requiem for their dead comrade; it's an anthem for a living American tradition of making mistakes, rueing them and starting afresh'. American, the land of the brave and the free, having forgotten the lessons of that war, thus redefines itself yet again as the land of transcendent promise.

It is significant that Vietnam is the one war with which mainstream America is only just beginning to draw parallels. The concept of the 'Vietnam syndrome' originally referred to the pathology of a nation that believed itself to have lost the war out of weakness of will. However, in the years since that war, the concept, if remembered, has taken on a new reality. Rather than it being seen as pathological to be obsessed by weakness, it is now deemed necessary to always be strong and resolute. The syndrome has been refigured in terms of what has long been called 'American exceptionalism'. Richard Nixon wrote an entire book claiming that America really won the war – 'it lost the peace', he said. And dozens of popular cultural moments in the meantime have confirmed this sense. During the TWA hostage crisis in 1985, President Reagan quipped into the microphone during a sound test that 'after seeing *Rambo* last night, I know what to do next time'. It was not a transcendental moment in itself, but it spoke of power that knew what it had to do. George W. Bush's State of the Union address on 30 January 2003 defending the Second Gulf War did not mention Vietnam, but he did

place the United States at the centre of a century of victories over power
and domination:

> Throughout the twentieth century, small groups of men seized control of great
> nations, built armies and arsenals, and set out to dominate the weak … In each case,
> the ambitions of Hitlerism, militarism and communism were defeated by the will of
> free peoples … and by the might of the United States of America.

In these strange times, despite the rules of war being completely rewritten,
the mainstream American sense of its own exceptionalism has continuities
that go back into the past. There are counter-examples to these themes, but it
can nevertheless be argued that they continue to be dominant in mainstream
thinking and practice. One continuing theme involves a mythical tribute to
the regeneration of peace through violence. It is the peace that always comes
after the conflict, like the freeze-frames at the end of *The Deer Hunter* or
Three Kings when life is returned to peaceful hometown normality. From
the Indian wars and the War of Independence to Vietnam and Kosova,
'peace' is always the backgrounded-but-transcendental moment that links
the community of fate across time. In Lynne Cheney's patriot primer,
discussed in Chapter 2, 'V is for the *valour* shown by those who've kept us
free', referring to the American military; W is for Washington, 'Brave in
battle and dignified always'; X is for marking the spot, including 'Lexington
and Concord, where the revolutionary war began' – but in arriving at Z she
ends with a sublime scene of children running on the beach as the sun rises.
'Z is the end of the alphabet, but not the end of America's story. Strong and
free, we continue to be an inspiration to the world.'[2]

A second theme is the essential virtue of *acting* to defend Truth, Infinite
Justice and the (American) Way. Defence always requires action. Despite
the failings (or heroism) of any one particular individual or institution in
the United States, or even of the state itself, there is always an active figure
of redemption. President Bush knows that he might be making a mistake
in the particularities of his actions, but (connecting the two themes) given
that an outsider has cut across the peace of the community of fate he has
no choice but to act. He will be forgiven for acting wrongly, but he would
not have been forgiven for appearing to acquiesce to an outsider's attack on
American soil. Like Mel Gibson in *The Patriot*, war is reluctantly entered
into, but enter the true patriot must. Again quoting from George W. Bush's
State of the Union address of 30 January 2003 (also discussed earlier in
Chapter 2):

> Whatever action is required, when action is necessary, I will defend the freedom
> and security of the American people … We will consult, but let there be no
> misunderstanding: if Saddam Hussein does not fully disarm, for the safety of our

people and for the peace of the world, we will lead a coalition to disarm him ... This country fights reluctantly, because we know the cost and we dread the days of mourning that always come ... And if war is forced upon us, we will fight with the full force and the might of the United States military – and we will prevail.

The figure of redemption that stands out in the Second Iraqi War is the teenager, Private Jessica Lynch. The Pentagon claimed that Private Lynch had been shot and stabbed in the course of being captured and mistreated. She was 'saved in a daring assault' on the Nassiriya Hospital by Army Rangers and Navy SEALS, filmed dramatically in blurred verisimilitude by a military night-vision camera. When the video footage of the rescue was shown, General Vincent Brooks declared that 'Some brave souls put their lives on the line to make this happen, loyal to a creed that they know that they'll never leave a fallen comrade.' Some media reports recognized the cultural reference to the Tom Hanks movie and dubbed the episode 'Saving Private Lynch'. Unfortunately for the Pentagon's straight-ahead mythologizing, there were eye-witnesses, other than the US military, who later complicated the story. Doctors in the Nassiriya Hospital said the whole event appeared staged. The Iraqi military had left the hospital at least a day before the assault. According to Dr Harith al-Houssona, Private Lynch had been assigned the only specialist bed in the building. She had been given

three bottles of blood, two of them from the medical staff because there was no blood at this time ... I examined her, I saw that she had a broken arm, a broken thigh and a dislocated ankle. Then I did another examination. There was no [sign of] shooting, no stab wound – only RTA, road traffic accident.[3]

In the aftermath, Private Lynch has no memory of the episode, and, contested details notwithstanding, the US administration still projects it as an important human-interest story. Their spokespersons continue to carry the line reinforced by Jerry Bruckheimer, producer of *Black Hawk Down* (2001), when he visited the Pentagon in 2001 to argue that what counts in presenting the valour of the US military is getting close and personal. For being in the wrong place at the right time, Private Lynch was awarded a Purple Heart, a Bronze Star and the Prisoner of War medal. Despite the revelations, the teenager, who had only just enlisted from an area of high unemployment, returned to the cheering crowds of rural West Virginia as a figure of simple, committed, active valour. As the war dragged on, other soldiers found themselves in a very different position. On the day that President Bush finally admitted directly that there was no evidence linking Saddam Hussein to the September 11 terrorist attacks, a small item appeared in the newspaper: 'a soldier from the 101st Airborne Division, based in Mosul, died of "non-hostile gunshot wounds" – usually a euphemism for suicide'. Officially at that time 297 US military personnel had been killed since the beginning of the war in March – of those, 189 were killed by hostile fire. Most of the rest were accidents.[4]

This brings us to a third theme, the contradiction of an abiding sense of home soil and the projection of a frontier that has no boundaries. Having its roots in an expansionist ideology called the doctrine of Manifest Destiny first proclaimed in 1845, American national interest has long been defined in terms that treated extensions of its frontier as part of its civilizing mission. With the first two themes we can, for example, rewrite them with Australian examples from Gallipoli to the doctrine of 'forward defence'. However, with this third theme of sacred-soil/extended-frontier the United States has an accentuated fear of the unbounded movements of others that goes beyond the fears that even mainstream Australia has evinced over the Tampa refugee crisis. The old domino theory and the necessity of defending the world against communists in Vietnam was reborn against drug runners in Panama, against Arab expansionists in Iraq, and now against terrorists in Afghanistan. Australia follows the United States into crusades.[5] By contrast the United States government feels that it simply has to be there. Notwithstanding the occasional recurrences of American 'isolationism', the norm is for US leaders to feel an overriding pressure to act across the frontiers of the world.

One way of carrying this baggage of the past into the new global disorder has been to project violence from a distance. The US war-machine has increasingly been remade around weapons of mass projection. The only lesson learned from Vietnam was not to get so many young compatriots killed and wounded: 58,000 Americans dead and 300,000 wounded. (We should also remember that over 1 million Vietnamese died.) Working forwards from the bombs dropped over Hiroshima and Nagasaki, weapons of mass projection are defended as increasingly calibrated responses, precisely targeted, and directed as much against infrastructure as against personnel. Many Americans know from the long-term effects in Iraq and Kosova that people continue to die long after the projection of terror has stopped, however the political decision makers equally know that the destruction of ways of life is quickly submerged in the complexity of immediate events.

With the attack on New York and Washington, cultures and structures continuous with the past have been overlaid by something new. America has been attacked by a group of people that apparently have no home and no name. Moreover, they are persons that are prepared to put their bodies on the line. It means that despite the enormity of the abstract war-machine, projecting power from a distance will not work in itself, not at least in the long term. In one respect the continuous War on Terror means going back to days of Vietnam when Americans too died in embodied combat. Despite all the facile suggestions that Bush has shown intelligence and restraint, it was mostly because he did not know what to do. Winter came to Afghanistan, and it became obvious that the cruise-missile solution did not work. A militarized 'peace' continues, combined with secret missions out of Kabul, closed even to the managed scrutiny of the world's media. 'Peace' came to Iraq with George W. Bush declaring that 'we have prevailed', and months later the war continues. There, US Marines die daily, and much more publicly. These military exercises, in their pretensions at least, make up a totalizing campaign that reneges on prior concerns about either just-war proportionality or the rights of those who have not been proven guilty.

TOWARDS A CONDITION OF META-WAR

The war in Iraq is continuous with the war in Afghanistan, but it has taken us a step further into what I have been calling the condition of meta-war, part of the new totalizing layer of globalization. As I have been concerned to say, we are in new and changing territory: a combination of strategic abstract strikes and embodied incursions that are effectively projected by a single hegemon at a widening series of fronts. This is where my position diverges from Tom Nairn's argument that America has now become the enemy of globalization (Chapter 3). The US war-machine is arguably extending globalization in new ways. There are a number of dimensions to the Second Gulf War that make it stunningly unique in military history. Never before has an invading military force been greeted by such sustained cultural-political opposition across the globe before the war had begun, including outsiders travelling into or staying in the zone of conflict as human shields. Without melodrama or undue emphasis, one Australian clergyman said that he would not be going into an air-raid shelter because the vast majority of Iraqi civilians would not have that luxury. Never before has a territorial invasion of a sovereign state been rationalized in terms of the necessity of war on a non-state-based, non-territorial network of enemies that have no documented connection to that state. Afghanistan set the stage for such a development, but then the rhetoric began with the rationale of apprehending a terrorist rather than effecting regime change. This time the rhetoric turned to the possible proliferation of weapons of mass destruction.

Never before have such strange bedfellows gathered together to defend a pre-emptive strike. Like Christopher Hitchens, Jose Ramos Horta, Nobel Prize winner in 1996, effectively sided with his old *bête noire* Henry Kissinger when he argued that 'if the anti-war movement dissuades the US and its allies from going to war with Iraq, it will have contributed to the peace of the dead'.[6] And never before has the will to global power been expressed through such blatantly contradictory language in the speeches and writing of the expeditionary leaders. On the one hand, we heard the rhetoric of unstinting patience in the face an evil threat, of reluctance to go to war to achieve peace, and of an ultimate divine mission to bring democracy to a downtrodden people. Even on the brink of war, President George W. Bush was staring cross-eyed into the autocue and expressing his belief that even though some Iraqi people might get caught in the maelstrom, it would be in their best interests. (Australia's Prime Minister John Howard missed the gravity of that rhetorical 'moment of truth' by arguing that Australia was going to war in its own national interest.) On the other hand, the lead into war was characterized by bluff, blackmail, lies and vicious character assassination. It was supported by a campaign of rhetoric that made the war seem inevitable and the projection of crude aggression the only alternative.

No pretense was made – as it had been in previous postmodern-dominated wars, the First Gulf War, Kosova and Afghanistan – that military violence would be clean, surgical and precise. Long before it came to power, the members of the current War Cabinet exhorted the path of pre-emptive strike, including with weapons of mass destruction if necessary, to 'deter any challenger from ever dreaming of challenging us on the world stage'. 'I want to be the bully on the block', said the Bush administration's gentleman general, Colin Powell, just after the First Gulf War.[7] Or, 'I made up my mind at that moment that we were going to war', said George W. Bush a decade on, just after being told that the second plane had hit the World Trade Center.[8] (Although, at that time, in true postmodern fashion, he had no idea on whom he was declaring war.) According to press reports that appeared much later than September 11, it was during the same fateful hour that President Bush 'declared war' that Defense Secretary Donald Rumsfeld had decided that the United States had to oust Saddam Hussein.

Overall, however, the uniqueness of the Second Gulf War is one of a convergence of developing trends rather than a simple break with the past. It is important to remember some of the longer-term structural conditions that lay behind the present condition. The Second Gulf War is the culmination of a historical shift in the dominant nature of war that goes back at least to one driving campaign in the Second World War, culminating in the dropping of a nuclear bomb on the civilian population of Hiroshima. This shift has been intensifying across the course of the late twentieth century and into the present. Understanding its nature helps us to understand the broader seriousness of the current situation in terms that include and go beyond the recent exposés of the various neo-conservatives who have been associated with the Project for a New American Century. Implicit in this argument is the suggestion that it would not have mattered much whether it was George W. Bush or Al Gore in power. Whether it was a neo-conservative, a neo-liberal or one of the adherents to Third Way politics at the helm, the current direction of United States foreign policy, in conjunction with the nature of its war-machine and the actions of its opposition, would have taken us to this period of escalated conflict, even if not necessarily to the particular all-out-war we saw in Iraq.

Conventional histories of post-world war international conflict tend to talk in terms of turning points between periods that are characterized by relative doctrinal clarity. In the aftermath of the Second World War, two superpowers faced each other in a nuclear stand-off. In the 1970s the tensions of the Cold War eased into a period of détente between the superpowers; then in 1989, the fall of the Berlin Wall signalled the beginning of a period characterized by a single hegemon, the United States. This also became the era of globalization in which conflict overwhelmingly involved intra-state violence, wars between erstwhile compatriots or neighbours over the political souls of their dissipating nation-states. While this history is half adequate, a quite different history can be written of a shift from war as a series of territorial conflicts to a condition of meta-war – that is, war without end or territorial boundary. The slogan of American Special Operations Forces is 'Anything, Anytime, Anywhere'. This is a condition of globalizing war that will probably never take the name of World War III. In this rendition of history we have been entering what Gore Vidal has, with devastatingly acuity, called the period of 'perpetual war for perpetual peace' (see Tom's Chapter 3 above).

One dimension of meta-war is that it is fought as a war without end – a collapsing of temporal limits. For a while now, politicians have talked ruefully about the decisiveness of winning the war, and the difficulty of winning the peace. However, we have gone another step. Like the previous War on Drugs, the present War on Terror cannot be won except as a series of provisional moments. Like the military operation in Afghanistan, superficial regime-change is relatively easily effected by the kind of massive military machine that the condition of meta-war sustains, but effecting long-term peace is a different matter. In the aftermath of a particular military campaign the process of what used to be called 'postwar reconstruction' now involves a continuing state of military pacification. In Afghanistan, Coalition troops, including Australia's SAS, are still engaged in a long slow war of strategic management as that country disintegrates, and one more place is added to the list of 'failed states'. In Iraq, US soldiers are ambushed daily with responses ranging from spraying the air with machine-gun fire to falling down and weeping by the side of the road. At the same time, on the home front in the United States the surveillance and internal security forces are on a permanent state of alert.

Another of the dimensions of meta-war is possibility of automating and projecting force from a distance, massively and quickly – a spatial overcoming. This possibility had its beginnings in the Second World War and was enhanced during the late twentieth century through the concurrent development of smart weapons and missile delivery systems and through new methods of organization, including computer simulation. It took two simultaneous directions. The first involved treating weapons as instruments of policy in their own right. Mutually Assured Destruction was both the outcome and limit of this first direction. The second direction involved automating and intensifying embodied attacks though such developments as the Rapid Deployment Force (RDF) of the 1980s. The idea here, first conceived in 1977, was that through super-efficient and flexible organization and transport systems a force of military personnel could be placed anywhere in the globe within days rather than months. Interestingly in the current situation, the RDF was first linked to the controversial Sinai 'Peacekeeping Force', a US-sponsored force to which Australia under Prime Minister Malcolm Fraser contributed troops despite 71.5 per cent disapproval from the Australian population. He lost the next election.

For a period during the 1990s, the projection of disembodied force took precedence over the projection of abstractly organized special ground troops. In Kosova, for example, months of bombing were used to win the war without risking troops on the ground. Some military strategists and some academics proclaimed the beginning of an age of pure electronic war. However, while books are now being written on *War in the Age of the Intelligent Machine* or *Postmodern War*,[9] this should not be taken to mean that wars will no longer involve soldiers on the ground or that civilians will be spared by precision machinery. Neither does the use of ground troops in the current war mean that we are returning to older forms of war-making. Rather, what we are talking about is the framing condition of war becoming increasing abstract and technologized, with an intensification of violence in the theatre of war that has a devastating effect on actual human bodies, either directly or through destruction of the social fabric.

In summary then, what the Second Gulf War indicates, as part of the meta-war on terror, is that war will potentially be fought across all levels of engagement from the embodied to the disembodied abstract, all the while being framed by the abstracted possibilities of high-tech weaponry, computerized organizational systems and a globalized military-industrial-communications complex. What the war brings together is the interconnectivity, or 'convergence' in the language of information systems analysis, of changing modes of practice – production, organization, communication and enquiry. This convergence under conditions of late capitalism and techno-science has taken the capacities of the modern war-machine to a new level of projected violence. In the meantime, individuals are being killed in ever-greater numbers, some by smart bombs, some by bulldozers pushing suffocating sand into their trenches, and some in the chaotic conditions of water and food shortages. Personally, I want to know what has happened to that Australian clergyman that I heard talking on the radio about his solidarity with the ordinary people of Iraq before the war started. He said that he would accept his fate outside the air-raid shelters because that was the fate of the people of Baghdad with whom he had worked for many years. His words resonated for me against two moments of religious rhetoric. The first was George W. Bush's final words in his State of the Union address on the eve of the Iraq bombing: 'We do not know – we do not claim to know all the ways of providence, yet we trust in them, placing confidence in the loving God behind all of life, and of history. May he guide us now. And may God continue to bless the United States of America.' The second was a satirical war-prayer written during the American occupation of the Philippines in 1905:

> O Lord our God, help us tear their soldiers to bloody shreds with our shells; help us to cover their smiling fields with the paler forms of their patriot dead; help us to drown the thunder of the guns with the shrieks of their wounded, writhing in pain; help us to lay waste their humble homes with a hurricane of fire; help us to wring the hearts of their unoffending widows with unavailing grief; help us to turn them out roofless with their little children to wander unbefriended the wastes of their desolate land in rags and hunger and thirst, sports of the sun flames of summer and the icy winds of winter, broken in spirit, worn with travail, imploring Thee for the refuge of the grave and denied it – for our sakes, who adore Thee, Lord, blast their hopes, blight their lives, protract their bitter pilgrimage, make heavy their steps, water their way with tears, stain the white snow with the blood of their wounded feet! We ask it, in the spirit of love, of Him Who is the Source of Love, and Who is the ever-faithful refuge and friend of all that are sore beset and seek His aid with humble and contrite hearts. Amen.[10]

The author was an American, Mark Twain. These words were not published until 13 years after his death because his editors thought that this 'moment of truth' was too sensitive for publication at such a time of high patriotism. Unfortunately, the kind of basic questioning of the culture of abstract global 'peace', a 'peace' that has brought us so much misery, seems as far off now as it was in Mark Twain's time. The difference was that then the harbingers of the successive wars-to-end-all-wars could not know how often history would be repeated as tragedy.

18
Post-2001 and the
Third Coming of Nationalism[1]

Tom Nairn

The falcon cannot hear the falconer;
Things fall apart; the centre cannot hold;
Mere anarchy is loosed upon the world,
The blood-dimmed tide is loosed, and everywhere
The ceremony of innocence is drowned ...
Surely some revelation is at hand;
Surely the Second Coming is at hand.

W.B. Yeats, 'The Second Coming', in *Michael Robartes and the Dancer* (1921)

Yeats foresaw the imminent era of nationalism and fascism in a famous poem of the 1920s, 'The Second Coming'. Today his words can hardly avoid assuming new significance, as other 'rough beasts' come forth in the wake of September 11, 2001. Their appearance compels us to look back and recognize some analogies with earlier versions of militarized authoritarianism, and not only with the British and Roman Empires that have recently been so favoured. The story of national*ism* is distinct from that of national identities and claims for nationhood or liberation. The latter asserted themselves from the eighteenth century onwards and were clearly linked to other Enlightenment themes. The former was a later development of the same process, emerging only in the 1870s, after the Franco-Prussian War, the American War of Secession, and the formation of the Italian and German states. National*ism* was distinctively a 'great nation' or supremacist idea, even though reproduced or aspired to everywhere else, in the imperialist climate of 1870 through the First World War ... and later. It has re-emerged in globalizing conditions, post-1989, contrary to every prophecy of the neo-liberal clerisy. However, global circumstances are unlikely to lead to a 'third coming', or ideological takeover like that of the post-Second World War. Things have evolved too far in other directions, and appear more likely to favour a return to national-identity politics *minus* – or against – the militarized '-ism' again prominent in post-2001 USA. Current reactions against the latter may indicate such a shift.

I suspect that W.B. Yeats' *Spiritus Mundi* must by now be disturbing all serious students of globalization who read poetry (so far, probably not enough of them). In 'The Second Coming' (1921) all will recall how he intuited a desert monster – 'with lion body and the head of a man, and a gaze blank and pitiless as the sun' – the rough beast of futurity shambling towards its inheritance, quite unlike the progressive bloke liberal theorists had been looking out for in 1922, or indeed that 'Last Man' imagined by Francis Fukuyama, way back in 1992.

The reasons for the renewed, ominous appropriateness of the words are all around us. Yeats' nightmarish vision was not of course confined to events in Ireland. He sensed a profound shift in the ground rules, the advent of forces and possibilities, somehow both novel and anachronistic (even atavistic) at the same time.[2] This seismic upheaval would change everything, from the international order to the beatings of the individual heart. Just after the appearance of 'The Second Coming', Mussolini's March on Rome signalled an apparent national will over both Left and Right. One hesitates before mentioning such debased coinage again: but (as a recent new biography points out) the fact is that the March was founded on the idea of a revolutionary 'Third Way'. It was supposed to represent a *via media* between capitalism and socialism. And it was made possible through a 'legal *coup d'état*', a takeover from above, by which King Vittorio Emmanuele III reinterpreted the constitution and will of the people. The US Supreme Court accomplished something rather similar in the year 2000. In both cases the result was power to what looked at first like a queerly mixed-up far Right.[3] This mix-up was speedily sorted out, by the ascendancy of 'radical' elements – the Fasci in Italy, the 'neo-Conservatives' in America – to rally the nation and let it recover from all the upsets. The convulsions in Ireland proved premonitory of many others, and Yeats could conclude: 'but now I know/ That twenty centuries of stony sleep/ Were vexed to nightmare by a rocking cradle'.

Today *we* know something analogous, since September 11 and the events that have followed. I have emphasized the Bush family's *coup d'état* in November 2000, but I know others are looking even further back, to the odd fevers of the millennium and the atmosphere of globalization's first *fin de siècle*. But whenever it started, there can surely be no doubt of its continuing and constantly deepening course. This forces us to ask new questions about some more deep-seated causes, and even more deeply mistaken judgements as to the general course of development following 1989 and the end of the Cold War. Yeats was addressing what became the rise of nationalism, fascism and Stalinism between the world wars. But just what is it that we should be addressing today?

HOMO IMPERIOSUS?

Well, what if the deeper issues the poet touched on so unforgettably at that historical moment were only one episode in a much longer-running drama – a drama not only continuing, but reasserting itself once more? I believe there are a number of reasons for thinking that something like this must indeed be the case. I'm not proposing a 'back to fascism' story. Bush's America, Blair's Britain and John Howard's Australia clearly don't amount to that. Yet they have plunged the world *forward* into a weird mix-up, which is being remedied (maybe not so temporarily) by styles of *authoritarianism* which, however distinct and contemporary, can't help recalling episodes from the past. We must assume these have a history – and not quite, or not only, the history of 'the West' proclaimed so loudly by politicians and tract writers since 2001. The empires of Great Britain and Ancient Rome have figured prominently in such apologias: a halo of 'liberalism' is suggested by the first, and one of ennobling and inescapable order by the second – the very ingredients called for by centurions and scribes of the imagined new order of Anti-Terrorism.

However, there seems to me quite a convincing case that the *série noire* should not be wholly omitted: the interwar world of fascism and unleashed ethnic nationalism. May these not also have been in certain ways an anticipation of today's dilemma – even a kind of crude 'trial run' for what may be the more durable authoritarianism of the early twenty-first century? And if this is so, then it must reflect rather deep level trends, towards which most the following remarks are directed. That is, at the level of the meaning and longer-term potential of 'nationalism' itself.

CHANGED UTTERLY

Any commentator has his or her own vantage point for these events. My own has been affected by travelling from one of the war-criminal triumvirate (Australia) to another (the United Kingdom). The thought that something profound and troubling was under way is unavoidable, even for someone long involved in disparaging and ridiculing things British. However, little is now expected of such a fossil-polity, the moral wreckage of its Iraqi war remains surprising. It is a society in which someone could bleed himself to death to escape state persecution, where nobody resigned, and the BBC stood accused of peddling disrespectful lies unto other nations, not just by the Murdoch press or a few resentful Tories, but by a Terminator-style *Labour* government. This is a regime behaving (as it were) more like Tsardom's last gasp than the inheritors of Gladstone and Clement Attlee. At the same time, the leader of this proudly authoritarian satrapy was escaping from such domestic embarrassment by soaking up 17 standing ovations from the US Congress before spending the following week sorting out 'coalition' affairs in East Asia. 'Coalition' means of course 'US State Department' – the further pursuit of the latter's crusade against actual or potential 'Axes of Evil' around the globe. Was this really Tony Blair, who used to be famous for his TV renditions of well-meaning, decent-bloke liberalism? Why has he turned into a janizary more blatant, more ostentatious, and far better rewarded than any servant of the old Ottoman Sultanate?

For two decades the globe had heard about little but the decline of the dreary old nation-state: lowering borders, less state interference, just one market under God ... and so on, and so forth. Neo-liberal pundits, books, learned articles and newspaper editorials beyond calculation, remembrance or forgiveness had poured forth this same message. That is, the long-overdue evaporation of nationalism. This had become part of the climate, the 'commonsense' of the entire *fin de siècle*. So how did it come about then, that following September 11, by far the greatest explosion of nationalism since 1945 has taken place *in the United States of America*? Not in 'remote', helplessly backward, benighted fringes, not among ethnic folk struggling to catch up, or trying pitiably to make the best of things – no, in the womb itself, the alleged identikit for global democracy. Not among rogues and beggars, but inside the motor of the globalizing process, supposedly at the heart of history.

Whatever had became of 'economic man' and the increasingly prominent economic woman of the 1990s? It had come to be taken for granted that they would now be above this kind of thing, and most probably for good. Yet at present, even after demolishing al-Qa'eda caves in Afghanistan, the hyperpower continues to confound all such expectations. It embarked on a huge armed attack upon a grotesque tyranny in another continent – a dictatorship which, however frightful, had had nothing to do with the 2001 atrocity. In order to do so with any semblance of reason, a mega-spectacular of lies was hastily staged in Washington, London and Canberra. These suggested that the Hussein tyranny had 'weapons of mass destruction', and *might be thinking* of using them unless pre-emptive action was taken. But whatever is discovered in time about all these 'might's and 'maybe's, there can be no doubt about the war's melodramatic assertion of both political and military *national* dominance. Like its predecessors, this assault was of course wrapped up in the ectoplasm of 'universal' this and that. But however dubious the WMDs and the role of petroleum may have been, the function of *nationalism* in this global theatre of operations was not.

Since the end of the war, the American and British occupation of Iraq has given rise to a new national movement there: a national liberation struggle, however fragmented, diverse and torn by internecine rivalries, however divided between the secular and the religious. The occupying powers deny this, naturally, just as previous conquerors did half a century ago, in India, in Algeria, in Indonesia, and dozens of other places. Such denials all ended in defeat and abandonment. Is there any serious likelihood of the present occupation ending differently? Ending, that is, other than with the victory of some variant of Iraqi nationalism, religious or secular, short or long term, blood-soaked or civic, defensive, aggressive or all mixed up? With the very thing decreed redundant by the Washington one-world clerisy, and the economic messiahs?

RISE AND RISE OF AN '-ISM'

One broad interpretation of this conundrum goes as follows: national*ism* was always far more important than either rightist-liberal or left-wing ideology conceded – as indeed Professor Liah Greenfeld has argued in her *The Spirit of Capitalism*.[4] It mattered to progress on a deeper, structural level. Economic growth and success were never matters of abstract belief, or of general economic principle alone: they arose out of, indeed by means of, an uneven development that required embodiment, and such social manifestation could only assume national forms. But as Professor Greenfeld shows (and had already demonstrated in her earlier book *Nationalism: Five Roads to Modernity*[5]) this manifestation was characteristically of larger, dominant or would-be dominant national societies. It was never essentially a concern of small or sidelined peoples, even if the latter were then compelled to react along similar lines – following their leaders, as it were – in what was to become the tidal motion of the nineteenth and early twentieth centuries. If that is right, then the tidal machine is still functioning. In fact it is functioning on a more global scale, and with greater means of violence than were ever previously deployed. The 'great nation' of this day still shows what it means, and the sidelined, oppressed and occupied still have no option but to fight back in the same old counter-nationalist terms, making their own pacts with the devil of progress.

It seems to me that what we need to focus on more closely is the '*-ism*' of nationalism. That is, we need to look at the formulation of nationality politics, national interests (and so on) as a hard-edged and indefinitely generalizable creed or doctrine. The term 'nationalism' slips all too easily off all of today's tongues. It has become popular discourse, the tabloids of all lands never tire of it, all shades of politician carry it on their shoulders, and academics in all cultures can still fortify their careers by denouncing it. After 'globalization', as before, it is part of the climate. But this was not always so. Nationality politics, romantic national revival, proclamations of national rights (and so on) were common from the later part of the eighteenth century onwards, and of course such manifestos famously culminated in the Springtime of Nations, the failed European revolutions of 1848. However, national*ism* was still not common currency in 1848. It actually disembarked and made itself at home slightly later in history, for interesting and still relevant reasons.

It may be salutary to recall here the point that the most celebrated single tirade of the nineteenth century against nationality-politics, Lord Acton's short essay 'On Nationality' in 1862, *does not employ the term*. Though by that time important enough to be reviled by fogeys, priests, landed aristocrats and the wealthy, nationality was (so to speak) not yet '-ism' worthy. It had not yet turned into a universal messianic or crusading creed and was not ready to join 'socialism', 'liberalism' and the other secular faiths who by then had been trying for some time to elbow old-fashioned religions out of their way. Although certainly on the ascendant, its moment had not fully arrived. Still, this '-ismic' phase lay not too far ahead.

However protracted the genesis of a discourse may be, the moment of actual birth remains very important, and in this case has been unduly neglected by theorists. It arrived, at last, in the 1870s – much later than would subsequently be recalled. It appeared first in French, where '*le nationalisme*' can be found in the *Grande Larousse* from 1874 onwards. In other words, it first surfaced in what had been *the* great power of the previous century. It was top-drawer, even metropolitan – from the international upper class, so to speak, rather than from the lower ranks, the romantic, emergent nationalities that had signalled their presences in 1848. The point is so important that it deserves emphasis. Romantic nationhood had been about, and making a nuisance of itself, for quite some time. However, the hard edge, the armoured carapace registered in the '-ism' of nationhood was from the outset an expression of *great-nation* will-power – an authority forced to 'mobilize' the new urbanized masses, to 'conscript' them ideologically in ways unknown to older societies. The military metaphors are inevitable and are not accidental. Nationality, national cultures, national identities are a broad spectrum of variables, touching on most aspects of living. But national*ism* is about one thing: *war* – or more rhetorically, about life-or-death options, preparing for such ordeals, or recovering from them in one piece.

The French will-power (or command-structure) in question here had been gravely wounded, and was indeed coping with revolt and injury, under conditions of defeat and demotion. '*Le nationalisme*' in the dictionary echoed the realities of a year or so before, in 1870–72 – that is, the humiliating defeat by Bismarck's Prussian army at Sedan, the terrifying social revolt of the Paris Commune, and the annexation of Alsace and Lorraine. And of course these impacted upon a national consciousness deeply imbued with grandeur, and a popular sense – by then generationally inherited – of civilized centrality, or even of supremacy. France was an empire long before the nationalist knuckle-dusters appeared in the mid 1870s. The Third Republic enjoyed an ancestry of revolutionary republican forms going back to 1789; but the *nationalist* republic was a novelty.

Nation-ism – this now fully armed ideology of nationality politics – sprang from a threatened consciousness of superiority and advantage. The adjectival form, 'national-ism' was appropriate for the subjective will which accompanied it. It registered the urge to 'mobilize' (or remobilize) an entire society in response to a mortal threat. The loss of what had long been an integral part of the older French state, Alsace and Lorraine, fostered a wounded sensibility, a popular consciousness of loss assuageable only by regained greatness, by the reassertive psychology of *La Revanche*. France had to pull itself together, to put Evil in its place and refashion identity for the sake of grandeur and recovery.

JINGOS AND CHAUVINISTS

From the mid 1870s onwards, all these elements flowed into the centre-stage appearance of nation-ism/'nationalism'. But the results were never confined to France alone. They became universally popular almost at once because they were felt to echo the times – that is, the climate of rising imperial conflict, where all states were threatened by analogous disasters, and hence obliged to undertake pre-emptive action. Axes of evil were everywhere, linked to fiercely competitive development. In the background of such aggressive international relations lay Social Darwinism, the new philosophy of a collective struggle for life and supremacy. Theorizations of the latter went back to the 1840s and 1850s, and received a great boost from popularizations of Charles Darwin's *Origins* after 1859. Landed, military and other elites liked the new climate because it was hierarchical and promised to keep the masses in line. But the newly literate masses liked it too, at least initially, because it seemed to be supplying a culture they could identify with – one that gave them a *meaningful* place unthinkable under the old regime.[6]

Then it was of course almost simultaneously projected backwards as well as downwards and outwards. Very quickly the idea arose that national-communal will-power must always have been there, at least *in nuce*, potentially, awaiting the birth-summons. The historical success and function of a concept brings this degree of projection with it – as it would later be called, 'reification', or 'essentialism'. In the later part of the twentieth century, nationalists would find themselves under daily sentence and conviction for such sins of an ahistorical projection, notably in smaller places. Actually, the history of the '-ism' in question made their trespasses inevitable. The entire point of post-1870s nationalism – which dominated the globe for a century – was that all societies were by nature like that. Hence Slovenian, Kashmiri, Welsh and Isle of Man nationalists had (and still have) little real option but to be like those of France, India, Germany, Britain, America, and so on (or as like them as they can be).

Confirmation of the historical character of this genesis can be found in two other directions: the jingos and the chauvins. This pair of notorious '-ism's is sometimes conceived as deplorable cousins of nationalism: subsequent redneck variants upon a more respectable, bourgeois model. In fact 'jingoism' arose at the same time as 'nationalism' itself, in the 1870s.[7] 'Chauvinism' was earlier: a French precursor of *le nationalisme*, produced in the milieu of the Parisian vaudeville theatre of the 1840s and 1850s. Their emblematic hero, the purely mythical Nicolas Chauvin, was a scarred yet loyal veteran of Napoleon's armies, an imperialist peasant seeking to inspire French youth to similar foreign adventures and conquests.[8] 'Chauvinism' conjoined rural blood and soil with external adventure and colonization, perceiving France as the natural epitome of a global order of things. In short, as I have to be in this context, national-ism was, and remains today, a big-headed phenomenon, because it has always been a great-nation phenomenon. It was born signalling a will to restored or newfound greatness, rather than to all-round rights or parity. It was really a prelude to, and a necessary condition of the successor '-ism' of empire – even though (to repeat the point) humanity's small battalions were then all forced to react with versions of the same creed, to the disgust of people like W.B. Yeats in Ireland or Saunders Lewis over in Wales. Authoritarianism and militarism were endemic to the '-ism', this creed built up both to express and to channel and control social transformation in a new climate of unceasing threat and warfare.

AUTHORITARIANISM REVIVED?

What Theodor Adorno would later analyse as *The Authoritarian Personality* (1951) found inevitable favour in this climate, a complex of attitudes quite compatible with a measure of democracy, or at least of representative government. Provided these things don't 'get out of hand', in the sense of disturbing or undermining the profounder will or 'fibre' of the nation. Indeed a nation is clearly better off with a popular voice – provided it manifests the 'right stuff' of (notably) recent US mythology. As the whole world is now uncomfortably aware, there's plenty of that still around in the globalizing world. There may even be a surfeit of it. If that's what we are indeed enduring, the 'Third Coming' unmistakably comports a kind of rejustified authoritarian ethos, under which dissent, popular opposition and demonstration are simultaneously permitted and ignored – that is, allowed as evidence of enlightenment when 'reasonable' (backing authority), but repressed as soon as they interfere with the larger realism authority requires. In a universe still prone to backsliding and Evil, the Axis of Good stands permanently in need of this pained realism.[9]

Oligarchy is the new socio-political nature that accords with neo-liberal capitalism. An old-fashioned term, of course, which most dictionaries define something like this: 'a form of government where most political power effectively rests with a small segment of society (typically the wealthiest or most ruthless elite)'. The Greek etymological origins of the word 'oligarchy' express the concepts of 'few' and 'rule'. Oligarchies are often controlled by a few powerful families whose children are raised and mentored to become inheritors of the power of the oligarchy, often at some sort of expense to those governed. This power may not always be exercised openly, the oligarchs preferring to remain 'the power behind the throne', exerting control through economic means.[10]

Oligarchies were familiar in antiquity, and also common in early modern times. But curiously, it is now clear how primitive globalization has recreated something quite close to these early modern circumstances. That is, the conditions of what Marxists once described as 'the rise of the bourgeoisie' in the Netherlands and England, and then in the American and French Revolutions. Outright totalitarian control and regimentation was now out of the question, after the collapse of both fascism and communism. But an earlier formula of indirect power was to hand – and as a matter of fact, quite strongly represented in the state forms and constitutions of two leading Atlantic nations, the United States and Great Britain. Both of these boasted oligarchic authority-structures, naturally disguised as in unceasing (if extremely slow) movement towards wider or 'mass' democracy.

The justification of astronomic inequality and visible corruption, the mass societal forebearance of putting up with misery now in the hope of later betterment, substituting economic goals for those of status and community – all this still can't do without identity-politics, and popular identification still cannot dispense with nationality. The neo-liberal *Geist* has to be grafted on to societies – 'imagined communities' – that live through *meaning*, and the sources of most meaning lie outwith its rather narrow confines. However, authority can always be reinforced by operation upon the 'imagined' dimension, a collective inheritance of meaning related to common, personal emotions.

During the interwar era, would-be great nations like Italy, Germany and Japan, defeated or marginalized by the more successful, resorted of course to these more extreme forms of the authoritarian creed. So indeed did the Russians, with their distinctive developmental variant of communism. At present the 'rough beast' is not, or not yet, driven to such extremes. It was generally felt that the American reaction to September 11, and the ensuing assaults on Afghanistan and Iraq had something 'inevitable' about them. They seemed to be derived from profounder sources than the risks to US profit margins, or the problems of guaranteeing petroleum supplies. They involved identity, passionate meanings, allegiance, and so on – in other words, the whole familiar panoply of big-style nationalism. The *Homo imperiosus* we now confront is therefore a far more determined character than that *Homo economicus* of whom far too much was made in the 14 years that followed the end of the Cold War. Look at him on the rebound today, in those 'more successful' nations that had been *the original leaders of the development race*. He is on the ascendant in those very early modern liberal democracies that, half a century ago, the fascists and Communists sought in vain to challenge and overtake.

Why is this so? Because these nations of the previous Anglo-liberal success, the victors of the Cold War, now feel threatened in themselves. And the rise of a new climatic authoritarianism has produced a pre-emptive war, hugely facilitated by the info-tech revolution (one of whose side-effects is obsession with presentation or 'spin', culture as power-tool – the kind of thing so salient in British New Labour's whole emergence, as well as in the recent David Kelly affair). Fascism in the old sense (uniformed, rural-based, blood-obsessed) is of course beyond the pale in industrialized countries, though it remains optional in parts of Asia and Africa. However, the 'authoritarian personality' has clearly recreated itself without such traditional appurtenances. It has managed to build up a new version of *La Revanche*, redemption with a vengeance, and in the case of the USA this is currently projected indefinitely into a distant future time, as a battle against Terrorism and Evil, the stirring of ever more 'rogue states', and so on.

Let me repeat the main point: these are not relapses into fascism. Rather, in the fuller retrospect that globalization now makes possible, fascism appears as a clumsy trial run for them. The new authoritarianism was pioneered in the former number one world power, Great Britain, first by Thatcherism and now Blairism. An analogous version of oligarchy was brought to the USA by Ronald Reagan, and borne onwards by the Third Way compromises of the Clinton period, before being abruptly confirmed by the Bush family's 2000 *coup d'état*. In the third active participant in the Iraq expedition, Australia, John Howard's neo-liberal regime reconstructed traditional authority after a milder variant of 'Clintonism' (the Labor government of Paul Keating) and confirmed it with a petty war against asylum-seekers in Australia.

One approach to discerning the lineaments of Third Way (or Third Coming) nationalism is simply to ask what the three Iraqi warmongers had in common in the period from the later 1990s up to the outbreak of hostilities? Economically, they shared an enthusiastic over-commitment to the neo-liberal model of development, an investment which made them in truth *dependent* on globalization. Not (I hasten to add) on global or one-world evolution as such, but on the specific and narrow dogmas of Free Tradery, competitiveness and ideological individualism that have blessed capitalist expansion since 1989. All three states had been fanatical worshippers of 'One Market Under God' (as Tom Franks memorably put it, and I have used as a shorthand phrase throughout this chapter). None of them could easily face a slump or downturn of this process – and least of all the United States, which now had to combine being the globe's main importer of goods, services *and* capital with protecting what was left of its own industries and agriculture.

Socially, all three countries faced profound and clearly structural uncertainties, deriving either from nationalist and secessionist threats (as in the UK) or from massive demographic shifts linked to immigration and minority cultural demands or restlessness (as in Australia and the USA). Also, all three suffered from political systems that were by nature ill-adapted to just those demands and tensions. That is, states 'liberal' but distinctly (and indeed proudly) old-fashioned, devoted to stability and continuity rather than to democratic innovation and experiment. This is of course blatantly so for both Britain and the USA, whose state-forms descend from the 1680s and the 1780s respectively. Australia may appear by comparison a stripling, since its independent variant of federalism goes back only to the year 1901 (see Chapter 9). But it should be recalled that this system was conceived as a replicant of the Westminster one. It was intended to stress stability and continuing royal authority, over against certain uncouth and disrespectful tendencies historically rather salient in the Australian population.

However, such economic, social and cultural unease discovered another solution available, one requiring no constitutional reform or smart social-engineering initiatives. This was, simply, warfare. A melodramatic foreign policy designed to pull the disintegrating and recalcitrant strands back together, to re-present and fortify traditional allegiances and identities. In the UK, Blair embarked well before the war on a practically non-stop world-statesman tour, designed to demonstrate how no globalizing world could possibly do without Great Britain. In Australia, John Howard's liberal regime undertook a peculiarly vicious war against 'illegal immigrants' and asylum-seekers with similar motives. That is, a nation consisting mainly of past immigrants (including the great Asian migration of the 1980s and 1990s) was to be integrated through a crusade against more of the same. Australians wanted to stand tall in this new world, as they had previously done via participation in the world wars of the old.

BLACK PLUTO'S DOOR

In the United States, it now tends to be forgotten how much widespread alarm and intellectual concern there was in the 'nineties about the disintegration of American identity and national responsibility. The drift and corruption of the later part of the Clinton period brought a climate where, for example, liberals like Christopher Lasch preached in his *The Revolt of the Elites* a recovery of 'national consciousness' by the US middle class, and Arthur Schlesinger Jr denounced multiculturalism gone mad in *The Disuniting of America*. And now? Well, just how changed, changed utterly, is shown rather well by the impressive book I read the other day, by *New York Times* journalist and reporter Chris Hedges. Its title is: *War is a Force that Gives Us Meaning*, and the two opening chapters are 'The Myth of War' and 'The Plague of Nationalism'.[11]

Naturally, these states continue to defend 'democracy', in the sense of their respective (and astonishingly decrepit) early-modern constitutions – while allowing the latter to moulder away *in practice* amid mounting popular abstention (except for the Australians, who have a more authoritarian solution: compulsory voting). In all three, nationalism remains decisively more important than democracy and constitutional reform. And this force that has poured so much meaning into the neo-liberal universe of 'globalization' is to be sanctioned by a presidential plebiscite in the US in 2005. That is, the general trend of the Third Coming will be validated by an acclamatory election (one cannot of course say 're-election') of George W. Bush in November 2004, quite possibly clearing the undergrowth further for the more resounding installation of Arnold Schwarzenegger in 2008. No doubt this is why the fate of the Romans has come to figure so prominently in that country's current paranoia. Eventually, the imperialism of the Romans dissolved into their own wider empire. But its contemporary successors are determined that pax Americana, the world they redeemed from communism, will *not* simply melt away into the successor condition of globalization. No, it will remain *theirs*. And to justify this rediscovered manifest destiny, Weapons of Mass Destruction (moral as well as physical) will always be found in Evil hands: the mandate of globalization, thus conceived, decrees that there can be but a single Axis of Good – to be maintained by legitimate nuclear force if necessary.

How can this prospect be related to the profoundly different narrative of romantic nationality? Well, I suspect this is actually an ideal time to be reviving and debating these issues. My suggestion earlier was that nationhood and modern nationality struggles long preceded 'national-ism' in that armour-plated and ideological sense that became so inescapable from the 1870s onwards. If this is so, then one can surely reasonably ask whether they will survive the demise of the '-ism'. If what we are enduring is the third *and the last* fling of great-power, big-headed, destinarian nationalism, then it can be maintained that a different style and demeanour of national identity will surely return – in its wake, or after its failure. Globalism is unlikely to mean universal transport into the neo-liberal or any other cosmopolis; but could it not possibly be built up in stages, by assorted democratic-national initiatives and experiments, consociational or confederal stratagems? Moves (for example) like the one which has been stalled in Northern Ireland for the whole of 2003?

I began by pointing out how Bushism and the Iraqi war have made us think again about nationalism. This is inevitably a gloomy perspective, evoking Yeats at his most portentous. However, the very same events have comported a contrary indication as well, in the shape of the even more extraordinary manifestations of resistance to these new big-nation histrionics. Millions and millions of people objected – far more than the protestors and peaceniks of the 1920s, and on a much more international stage, and probably with more lasting effects. These effects will be both practical and conceptual, and obviously I can't at this stage embark on the politics of the former. One remark about the conceptual side of the response may be worth making, however. While going through great ideal schisms like this, people require new stories and myths to support their instincts, novel indicators of possibility and lines of advance. On the philo-American side, for example, we see a theory like Robert Kagan's: post-Cold War Americans are now solemnly encouraged to see themselves as 'from Mars', in contrast to wavering or irresponsible Europeans who are 'from Venus'. It was never clear where the rest of humanity might be located in this solar-system order. The asteroid belt, perhaps? This may be little more than a feeble echo of old-fashioned Social Darwinism, but it serves a purpose none the less – that of reminding the opposition, and perhaps specially opponents from small cultures like Ireland and Scotland, that they too need new songs, if only to live through the reign of such high-horse notions.

Today they are enormously better equipped to do so than was the case in Yeats' time. The ridiculous contradictions of the latest paradise, neo-liberalism, have had the side-effect of liberating opponents from counter-utopias as well. After communism and neo-conservatism, humankind is due a holiday from '-isms'. One response, admittedly, may be a reversion to religious fundamentalisms, whether of the Mid-East or the Mid-West. However, I doubt if these can now get far. The new conceptual infrastructure they would need is simply unavailable. So much more is now known about 'human nature', that ayatollahs of all lands and colours are really disarmed in advance. Even while the clammy orthodoxies of neo-liberal economics were being foisted upon us under first-stage globalization, great advances were under way in social anthropology, archaeology, and the study of both the brain and the common psyche – enough, surely, to take us forever beyond the fantasmagoric level of Axes of Evil *or* Good.

So let me end both this chapter and *Global Matrix* by quoting (again) from a different poem, something that is appropriately both ancient and up to the minute: Seamus Heaney's translation from Virgil, already referred to at length in Chapter 16. This poem has rarely been out of my mind since I discovered it in America in 1998, when the paperback of Heaney's collection *Opened Ground* first came out. I didn't at the time know just what it was touching on, at such a deep level, or why it practically haunted me for years. It's *The Golden Bough*, where Aeneas finds himself close to the ultimate source of truth, the secrets of genuine human existence, hidden in the Underworld, Hades. They are supposedly guarded by monsters, the awful black dog Cerberus, or Pluto. While Aeneas is waiting in suspense down there, a bit of gnomic advice is offered:

> Aeneas was praying and holding on to the altar
> When the prophetess started to speak: 'Blood relation of Gods,
> Trojan, son of Anchises, the way down to Avernus is easy.
> Day and night black Pluto's door stands open.
> But to retrace your steps and get back to upper air,
> This is the real task and the real undertaking.'[12]

Yes, the 'upper air' of a more common world, 'globalized' in the sense of shared, more equal – and at the same time more diverse and more self-consciously diverse. But what can that represent except a reprise of the very themes to be discussed here, in Charles Stewart Parnell's birthplace, at Avondale, County Wicklow – 'romantic nationality' in plain clothes, as it were, liberated at last from the straitjacket of the '-ism', from the uniforms, from industrialized nostalgia, 'us and them' minus the paranoia, the chest-beating and the genocide?

Notes

PREFACE

1. Jonathan Swift, *Gulliver's Travels*, Oxford University Press, Oxford, 1998 (1726), pp. 161–2.
2. *Ibid.*, p. 162.
3. From the 'back-cover' sleeve of the Village Roadshow video, *The Matrix*, written and directed by Andy and Larry Wachowski.
4. *Star*, 16 August 2003.
5. *GQ Magazine*, September 2003.

I INTRODUCTION: MAPPING NATIONALISM AND GLOBALISM

1. John Lukacs, *The End of an Age*, Yale University Press, New Haven, 2002.
2. William H. McNeill and J.R. McNeill, *The Human Web*, Norton, New York, 2003.
3. Emmanuel Todd, *Après l'Empire*, Gallimard, Paris 2002, English translation forthcoming as *After the Empire*, Columbia University Press, New York, 2004.
4. Manfred Steger, *Globalism: The New Market Ideology*, Rowman and Littlefield, Lanham, 2002.
5. The Spanish painter Goya produced a famous series of dark premonitory images, after experiencing the horrors of the French occupation of Spain – in many ways a forerunner of nineteenth- and twentieth-century imperial and colonial conflicts. The best-known is 'El Coloso', The Colossus (1808–12) in the Prado Museum in Madrid, which shows a gigantic figure turning his back upon a terrified, fleeing humanity the size of ants. It has always been noted as one of the greatest yet most enigmatic images of modern times. Robert Hughes' recent biography of the artist describes the background of this and other dark masterpieces as an illness that forced Goya to brood upon what he (and many others) had seen, during a foreign military invasion intended to impose 'regime change' upon a notoriously backward, superstition-ridden land bent on holding back progress. Interestingly, the idea may have been associated with the work of a Basque poet of the period, Juan Bautista Arriaza, whose *La profecia de los Pirineos* (1808) imagined a giant spirit of resistance, arising against the invaders. See Robert Hughes, *Goya*, Harvill Press, London, 2003, pp. 286–7.
6. David Hume, *A Treatise of Human Nature*, Edinburgh, 1739–40. The most valuable recent edition is the Oxford Philosophical Text, edited by David and Mary J. Norton: see Book 2, Part 3, Section 3, 'Of the influencing motives of the will', p. 266. The 'crooked timbers' started with Immanuel Kant: 'Out of the crooked timber of humanity no straight thing was ever made' (*Kant's Gesammelte Schriften*, Berlin, 1900–) vol. 8, p. 23. It was Isaiah Berlin's favourite quote, recurring throughout his collected essays, *The Proper Study of Mankind*, New York, 1997, as it will through this volume.
7. John Dalberg Acton, from *Essays on Freedom and Power* (1862), excerpted in Gopal Balakrishnan, ed., *Mapping the Nation*, Verso, London, 1948, p. 37.
8. Here, and throughout the book, 'globalism' is treated firstly as the inclusive category for associated terms such as 'globalization', 'globalizing' and 'global formation'. This is similar to the way that the concept of 'nationalism' is used in the literature to stand in for the cluster of associated but differently defined terms – 'nation', 'nation-state',

'nation formation', and so on. Secondly, when made explicit, the concept of 'globalism' has a more specific reference as the ideology or subjectivity of globalization. Similarly, 'nationalism' is used to refer to the ideology or subjectivity of nation formation, in both cases – ideological or subjective – a much broader notion than the politically expressed desire to form a nation-state.

9. Alan Shipman, *The Globalization Myth*, Icon Books, Cambridge, 2002, p. 5.
10. Ernest Gellner, *Thought and Change*, Weidenfeld and Nicolson, London, 1964; Eric Hobsbawm, *Nations and Nationalism since 1780*, Cambridge University Press, Cambridge, 1990; Benedict Anderson, *Imagined Communities*, Verso, London, 2nd edn, 1991.
11. Perry Anderson, *A Zone of Engagement*, Verso, London, 1992, p. 205.
12. Anthony D. Smith, *The Ethnic Origins of Nations*, Basil Blackwell, Oxford, 1986; *Nationalism: Theory, Ideology, History*, Polity Press, Cambridge, 2001.
13. Benedict Anderson made this point very strongly, in a lecture delivered (appropriately) at the National Library of Taiwan in April 2000. He concluded that 'any sharp and unequivocal distinction between Eastern and Western, Asian and European, nationalism is impossible to justify, either theoretically or empirically'.
14. Benedict Anderson, 'Eastern and Western Nationalism', *Arena Journal*, new series no. 16, 2000/1, pp. 121–31.
15. 'England' might be one counter-example, but prior to the nineteenth century we would still call it a 'traditional nation' (that is, genealogically extended but bound by class-based delimitations) rather than a 'modern nation'.
16. For example, between 1994 and 2002 there were eight new members, representing a population total of 19,085,022 souls, giving an average size of 2,385,627 per admission – small but not derisory. However, if it is borne in mind that two of the candidates were Serbia-Montenegro and Switzerland – manifest belated 'exceptions' for quite different reasons, one a palpable phoney – then a more realistic picture emerges. The six-year period saw six real newcomers, representing an average population of 192,711 on an average land area of 17,064 km² (approximately the same as Fiji, or the US state of New Jersey). The dominant trend is certain to continue over the period of (say) 2004–50, albeit with some further large belated entries, like Taiwan and Kurdistan. There are then likely to be at least 230–240 members, predominantly of once-despised mini- or micro-states (and that number can be more easily imagined as rising than as falling). This is still nothing like the thousands of 'ethnic' or ethno-linguistic and national communities bequeathed from the longer range evolution of *Homo sapiens*. But equally, it will be almost as far removed from the tidied-up straight-timbers club formerly deemed 'tolerable' by all protagonists of Giant-style International Relations, and the Security industry.
17. The 'X Factor' has been insinuated into the new controversies by Francis Fukuyama in his recent work *Our Posthuman Future: Consequences of the Biotechnology Revolution*, Profile Books, London, 2002. The author argues that genetic manipulation must be prevented from interfering with the human soul, which reappears in relabelled and ill-fitting postmodern attire as a precious, if rather shambolic, 'X Factor': the shy tribute of neo-liberal enthusiasm to its own downfall? Tom Nairn has published a critique of the strange episode in the *International Journal of the Humanities* (available at <http://HumanitiesJournal.Publisher-site.com/>). See also Simon Cooper, 'The Small Matter of Our Humanity', *Arena Magazine*, no. 59, 2002, pp. 34–8.
18. For a more explicit elaboration of such an approach see the writings of theorists such as Geoff Sharp, John Hinkson and Simon Cooper in the pages of *Arena Journal*.

2 GLOBAL ENCHANTMENT: A MATRIX OF IDEOLOGIES

1. The metaphor of the genie is significantly different from the metaphor of the juggernaut used by Anthony Giddens (*The Consequences of Modernity*, Polity Press, Cambridge, 1990)

or the Hindu god Shiva used by Manfred Steger (*Globalism: The New Market Ideology*, Rowman and Littlefield, Lanham, 2002), except that it is simultaneously old and new. It is used here because it highlights historical tensions of meaning that are relevant to globalization now: in this instance between the evil genie of the darker Arabian tales and the rock-and-roll cowboy-style genie of Hollywood's *Aladdin*. A shorter version of this chapter was published in Manfred Steger's anthology, *Rethinking Globalism*.

2. The concept of a 'matrix' carries in its multiple meanings the contradictorily embodied/disembodied nature of abstracted social relations that the present study is attempting to describe. In its most general meaning a matrix is a setting in which something takes form, has its origin or is enclosed. In obstetrics 'matrix' refers to the body of the womb. By contrast, in mathematics it refers to a regularized array of abstract elements. And in engineering (my personal favourite given the current expressions of globalism) it refers to a bed of perforated metal placed beneath an object in a machine press against which the stamping press operates.

3. George Meyerson, *Heidegger, Habermas and the Mobile Phone*, Icon Books, Cambridge, 2001.

4. And of course they are not intrinsically bad, but then neither, it should be said, are their opposites: isolation, bounded or immobile placement, insecurity, authority, closure and lack of choice. It is again indicative that despite, or perhaps because of, the abstract distance that constitutes the modern/postmodern reader as intellectually trained, 'we' are likely to find such an alternative list confronting. We may know in our intellects that judgement on what is good or bad depends in all cases on negotiating the ethical principles that undergird human practice. However, in our liberal heart-of-hearts, social outcomes such as closure or lack of choice appear intrinsically bad.

5. Francis Fukuyama, *The Great Disruption: Human Nature and the Reconstitution of Social Order*, Profile Books and the Free Press, London, 1999.

6. At this stage 'smashing the infidels' meant civilizing them by means of sword and burning oil, not engaging in genocide.

7. William Arthur Heidel, *The Frame of the Ancient Greek Maps*, Arno Press, New York, 1976.

8. See Jeremy Black, *Maps and History: Constructing Images of the Past*, Yale University Press, New Haven, 1997, pp. 2–3, on Standen's thesis about the ahistorical depiction of the Great Wall, whether or not it had been built.

9. A stylized map of the empire, about twelve-feet long and rolled out like a narrow scroll. It is known from a thirteenth-century copy. In modern cartographical terms it is unrecognizably distorted. Made more than 2,000 years earlier is a Mesopotamian clay tablet with a circular Assyroncentric map showing the Euphrates joining the Persian Gulf and surrounded by the 'Earthly Ocean'. See Norman J.W. Thrower, *Maps and Man: An Examination of Cartography in Relation to Culture and Civilization*, Prentice-Hall, Englewood Cliffs, 1972.

10. Christian Jacob, 'Mapping in the Mind: The Earth from Ancient Alexandria', in Denis Cosgrove, *Mappings*, Reaktion Books, London, 1999.

11. Justin Rosenberg, *The Follies of Globalisation Theory: Polemical Essays*, Verso, London, 2000.

12. This point is influenced by Leslie Sklair (*The Transnational Capitalist Class*, Blackwell, Oxford, 2001) though the emphasis on 'the intellectually trained' gives his argument a different slant.

13. Roland Robertson, *Globalization*, Sage Publications, London, 1992. His historical mapping of the 'phases' of globalism is the subject of chapter 3 in that book.

14. Giddens, *Consequences of Modernity*; Martin Albrow, *The Global Age*, Polity Press, Cambridge, 1996.

15. *Empire*, EMAP consumer magazines, first published in the UK in 1992, began publication in Australia in 2001. Website: <www.empireonline.com.au>. While it is unlikely that the marketing department of the magazine directly considered the resonance with Antonio Negri and Michael Hardt's wildly popular academic book *Empire* (Cambridge, MA: Harvard University Press, 2000), the overlap of names is, to use a Marxist refrain, probably no coincidence. At the very least it indicates an ideological confluence – 'empire' has again become a sexy theme.

16. Asa Briggs and Peter Burke, *A Social History of the Media: From Gutenberg to the Internet*, Polity Press, Cambridge, 2002.

17. See, for example, Ulrich Beck's presumptive definition of the globalization as denoting 'the processes through which sovereign national states are criss-crossed and undermined' (*What is Globalization?*, Polity Press, Cambridge, 2000, p. 11). This also put me at odds with Mohammed Bamyeh (*The Ends of Globalization*, University of Minnesota Press, 2000) and his arguments about the death of the nation-state.

18. Lynne Cheney with Robin Preiss Glasser, *America: A Patriotic Primer*, Simon & Schuster, New York, 2002.

19. Jonathan Steele, 'The Bush Doctrine Makes a Nonsense of the UN Charter', *Guardian*, 7 June 2002.

3 GLOBAL TRAJECTORIES: AMERICA AND THE UNCHOSEN

1. Earlier versions of this chapter appeared in *Arena Journal* and on the Open Democracy website.

2. Gore Vidal, *Perpetual War for Perpetual Peace*, Nation Books, New York, 2002.

3. Thomas Frank, *One Market Under God*, Vintage, London, 2002.

4. Open Democracy (<www.opendemocracy.net>) 16 September 2002.

5. Anthony Giddens, *Runaway World*, 2nd edn, Profile Books, London, 2002.

6. David Held and Paul Hirst (<www.opendemocracy.net>) January 2002.

7. George Soros, *The Crisis of Global Capitalism*, Public Affairs, New York, 2002; George Soros, *George Soros on Globalization*, Public Affairs, New York, 2002. More recently, Soros's *The Bubble of American Supremacy* (Public Affairs, New York, 2004) is an astringent denunciation of George W. Bush's Republican regime and war policy.

8. J.X. Inda and R. Rosaldo, eds, *The Anthropology of Globalization*, Blackwell, London and New York, 2002; Peter L. Berger and S. Huntingdon, eds, *Many Globalizations*, Oxford University Press, Oxford, 2002.

9. James Ferguson, 'Global Disconnect: Abjection and the Aftermath of Modernism', in Inda and Rosaldo, *The Anthropology of Globalization*, p. 143.

10. Liah Greenfeld, *Nationalism: Five Roads to Modernity*, Harvard University Press, Cambridge, MA, 1993.

11. Amy Chua, 'A World on the Edge', *The Wilson Quarterly*, vol. 26, no. 4, 2002, p. 66.

12. Thomas Friedman, *The Lexus and the Olive Tree*, Farrar, Strauss & Giroux, New York, 2000, p. 12.

13. Open Democracy (<www.opendemocracy.net>) 17 December 2002.

14. Emile Durkheim, *Suicide: A Study in Sociology*, Routledge & Kegan Paul, London, 1970, p. 221.

15. Michael Ignatieff, 'The Burden', *New York Times*, 5 January 2003.

16. Ibid.

17. Michael Ignatieff, *Blood and Belonging*, Vintage, London, 1994.

18. Donald Mackenzie, 'Tacit Knowledge, Weapons Design, and the Uninvention of Nuclear Weapons', *American Journal of Sociology*, vol. 101, no. 1, July 1995, pp. 44–99.

19. William Arkin, 'The Nuclear Option in Iraq', *Los Angeles Times*, 26 January 2003.

20. Scott Ritter, 'L'Apocalypse', *Le Monde*, 29 October 2002.
21. Roberto Unger's 'Boutwood Lectures' <www.sopde.org>, 2002; Michael Hardt and Antonio Negri, *Empire*, Harvard University Press, Cambridge, 2000.
22. Gopal Balakrishnan, 'Hardt and Negri's Empire', *New Left Review*, new series no. 5, September–October 2000, pp. 142–8.
23. Unger, 'Boutwood Lectures', <www.sopde.org>, 2002.
24. Open Democracy (<www.opendemocracy.net>), 25 September 2002.
25. *Washington Quarterly*, Autumn 2002, p. 86.
26. John Keane, 'Whatever Happened to Democracy?' Institute for Public Policy Research, 27 March 2002, also available from <csd@westminster.ac.uk>.
27. *Washington Quarterly*, Autumn 2002, p. 95.

4 GLOBAL TENSIONS: A CLASH OF SOCIAL FORMATIONS

1. This chapter developed out of an earlier essay that appeared in the journal *Communal/ Plural*.
2. *Back to the Future*, 1985, directed by Robert Zemeckis; *Pleasantville*, 1998, directed by Gary Ross; and *The Truman Show*, 1998, directed by Peter Weir. *Back to the Future* is one of the 20 highest grossing films of all time. It spawned two sequels, an animated television series, and became the stock-in-trade title for dozens of books, some with dubious claim to using it. One example is an instructively entitled attempt to bring 'dry documents' back to life for a people who have never seen them as dead: *Back to the Future: Reclaiming America's Constitutional Heritage*, 1998.
3. Neal Stephenson, *Snow Crash*, Penguin, Harmondsworth, 1992; William Gibson, *Virtual Light*, Bantam Books, New York, 1993. Richard Rorty (*Achieving Our Country: Leftist Thought in Twentieth-Century America*, Harvard University Press, Cambridge, MA, 1998) uses *Snow Crash* as paradigmatic of a 'rueful acquiescence' about the end of good old-fashioned national pride.
4. The continuing tension here with McDonald's still seen to be a pre-eminently global corporation, is exemplified by the violent targeting of one of their outlets in Davos at the 2000 World Economic Forum. Going back further, in 1985, London Green Peace organized an International Day of Action against McDonald's. Leaflets were distributed, which over the next few years became the basis for a libel trial that was to take two and a half years, concluding in June 1997. The action taken against two community activists in London became known as the McLibel Trial.
5. *Cambodia Daily*, 13 July 1994.
6. In the early 1990s, Roland Robertson (*Globalization: Social Theory and Global Culture*, Sage, London, 1992, pp. 173–4) used the concept advisedly. However, by the middle of the decade it unreservedly took a central place in his writings ('Glocalization: Time-Space and Homogeneity-Heterogeneity' in Mike Featherstone, Scott Lash and Roland Robertson, eds, *Global Modernities*, Sage, London, 1995).
7. Steve Silberman, 'Just Say Nokia', *Wired Magazine*, vol. 7, no. 9, 1999, downloaded from <www.wired.com/wired/archive>. In 1998, of 165 million mobile phones sold in the world – that is, more mobile telephones than cars and computers combined – Nokia manufactured 41 million units.
8. See the article that originally came out of my contribution to the Academica Sinica conference organized by Alan Chun: 'Beyond a Postnationalist Imaginary: Grounding an Alternative Ethic', *Arena Journal*, new series no. 14, 1999/2000, pp. 53–74. The present chapter draws on material presented there.
9. Arjun Appadurai, *Modernity at Large: Cultural Dimensions of Globalization*, University of Minnesota Press, Minneapolis, 1996, chapter 8, 'Patriotism and Its Futures'.

10. The quote comes from Appadurai (*Modernity at Large*, p. 169) but the sentiment ranges widely from postmodernists to radical liberals: for examples of the latter group, see from the Left, Jean-Marie Guéhenno, *The End of the Nation-State*, University of Minnesota Press, Minneapolis, 1995; and from the Right, Kenichi Ohmae, *The End of the Nation State: The Rise of Regional Economies*, HarperCollins, London, 1996.

11. Benedict Anderson, *Imagined Communities*, Verso, London, 2nd edn, 1991; Eric R. Wolf, *Europe and the People Without History*, University of California Press, Berkeley, 1982.

12. Bruce Robbins ('Actually Existing Cosmopolitanism', in Pheng Cheah and Bruce Robbins, eds, *Cosmopolitics: Thinking and Feeling Beyond the Nation*, University of Minnesota Press, Minneapolis, 1998, p. 3) represents a critical cosmopolitanism that largely avoids the valorization of mobility and detachment endemic in postmodern cosmopolitanisms, but in criticizing its critics he occasionally falls off the balancing beam. Pheng Cheah's introductory chapter, 'The Cosmopolitical – Today' in the same volume turns the critique back on the postnationalists, convincingly arguing that cosmopolitanism need not be postnational.

13. Appadurai, *Modernity at Large*, p. 170.

14. Among the many articles and books now written on Rwanda, I am particularly indebted to Mahmood Mamdani, 'From Conquest to Consent as the Basis of State Formation: Reflections on Rwanda', *New Left Review*, no. 216, 1996, pp. 3–36; and Gérard Prunier, *The Rwandan Crisis: History of a Genocide*, Columbia University Press, New York, 1997. The figures are all approximations, but I have cross-checked multiple sources. For a good overview of other relevant literature see Alexander Johnston, 'Ethnic Conflict in Post Cold War Africa: Four Case Studies', in Kenneth Christie, ed., *Ethnic Conflict, Tribal Politics: A Global Perspective*, Curzon Press, Richmond, 1998.

15. See Michael Herzfeld, *The Social Production of Indifference: Exploring the Symbolic Roots of Western Bureaucracy*, University of Chicago Press, Chicago, 1992. This 'indifference' can itself in turn become the basis of state-legitimized violence from a distance. Rationalized violence, as evidenced in the wars over Iraq and Kosova, is however usually *framed* at a more abstract or technologically mediated level. In practice, of course, war is fought across the various levels of embodiment to disembodiment, but the *framing* of war has become increasingly abstract over the course of history even if the flesh-and-blood bodies of civilians increasingly bear the brunt of military action.

16. Mahmood Mamdani, 'From Conquest to Consent'; Jacques J. Maquet, *The Premise of Inequality in Ruanda*, Oxford University Press, London, 1961, pp. 124–8, 148–52.

17. Mamdani, 'From Conquest to Consent', p. 12. See also Wm. Roger Louis, *Ruanda–Urundi: 1884–1914*, Clarendon Press, Oxford, 1963, part 2.

18. See René LeMarchand, *Rwanda and Burundi*, Pall Mall Press, London, 1970, on the complications of using the terminology of caste and class in relation to the Tutsi.

19. Despite these putative embodied differences, witnesses after the 1994 massacres talked of the executioners often demanding identity cards to determine if they were killing the right people.

20. The Rwandan Patriotic Front (RPF), which again reversed the power hierarchy and returned the Tutsi to government in the wake of the 1994 genocide, had been formed in 1987 in Uganda. The unevenness of the process and how it spread beyond the borders of one nation-state is indicated by the fact that the RPF leader, Paul Kagame, had up until the early 1980s considered himself Ugandan. To carry the story forward: in August 1998, Tutsi-led rebels backed by Rwanda claimed control of two-thirds of the Democratic Republic of the Congo. Angolan, Namibian and Zimbabwean troops were sent in to support President Kabila. The European nations, including former colonial power Belgium, organized a foreign evacuation. In Rwanda there are still rumoured to be Hutu rebel movements in the jungle.

21. Tone Bringa, *Being Muslim the Bosnian Way: Identity and Community in a Central Bosnian Village*, Princeton University Press, Princeton, 1995.

22. Trond Gilbert, 'Ethnic Conflict in the Balkans: Comparing ex-Yugoslavia, Romania and Albania', in Christie, *Ethnic Conflict, Tribal Politics*, p. 67. Michael Keating ('Minority Nationalism or Tribal Sentiments') writing in the same volume rightly distances himself from the moral assumptions of the civic-ethnic nationalism sentiments, but then falls for the parallel moral dichotomy. The new nationalisms, he writes, 'may be benevolent, democratic and progressive [that is, good], or represent a retreat into tribalism [that is, bad]' (p. 35).

23. *New York Times*, 13 October 1991. On representations of the war, both academic and popular, see David Campbell, *National Deconstruction: Violence, Identity and Justice in Bosnia*, University of Minnesota Press, Minneapolis, 1998, pp. 53–81.

24. Gilbert, 'Ethnic Conflict in the Balkans', p. 67. This claim forgets, for example, the self-proclamations of Celtic tribal roots by the southern leagues of the United States, that is, in the 'pre-eminent Western civic nation' upon this planet. See Edward H. Sebesta, 'The Confederate Memorial Tartan', *Scottish Affairs*, no. 31, 2000, pp. 55–84.

25. *Ibid.*, p. 76. While I basically disagree with the analysis, this is not to say that tribalism is not crucial to understanding Balkan history or that it is irrelevant to its present. In the present there can be said to be elements of tribalism to the extent that the organized gangs, that emerged with the collapse of Communism, became an emcompassing way of embodied life for some people. On the past and its incorporation into the traditional state and society see M.E. Durham, *Some Tribal Origins, Laws and Customs of the Balkans*, George Allen & Unwin, London, 1928.

26. Carolyn Marvin and David W. Ingle, *Blood Sacrifice and the Nation: Totem Rituals and the American Flag*, Cambridge University Press, Cambridge, 1999.

27. *Ibid.*, p. 1.

28. *Ibid.*, pp. 22–3. This is the subject of their chapter 9.

29. *Ibid.*; compare, for example, pp. 22 and 192; 19 and 22; 29, 25, 42, 43 and 11; 42–3 and numerous discussions of the flag's textual representations; 20 and 29; 32, 54 and 215.

30. See Anderson, *Imagined Communities*, chapter 11, on the modern issue of remembering and forgetting. Here I am stretching the concept in a way that Anderson perhaps did not intend.

31. The term 'global nation' comes from John Wiseman's book of the same name: *Global Nation?*, Cambridge University Press, Cambridge, 1998.

5 FETISHIZED NATIONALISM?

1. Special thanks to Peter Cocks for his never-ending arguments with me on nations and nationalism, and for his energetic bibliographical work despite, but also in the service of, those arguments. Thanks to Wendy Brown for provocative comments, to Amrita Basu for insightful criticisms, and to Paul Shepard for helpful suggestions on earlier drafts of this chapter. This chapter is an edited version taken from *Arena Journal*, but other versions appeared in the electronic journal *Theory & Event* and in my book, *Passion and Paradox: Intellectuals Confront the National Question*, Princeton University Press, Princeton, 2002.

2. I take a longer look at Ernest Gellner and Benedict Anderson in another article, 'From Politics to Paralysis: Critical Intellectuals Answer the National Question', *Political Theory*, vol. 24, no. 3, 1996, pp. 518–37.

3. Or as Nairn puts it, of neo-nationalism, which he describes as 'comparable to elemental nationalism in being a forced by-product of the grotesquely uneven nature of capitalist development', but a by-product that 'occurs at a far more advanced stage of general development, in areas ... on the fringe of the new metropolitan growth zone'. See Tom Nairn, *The Break-up of Britain*, London, New Left Books, 1977, p. 128.

4. By 'geographical conception of place', Said means an appreciation of how the 'physical, political, historical, social and ideological features' of the earth contribute 'each in its own way to ... culture'. Edward Said, 'Narrative, Geography and Interpretation', *New Left Review*, no. 180, 1990, p. 83.

5. Nairn, *The Break-up of Britain*, p. 125. See also G. Lamming, *The Pleasures of Exile*, Allison and Busby, London, 1984. The imperial relation determined not only the predicament of West Indian writers but also the fact that they automatically thought to resolve it by travelling to London. It is one of the many ironies of postcolonial experience that they eventually found their first audience there.

6. For an especially hot-headed concentration on Great Britain, see Nairn's runaway attack on the British monarchy and its 'archaism, trash, quaintness and a burdensome family *Schmalz*' in his book *The Enchanted Glass: Britain and its Monarchy*, Radius, London, 1988, p. 371. One cannot help but speculate on the sources of Nairn's animus here. Is it motivated solely by an ethnic hostility to the English? Unlikely. A political hatred of empire? More likely. A Marxist irritation with England for remaining stalled at an early stage of capitalist development and refusing to 'modernize' into the standard nation-state form to become a 'Little England' to match the mainstream of modern nation-building and identity imposed on most peoples (Nairn, *The Enchanted Glass*, p. 257)? Very likely. It is more likely, however, that such animus is motivated by some combination of the lot, as well as by Nairn's fundamental populism, which always puts him on the side of democracy against royalty.

7. Nairn, *The Break-up of Britain*, p. 317.

8. *Ibid.*, p. 354.

9. *Ibid.*, pp. 340, 353.

10. *Ibid.*, p. 85.

11. *Ibid.*, p. 319.

12. Scholars and proponents of nationalism who dislike the book usually dislike it for this reason. See, for example, Craig Beveridge and Ronald Turnbull's *The Eclipse of Scottish Culture*, Polygon, Edinburgh, 1989. In their chapter 'Scottish Nationalist, British Marxist: The Strange Case of Tom Nairn', Beveridge and Turnbull respond to Nairn's early essays, culminating in *The Break-up of Britain*. They also see him as 'a strange case' because of his mixture of nationalism and Marxism, but their complaint against him, almost the opposite of what mine will be, is that Nairn defends nationalism for Marxist purposes. See also the Scottish nationalist John Herdman's objection to Nairn for treating the 'sweeping away of archaic or predatory social forms' and the 'mobilising of populations for socio-economic development' as the purpose of nationalism, when that purpose, according to Herdman, is really 'the mobilising of populations for spiritual development'. See Herdman, *Whither Scotland*, D. Glen, ed.,Victor Gollancz, London, 1971, p. 109.

13. Nairn, *The Break-up of Britain*, pp. 332, 335. The idea of force is the key to Nairn's difference from Gellner who also sees nationalism as a form of 'good' mystification.

14. *Ibid.*, p. 323. Although unacknowledged by contemporary theorists, Rosa Luxemburg anticipates the argument that nationalism is a modern phenomenon that invents itself as age-old. For the most prominent example of a thinker who is more generous to nationalism, see Benedict Anderson in his *Imagined Communities*, Verso, London, 1991. For an example of a thinker who is less generous, see Eric Hobsbawm, *Nations and Nationalism since 1780*, Cambridge University Press, Cambridge, 1990.

15. H. Arendt, *The Ends of Totalitarianism*, Harcourt Brace Jovanovich, New York, 1973, pp. 231–2.

16. Nairn, *The Break-up of Britain*, p. 348. Hence the title of Nairn's famous final chapter, 'The Modern Janus'.

17. *Ibid.*, p. 329.

18. *Ibid.*, p. 360.
19. They are left unclear for a reason that Eric Hobsbawm sums up in a nutshell: 'there is no way of turning the formation of "national communities" (i.e. the multiplication of nation states as such) into a historic engine for generating socialism either to replace or to supplement the Marxian historic mechanism'. Hobsbawm, 'Some Reflections on *The Break-up of Britain*', *New Left Review*, no. 105, 1977, p. 12.
20. In, respectively, Nairn, 'Beyond Big Brother', *New Statesman & Society*, no. 30, 1990; and 'All Bosnians Now?', *Dissent*, Fall 1993, p. 403.
21. Nairn, 'Beyond Big Brother', p. 30.
22. Nairn, 'All Bosnians Now?', pp. 407 and 408.
23. Nairn, 'Demonizing Nationalism', *London Review of Books*, 5 February 1993, p. 5.
24. *Ibid.*, pp. 6 and 3. The other progressive actors were the 'democratic rebellion against one-party autocracy and state terror', and the 'national mould into which these revolts were somehow inevitably flowing'.
25. Nairn, 'Internationalism and the Second Coming', *Daedalus*, Summer 1993, pp. 163, 164. Another example: 'Socialism has to find new, post-1989 bearings, although some will find this a charitable description of its plight ... The alternative lies within what used to be called the enemy.'
26. Nairn, 'Beyond Big Brother', p. 30.
27. Nairn, 'Does Tomorrow Belong to the Bullets or the Bouquets?', *Borderlands: Nations and Nationalism, Culture and Community in the New Europe*, a special supplement to the *New Statesman & Society*, 19 June 1992, p. 30.
28. Nairn, 'Internationalism and the Second Coming', p. 160.
29. *Ibid.*, p. 161.
30. Nairn, 'Beyond Big Brother', p. 32.
31. Nairn, 'Does Tomorrow Belong', p. 30. His preliminary thought is that while 'at one level' modern socio-economic factors give rise to nationalism by lending 'political and military salience' to an older ethnic variety, 'on another level'.
32. Nairn and J. Osmond, 'This Land is My Land, That Land is Your Land', in *Borderlands*, p. 3.
33. Nairn, 'All Bosnians Now?', pp. 404, 406.
34. *Ibid.*, pp. 407, 408.
35. Nairn, 'Breakwaters of 2000: From Ethnic to Civic Nationalism', *New Left Review*, no. 214, 1995, p. 94.
36. Nairn, 'Internationalism and the Second Coming', p. 158.
37. Nairn, 'Breakwaters at 2000', p. 98. Nairn uses this phrase while scoffing at those who are horrified by the tendency 'against gigantism, and in favour of identity delusions'.
38. Nairn, 'Demonizing Nationalism', pp. 5, 6.
39. *Ibid.*, p. 3.
40. Nairn, 'Breakwaters of 2000', p. 101. Nairn quotes from Michael Ignatieff's *Blood and Belonging: Journeys into the New Nationalism*, Vintage, London, 1994.
41. For two critiques of the civic/ethno national divide, see Bernard Yack's 'The Myth of the Civic Nation' and Nicholas Xenos' 'Civic Nationalism: Oxymoron?', in *Critical Review*, vol. 10, no. 2, Spring 1996, pp. 193–211 and 213–31.
42. Nairn, *The Break-up of Britain*, p. 341.
43. Nairn, *The Enchanted Glass*, pp. 231–8.

6   AMBIGUOUS NATIONALISM: A REPLY TO JOAN COCKS

1. My reply here is to Joan Cocks' version of Chapter 5 in the present volume that was published in her *Passion and Paradox: Intellectuals Confront the National Question*,

Princeton University Press, Princeton, 2002. Her chapter there is titled 'In Defense of Ethnicity, Locality, Nationality: The Curious Case of Tom Nairn', pp. 111–32. *The Break-up of Britain*, the book referred to, was first published in 1977, but has recently come out in a new edition, with a 2003 Introduction and update, published by Common Ground of Melbourne: ISBN 1 86335 508 1 (1 86335 509 X as a downloadable PDF format).

2. 'Out of the crooked timbers of humanity no straight thing was ever made', Kant's *Gesammelte Schriften* (Berlin, 1900–), vol. 8, p. 23. The saying was frequently repeated throughout the works of another of Cocks's subjects, Isaiah Berlin, and he used it as the title of one of his collections of essays. In the most extensive of his collections, *The Proper Study of Mankind*, the phrase recurs in three different places.

3. The most incisive commentary on 1989 and after came from the greatest twentieth-century theorist of nationalism, Ernest Gellner, in his essay 'Homeland of the Unrevolution' in *Daedalus*, Summer 1993. See also his 'From the Ruins of the Great Contest', *Times Literary Supplement*, 17 March 1992.

4. Cocks, *Passion and Paradox*, pp. 128–9.

5. The text opens Gopal Balakrishnan's invaluable reader, *Mapping the Nation*, Verso Books, London, 1996, pp. 17–38. Acton was opposed to 'the cashiering of monarchs, or the revocation of laws', and believed that 'the notion of the sovereignty of the people' was to blame, the sin of democracy assuming national disguise. That actual sovereigns from his own social class would soon steal the same clothes, and commit much more frightful crimes with them, did not occur to such a decent fellow.

6. Christopher Hitchens used the phrase in an essay on the second anniversary of September 11 2001, in the internet magazine *Slate* (8 September 2003): 'What is required is a steady, unostentatious stoicism, made up out of absolute, cold hatred and contempt for the aggressors, and complete determination that their defeat will be utter and shameful. This doesn't require drum rolls or bagpipes or banners.' Was he unaware that these were the sentiments of a newly reinvigorated Frenchness of the far Right – of the progenitors of the anti-Dreyfusard agitation of the 1890s? Transliterated into twenty-first-century USA, the implications appear straightforwardly neo-conservative and militarist – but of course, now upon the global scale of the war to extirpate terrorism.

7. Originally given as an address to the Charles Stewart Parnell Society at Avondale House, Co. Wicklow, Ireland, August 2003. Some of the ideas there were also published on the Open Democracy website, earlier in 2003, and can be found on <www.opendemocracy. net>.

8. Carl Dennis, from the volume *Climbing Down* (1975). The references were mainly to the Vietnam War. The author won the Pulitzer Poetry Prize in 2002 for *Practical Gods*.

9. Worst of all, I see from the monthly 'Index' of *Harper's Magazine* (December 2003) that 54 per cent of US citizens still think President Bush was elected by a majority.

10. A sub-note may be relevant here too: the author bears scar tissue from an embarrassingly long trail of identity 'decisions' and failed chameleon acts. Italy, England, France, the Netherlands, Ireland and now Australia feature in this street-corner performance – worth mentioning only because (of course) they derived from what was felt to be the insupportability of the 'real' (Scottish) identity one was landed with. But they could not help being perpetuations of this identity dilemma. About the time *Break-up* appeared, I recall the secretary of the Transnational Institute in Amsterdam, Helen Hopps, being so amused by these antics she said: 'No, no … the ice-cream's been ordered, you're allowed new toppings, but you can't change the flavour!'

11. I take the phrase 'fatherless world' from Emma Rothschild's recent brilliant retrospect on the Enlightenment and since, *Economic Sentiments: Adam Smith, Condorcet, and the Enlightenment* (Harvard University Press, Cambridge, MA, 2001): 'Smith and Condorcet

lived in an imaginative universe which was prodigiously uncertain by the orderly standards of the early twenty-first century; a fatherless world' (p. 252). But of course since she wrote this, standards have dropped alarmingly, and fatherlessness is again strongly on the increase.

12. Cocks, *Passion and Paradox*, p. 41.

13. *Ibid.*, p. 74.

14. Roman Golicz, 'The Russians Shall Not Have Constantinople', *History Today*, vol. 53, no. 9, September 2003, pp. 39–45.

15. *Karl Marx* (W.W. Norton, London and New York, 1999), chapter 12, 'The Shaven Porcupine', pp. 364–5.

16. *The Ethnological Notebooks of Marx*, Van Gennep, Netherlands, in association with the International Institute for Social History, 1972 and 1974, p. 85.

17. Stephen Jay Gould mentioned the episode in his paper 'A Darwinian Gentleman at Marx's Funeral', in *Natural History*, September 1999, and observes: 'I must say I have never read a more absurd or more poorly documented thesis [than Trémaux's book] … If Marx really believed that such unsupported nonsense could exceed the Origin of Species in importance, then he could not have properly understood the power of Darwin's facts and ideas.' Amazingly, Gould's evaluation of Trémaux errs if anything on the side of kindness. The book's conclusion ends with a re-evocation of Biblical prophecy: Man represents God's repose, at the end of the Seventh Day of Creation – 'as St Augustine said' – when the finest and richest layers of soil appeared, capable of supporting humankind. The book also contains an astounding analysis of the causes of cretinism – attributable to the particular silts deposited in certain Alpine river valleys (*Origines et Transformations de l'Homme, et des Autres Etres*, Paris, 1865, pp. 484–5).

18. In *Pariah: Misfortunes of the British Kingdom*, Verso, London, 2002, I look at a wider range of such phenomena in Blair's Britain, including the dilemmas of recent inner communities in Southern and Central England. The book has an appendix with an interchange between the author and British-Asian journalist Yasmin Alibhai-Brown on this subject.

19. The most celebrated specimen is Malaysian Premier Mahatir Mohammed's speech of 2003, in which we find the whole miserable tale of 'Jewish conspiracy' gruesomely resurrected as a way of accounting for the Middle East War, and American obsession with Terrorism. This was a roundabout way of expressing anti-Americanism, of course, in an area where there are almost no Jewish communities – but where populist authoritarianism remains important, and quite capable of refuelling by hostility towards other diasporic minorities, like the Chinese.

20. See via <opendemocracy.net>.

21. *Après l'empire*, Gallimard, Paris, 2002, English translation forthcoming as *After the Empire*, Columbia University Press, New York, 2004.

22. Cocks, *Passion and Paradox*, p. 124.

23. See Perry Anderson, *A Zone of Engagement*, Verso, London and New York, 1992, 'Max Weber and Ernest Gellner: Science, Politics, Enchantment', pp. 204–5. Biographical notes on Gellner (including my own) often indicate how half-heartedly or intermittently he followed his own theoretical prescriptions. He was quite aware of the contradiction himself, and indeed mentioned it in a reply to Anderson's essay. There were significant national motives in his return from Cambridge to Prague in the early 1990s, as in his reaction to Bohemian themes, and his judgement, for example, of the Czech–Slovak separation of the same years.

24. 'The primordialist-constructivist debate today' in Daniel Conversi, ed., *Ethnonationalism in the Contemporary World: Walker Connor and the Study of Nationalism*, Routledge, London, 2002.

7 DARK NATIONALISM OR TRANSPARENT POSTNATIONALISM?

1. A couple of sections of this chapter were originally published in *Arena Journal*.
2. 'Being' refers to the ontological depth of social relations – from whence come issues of identity formation and social integration. A fuller expression of this position would firstly make it clear that in practice 'being' and 'doing' are always mutually constitutive and can only be separated out for analytical purposes. Secondly, it would make clear that the kind of critically reflexive comunitarianism that I am espousing involves a fine balance between an embeddedness within bounded social relations and a critical reflexivity which continually interrogates embedded particularism from the distance of abstract universalism.
3. Tom Nairn, *Faces of Nationalism: Janus Revisited*, Verso, London, 1997.
4. Originally published as Joan Cocks, 'Fetishizing Ethnicity, Locality, Nationality: The Curious Case of Tom Nairn', *Arena Journal*, new series no. 10, 1998, pp. 129–50.
5. First published in *New Left Review* in 1975 and reprinted as chapter 9 in Tom Nairn, *The Break-up of Britain: Crisis and Neo-Nationalism*, Verso, London (1973), 2nd edn 1981. See pp. 334–5.
6. *Ibid.*, pp. 348–9.
7. As well as her *Arena Journal* article, see Joan Cocks, 'From Politics to Paralysis: Critical Intellectuals Answer the National Question', *Political Theory*, vol. 24, no. 3, 1996, pp. 518–37.
8. Julia Kristeva, *Nations Without Nationalism*, Columbia University Press, New York, 1993, p. 3.
9. *Ibid.*, pp. 15–16.
10. Joan Cocks' phrase (from Chapter 5, 'Fetishized Nationalism?') referring to Nairn, and critically suggesting that this careful balancing act has not been sustained by that author over the last decade.
11. Nairn, chapter 4 of *Faces of Nationalism*.
12. See the massive tome by Jean L. Cohen and Andrew Arato, *Civil Society and Political Theory*, MIT Press, Cambridge, MA, 1992. Gellner acknowledges this heritage, and sets it against the older version developed by the Enlightenment Scottish philosopher, Adam Ferguson.
13. Ernest Gellner, *Conditions of Liberty: Civil Society and its Rivals*, Penguin Books, London, 1996, pp. 187 and 188.
14. *Ibid.*, p. 193
15. Nairn, *Faces of Nationalism*, p. 85.
16. *Ibid.*, p. 89.
17. These base principles might include reciprocity-cooperation, autonomy-freedom, equality-participation, solidarity-authority and nature-culture – with these principles debated and worked through the various modes of practice and over varying levels of space-time extension and social integration.
18. Arjun Appadurai, *Modernity at Large: Cultural Dimensions of Globalization*, University of Minnesota Press, Minneapolis, 1996, p. 177. For a variety of different takes on the same question see Martin Albrow, *The Global Age: Society and State Beyond Modernity*, Polity Press, Cambridge, 1996; Homi K. Bhabha, *The Location of Culture*, Routledge, London, 1994; Frederick Buell, *National Culture and the New Global System*, Johns Hopkins University Press, Baltimore, 1994; Peter Cochrane and David Goodman, 'The Great Australian Journey: Cultural Logic and Nationalism in the Postmodern Era', in Tony Bennett, Pat Buckridge, David Carter and Colin Mercer, eds, *Celebrating the Nation: A Critical Study of Australia's Bicentenary*, Allen & Unwin, St Leonards, NSW, 1992; Mike Featherstone, *Undoing Culture: Globalization, Postmodernism and Identity*, Sage

Publications, London, 1995; Richard Kearney, *Postnationalist Ireland: Politics, Culture, Philosophy*, Routledge, London, 1997.

19. The 'we' here refers to the 'intellectually trained', a grouping that partially through being trained in the art and technique of analytical dismemberment, becomes 'instinctively' ambivalent about the classically conceived closures of modern national community. Notwithstanding examples to the contrary, in the late twentieth century this ambivalence has often moved to acute discomfort. We have to be careful that our framing mode of enquiry does not lead us to treat ideologies of openness, freedom and autonomy as naturally good things.

20. The term 'banal nationalism', coined by Michael Billig (*Banal Nationalism*, Sage Publications, London, 1995), or what I would call the 'new civic nationalism' describes a kind of nationalism that cannot see itself as such. It is the flagged patriotism of those who naturalize their attachments to constitution and country as civic loyalty rather than as intense 'primordial' passion.

21. Appadurai, *Modernity at Large*, chapter 8, 'Patriotism and Its Futures'.

22. Bruce Robbins ('Actually Existing Cosmopolitanism', in Pheng Cheah and Bruce Robbins, eds, *Cosmopolitics: Thinking and Feeling Beyond the Nation*, University of Minnesota Press, Minneapolis, 1998, p. 3) represents a critical cosmopolitanism that largely avoids the valorization of mobility and detachment endemic in postmodern cosmopolitanisms, but in criticizing its critics he occasionally falls off the balancing beam. Pheng Cheah's introductory chapter 'The Cosmopolitical – Today' in the same volume turns the critique back on the postnationalists, convincingly arguing that cosmopolitanism need not be postnational.

23. Appadurai, *Modernity at Large*, p. 159.

24. The quote comes from Appadurai (*ibid.*, p. 169) but the sentiment ranges widely from postmodernists to radical liberals: for examples of the latter group, see from the Left, Jean-Marie Guéhenno, *The End of the Nation-State*, University of Minnesota Press, Minneapolis, 1995; and from the Right, Kenichi Ohmae, *The End of the Nation State: The Rise of Regional Economies*, HarperCollins, London, 1996.

25. Iris Marion Young, 'The Ideal of Community and the Politics of Difference', in Linda J. Nicholson, ed., *Feminism/Postmodernism*, Routledge, New York, 1990.

26. Julia Kristeva, *Nations without Nationalism*, Columbia University Press, New York, 1993, p. 3.

27. Robbins, 'Actually Existing Cosmopolitanism', p. 3.

28. And even then, as Robbins writes in another essay in *Cosmopolitics* ('Comparative Cosmopolitanism', p. 253), 'Hidden away in the miniaturizing precision of "locality" with its associations of presence and uniqueness, empirical concreteness, complex experience, and accessible subjectivity, has been the nostalgia for a collective subject-in-action that is no longer so easy to localize.' On the philosophical complexities of 'place' see Edward S. Casey, *The Fate of Place: A Philosophical History*, University of California Press, Berkeley, 1998. On the levels of theoretical abstraction from which one can examine a particular local place see Elspeth Probyn, 'Travels in the Postmodern: Making Sense of the Local', in Linda J. Nicholson, ed., *Feminism/Postmodernism*, Routledge, New York, 1990.

29. Hildegarde Hannum, ed., *People, Land, and Community*, Yale University Press, New Haven, 1997; William Vitek and Wes Jackson, eds, *Rooted in the Land: Essays on Community and Place*, Yale University Press, New Haven, 1996.

30. Liah Greenfeld, *Nationalism: Five Roads to Modernity*, Harvard University Press, Cambridge, MA, 1992, p. 11.

31. Kearney, *Postnationalist Ireland*, p. 23.

32. Appadurai, *Modernity at Large*, pp. 175–6.

33. See David Harvey, *The Condition of Postmodernity: An Enquiry into the Origins of Cultural Change*, Basil Blackwell, Oxford, 1989; and also Manuel Castells, *The Information Age: Economy, Society and Culture: Vol. 1, The Rise of the Network Society*, Blackwell Publishers, Cambridge, MA, 1996.
34. *Rocky IV*, 1985, a United Artists film, written and directed by Sylvester Stallone.
35. Bhabha, *Location of Culture*, p. 172.
36. The following section is a rewriting of an earlier attempt to discuss the principles underlying an alternative regime of production and working life: Paul James, 'Reconstituting Work: Towards an Alternative Ethic of Social Reproduction', *Arena Journal*, new series no. 10, 1998, pp. 85–111.
37. Claus Offe and Rolfe G. Heinze, *Beyond Employment: Time, Work and the Informal Economy*, Polity Press, Cambridge, 1992.
38. Geoff Sharp, 'Constitutive Abstraction and Social Practice', *Arena*, no. 70, 1985, pp. 48–82. The irony here is that under the rubric of the 'ideology of autonomy', market relations in fact set up unacknowledged structures of authority (power) which limit the *de facto* freedoms of people in ways that close-knit communities could not sustain.
39. Within the *Arena* circle of writers it is Nonie Sharp who has done most to elaborate the concept of reciprocity – mostly in relation to tribal society. See her book *The Stars of Tagai*, Aboriginal Studies Press, Canberra, 1993.

8 UKANIA: THE RISE OF THE 'ANNUAL REPORT' SOCIETY

1. David Good, *The Economic Rise of the Habsburg Empire: 1750–1914*, University of California Press, Berkeley, 1984.
2. Anthony Barnett, *This Time: Our Constitutional Revolution*, Vintage Books, London, 1997.
3. Robert Musil, *The Man Without Qualities*, Picador, London, 1997.
4. Barnett, *This Time*, p. 145.
5. *Ibid.*, p. 273.
6. Cited in Tom Nairn, *After Britain: New Labour and the Return of Scotland*, Granta Books, London, 2000, p. 55.
7. Cited in *ibid.*
8. Cited in *ibid.*, p. 77.
9. Benedict Anderson, 'The Goodness of Nations', in his *The Spectre of Comparisons: Nationalism, South-East Asia and the World*, Verso, London and New York, 1998.
10. William Rees-Mogg, 'Remember the Bounty Mr Blair', *The Times*, 16 November 1998.
11. Julian Barnes, *England, England*, Jonathan Cape, London, 1988, p. 109.

9 AUSTRALIA: ANTI-POLITICS FOR A PASSIVE FEDERATION

1. An earlier version of this chapter first appeared in *Arena Journal*.
2. *Age Good Weekend*, 5 May 2001.
3. Hugh MacKay, *Reinventing Australia*, Angus and Robertson, Pymble, 1993.
4. Michael Billig, *Banal Nationalism*, Sage Publications, London, 1995.
5. Gary Grey, Address to the National Press Club, Canberra, 22 March 2000.
6. *The Australian*, 19 February 2000.
7. Paul Keating, 'Speech at Corowa', *Papers on Parliament (32)*, Australian Senate Publications, Canberra, pp. 63–4.
8. Civics Expert Group, *Whereas the People. Civics and Citizenship Education*, Australian Government Publishing Service, Canberra, 1994, p. 3.

9. *Ibid.*, p. 15.
10. Department of Immigration and Multicultural Affairs, *A New Agenda for Multicultural Australia*, Commonwealth of Australia, Canberra, 1999, p. 6.
11. Australian Citizenship Council, *Australian Citizenship: A New Century*, Canberra, Commonwealth of Australia, 2000, p. 4.
12. <www.onenation.com.au/New_Pages/Main_Frames/Main_Frame.html>, 5 September 2000.
13. <www.centenary.gov.au/happen/nation_endorse.htm#criteria>, 8 March 2000.
14. *Ibid.*
15. <www.centenary.gov.au/media/release/20000124.html>, 24 January 2000.
16. <www.centenary.gov.au/resource/neworld.htm>, 8 March 2000.
17. *Women's Weekly*, December 2000. Interestingly, one of the government's education advertials, 'What kind of country?' in the *Women's Weekly* (October 2000), featured a cover of the *Weekly* itself.
18. <www.centenary.gov.au/happen/nation_endorse.htm#criteria>, 8 March 2000.
19. <www.centenary.gov.au/centenary/cent_who.htm>, 2 March 2000.
20. <www.centenary.gov.au/resource/ceo2.htm>, 8 March 2000.
21. <www.centenary.gov.au/resource/inclusiveyear.htm>, 8 March 2000.
22. <www.centenary.gov.au/resource/tellstory.htm>, 8 March 2000.
23. <www.centenary.gov.au/media/release/3179.html>, 8 March 2000.
24. <www.centenary.gov.au/happen/happen_grants.htm>, 8 March 2000.
25. *Ibid.*
26. David Headon and John Williams, *Makers of Miracles: The Cast of the Federation Story*, Melbourne University Press, Melbourne, 2000.
27. <www.centenary.gov.au/resource/pt1/whatkind_body.htm>, 8 March 2000.
28. *Ibid.*
29. A.D. Smith, 'Nationalism and the Historians', in G. Balakrishnan, ed., *Mapping the Nation*, London, Verso, 1996, p. 175.
30. <www.cofq.qld.gov.au/qld_story_overview.html>, 8 March 2000.
31. Luke Trainor, *British Imperialism and Australian Nationalism: Manipulation, Conflict and Compromise in the Late-Nineteenth Century*, Cambridge University Press, Cambridge, 1994, p. 158.
32. *The Australian*, 20 June 2000.
33. Helen Irving, *To Constitute a Nation: A Cultural History of Australia's Constitution*, Cambridge University Press, Cambridge, 1999, p. 134; John Hirst, 'Federation and the People: A Response to Stuart Macintyre', in *Papers on Parliament (32)*, Australian Senate Publications, Canberra, 1993. Helen Irving is director of the 1901 Centre at the University of Technology Sydney set up with money from the National Council for the Centenary of Federation. The Centre is part of the Federation industry. The website for the 1901 Centre encourages general enquiries and notes that 'written information can be provided for a negotiated fee'. (<www.uts.edu.au/fac/hss/Departments/1901/1901_centre.htm>) Donald Horne is among the many names listed as members of the 1901 Committee.
34. Stuart Macintyre, *A Concise History of Australia*, Cambridge University Press, Cambridge, 1999, p. 136.
35. *Ibid.*, p. 139.
36. Noel McLachlan, *Waiting for the Revolution: A History of Australian Nationalism*, Penguin Books, Ringwood, 1988, p. 168.
37. Roslyn Russell and Philip Chubb, *One Destiny: The Federation Story, How Australia Became a Nation*, Penguin Books, Ringwood, 1998, pp. 7–14.
38. <www.centenary.gov.au/resource/pt1/whatkind_body.htm>, 8 March 2000.

39. Australian Citizenship Council, *Australian Citizenship*, pp. 9–10.
40. *Ibid.*, p. 13.
41. Department of Veterans' Affairs, *Australians at War: Key Dates and Data since 1901*, Commonwealth of Australia, Canberra, 1999, p. 3.
42. McLachlan, *Waiting for the Revolution*, p. 182.
43. Russell and Chubb, *One Destiny*, p. 13.
44. National Archives of Australia: A6443, 281.
45. National Archives of Australia: A6443, 281.
46. Henry Reynolds, *Why Weren't We Told? A Personal Search for the Truth About Our History*, Viking, Ringwood, 1999, p. 151. We note the controversy over these figures, but just as we consider that the controversy over how many Jews died in the Holocaust does little to take forward an understanding of the problem, our argument here does not depend upon one-by-one empirical confirmation of the numbers of dead.
47. John Hutchinson, *Modern Nationalism*, Fontana Press, London, 1994, chapter 6.

10 LATE BRITAIN: DISORIENTATIONS FROM DOWN UNDER

1. An earlier version of the present chapter appeared in Gerry Hassan and Chris Warhurst, eds, *Tomorrow's Scotland*, Lawrence & Wishart, London, 2002.
2. I arrived in Australia during the run-up to the 2001 Australian election, which was dominated – to an extent even unimaginable by UK standards – by the issues of asylum-seekers, immigration and race. This was symbolized by the international news event of the Norwegian freighter carrying asylum-seekers which was refused permission to land.
3. I followed the 2001 UK election quite closely, from the beginning of the year until after polling day, for a book project that I was writing at the time: T. Nairn, *Pariah: Misfortunes of the British Kingdom*, Verso, London, 2002.
4. See David Seawright's chapter in *Tomorrow's Scotland*, Lawrence and Wishart, London, 2002, edited by Gerry Hassan and Chris Warhurst, on the post-election reaction to the Conservatives' solitary victory in Galloway and Upper Nithsdale.
5. See S. Walters, *Tory Wars: Conservatives in Crisis*, Politico's Publishing, London, 2001; A. Seldon and P. Snowdon, *A New Conservative Century?*, Centre for Policy Studies, London, 2001; D. Seawright, *An Important Matter of Principle: The Decline of the Conservative and Unionist Party*, Ashgate, Aldershot, 1999.
6. See R.H.S. Crossman, 'Introduction' to W. Bagehot, *The English Constitution*, Fontana, London, 1963, for an informed labourist analysis of the supposed democratization of this mystifying structure.
7. See D. Mackie, 'The Non-Voting Party', in J. Glover, ed., *The Guardian Companion to the General Election 2001*, Atlantic Books, London, 2001, pp. 122–4.
8. The official figure was that '25 per cent of voters' supported New Labour in the 2001 general election. However, the UK electoral roll is notoriously out of date. Nobody knows how many potential voters have absented themselves from registration over the period since Mrs Thatcher's Poll Tax, at the same time as many immigrants have failed to enrol. 'Keeping out of trouble' has become a way of life, possibly for millions, the implication being that the 'NVP' is a lot bigger than statistics recognized – and therefore that 25 per cent of voters represents less than a quarter of the real voting-age population.
9. There is a widespread consensus that voting participation is irrevocably failing across Europe and the West, but this hides disparate trends and turnouts. In 2001 the Italian general election produced an 83 per cent turnout, whereas the Polish election, after a decade of non-Communist government, produced a derisory turnout of 47 per cent.

10. *Basildon: The Mood of the Nation*, Demos, London, 2001, p. 11: 'The Basildonians ... see their own prospects for self-improvement as good, but not the future of society as a whole.'

11. *Hansard*, 11 December 2000, Col. 351.

12. *The Economist*, 9 June 2001.

13. Jim Bulpitt, *Territory and Power in the United Kingdom*, Manchester University Press, Manchester, 1983.

14. Paul Kennedy, *The Rise and Fall of the Great Powers*, Unwin Hyman, London, 1988.

15. A. Barnett, *Iron Britannia*, Allison and Busby, London, 1982. Barnett's essay, subtitled, 'Why Parliament Waged its Falklands War', is a wonderful polemic about post-imperial decline, the meaning of 1940 and the creation of 'Churchillism'.

16. Hailsham's remarks were representative of right-wing fears and fantasies about democracy and ungovernability. See A. King, ed., *Why is Britain Becoming Harder to Govern?*, BBC, London, 1976; R. Moss, *The Collapse of Democracy*, Temple Smith, London, 1975.

17. J. Freedland, 'I Think We should do', *Guardian*, 18 June 2001.

18. I. Crewe, 'Elections and Public Opinion', in A. Seldon, ed., *The Blair Effect: The Blair Government 1997–2001*, Little Brown, London, 2001, pp. 67–96. Crewe explains the key significance of 'depopulating industrial and inner-city areas' for reinforcing New Labour dominance.

19. D. Butler and D. Kavanagh, *The British General Election of 2001*, Palgrave Macmillan, London, 2001.

20. See Walters, *Tory Wars*.

21. Hans Nichols, 'The Extinction of the Tory Party', *Guardian*, 8 October 2001.

22. Post-1997 there was an avalanche of books on the theme of the death of England and Britain: J. Paxman, *The English: A Portrait of a People*, Michael Joseph, London, 1998; R. Scruton, *England: An Elegy*, Pimlico, London, 2001; S. Heffer, *Nor Shall My Sword: The Reinvention of England*, Weidenfeld and Nicolson, London, 1999; P. Hitchens, *The Abolition of Britain: The British Cultural Revolution From Lady Chatterley to Tony Blair*, Quartet Books, London, 1999; J. Redwood, *The Death of Britain: The UK's Constitutional Crisis*, Macmillan, London, 1999; A. Marr, *The Day Britain Died*, Profile, London, 2000.

23. Liah Greenfeld, *Nationalism: Five Roads to Modernity*, Harvard University Press, Cambridge, MA, 1992.

24. Kevin Pask, 'Late Nationalism: The Case of Quebec', *New Left Review*, no. 11 (second series) 2001, pp. 49–50.

25. G. Hassan and J. McCormick, 'The Future of Britishness', *Soundings*, no. 18, 2001, pp. 118–34.

26. G. Brown and D. Alexander, *New Scotland, New Britain*, Smith Institute, London, 1999. See Hassan and McCormick, 'After Blair', pp. 125–8.

27. It is no accident that the demise of two-party Ukania 1945–70 has seen the development of more pluralist political systems in Scotland, Wales and Northern Ireland. Northern Ireland has a highly competitive four-party system at both Westminster and Stormont, while the Scots and Welsh have four-party systems at a devolved level, but the continuation of Labour one-party rule at Westminster. England has a political system where Labour predominates, but which currently sits with ill ease between a two-party system and one-party dominance, neither one nor the other. The interaction between these different political systems – the tensions, dynamics and evolution – will have a major influence on the future shape of the UK.

28. Lewis Carroll, 'The Queen's Croquet Ground', *Alice's Adventures in Wonderland* (1865), in R. Gassar, ed., *The Illustrated Lewis Carroll*, Juniper Books, London, 1978, pp. 64–71.

29. On this theme see my *The Break-up of Britain*, Common Ground Publishing, Melbourne, 3rd edn, 2003, the original version of which was written 25 years ago and published by New Left Books.

11 NORTH AMERICA: THE MISFORTUNES AND 'DEATH' OF ETHNICITY

1. From 'As Birds Bring Forth the Sun', 1985, in the collection *Island* (Vintage, London, 2002, introduction by John McGahern), p. 320. The other book referred to below is the novel *No Great Mischief* (Vintage, London, 2000).
2. See Thomas Hylland Eriksen, *Ethnicity and Nationalism: Anthropological Perspectives*, Pluto Press, London, 1993, chapters 1 and 2. Eriksen is quoting from Roland Cohen at this point, writing in the *Annual Review of Anthropology* for 1978.
3. See Godfrey Hodgson's *The Gentleman from New York*, Houghton Mifflin, New York, 2000.
4. See 'Moynihan as Devil' at <www.klausfiles.com>. One of his more important crimes was perpetrated as US Ambassador to the United Nations in 1975. He failed to propose any opposition to Indonesia's invasion in 1975 of East Timor, then still a Portuguese colony seeking independence. In his UN memoir, *A Dangerous Place*, Moynihan boasts: 'the United States wished things to turn out as they did, and worked to bring this about. The Department of State desired that the United Nations prove utterly ineffective in whatever measures it undertook. This task was given to me, and I carried it forward with no inconsiderable success.' Thus an exponent of 'Irish-American' ethnicity was at least partly responsible for the resultant massacres of East Timor's ethnic population. Benedict Anderson has estimated that Indonesian 'integration' of East Timor took the lives of one third of the local population between 1975 and 1980. The carpet towards this was unrolled during Moynihan's Ambassadorship, and is very flatly described on pages 245–6 of *A Dangerous Place* (1979). The episode is omitted from the biography of Moynihan cited in the previous footnote: Hodgson's *The Gentleman from New York*.
5. 'Clearances', in MacLeod's *Island*, p. 418. This is approximately a century after the same process in Ireland, described by Declan Kiberd in *Inventing Ireland*, Granta, London and New York, 1996: 'It was only in the mid-19th century that the native language declined, not as an outcome of British policy so much as because an entire generation of the Irish themselves decided no longer to speak it. O'Connell said that the superior utility of English was such that even a native speaker like himself could witness without a sigh the gradual disuse of Irish ...' (pp. 615–16).
6. Macleod, 'Clearances', *Island*.
7. MacLeod, *No Great Mischief*, p. 127.
8. See *ibid.*, pp. 139–43.
9. *Ibid.*, pp. 141–2.
10. *Ibid.*, p. 235.
11. *Ibid.*, p. 261.
12. MacLeod, 'The Return', *Island*.
13. 'From the Lone Shieling: Alistair MacLeod', *Raritan*, vol. 21, no. 4, 2002, pp. 149–61.
14. *Ibid.*, p. 150.
15. *Ibid.*, p. 156.
16. *Ibid.*, p. 161.
17. Macleod, 'Clearances', *Island*, p. 426.
18. William H. McNeill and J.R. McNeill, *The Human Web*, W.W. Norton, New York, 2003: 'Big Pictures and Long Prospects', pp. 326–7.

12 CENTRAL ASIA: CONTINUITIES AND DISCONTINUITIES

1. An earlier version of this chapter appeared in *National Identities*.
2. Ernest Gellner, *Nations and Nationalism*, Blackwell, Oxford, 1983, p. 48.
3. Ernest Gellner, 'The Coming of Nationalism and Its Interpretation: The Myths of Nation and Class', in Gopal Balakrishnan, ed., *Mapping the Nation*, Verso, London, 1996.
4. Anthony D. Smith, 'Nations and Their Pasts', *Nations and Nationalism*, volume 2, no. 3, 1996, pp. 358–65; and Tom Nairn, 'Breakwaters of 2000: From Ethnic to Civic Nationalism', *New Left Review*, no. 214, 1995, pp. 91–103. While it might seem strange writing about Anthony Smith in the same vein as the other modernist writers, even his latest work misses the contradictory layering of the ontological formations of traditionalism, modernism and postmodernism.
5. Benedict Anderson, *Imagined Communities: Reflections on the Origins and Spread of Nationalism*, Verso, London, 2nd edn, 1991.
6. Ernest Gellner, *Culture, Identity and Politics*, Cambridge University Press, Cambridge, 1987.
7. E. Hobsbawm, 'The Nation as Invented Tradition' in John Hutchinson and Anthony D. Smith, eds, *Nationalism*, Oxford University Press, Oxford, 1994. See the critique of this position in John Hutchinson, *Modern Nationalism*, Fontana Press, London, 1994.
8. Etienne Balibar and Immanuel Wallerstein, *Race, Nation, Class: Ambiguous Identities*, Verso, London, 1991.
9. For an explanation of this approach see P. James, *Nation Formation: Towards a Theory of Abstract Community*, Sage Publications, London, 1996, as well as writings by theorists such as Geoff Sharp and John Hinkson in *Arena Journal*.
10. Gellner, 'The Coming of Nationalism', pp. 130–1.
11. M. Haghayeghi, *Islam and Politics in Central Asia*, St Martin's Press, New York, 1995.
12. A. Rashid, *The Resurgence of Central Asia: Islam or Nationalism?*, Oxford University Press, London, 1994, pp. 15–16.
13. *Ibid.*, p. 85.
14. Haghayeghi, *Islam and Politics*, p. 2.
15. Rashid, *The Resurgence of Asia*, p. 85.
16. M. Haghayeghi, 'Islamic Revival in the Central Asian Republics', *Central Asian Survey*, vol. 13, no. 4, 1994, pp. 251–2.
17. Haghayeghi, *Islam and Politics*, p. 77. This infusion of Sufism into Islam continues today.
18. Haghayeghi, 'Islamic Revival', p. 251.
19. D. Hiro, *Between Marx and Muhammed: The Changing Face of Central Asia*, HarperCollins Publishers, London, 1995.
20. Admittedly, the Russian advance did spur the amir of Bukhara to attempt to modernize his state apparatus between 1826 and 1860. However, whilst feudal chiefs were purged from the administration in favour of professional bureaucrats and taxes were increased as part of a more general fiscal reorganization, the possibility that such processes could eventually have led to nation formation, a contestable proposition at best, is a moot point in light of the subsequent Russian takeover of the khanates. See Rashid, *The Resurgence of Asia*, p. 86.
21. Roland Robertson, *Globalization: Social Theory and Global Culture*, Sage Publications, London, 1992.
22. Rashid, *The Resurgence of Asia*.
23. Hiro, *Between Marx and Muhammed*, p. 5.
24. R.R. Anderson, *et al.*, *Politics and Change in the Middle East: Sources of Conflict and Accommodation*, Prentice Hall, New Jersey, 4th edn, 1993, p. 54.

25. Y. Onaran, 'Economics and Nationalism: The Case of Muslim Central Asia', *Central Asian Survey*, vol. 13, no. 4, 1994, p. 493.

26. Hiro, *Between Marx and Muhammed*, p. 5.

27. Onaran, 'Economics and Nationalism', p. 494.

28. We use the term 'state-nations' to describe the states forged by national-minded elites in nineteenth-century Europe (for example, Italy, Germany) and in which the development of national consciousness amongst the masses had yet to occur.

29. E. Weber, *Peasants into Frenchmen: The Modernization of Rural France 1870–1914*, Stanford University Press, Stanford, 1976.

30. S. Sabol, 'The Creation of Soviet Central Asia: The 1924 Delimitation', *Central Asian Survey*, vol. 14, no. 2, 1995, p. 236.

31. *Ibid.*, pp. 237–8.

32. *Ibid.*, p. 241.

33. For a sympathetic discussion of the differentiated layers of nationalism in the context of South Asia see Partha Chatterjee, *The Nation and its Fragments: Colonial and Postcolonial Histories*, Princeton University Press, Princeton, 1993. On Central Asia see Shahram Akbarzadeh, 'A Note on Shifting Identities in the Ferghana Valley', *Central Asian Survey*, vol. 16, no. 1, 1997, pp. 65–8.

34. Onaran, 'Economics and Nationalism', p. 495.

35. *Ibid.*, pp. 82–3.

36. A.M. Khazanov, 'The Ethnic Problems of Contemporary Kazakhstan', *Central Asian Survey*, vol. 14, no. 2, 1995, p. 245.

37. F. Braudel, *A History of Civilizations*, Penguin Books, Melbourne (1963), 1994, p. 462.

38. D.S. Carlisle, 'Uzbekistan and the Uzbeks', *Problems of Communism*, no. 40, September–October 1991, p. 26.

39. Onaran, 'Economics and Nationalism', p. 496.

40. This refers not only to the slow demise of the feudal mode of production but also to the gradual diminution in the concrete manifestations of traditional identities from the Reformation onwards. Whilst one is inclined to retroject an individualistic and private conception of religion onto premodern Europeans, practices such as the trade in relics, the cult of saints and the pilgrimages to holy places throughout Europe indicate the highly public, social and 'lived' nature of religion and invites comparisons with the cult of the holy sites in contemporary Central Asia. It was only the very gradual demystification of the world in Europe that makes the traditionalized modernity of Central Asia and the existence within Central Asians of opposing ontologies seem so incomprehensible. See M. Maffesoli, *The Time of the Tribes: The Decline of Individualism in Mass Society*, Sage Publications, London, 1996, pp. 59, 111 and 131.

41. Rashid, *The Resurgence of Asia*, p. 98.

42. The fact that *Birlik* was able to mobilize 50,000 people to protest for the adoption of Uzbek as the national language in the Uzbek capital of Tashkent in 1989 is demonstrative of the presence of broad-based national subjectivities in Central Asia. See Rashid, *The Resurgence of Asia*.

43. The Islamic revolution in nearby Iran in 1979 and the Soviet war against Afghanistan, a country containing large numbers of Uzbeks and Tajiks who fled the Soviets in the 1920s and 1930s, no doubt assisted the Islamic renaissance in Central Asia.

44. Rashid, *The Resurgence of Asia*, p. 100.

45. M.E. Subtelny, 'The Cult of Holy Places: Religious Practices Among Soviet Muslims', *Middle East Journal*, vol. 43, no. 4, 1989, p. 597.

46. M.H. Yavuz, 'The Patterns of Political Islamic Identity: Dynamics of National and Transnational Loyalties and Identities', *Central Asian Survey*, vol. 14, no. 3, 1995, p. 343.

47. Subtelny, 'The Cult of Holy Places', p. 601.
48. Y. Ro'i, 'The Islamic Influence on Nationalism in Soviet Central Asia', *Problems of Communism*, July–August 1990, pp. 54 and 59.
49. J. Janabel, 'When National Ambition Conflicts with Reality: Studies on Kazakhstan's Ethnic Relations', *Central Asian Survey*, vol. 15, no. 1, 1996, p. 15.
50. V. Tishkov, '"Don't Kill Me, I'm a Kyrgyz!" An Anthropological Analysis of Violence in the Osh Ethnic Conflict', *Journal of Peace Research*, vol. 32, no. 2, 1995, p. 147.
51. O. Brenninkmeijer, 'Tajikistan's Elusive Peace', *The World Today*, no. 53, February 1996, p. 42.
52. This position is supported by Shahram Akbarzadeh, 'Why Did Nationalism Fail in Tasjikistan?', *Europe-Asia Studies*, vol. 48, no. 7, 1996, pp. 1105–29.

13 DEMOCRACY AND THE SHADOW OF GENOCIDE

1. This chapter was first published in *Arena Journal*, no. 16, as 'Democracy and Genocide'.
2. For extracts and summaries of Mann's book, see the website <www.theglobal-site.ac.uk/press/103mann.htm>.
3. Ryszard Kapuscinski, 'On the Nature of Genocide', *Le Monde Diplomatique*, March 2001.
4. Zygmunt Bauman, *Modernity and the Holocaust*, Polity Press, Cambridge, 1989.
5. Michael Ignatieff, 'Lemkin's Word: The Danger of a World Without Enemies', *New York Review of Books*, vol. 46, no. 9, May 1999.
6. See Alistair MacLeod's novel of the same name, *No Great Mischief*, Jonathan Cape, London, 2000, a great mediation on the limitations and futility of Ignatieff's 'tribal' inheritance, as found among the Highland Scots of present-day Novia Scotia and Quebec.
7. Linda Melvern, *A People Betrayed: The Role of the West in Rwanda's Genocide*, Zed Books, London and New York, 2000.
8. Kapuscinski, 'On the Nature of Genocide'.
9. Michael Mann, *The Dark Side of Democracy: Explaining Ethnic Cleansing*, Cambridge University Press, Cambridge, 2004.
10. Ignatieff, 'Lemkin's Word'.
11. Melvern, *A People Betrayed*, p. 218.
12. A good example was given in Fred Halliday's lecture, 'On the Perils of Community'. He points out there that the longer past supports much more ambiguous generalization than ideologists of ethnicity have assumed: 'At the purely anthropological level, one can only note that curiosity about the other, the alien, the new, is at least as prevalent as clinging to one's own. Every aspect of human existence involves a combination of searching for similarity and difference ...' (*Nations and Nationalism*, vol. 6, no. 2, 2000, p. 166).
13. A good account of the Tasmanian genocide is to be found in Ian Hernon's 'The Black War: Tasmania 1824–30', in *The Savage Empire: Forgotten Wars of the Nineteenth Century*, Sutton Publishing, Gloucester, 2000.
14. *Correspondence of Charles Darwin*, Vol. 1, ed. by F. Burkhardt, Cambridge University Press, Cambridge, 1985, pp. 489–91.
15. Gavin de Beer, *Charles Darwin: Evolution by Natural Selection*, Greenwood Press, Westport, CT, 1976, pp. 53–4.
16. Matthew Kneale, *English Passengers*, Hamish Hamilton, London, 2000.
17. 'Querulous toe-rags', according to the short Manx-English dictionary that Mr Kneale (*ibid.*) helpfully appends to his novel.
18. *Ibid.*, p. 407.
19. Kapuscinski, 'On the Nature of Genocide'.

14   NATIONALISM AND THE CRUCIBLE OF MODERN TOTALITARIANISM

1. An earlier version of this chapter first appeared in *New Left Review*.
2. David Clay Large, *Where Ghosts Walked: Munich's Road to the Third Reich*, Basic Books, New York and London, 1997, p. 158.
3. Large, *Where Ghosts Walked*, p. 165.
4. Leon Feuchtwanger, quoted in *ibid.*, p. 158.
5. *Ibid.*, p. 39.
6. See Benedict Anderson, *Imagined Communities: Reflections on the Origin and Spread of Nationalism*, Verso, London, 1991.
7. Large, *Where Ghosts Walked*, p. 164.
8. Karl Alexander von Müller, cited in Large, *Where Ghosts Walked*, p. 165.
9. I have further explored these issues in my *Faces of Nationalism: Janus Revisited*, Verso, London, 1997.
10. Thomas Mann, quoted in Tom Nairn, 'Reflections on Nationalist Disasters', *New Left Review*, vol. 1, no. 230, July–August 1998, p. 149.
11. Isaac Kramnick and Barry Sheerman, *Harold Laski: A Life on the Left*, Hamish Hamilton, London, 1993.
12. Donald McKenzie, 'Tacit Knowledge, Weapons Design, and the Uninvention of Nuclear Weapons', *American Journal of Sociology*, vol. 101, no. 1, July 1995, pp. 44–99.
13. Ben Kiernan, *The Pol Pot Regime: Race, Power and Genocide in Cambodia Under the Khmer Rouge*, Yale University Press, New Haven, CT, 1996.

15   CONTROL AND THE PROJECTION OF A TOTALIZING WAR-MACHINE

1. An earlier version of this chapter appeared in *Arena Journal*.
2. The concept of the 'war-machine' is used here to denote the institutionalization of the means of military violence and control, organized in the contemporary period usually by a state. It is thus used in an antithetical sense to Gilles Deleuze and Felix Guattari (*Nomadology: The War Machine*, Semiotext(e), New York, 1986) when they say that 'The war machine is the invention of nomads (insofar as it is exterior to the State apparatus and distinct from the military institution' (p. 56). The only resonance of their approach in the current chapter is my argument that the modern war-machine is being overlaid by postmodern techniques of organization and extension of force that emphasize the advantages of deterritorialization outside of its own borders. The compound concept of the '*abstract* war-machine' is intended to emphasize this new layer of effecting power in a way that aims to overcome the friction of distance and time.
3. With thanks to Monika Naslund, Victims and Witness Support Section, International Criminal Tribunal for the Former Yugoslavia.
4. On 17 June 1999, the British Foreign Office Minister Geoff Hoon, the man who also talked of the 'certainty' of Saddam having weapons of mass destruction, was reported as claiming that 10,000 persons had been killed in 100 massacres in Kosova. The trial papers for the International Criminal Tribunal for the Former Yugoslavia, (*Indictments: Slobodan Milošević*, PIS, The Hague, 2001) list Račak as the only massacre site occurring before the NATO bombing began.
5. Hannah Arendt, 'Eichmann in Jerusalem', in Alexander Laban Hinton, ed., *Genocide*, Blackwell Publishers, Oxford, 2002.
6. W.G. Sebald, *On the Natural History of Destruction*, Hamish Hamilton, London, 2003, citations from pp. 16 and 20.
7. *Indictments: Slobodan Milošević*, 2001.

8. A dangerous juxtaposition, I know, but it is important to make. At the same time, in making these large and general claims we need to stay acutely aware of both subtle and profound differences. For example, I have already juxtaposed the Nazi total solution for the Jews and the Jewish attempt at totalizing control in Palestine. However, I do not intend to suggest that Israel's so-called 'security fence' and its use of tanks and helicopter gunships to effect control in the Palestinian ghettos can be grouped in category of 'genocidal' along the lines of the systematic Holocaust in the 1940s that wrenched people out of parallel ghettos.

9. Cited in Arendt, 'Eichmann in Jerusalem', p. 98.

10. Michael Hardt and Antonio Negri, *Empire*, Harvard University Press, Cambridge, MA, 2000, pp. xii–xiii.

11. David Lyon, *Surveillance after September 11*, Polity Press, Cambridge, 2003, pp. 96–7.

12. This naming is the postmodern war-machine's equivalent of the neo-traditional concept of the 'human bomb'. On the latter see Nasra Hassan's stunning feature article on the subjectivity of the suicide bombers: 'Human Bombs', *The Age*, 20 January 2002.

13. Cited from the Defense Advanced Research Projects Agency (DARPA) website <www.darpa.mil/body/newsitems/pdf/falcon_ph_1.pdf> and reported in the *Guardian Weekly*, 3 July 2003.

16 TERRORISM AND THE OPENING OF BLACK PLUTO'S DOOR

1. Brendan O'Leary, 'The Right to Rights', Open Democracy (<www.opendemocracy.net>), 18 September 2001.

2. Fouad Ajami, *The Arab Predicament*, Cambridge University Press, Cambridge, 1992, p. 251.

3. Roger Owen, *State, Power and Politics in the Making of the Middle East*, Routledge, London and New York, 2000.

4. *Ibid.*, p. 246.

5. Fred Halliday, 'No Man is an Island', *Observer*, 16 September 2001.

6. Murat Belge, 'Inside the Fundamentalist Mind', Open Democracy (<www.opendemocracy.net>), 4 October 2001.

7. John Down, Open Democracy on-line discussion forum (<www.opendemocracy.net>), 14 September 2001.

8. David Held, Open Democracy on-line discussion forum (<www.opendemocracy.net>), 14 September 2001.

9. David Held and Mary Kaldor, 'New War, New Justice', Open Democracy (<www.opendemocracy.net>), 28 September 2001.

10. Perry Anderson, 'Scurrying Towards Bethlehem', *New Left Review*, no. 10, 2001, pp. 5–30.

17 META-WAR AND THE INSECURITY OF THE UNITED STATES

1. Andrew Sullivan, 'This is What a Day Means', *New York Times Magazine*, 23 September 2001.

2. Lynne Cheney, *America: A Patriot Primer*, Simon & Schuster, New York, 2002, no page numbers. The accompanying quote from Ronald Reagan, 'I know that for America there will always be a bright dawn ahead', is a quotation from his personal-political letter to the nation saying that he had Alzheimer's disease.

3. *The Age*, 18 May 2003; see also *The Australian*, 24 July 2003.

4. *The Australian*, 19 September 2003. Bush's admission effectively reversed Secretary of State Colin Powell's testimony to the United Nations, which included drawing links between Saddam Hussein and Osama bin Laden.

5. The term 'crusades' was withdrawn from the lexicon of the US establishment after the obvious reference to an earlier 'clash of civilizations' in the Middle Ages, Christian and Islamic, was pointed out.

6. *The Age*, 27 February 2003.

7. Cited in David Armstrong, 'Dick Cheney's Song of America', *Harper's Magazine*, October 2002, p. 78.

8. Dan Balz and Bob Woodward, 'The First Twenty-Four Hours', *Washington Post*, syndicated to *The Sunday Age*, 3 February 2002.

9. Manuel de Landa, *War in the Age of the Intelligent Machine*, Zone Books, New York, 1991; Chris Hables Gray, *Postmodern War: The New Politics of Conflict*, Routledge, London, 1997.

10. Mark Twain, 'The War Prayer', cited in Lewis H. Lapham, 'The Road to Babylon', *Harper's Magazine*, October 2002, p. 41.

18 POST-2001 AND THE THIRD COMING OF NATIONALISM

1. This chapter is based on a paper prepared for the annual meeting of the Charles Stewart Parnell Society, held at Avondale, County Wicklow, in August 2003. My thanks are due to the Society for the opportunity, and for permission to publish the text.

2. The long delay in publishing the poem meant it was interpreted at first mainly a comment on Irish matters, rather than the postwar condition of the world. But subsequent reinterpretations by Terence Brown and Seamus Deane have shown the original sense. See Terence Brown, *W.B. Yeats: A Biography*, Gill & Macmillan, London, 2000, pp. 270–2.

3. See Nicholas Farrell, *Mussolini: A New Life*, Weidenfeld, London, 2003, chapter 9, 'Power: Year One of the Fascist Era', pp. 124–5; also Adrian Lyttelton, *The Seizure of Power: Fascism in Italy 1919–1929*, Scribner, New York, 1973.

4. Liah Greenfeld, *The Spirit of Capitalism: Nationalism and Economic Growth*, Harvard University Press, Cambridge, MA, 2001.

5. Liah Greenfeld, *Nationalism: Five Roads to Modernity*, Harvard University Press, Cambridge, MA, 1992.

6. Perhaps the best account of the genesis of *'le nationalisme'* is Henri Guillemin's *Nationalistes et 'Nationaux', 1870–1940*, Gallimard, Paris, 1974, unfortunately long out of print. This traces the strange mixture of opportunism, imposition and populism that presided over the formation of the Third Republic.

7. See recent comments by Roman Golicz in 'The Russians Shall Not Have Constantinople: English Attitudes to Russia, 1870–1878', *History Today*, November 2003: 'We don't to fight, but by jingo if we do/ We've got the ships, we've got the men, and got the money too ...'. Effortless translation can be made into the US media-English of 2001–04. The music-hall singer who coined the phrase in January 1878, 'the great Macdermott', later produced a second ballad sneering at the liberal 'scribblers' who questioned jingoism. As Golicz observes, the most 'highly placed Jingoes in Britain were Disraeli and Victoria ...', and an Irish politician of the moment stated that 'It seemed as if the whole country had gone mad.'

8. See Gérard de Puymège's brilliant study, *Chauvin: Le Soldat-Laboureur. Contribution à l'étude des Nationalismes*, Gallimard, Paris, 1993. An opera about Chauvin was put on in New York in 1998–2000, and the accompanying text contained the following: 'Ultimately, chauvinism is the fanatical attack of the true believer on the government, stirring to life

a complacent and even "decadent" society through a leader who knows the process of religiofication to ignite a national virility. Such fanaticism is an important invention, "a miraculous instrument for raising societies and nations from the dead – an instrument of resurrection".' Comment is superfluous. The libretto was by John Deephardt and the music by Malcolm J. Hill: see <www.ChauvinGrandOpera.TheOpera.com>.

9. The term comes from the most brilliant analysis of the current convulsions yet to appear, Emmanuel Todd's *Après l'Empire: Essai sur la Décomposition du Système Américain*, Gallimard, Paris, 2002 (English translation forthcoming as *After the Empire*, Columbia University Press, New York, 2004). See p. 41 in 'Le Mythe du Terrorisme Universel'. The author hopes that there will soon be left only a single member of the 'Axis of Good'; but alas, it may take some time for the UK, Australia and other coalitioneers in Eastern Europe to come to their senses.

10. *The Wikipedia*, at <www.wikipedia.com>.

11. Chris Hedges, *War is a Force that Gives Us Meaning*, Public Affairs, Oxford, 2003.

12. Seamus Heaney, *The Golden Bough*, from Virgil's *Aeneid*, Book VI. Reproduced in *Opened Ground: Poems 1966–96*, Faber, London, 1998.

Index